AIRSHOW

AIRSHOW

A YEAR IN THE LIFE
OF THE WORLD'S LARGEST
MILITARY AIR SHOW

Graham Hurley

Best wishes.

[signature]

ORION

The right of Graham Hurley to be identified as the
author of this work has been asserted by him in
accordance with the
Copyright, Designs and Patents Act 1988

First published in Great Britain in 1998 by
Orion
An imprint of Orion Books Ltd
Orion House, 5 Upper St Martin's Lane, London
WC2H 9EA

A CIP catalogue record for this book is available
from the British Library

ISBN 0 75281 793 0

Filmset by Selwood Systems, Midsomer Norton
Printed in Great Britain by
Butler & Tanner Ltd, Frome and London

To
Flying Officer Stanley Hurley
255 Squadron, RAF

Fly hard. Fly well. Fly safe.

Air Chief Marshal Sir Richard Johns
24 July '98

Improvise. Adapt. Overcome.

RIAT site team motto

Contents

Who's who? ... in *Airshow*

Air Chief Marshal Sir **Roger Palin**,
KCB, OBE, MA, FRAeS, FIPD
Controller, Royal Air Force Benevolent Fund
Chairman, Royal International Air Tattoo
 (RIAT)

Fred Crawley, CBE, FCIB, CIMgt
Treasurer, Royal Air Force Benevolent Fund
Deputy Chairman, RIAT

Paul Bowen
Director, RIAT

Tim Prince
Director of Operations, RIAT

Sqn Ldr **Wally Armstrong**, MBE, RAF
(Ret'd)
Deputy Director, Hospitality International
 and Catering Services, RIAT

Amanda Butcher
Deputy Director, RIAT

Gordon Harris, OBE
Deputy Director, Admin and Personnel, RIAT

David Higham
Deputy Director, Aviation Trading, RIAT

Caroline Rogers
Deputy Director, Business Development, RIAT

Gp Capt **John Thorpe**, AFC, RAF
Director of Flying, MoD(PE)
Deputy Director, Air Operations, RIAT

Tony Webb
Deputy Director, Public Affairs, RIAT

Sue Allen
Aircraft Participation Manager, RIAT

Graeme Bowd
Producer, Central Television

Gp Capt **Geoff Brindle**, RAF
General Co-ordinating Officer, HQ, Royal
 Airforce of Oman
Chairman, Flying Control Committee, RIAT

Tim Cairns, RN (Ret'd)
Event Services Manager, RIAT

Clive Elliott
Business Development Manager, RIAT

Patti Heady
Senior Press Officer, RIAT

Catherine Iddon
Site Manager, RIAT

Wg Cdr **Mel James**, OBE, RAF (Ret'd)
Engineering Services Co-ordinator, RIAT

Gp Capt **Kevin Leeson**, BSc, CEng, FIEE, RAF
Tornado Fleet Manager, HQ, RAF Strike Command
Protocol and VIP Programmes Co-ordinator, RIAT

Sqn Ldr **Paul Lindsay**, MBE, RAF
Logistics Command, RAF Wyton
Engineering Services Manager, RIAT

Jonathan McNicholas
Executive Producer, Onyx Productions

Sean Maffett
Broadcaster and Journalist
Senior Commentator, RIAT

Peter March
Aviation Journalist
Programme Editor and Senior Photographer, RIAT

Col **Brian Robertson**, RAMC(V)
General Practitioner, Aldershot
Commanding Officer, 306 Field Hospital (V)

Gp Capt **David Roome**, OBE, MRAES, RAF
Head of Business Planning and Finance, Training Group Defence Agency
Flying Display Manager (Berlin Airlift and RAF Eightieth Anniversary Pageants)

Gill Sharpe
Personnel Manager, RIAT

Heidi Standfast
Marketing Manager, RIAT

Jack Taylor
Emergency Services Co-ordinator, RIAT

Wg Cdr **Ian Sheeley**, RAF
OC, RAF Brize Norton Radar
Flying Display Manager, RIAT

Sue Vizor
Finance Manager, RIAT

Tom Watts
Exhibition and Trade Fair Manager, RIAT

Supt **Peter Williams**
National Assistant Secretary, Police Superintendents' Association of England and Wales
Admissions Co-ordinator, RIAT

Acknowledgements

This book began life a little over a year ago, at the 1997 Royal International Air Tattoo. At the invitation of Hugh Lohan, I penned a little piece for his daily newsletter. Wandering around with a notebook and a pencil gave me just an inkling of what must lie behind an event as vast as the Air Tattoo, and my usual nosiness did the rest. Hugh was kind enough to say he liked the piece. Proposing a book-length version – same style, same curiosity – was irresistible.

Without the trust and support of a small army of full-time staffers – RIAT's shocktroops – the project would have been stillborn. Over the last year, I've made some wonderful friendships and picked some fine brains. My thanks to Sue Allen, Wally Armstrong, Emma Baylis, Amanda Butcher, Tim Cairns, Arlene Carson, Clive Elliott, Paddy Feenan, John Hamilton, Patti Heady, Gordon Harris, David Higham, Mel James, Catherine Iddon, Christina Iddon, Helen Knight, Claire Lock, Lyn Miller, Lesley O'Brien, Heather Robinson, Caroline Rogers, Brenda Sawyer, Nikki Slade, Gill Sharpe, Heidi Standfast, Lisa Tarbett, Sarah Taylor, Sue Vizor, Tom Watts and Mandy White. Heroes all.

Outside the confines of Buildings 15 and 16, a cadre of key players lent me their time and their memories over the year. My thanks to Roger Beazley, William Beeston, Geoff Brindle, Mike Chapple, Les Garside-Beattie, Rod Dean, Supt Adrian Grimmitt, Tony House, Brian Hughes, Supt John Horam, Hazel Jones, Inspector Ian Jones, Mel

Kidd, Kevin Leeson, Vic Norman, Rick Peacock-Edwards, Sylvia Quayle, Dr Brian Robertson, Ken Robertson, Jack Taylor, John Thorpe, Brian Trubshaw, Ian Sheeley, Mike Sweeney, Peter Williams, and Chris Yeo.

Sean Maffett and Peter March have survived successive Air Tattoos for longer than most and were generous enough to act as Pathfinders, as did Tony Webb. I owe a large debt of gratitude to all three. Janet Wright's hospitality and kindness softened an often brutal schedule, and helped make my visits to Fairford such a delight.

Over the show itself, my canvas inevitably broadened. My thanks to Flt Lt Peter Astle, Bob Arnott, Peter Atkinson, Ian Beadle, Iain Bell, Mark Biddle, Barney Bruce, Guy Bowen, Simon Boyle, Flt Lt Bernie Brennan, Harry Burgoyne, Andy Chapman, Paul Emery, Peter Finch, Chris Fopp, Alan Foulis, Dave Frayley, David George, Tonya Glover, Liz Harlaar, Jane Hartle, Jo Haskins, Philippa Hayday-Brown, Geoff Hayhoe, Dave Humphrys, Jack Hurley, Denise James, Robin Jackson, Master Engineer Doug Johnson, John Jones, SSgt Mark Kingston, Bob Lamburne, Paul Lindsay, Antony Maslin, Flt Sgt Ian McCabe, Ian Matthews, Tony Morris, Julie Morrissey, Michelle Moore, Catherine Moubray, Capt Paul Neumann, Robby Robinson, Capt Michael Sauer, Mike Scaddan, Sue Stafford, Flt Lt Dom Stamp, Brian Strickland, Bob Taylor, Tony Thomas, Tony Twiggs, Capt Gyula Vari, Mark Williams, and Mike White.

RAF Fairford is currently leased to the USAF. Lt Col Frank Robinson and Capt Dan Jagt were generous and supportive hosts. My thanks to them both.

The media world forms a minor sub-plot in this book. Thank you to Andy Bethel, Graeme Bowd, Tony Howard, Jonathan Ruffle, Jonathan McNicholas, Kris Pyle and Colin Webb. A special thank you, as well, to Simon Spanton, my editor at Orion, who nursed the project through to completion, and to my wife, Lin, who kept her eyes peeled for bandits.

Group Captain David Roome features heavily in the pages that follow. He taught me a great deal about the silky arts of airshow choreography and was impressively nerveless when his aerial ballet hit severe turbulence. I can't imagine that he ever planned to become the star of a book like this but life, as they say, is full of surprises.

At the Royal Air Force Benevolent Fund, Mary Bentley and Ann Dewar were unfailingly helpful. Fred Crawley, Deputy Chairman of the Board of Benevolent Fund enterprises, trusted me with some wise and candid insights for which I am deeply grateful, while Air Chief Marshal Sir Roger Palin – Fund Controller and Chairman of Benevolent Fund Enterprises – was never less than totally supportive. Without his backing, this book would never have happened. I hope it meets his every expectation.

Above all, my thanks must go to Paul Bowen and Tim Prince. The Royal International Air Tattoo has always been their baby. They conceived it, nurtured it, watched it grow into a world beater, and for one brief year they were courageous enough to lend it to me. The experience of writing this book has been a rare pleasure. Meeting the team they've built around them has taught me a great deal. My thanks to you all.

....

CHAPTER ONE

19 July 1997

It's half past three on a hot, cloudless midsummer afternoon. I'm riding in the front of a Volvo estate, crossing the main runway at RAF Fairford in Gloucestershire. Behind me, an enormous crowd has just watched the first stealth bomber ever to make a public landing in the UK.

The aircraft is a Northrop Grumman B-2A Spirit. Ten minutes ago it swam in from the west, an eerie silhouette flanked by two F-15 Eagle fighters. Black against the brilliant blue of the sky, it had no tailplane, no fuselage, none of the comforting trademarks of a normal aeroplane. It slipped overhead, framed by tens of thousands of cameras, an intruder so alien that it silenced even conversation. There was an extraordinary hush. For once, in a world of hype, the star of the show exceeded every expectation. People just stared.

Now, the B-2 is discreetly tucked away at the far end of the airfield. The Americans have thrown a protective cordon around it, a ring of grim-faced soldiers with – no doubt – orders to shoot on sight. In the arsenals of the west, the B-2 is still cutting edge. A 160-ton aeroplane with a radar profile the size of a golf ball, it can deliver a 50,000lb bombload – nuclear or conventional – with startling accuracy. One of the reasons Saddam Hussein blinked in his latest eyeball-to-eyeball confrontation with the Americans over weapons inspections was undoubtedly the existence of this sinister miracle of hi-tech engineering.

The driver of the Volvo drops me a hundred metres from the B-2.

In a minute or two a convoy of limousines will arrive with a dozen or so VIPs to inspect the beast. Royalty will be there, and General Fogelman, Chief of the US Air Force, together with a clutch of top names from the aerospace industry. A ladder unfolds from the black belly of the aircraft and the B-2's crew clamber down, awaiting the VIPs' arrival. I wonder how they're feeling after their transatlantic crossing, and I wonder too how they'll manage a half-decent conversation over the deafening whine from the single idling turbine.

The Daimlers appear. Someone lends me a pair of binoculars and for the next twenty minutes I watch the visiting dignitaries pick their way over the umbilicals, gazing up at the starship, pausing from time to time to point a wondering finger at this feature or that. It's probably fanciful but from a hundred metres I swear they're as gobsmacked as everyone else. This aircraft is as awesome and top secret as any piece of hardware on earth.

Among the VIPs I recognise the organiser of the airshow. His name is Paul Bowen, a portly figure in a beautifully cut suit. Paul and his co-director Tim Prince are the guys who have nurtured this event, helped it to grow from a cheerful day out on a wartime airfield north of London to this monster, must-attend date on the international aviation calendar. The driver of the Volvo has been telling me that the Royal International Air Tattoo is now the world's biggest military airshow, and – my eyes still glued to the B-2 – I believe him.

Paul is talking to the Duke of Kent and General Fogelman. All three of them appear to be sharing a joke. Paul seems totally at home, proprietorial almost, *mein host* at the party of his dreams. It's an extraordinary moment: the suited figures swimming in the binoculars, the hot tang of Avtur in the still air, the shattering roar as a pair of MiG-29s on re-heat thunder down the nearby runway.

Standing beside the Volvo, I rack the focus on the binos, steadying myself against the passenger door. I haven't seen Paul Bowen for more than three decades. Half a lifetime ago, he and I were at school together. For a couple of years we even shared a dormitory – a claustrophobic, poorly lit room with knots in the floorboards and a permanent smell of stewing cabbage from the kitchens below. For reasons I never understood, the dormitory was called Lower Blue.

Paul was a passionate Boy Scouter, and the king of the hundred metres freestyle. The latter talent took him to evening training sessions at nearby Walthamstow Baths, and he'd return past lights out, laden with double-wrapped bundles of haddock and chips. I remember the stink of the vinegar and the trouble we'd have afterwards, trying to dispose of the greasy balls of sodden newsprint. Now, through my borrowed binoculars, this same Paul Bowen is shaking hands with the pilot of a B-2 stealth bomber. Thanks for coming over. Thanks for dropping in. Amazing.

I shake my head – part disbelief, part admiration. It's a brilliant scoop – not just the B-2, but the whole event. The traffic queues start ten miles out. An army of four-and-a-half thousand volunteers are marshalling the crowds on the airfield. There's eight hours of flying, umpteen national aerobatic teams, fifty-two participating air forces. The static display line – parked, state-of-the-art aircraft you can ogle and snap and actually *touch* – stretches nearly two miles. When I finally do the sums it turns out that the show has pulled in no less than 486 aeroplanes. That makes my old chum from Lower Blue – for one brief, unforgettable weekend – the commander of the world's ninth biggest airforce. Paul was never less than ambitious, but how come he's managed to work this extraordinary magic?

I write novels for a living. Paul's invitation to spend a couple of days at the airshow has given me invaluable background for my latest book. But here, in front of me, is a real-life story on the grandest possible scale, and for days afterwards I find myself musing on what it must have taken to put it all together. Impressive is too small a word to describe what I saw that July weekend. Genius, I decide, smells ever-so-faintly of haddock and chips.

A week or so later I return to Fairford. Paul sits behind an enormous desk, flanked by souvenirs from twenty-six years of Air Tattoos. Among the colour blow-ups awaiting inspection in his bulging in-tray is a shot of the B-2 crouched over a gaggle of grey suits. The image is stencilled on my brain. Apart from anything else, it's the reason I've levered myself into his crowded diary.

I explain that I'd like to write about next year's air show, telling the story from the inside. I use phrases like fly-on-the-wall and as-it-happens. A couple of phone calls to specialist aviation journalists have confirmed just how prestigious this event has become. Not just the Tattoo and the flying, but everything else that goes with it. Beneath the sheltering umbrella of the RAF Benevolent Fund, Paul's organisation runs concert tours, sells merchandise, brokers deals, organises air shows all over the world. Ironically enough, he even publishes books.

He asks for more detail. Three years surviving Lower Blue counts for a lot, but he's understandably wary – these documentary projects can have a sizeable downside. The Benevolent Fund Board are sometimes wary of media exposure. The big hitters in the aerospace business are deeply serious people. The Air Tattoo floats on a raft of multiple sponsorship, and Paul would hate for any of them to get upset.

I do my best to quieten his fears but when he talks about me getting deep inside his organisation I have to admit that he's right. Without total access – and real candour – the thing won't fly.

He nods, then looks up.

'Readership?'

'As wide as possible.'

'And we can sell it through our catalogue?'

'Delighted.'

He reaches for his fifth cigarette, brooding. In the end, as we both know, it has to be an act of faith. Finally, he looks up again. The old grin is back. Lower Blue. Rain at the window. Chips bloody everywhere.

'Let's do it,' he says.

....

CHAPTER TWO

October 1997

Two and a half months later I'm back at Fairford with my notepad and pencil, embarking on a nine-month journey that will take me to next year's airshow. I want, above all, to burrow deep into the organisation responsible for what USAF General Al Hansen has recently described as 'without doubt, the best air show in the world'.

The Royal International Air Tattoo, or RIAT, is actually run by an outfit that terms itself Enterprises. Enterprises is shorthand for Royal Air Force Benevolent Fund Enterprises, and is in essence the trading arm of the charity charged with the care and welfare of ex-servicemen.

Headquartered in a couple of bleak-looking, single-storey, pre-cast hutments (listed on the Fairford airfield map as Buildings 15 and 16), Enterprises employs fifty full-time staff. This team carries the torch for RIAT from summer to summer, and just now three of them are sitting at a table in the dining room with a nice view of the lunchtime salad bar.

The scent of a delicious chicken murglai still hangs in the air. Laid out on the table between us are photocopied pages from the 1997 *Guide to the World's Airforces*. Bent over the master copy is Sue Allen. Slim, tenacious, attractive, Sue is in charge of assembling the small armada of hardware that is the very centre of the Air Tattoo, and this afternoon she's tasked with going through each of the world's air arms, putting together wish-lists of military aircraft, the raw ingredients for next year's show. In five weeks' time, with colleague Amanda Butcher, Sue will decamp to London for a ten-day blitz on a succession of foreign air attachés. In embassy after embassy, today's lists will form the basis for a carefully paced conversation, seeded with all manner of RIAT delights. More of that later.

Paul Bowen is with Sue and Amanda at the table. Amanda is in her forties, a spirited ex-Wing Commander who has swapped the comforts of RAF Lyneham for the hectic pace of life in Building 15. Just now, the three of them are deep in thought about the hardware listed for the Japanese Self Defence Force. The Japanese embassy, it seems, has recently acquired a new air attaché. To date they've resisted invitations to RIAT, but a new face at 101 Piccadilly just might make a difference.

Paul, resting briefly between cigarettes, thinks it's worth a shot.

'Look,' he growls. 'They'll soon be flying the 767 AWACs. Be nice to get hold of one of those.'

Sue has a handful of gaily coloured high-lighters. Pink is for surveillance aircraft. She's about to add the big Boeing to the RIAT list when Paul spots another goodie.

'What about that Shinmaywa US-1A? I can't remember when we last had an amphibian SAR. And they're flying the Kawasaki EP-3. Perfect for SkyWatch.'

Sue uncaps another high-lighter. God knows what green stands for. I scribble down the aircraft designations, desperately trying to get the letters in the right order. EP-3? P-3Cs? RAS? SAR? I look up, meaning to check, but Paul has already abandoned Japan for Jordan. King Hussein, it seems, is an old friend of RIAT. Every July without fail he flies in from Amman, and this support has extended to helping fund RIAT's flying scholarships for the disabled. Paul dictates a list of aircraft. Within twenty seconds he's added several hundred million pounds' worth of hardware to the flying programme and static display line.

Amanda reaches for the next page. 'What about Latvia? We could have *all* of their airforce.'

'No point.' Paul shakes his head. 'They haven't got the range.'

'Libya?'

'Not allowed. Foreign Office would go ballistic.'

'Israel?'

'They'd love it. Especially if we invited the Libyans.'

'But the Libyans can't come.'

'Quite.'

Paul turns to page twelve and begins to muse about Malaysia. The Malays have some impressive kit and British Aerospace are keen to sell them more, but there appears to be some problem over last year's fuel bill.

Paul glances up at Amanda. 'What do you think?'

'It's a long way.'

'You're right. Next.'

More airforces come under the hammer. The Maltese are small and interesting and very definitely on-side. The Mexicans fly an old DC-6 which might fit nicely with one of next year's show themes. The Omanis operate Skyvans which still return to the UK for major overhauls. The list of aircraft grows and grows as Sue's high-lighters race across the smudged photocopies.

We get to Pakistan.

'Mirage IIIs …' Paul at last shreds the cellophane from a fresh pack of Superkings. 'Now they'd be really nice.'

Sue's hand hovers over the high-lighters. Blue is definitely for fighters. I know about the Mirage III – a beautiful delta-winged French interceptor I once saw at an air show in the Pas-de-Calais.

'They don't tank, do they? The Pakistanis?'

Amanda is frowning. Heads bow over the entries for Pakistan. Among the F-6s, A5s and C-130s there appears to be no sign of any mid-air refuelling capability. I'm still wondering what this tells us about Islamabad's war plans when Paul moves briskly on to the next airforce. Pakistani Mirage IIIs, tasty as they are, would never make it to Turkey, let alone Fairford.

'Paraguay?'

'Desperate to get in. Might be an MoD problem, though.'

'Peru?'

'They've got a DC-8F, the long-range cargo version. Be nice on the static line.'

'Hmm ...' Paul's not convinced. 'It's a hell of a way to come, especially if we pick up the fuel bill. Those old DC-8s drink the stuff. What about Poland? They're flying a MiG-29 four-ship.'

Sue's worried about ending up with too many aerobatic teams. 'We've already got the Ukrainians. And that's a six-ship. They've got *Fishbeds* and *Flankers*, though, and they do solo displays. That'd be really nice, wouldn't it?' She looks up. 'Paul?'

Something else has caught Paul's eye. 'Hey, look. Romania's got an H-5R. Just think of the anoraks. Has to be on the list. Definitely.'

Sue pauses for a moment to check whether the bid is serious. Romania is evidently a treasure trove of classic Russian hardware. Paul reels off the aircraft, undeterred by Amanda's quiet reminder that most of them are too knackered to fly. Il-28s. An-24s. Su-7s. Yak-52s. I'm still writing as fast as I can. Most of it's totally impenetrable, and while Paul launches a discussion about the sorry state of Romanian aviation I risk a look at my notes. The last five pages are a tangle of acronyms, aircraft types and serial designations that resembles a nightmare hand at Scrabble. SAR? P-3Cs? An-24s? *Fitters*? *Flankers*? Four-ships? Six-ships? H-5Rs? What on earth are these people talking about? As the conversation moves on to yet another country I scribble a note to myself: MFOL – Must Find Out Later.

I glance up. The girls are in stitches. Not about aircraft this time, but one of the air attachés. According to Sue he's slim, tanned and totally irresistible. Better still, he's rumoured to have recently turned down a suggested move to Washington.

Pencil poised, I press for more details. 'He's on the list then, this guy? You'll definitely be seeing him?'

Amanda nods. 'Day One,' she confirms. 'Last call of the afternoon. Just before we hit the pub.'

So how come Paul Bowen and his team can trawl the world's airforces with such an amazing degree of confidence? What is it about the Royal International Air Tattoo that last year attracted nearly five hundred aircraft?

The headquarters of the RAF Benevolent Fund lies at the northern end of Portland Place. At the helm is the Fund Controller, Air Chief Marshal Sir Roger Palin. It's his job to supervise the raising and distribution of monies to serving and retired RAF personnel who might suddenly find themselves in financial need. Only this morning he was chairing the Main Grants Committee, considering applications for Fund assistance. Last year alone, Sir Roger was in charge of the disbursement of more than £12.4 million in direct welfare, and the number of cases tackled by the Fund in 1996 numbered over 20,000. In addition to that, the Fund grant-aids no less than forty-eight other associated charities.

Now retired from the RAF, Sir Roger occupies a modest, windowless office at the back of Benevolent Fund headquarters. He has a firm handshake and an easy smile. Noticing the framed prints of aircraft on the wall – a Phantom, a Tornado – I assume rightly that he was a fast jet man.

'Did you have a favourite aircraft? As a matter of interest?'

'Very much so.'

'What was it?'

'The Lightning.' He beams at me. 'A triumph of power over aerodynamics.'

The Lightning, as it happens, used to feature in my Eagle comic centrespreads, a brutal-looking aluminium tube with stubby little swept-back wings and a couple of meaty Avons mounted one on top of the other in the slender fuselage. The shattering roar of a Lightning on reheat was, for me, one of the defining moments of mid-adolescence, and the sight of this frontline interceptor powering upwards in a near-vertical climb was as close to sex as the late Fifties permitted. But what was it like for the pilot?

'Wonderful,' Sir Roger nods. 'Quite wonderful. Single-seat. Limitless power. What else could a man possibly want?'

We fall to discussing the International Air Tattoo. The word 'Royal' is a recent addition, an acknowledgement that the event has won its establishment spurs. When Sir Roger became Fund Controller back in 1993, the annual spectacular was – more simply – IAT.

'What did you make of them?'

'Wonderful crowd. Great bunch of people.'

'Have you ever come across anything like it before?'

'The show or the organisation?'

'The organisation.'

'No.' He shakes his head. 'Never.'

This is important. On even the briefest acquaintance, it's already obvious that Paul Bowen and Tim Prince have, between them, nurtured a very odd organisation indeed. The core operation is staffed by civilians, yet everything they do has a military dimension. Enterprises shelters under the umbrella of one of the country's largest charities, yet their conduct in the marketplace is as hard-nosed as the most commercial of companies.

Sir Roger offers a vigorous nod. 'We have to be commercial. We're competing with the biggest and the best out there. Alton Towers. The Henley Regatta. The Silverstone Grand Prix. To do that, you've got to create awareness. And to do *that*, as everyone says, you've got to have money. Have we got money? No we haven't. Do we want to be out there with the leaders? Yes, we do.'

Money. By far the biggest money-spinner to come out of Buildings 15 and 16 is the annual Air Tattoo. This year's show, after expenses, is predicted to contribute a fat £400,000 to Sir Roger's Benevolent Fund. That's a figure of which Paul and Tim are rightly proud, but the arithmetic behind it is hideously complicated. For one thing, the team down in Fairford is not allowed to hazard a single penny of Benevolent Fund money on any of its money-raising activities. That means that the airshow – and all the other elements in the RIAT operation – have to be self-financing.

Another nod from Sir Roger, even more emphatic. 'Absolutely. Enterprises raises money for the Fund. The cash flows are strictly one-way. There's working capital available in a development trust, but the Fund itself is ring-fenced. It's very important to recognise that fact. In no sense is the Fund ever at risk.'

Whether or not this is a tribute to Paul and Tim and their cadre of full-time staff, I don't know – but in my mind's eye I'm back in July, clambering into a Volvo estate car, heading for the B-2 stealth bomber. The crowd that day exceeded 100,000, and without RIAT's army of helpers – 4,500 and counting – the event would never have happened.

Another puzzle: an organisation which depends almost wholly on unpaid volunteers.

The word 'volunteer' lights a fire in Sir Roger. He visibly warms to the concept, and to the reality. As Controller of the Benevolent Fund, he automatically became Chairman of Enterprises. And as Chairman of the Fairford organisation, he pledged himself to safeguard what he calls 'the spirit and the essence' of the volunteers.

'That's one of the things that makes the show so special. When you talk about volunteers, you're talking about people from all walks of life. Some of them are pretty high-profile people; others might not even have a job. But on the day they're given enormous responsibilities and they just muck in – get down and *do* it.'

The notion gladdens him. You can see it in his face. Was this a surprise – when he first encountered it?

'A surprise? I was horrified. I came from a service background. I'd known the RAF at every level. We lived in a world of rules and regulations, of dos and don'ts. IAT wasn't like that. You either could or you couldn't do something. Results were the only thing that mattered.'

'Meaning …?'

'Meaning that I'd happen across some callow youth, maybe an RAF man, but someone – you know – pretty lowly. And there he'd be, out on the apron, waving in a B-52. A *B-52*. The mind boggled.'

The thought of the Air Chief Marshal watching a twenty-two-year-old volunteer helping park an American eight-engined bomber raises a smile. But did it really matter? As long as the job got done?

'Not at all. Of course it didn't. And that's why Servicemen, in particular, love helping out. RIAT gives them more hands-on experience than they'd ever get in uniform. It becomes addictive. They can't wait to come back next year.'

I brood on his answer for a moment or two. Something else that has struck me about Paul and Tim – and the hum of activity in Building 15 – is an absolute commitment to progress. Year on year, the show must get better, bigger, bolder. Like a shark, RIAT must keep moving forward to survive.

Sir Roger nods. 'That's true. Maybe not bigger, not in the physical sense. There are all kinds of reasons why we might reach a limit on aircraft and spectators. But better, most certainly. And bolder, too.'

Bold is an attractive word, slightly missionary in flavour. It smacks of that blend of showbusiness, risk-taking and hard commercial logic that seems so close to the heart of the Fairford operation. In terms of the air display it's been a fantastic success, pulling in huge crowds year after year. But doesn't it also take us straight back to this odd marriage between charitable good works and buccaneering free enterprise that seems – to the onlooker – just a little bit uncomfortable?

Sir Roger looks briefly concerned. 'You mean we're hazarding money?'

'Bluntly, yes.'

'Then you're wrong.' He reaches for a sheet of paper. 'Look – the way Tim and Paul have set it up, we pre-sell most of the show. Attendance tickets are mostly bought way in advance. Corporate sponsorship brings in lots of money early. By July, if we're on track, the show has paid for itself.'

'How much?'

'This year?' He frowns. 'Two and a half million.'

'You mean the expenses?'

'Yes.'

'Two and a half *million*? To run an airshow?'

'Yes. But as I say, the bulk of that we've covered. It's the last 15,000 through the gate that really matters. That's our profit. That's what comes to the Fund.'

I gaze at the pencilled figures. I was never convinced by magic. 'You're telling me the show pays for itself before a single plane's taken off?'

'Absolutely. That's one of the clever bits. That's why it's run the way it's run. You don't believe me? Go back to Fairford. Talk to David Higham. Talk to Clive. Talk to Heidi.'

Heidi Standfast used to be a shepherdess. With her blonde hair and her cornflower-blue eyes goes a certain briskness of manner. Like so many of the team, she seldom works less than a sixty-hour week.

'It's all about footfall,' she tells me.

'It's all about *what?*'

Heidi favours me with the ghost of a smile. It might signal amusement, but I'm not sure. 'Footfall is a term we use in marketing,' she
explains. 'It's a measure of the number of people going through a
store, or past a market stall, or whatever. Basically we're talking
bodies.'

'You mean money?'

'Yes.' The smile broadens. 'Money.'

With an HND in livestock production, Heidi spent a year in Africa,
working on a 3,000-acre estate. Back in England, after a BA in
marketing, she joined a Dutch publishing company, becoming a senior
sales executive. But while she loved the challenge of the marketplace,
she never felt happy living in London. A move back to her native
Wiltshire brought her a job at Fairford – and now, from her busy
office in Building 16, she pilots the RIAT marketing operation.

By this stage I'm becoming seriously intrigued by this strange,
higgledy-piggledy organisation that Paul and Tim have bolted together
over the years. Heidi came down from the bustle of the big city. How
on earth did it feel when she first arrived on this bleak, windswept
airfield?

She takes her time answering. You get the feeling she's thought this
through before. Probably often.

'It was pretty scary in some ways,' she says at last. 'It's the kind of
place where either your face fits or it doesn't.'

'What does that mean?'

'It means that they do things a certain way. They give you lots of
challenges, loads of responsibility, and then it's up to you to go and
sort it out. They're not really interested in problems. Only solutions.'

'They?'

'Paul and Tim.'

I make sure she knows I'm writing all this down. It's a tribute to
the place that someone like Heidi has the confidence to be so frank.
She comes back at me. She's engaged now, opening up.

'I've been here nearly seven years now and I love it. The pay's
probably twenty-five per cent less than the market rate, but that
doesn't seem to matter. It's a really can-do company. They work you

really hard – actually you work *yourself* really hard – but then you play hard too.' She grins. 'It tests you all the time. There's lots of graft and lots of laughter. That's why I love it so much.'

'*Need* it so much?'

She looks me in the eye. Then nods. 'Yes. They make you proud of what you do. And that's important.'

We talk about the faces that don't fit. At the edges of the organisation there appears to be a tremendous coming and going of new recruits, folk who sample the RIAT culture for a month or two and then beat a retreat, thoroughly alarmed. From this perspective, the company seems slightly Jesuitical. You're either in, body and soul, or you call it quits. It's no kind of life for the timid.

Heidi agrees. 'That's true. You've got to want to do it. And you've got to be the kind of person who's never put off. If you want a half-decent private life, it can be difficult. Leading up to show time we're working all the hours God gives, but even now there's always something new to get your teeth into.'

Earlier in the day, I noticed Heidi in the dining room, locked in conversation with a visitor. The table between them was spread with bulging files, sales graphs, calculators and all the other tools of the marketing biz – and now I'm nosy enough to enquire further. The visitor, it turns out, was an executive from Waitrose. The supermarket chain was one of the key sponsors for this year's show, and the meeting offered the chance for an in-depth review of exactly how things had gone.

'Were they pleased?'

'Very. In fact they were delighted.'

Waitrose are one of two retail outlets to sell tickets in advance of the show. A £4.50 saving on a £24 adult ticket is a discount worth having, and I begin to sense the logic in the RIAT marketing plan when Heidi tells me that eighty-six per cent of tickets for the Air Tattoo are sold ahead of the show. Two-thirds of these sales come through Waitrose and Victoria Wine, RIAT's favoured high-street outlet, while the rest are sold through a direct-response mail operation within RIAT itself. Eighty-six per cent of well over a million pounds must offer a great deal of comfort when the money's sitting in the bank and the longer Heidi talks the more I understand the gleam in Sir Roger's eye. Most of the financial risk has indeed been squeezed out of the Air Tattoo. These people really have got it taped.

'Why Waitrose?' I enquire.

'Because it offers us exactly the right kind of audience profile.'

'Meaning?'

'Meaning that Waitrose attract lots of ABC1s. You know the kind – two-point-two children, lots of consumer goodies, lifetime subscription to the *Daily Mail*. Upmarket, but not *too* upmarket.'

'Is that important?'

'Important? Of course it's important! This year, fifty-eight per cent of people coming through the gate were ABC1s, and quite a lot of that's because of Waitrose. ABC1s have money, disposable income. And if they've paid for their tickets in advance then they've probably got a brand-new wage packet in their pockets. That's what we're after. Maximising the spend.'

Put this way, the marketing plan sounds cold, almost predatory. Heidi disagrees.

'It's common sense,' she says. 'We're here to protect the bottom line, and you can only do that by constantly increasing revenue flows. People will only part with money if you offer them something attractive. So that's what we try and do.'

I make a careful note of the phrases, slightly awed by this blizzard of marketing-speak.

'So how does it work? The sponsorship?'

'Easy.' Heidi leans forward, tallying the key points on the fingers of one hand. 'Waitrose agree to sell tickets through their stores, that's the first thing. Secondly, they sign up to sponsor our welcome leaflet. That's a little brochure we distribute free to every incoming car. It gives you a map, tells you where the loos are, tells you what to do if you lose the kids. That kind of thing.'

'How many do you print?'

'Sixty thousand.'

'And Waitrose?'

'Pay for it.'

'And do they pay for anything else?'

'Yes, the Jubilee Gardens. They sponsor that too.'

The Jubilee Gardens, she explains, is a special enclosure fenced off from the passing hordes. A £12 ticket will buy you a deckchair, a fabulous view of the flying, and a chance to buy a range of Waitrose goodies, from fresh baps to chilled champagne. Heidi's infatuation with the ABC1s begins to make sense.

'And you get takers? For the Jubilee Gardens?'

'It's a sell-out.'

'How many tickets?'

'Twelve hundred.'

'So who gets the income from the tickets?'

'We do.'

'And who pays all the expenses?'

'Waitrose.'

Nice. Heidi, hugely amused, rattles through the other 'added-value' hospitality options available to paying members of the public, and it's at this point that I begin to sense the way the Air Tattoo has become a mosaic of sponsorship opportunities – marketing code for the conversion of every square inch of prime Fairford turf into hard cash.

Buy your £19.50 ticket in advance or your £24 ticket on the gate, and the moment you enter the show you'll be faced with a tempting choice of 'enhanced spectator opportunities': The Friends of the Royal International Air Tattoo Grandstand; The Public Grandstand; The Park and View Enclosure; The Photo Bus. None of these privileged seats is obligatory, of course – most spectators simply wander up and down – but each bum on each paid-for seat adds another sandbag to the protection of RIAT's bottom line, a wise and necessary precaution when a hundred other public events are competing for what Heidi calls 'the leisure pound'.

Beyond Heidi, in the battle for air show revenue, lie other RIAT warlords. Corporate hospitality, for instance, has become enormously important, and I'm relishing the chance to get to grips with this glitzy corner of the RIAT operation. But here, in the foothills of Heidi's marketing empire, there's still something that bothers me. Waitrose must be parting with a sizeable sum of money. What do they get in return?

Heidi fixes me with those amazing eyes. 'Is that a serious question?'

I confess that it is, and with enormous patience she goes through it all again. How they value the tie-up with the world's largest military air show. How they love the association with a big family day out. And how, to everyone's delight, the in-store sale of tickets actually brings in business during a traditionally slack couple of months in the supermarket year.

'You mean *extra* business? Because they're selling your tickets?'

'That's right.' Heidi's grinning fit to bust. 'We call it footfall.'

A little dazed, I wander into the car park to gather my wits. It's nearly dark, a grey day with a whisper of wind from the west. You can smell rain in the air.

I walk across the car park. Beyond the chain-link fence lies the airfield – 10,000 feet of runway and the usual assortment of hangars, revetments and heavy-duty pipework. Since the 1950s, the airfield has been leased to the US Air Force. There's no hint of this on the local signposts – they all say RAF FAIRFORD – but jurisdiction on-base belongs to the Americans. Giant B-52s bombed Iraq from here during the Gulf War, and one of Paul Bowen's more sobering memories was the speed with which the Americans converted sleepy old Fairford into a bustling frontline bomber base. The locals, it seems, didn't get unduly alarmed – a squadron or two of B-52s were nothing compared to the annual Air Tattoo – but there must have been a measure of relief when Saddam threw in the towel and Fairford returned to its normal torpor.

Away to the east a red light glows on top of a water tower, and I half-close my eyes a moment, trying to recall the names stencilled on the big operational maps of the airfield that the RIAT teams use in July. Apron Red Alpha. Apron Green Bravo. Crash Gate P. Fire Lane Four. Silver Control. To some, myself included, there's a kind of rough, martial poetry in these names. They're not, after all, simple designations on a map, but have a dimension beyond that. To understand their importance, the way they link together, the way they conjure order out of chaos, is to become part of the airshow itself.

I turn and look at the rows of lit windows in Buildings 15 and 16, the heads bent over computer terminals, the phones clamped to ears, the rows and rows of files in office after office. It is, without doubt, a huge operation – but to believe that it's simply commercial would be wrong. There's a pulse here, a certain excitement, and even in the dog-days of late October it's possible to feel it.

'You're serious? About this pulse thing?'

'Yes.'

I'm sitting in Tim Prince's office. It's dark outside and Tim is behind his desk, listening to me trying to put this feeling into words, trying to understand how hard it must be to spend fifty-one weeks a year getting ready for the fifty-second.

'We do lots of other things. You know that, don't you?'

I nod. Tim and Paul's organisation puts together touring concerts with the RAF Bands. It sends out catalogues to a huge database of current and ex-servicemen. It accepts commissions to run airshows elsewhere in the world. But in the very middle of the RIAT year, dominating everything else, are those five giddy days in July. How come it got so big? Did anyone ever sit down and *plan* it this way?

'Not at all.' Tim offers a wry smile. 'In fact I never expected it to go anywhere.'

'You mean that?'

'I do. At the start of it all we were very hand-to-mouth. We had loads of tactics but absolutely no strategy. Show us a problem and, sure, we'd try and solve it – but beyond that we didn't really bother. We did it because it was fun.'

The word fun sits easily with Tim Prince. He's a slim, sandy-haired, bespectacled figure with an infectious grin and a deceptively mild manner. Given a second go at life, I suspect he could have become a very good GP. He has a natural bedside manner – detachment warmed by real concern. In the event, though, he never went near a medical school. Partly because he was mad about aeroplanes. And partly because he met Paul Bowen.

Tim Prince and Paul Bowen go back a long way. They bumped into each other in the late Sixties when they were both cadets at the School of Air Traffic Control at Bournemouth's Hurn Airport. They were never close socially, but after Hurn they both found themselves at the RAF's Aircraft and Armament Experimental Establishment at Boscombe Down. It was a perfect posting – three runways, a huge variety of aircraft, and a feeling of being in the dress circle as far as the cutting edge of military aviation was concerned. Nearly thirty years later they remain very different in character and attitude, a fact that neither of them has any difficulty in pointing out.

'I was always the rough one,' Tim contends, 'while Paul was a bit posher. Socially, he's completely fearless. Show him any door and he'll open it without a moment's thought. He's very punchy. He has enormous self-confidence. Me? I'm a nuts-and-bolts guy. I'm as happy fixing a slide projector as I am going up to Derby to talk to the Rolls-Royce bosses. To be honest, if you gave me a choice, I'd burn the suit and tie.'

This picture Tim likes to paint of himself – low profile, slightly retiring – is less than complete. It's true that Paul Bowen casts a long shadow – the years have lent his undeniable self-confidence a certain physical weight – but as the show comes round and the pressure builds it's often Tim who refuses to bend before an unreasonable demand from a foreign aerobatic team, or a last-minute change of plan from someone who should know better. That, at least, is the way I've been hearing it.

True?

'Maybe.' Tim gazes at me. 'Why do you ask the question?'

'Because I'm intrigued. The pair of you are so different. Yet, without the chemistry ...' I leave the sentence unfinished, gesturing up at the framed photos on the wall. A hundred thousand people in the summer sunshine. The B-2 stealth bomber. Hardly something that happens by accident.

Tim shrugs the intended compliment aside. He's more aware than most of the sheer scale of the event he and Paul have created, yet this passionate devotion to the small print remains. It's nice to get the headlines and the awards and become – to some degree – the elder statesmen on the airshow circuit, but fathering RIAT from year to year is still a drug, every bit as addictive as anything you can buy on the street.

So where's the buzz in being in charge? Where's the satis-faction?

'It's all kinds of things. The power, obviously, and the excitement – they're really important. We've built this thing, this monster, and keeping it under control can be a nightmare. You see this?' He produces a big orange carrier bag. 'Every Friday night this comes home with me. Full.'

'*Every* Friday?'

'Without fail. Most nights, if I'm lucky, I'll be home by half eight. Most weekends, thanks to the bag, I just go on working. I haven't taken annual leave for the last three years. Even Christmas has become a catch-up time.'

'Still married?'

Tim concedes the point with a wry nod. 'I'm lucky,' he says. 'My wife's amazingly tolerant. She's built a life of her own, because she's had to. And the kids? Well, they're more or less grown up now, but I'm sure I haven't seen as much of them as I've wanted to. So you're right. There are losses as well as gains.'

Give or take a year or so, Tim and I happen to be the same age. Meeting Paul again after thirty years has set me thinking about the paths life maps out for us, where they may lead, and exactly how much say we have in deciding whether or not to pursue them.

I offer the thought to Tim. It raises a smile. 'There's something in that,' he agrees. 'When I first went to Boscombe Down I was working twenty-three hours a week. I had lots of money in my pocket and lots of spare time, and I used to sit in one of those wonderful coffee shops in Salisbury, just gazing out of the window, being a bum. Now? Now I'm a workaholic. I make a million decisions a day. I'm forever on the phone, or on trains, or on aeroplanes. There's never enough time to get everything done and I absolutely love it.'

'Why?'

'*Why*?' The question seems to puzzle him. 'Because ...' he frowns. 'Because I still get this huge charge out of people. We're a volunteer organisation. Without the volunteers there'd be no IAT, no Royal IAT, no nothing. They come back to us year after year, and year after year they do more than any of them thought possible. That's it, you see. That's the charge. Seeing the way these guys extend themselves, go beyond themselves, that's incredible to watch.'

This is beginning to sound like RIAT's house style. Heidi's word for it was can-do.

'She's right. I'm not saying that Paul and I set the pace or anything like that, but we've always loved making the impossible possible. Now that's a wonderful way of looking at the world, but you'd be amazed at how much it upsets some people. Take some of our colleagues in the airshow business. A lot of them don't like us at all. They think we're a pair of poseurs. They think we make it up as we go along.'

'And do you?'

'We certainly used to, yes. But that's exactly the point. We did that, we made up our own rules, because otherwise there weren't any. Now, of course, it's all a bit different.'

He breaks off, eyeing the orange bag, and for a moment I wonder whether a life as high-pressured as Tim's leaves any time at all for quiet reflection. Probably not, I conclude, as he asks his PA for the fourth coffee of the afternoon and settles down to brief me about next summer's show.

In essence, the Royal International Air Tattoo revolves around three themes. Next year, 1998, marks the eightieth anniversary of the RAF, and so the public days – Saturday and Sunday – will be structured to reflect this. Various elements in the eight-hour flying display will echo the anniversary and each afternoon will climax with a special eighty-minute tribute featuring a huge range of aircraft, old and new. This tribute, Tim assures me, will be specially choreographed, and the display will end with a unique flypast in front of a hand-picked bunch of RAF veterans.

'How many veterans?'

'Eighty.'

'And how many aircraft?'

'Take a wild guess.'

I write down the figure 80, still wondering about the choreography. What, exactly, does this word mean?

Tim sips coffee. 'Not sure yet,' he says. 'Paul's got one or two ideas.'

That sounds ominous and I say so. Tim grins. It's very difficult trying to work out the exact balance within this relationship of theirs, but I rather fancy that Tim, in his quiet way, is as much of a risk-taker as the wildly entrepreneurial Paul Bowen.

'You have to take risks,' Tim admits. 'You have to keep pushing the envelope out. If we don't raise our game, we're dead.'

'But how do you do it?'

'Well, that's the trick, isn't it? You keep looking. You keep asking yourself questions. You keep asking yourself why you do something this way and not that. Take all this stuff about the Theatre of the Air. Have you heard about that yet?'

I tell him I haven't. It sounds a wonderful phrase. What does it mean?

'It means admitting that what we do is a branch of showbusiness. Just think about night displays. They happen. I've seen one.'

'*Night* displays?'

'That's right. I went to a show in Austria recently. It was run by a pal of ours. It started at dusk. They lit gasoline fires beside the runway. There was a huge conflagration, serious stuff, and then they sent in this big old Antonov water-bomber to dump on the fires. They put coloured lights through the spray, then flew Hueys through the smoke, lights on, low level. They were playing the *Close Encounters* theme through these huge speakers and the Hueys were out there, performing to the music. If you want to talk about choreography and the Theatre of the Air and stuff like that then you should go and have a look.'

'Are they doing it again?'

'No.'

'Why ever not?'

'They got banned.'

'Why?'

'Because it was too bloody dangerous.' He shakes his head regretfully, still warmed by the memories, then fills me in on the rest of next year's show.

As well as the RAF's eightieth, RIAT will be marking the fiftieth anniversary of the Berlin Airlift, the year-long food and fuel shuttle that saved West Berlin from the Soviet army. At this early stage, Tim and Sue Allen are scouring the planet for DC-3s, the legendary twin-engined Dakota that provided the Airlift's mainstay. Given enough aircraft, RIAT will be staging an anniversary re-enactment of the landing and turnaround routines, an against-the-clock operation that saw another aircraft on the glideslope every ninety seconds.

'How many aircraft do you need?'

'It's early days but I think twelve will do it.'

Twelve? I think back to my sixth-form days on the A level history course. As far as I remember, the Allies were flying hundreds of aircraft aday into Tempelhof and Gatow. I'm about to query the wisdom of this kind of token historical tableau when I remember something else. Paul Bowen never bothered with the sixth form. By the time we were all scribbling essays about the Italian Risorgimento, he was out there. Doing it.

'Twelve sounds ideal,' I say thoughtfully. 'A dozen Daks should do nicely.'

Tim accepts my capitulation with good grace. Already he's outlining next year's operational theme, a hook for foreign air arms which RIAT baits with flying competitions, in-depth, high-level symposiums, and some nice bits of trophy glassware.

'We're calling it SkyWatch next year,' he tells me. 'Basically it's J-Stars and AWACS, ELINT and spooky-dooky Blackbirds, all that stuff. What you can see from 50,000 feet. Why the eye in the sky can pick up the filling in your sandwich. We may even fly some UAVs. Should be brilliant.'

'UAVs?'

'Unmanned Aerial Vehicles. The Israelis have got hundreds. We're talking to someone about getting one over.'

'Isn't there a safety problem here? A hundred thousand people? No one in the cockpit?'

'Not at all!' Tim laughs. 'It's the pilots who give us the problems.'

For a minute or two he explores the SkyWatch theme a little further, and I take notes as he outlines what these highly specialised surveillance and recce aircraft will be able to contribute to the weekend's flying. A lot of the equipment is top secret, but there'll certainly be scope for downlinking data and pictures to giant screens among the crowd.

The mention of giant screens brings me back into the conversation. For twenty years I worked as a producer for ITV. I did lots of outside broadcasts. I know about giant screens.

'You're having Jumbotrons?'

'That's the plan.'

'How many?'

'We've got quotes for four.'

'How much?'

He hesitates. So far, everyone's been remarkably candid about money – and Tim, in the end, sees no point in hiding the figures. 'They're asking a hundred grand,' he says.

I try and do the sums in my head. Giant screens are only as effective as the material you feed them. That means laying hands on a mobile outside broadcast scanner, cabled and remote cameras, outfield links, full technical back-up, the whole caboodle. I glance up.

'You'll obviously be using these screens throughout the day. Not just for SkyWatch.'

'Of course.'

'So what goes on them?'

'You tell me.' The faintest smile plays around his mouth. Paul must have told him about my programme-making days.

'Downlinked pictures from the aerobatic displays?' I suggest. 'Close-up ground-to-air coverage?'

'Sounds great.'

'Archival packages for the Berlin Airlift? Veteran profiles for the RAF eightieth?'

'Perfect.'

'Are you serious?'

'Always.'

As a creative challenge it sounds enticing, but the sums involved are awesome. Add a production crew to the hardware and the technicians and you're looking at serious money.

'Including the screens, you might be up for a hundred and fifty thousand,' I say. 'Minimum.'

'Dollars or pounds?'

'Pounds.'

Tim doesn't even blink. Perhaps this is what he means by the word impossible.

'So how would you fund that kind of expense?' I enquire. 'As a matter of interest.'

Tim gazes at his empty cup then leans back in his chair, his hands clasped behind his head. 'You're staying with Paul tonight,' he says cheerfully. 'Why don't you ask him?'

Paul Bowen lives up in the Cotswold hills. The house, to my delight, is called Three Greens. Three green lights in the cockpit tell any pilot that his undercarriage is extended and locked. The thought of Paul Bowen coming down to earth is – at this moment – wholly appropriate.

After supper we retire with a bottle of rather good Pinotage.

'We have to go with the Jumbotrons,' he insists. 'It has to be done.'

'But how? How do you raise that money?'

'Sponsorship. Someone'll be happy to pay. It's a really exciting development.'

With the latter, I can't help agreeing. Imagine next year's show. The Red Arrows are running in from the west. A hundred thousand pairs of eyes look skywards. Everyone can see the diamond nine. Everyone – in telly terms – has the wide shot.

'So we put the cameras in the cockpit,' I suggest, 'and give them the close-up.'

'Of course. And helmet-mounted, too. We did that last year, for the video. It looked brilliant.'

Paul's one step ahead of me. I've been out of the game too long. We power on, pushing ever deeper into the corners of the display envelope, and as we do so I begin to understand what makes this thing so infectious. The world's sexiest planes. The world's top pilots. Ours for a whole weekend. To do whatever we like with.

'Take the Berlin Airlift,' I say. 'You're planning on vintage transport on the runway for the unloading sequences. Brilliant idea – but all the crowd will see are dots in the distance. So we put in a couple of hand-held cameras, linked back to the scanner and the screens.'

'Of course.'

'So you're there, in the thick of it.'

'Sure. Then the gooney birds take off, the DC-3s. Twelve of them. Think of the noise.'

We sip glasses of Pinotage, thinking of the noise. My qualms about historical tableaux have disappeared. Twenty-four Pratt & Whitneys. Magic. Paul begins to brood about another idea.

'Did Tim mention the eightieth flypast? The veterans taking the salute?'

I tell him he did.

'And did he mention what I had in mind?'

'No.'

Paul leans forward in his armchair, his hands slicing the air over the low table. He's planning on vertical stacks of aircraft for the fly-by, each one representing a particular phase in the RAF's history. He wants to sequence the stacks by aircraft type – bombers, transports, trainers, etc – and he wants to launch with fighters. This first stack will feature the Camel at the bottom and a Eurofighter 2000 at the top. The Camel is an ancient World War One biplane. Eurofighter is the state-of-the-art multi-national interceptor, due to replace the Tornado.

I try and visualise what Paul has in mind. It isn't easy to come up with something totally new.

'So how many aircraft? In between the Camel and the Eurofighter?'

'Dunno.' Paul starts to count. 'Camel. Hind. Hurricane. Spitfire. Meteor. Vampire. Harrier. Tornado. Eurofighter.'

'That's nine.'

'OK, nine.'

'And they're all stacked up?'

'Yes.'

The problem here is relative speed. The Camel, on a good day, might make sixty knots. At anything less than 130 knots, Eurofighter will fall out of the sky. So how do they stay in a vertical stack?

'They don't.'

Paul's hands are spaced out now, one behind the other. The top hand is the Eurofighter. The bottom, the Camel. The Eurofighter gains on the Camel and, exactly in front of the eighty watching veterans, they find themselves vertically stacked.

'And the seven in between?'

'They're stacked too. It all comes good in front of the veterans.'

'And you'll repeat this? With other kinds of aircraft?'

'Yep. Trainers. Bombers. Maritime. Transport. GA.'

'GA?'

'Ground Attack.'

I swallow another mouthful of Pinotage, trying to imagine the sky full of briefly coalescing vertical stacks. I'm no expert but the plan seems wildly ambitious.

Paul beams. In his mind's eye all the practical problems – wind, safety margins, pilot error – have already been solved, and RIAT 98 is presenting the world's first vertically stacked flypasts. I try, very tactfully, to sound a warning note but he shakes his head, convinced the concept will work, convinced the concept *has* to work. And as he begins to uncork another bottle I realise that this is one of the keys to RIAT's success. You start, illogically enough, with the end result. You draw yourself a little cartoon, and you try it out on one or two people you trust, and when they shake their heads and say it's impossible you go out and find the very best guy in the field, and with a bit of arm-twisting and a lot of luck he'll make it all come true.

'Am I right?'

The grin again. Big. Bold. Completely undaunted. 'Of course you are. That's what makes it fun.'

We talk long into the night. The first Air Tattoo was twenty-seven years ago, but I remember freezing spring weekends even earlier than that when we dodged out of school and piled into the back of an ancient Land Rover and drove the fifteen miles up the road to the old Battle of Britain airfield at North Weald. Paul's home was nearby – his father was secretary at St Margaret's Hospital – and it was already obvious that Paul, like his dad, had been bitten by the aviation bug.

That first show, in 1971, took place at North Weald, but it was quickly apparent that the strip was too small for the plans Paul and Tim were hatching. What they needed was a proper airbase, some-where with extensive facilities – and an exhaustive countrywide tour finally took them to Greenham Common near Newbury, where the Americans were only too willing to open the gates of their base to these two fresh-faced young air traffic controllers with plans for a little yearly entertainment.

There's a part of Paul Bowen that thrives on anecdote. Over the years the Tattoo has generated a constant supply of stories, and Paul embellishes them with enormous gusto. From the Greenham Common days come two favourites of mine. One of them features a woman who'd leased a tiny, far-flung part of the airbase. Among other things, she kept rabbits. Their hutches were a couple of hundred metres from the lift-off point on the runway, and a brace of Phantoms on re-heat gave the bunnies a serious fright. Their owner hauled Paul and Tim across the airfield to view her quivering livestock and demanded to know what they intended to do about them. Paul and Tim went into a huddle. Seconds later, they came up with the answer. Treble-glazed bunny hutches. Courtesy of IAT.

The other story is equally telling, though a good deal less funny. It was the Friday of airshow week, the day before the gates opened to the public. One of the star attractions was to be the presence of a giant USAF B-52 bomber, always a crowd-pleaser. Paul had pulled lots of strings to lay hands on the plane and was absolutely determined that it should get top billing. The aircraft was inbound from the States when the captain made radio contact. Paul and Tim, in the Operations Room, heard him announce that he was having problems with the gear. Without the undercarriage down and locked – three greens – the giant bomber would come to grief on the runway. With an aircraft that size, it would take the rest of the weekend to clear up the mess.

Tim and Paul and the American base commander, Les Gibson, discussed their options. The sensible decision was for the pilot to divert to the big USAF base at Mildenhall. Not only were they better equipped to deal with this kind of emergency, but the diversion would leave the rest of the IAT flying display intact. Paul wasn't convinced. He knew from Les that B-52s regularly suffered from faulty micro-switches, giving false readings.

Minutes later, the big bomber appeared overhead. A pair of bin-oculars revealed the gear to be down but there was no guarantee that the wheel supports would be locked in place.

What to do? Tim was emphatically in favour of Mildenhall. Paul was prepared to bet on the microswitch. Tens of thousands of people were already dreaming of seeing the B-52. How could he possibly let them down?

I stir on the sofa. 'So what happened?'

'We cleared it to land. Full emergency alert. Fire trucks. Ambulances. The lot.'

'And?'

'It was the microswitch.'

Paul is the first to admit that the decision was a gamble. Had the aircraft pancaked on the runway, the weekend's flying programme would have been wiped out. But the story has rightly become an IAT classic, not least because it demonstrates the iron faith in luck and judgement that appears to underpin so much of the Air Tattoo.

Paul and Tim decamped from Greenham Common after the 1983 show, driven out by the arrival of yet more cruise missiles. Two years later they produced the first of the Fairford IATs, attracting 200,000 people with an ambitious flying display and a static line of aircraft more than two miles long. By now, IAT had become a major entry in the international aviation calendar, though Tim and Paul were often far too busy to take stock.

It's two in the morning. The second bottle of Pinotage lies empty between us.

'It's funny,' Paul muses, 'there are moments when it suddenly hits you. I remember when we first pitched to Lockheed for sponsorship, years and years ago. Tim and I flew over to Atlanta, and they made a great fuss of us, and we put on our best suits, and up we went to the main boardroom, and I remember looking round at all the faces and thinking, "Christ, we're in the big league now."'

Lockheed evidently liked what they heard and, since that first encounter, their support for the show has grown and grown. In their wake, over the last decade or so, have come other giants from the aerospace industry. Paul tallies the list of names with enormous relish. Boeing, Hughes, Raytheon, Northrop-Grumman, British Aerospace and Rolls-Royce all pitch their tents at Fairford, each company only too happy to sponsor this element or that in the five-day programme of events. Already, in the long run-up to the 1998 show, projections for RIAT's share of the corporate cake are edging towards £600,000, another fat wodge of money in Enterprises' bank account. Quite how this translates on the ground – enclosures, tents, hospitality, protocol – I've yet to discover, and I'm still battling to get this dimension into some kind of perspective when Paul returns to the jumbo screens.

'We have to do it,' he repeats. 'Every year we have to do something new. We can't stand still. Ever.' He looks across at me. 'This year they called us the best air show in the world. Frightening, isn't it?'

I head up to bed minutes later. There's a room set back from the top landing which catches my attention. Through the open door, half lit, I can see the glint of a model railway. The engines – classics from the Fifties and Sixties – are exquisitely painted. The rolling stock include carriages I can remember from my schoolboy days. Even the tiny signals look totally authentic. It's a little world of its own in there, perfectly realised, brilliantly mounted.

I hear footsteps coming up the stairs behind me. It's Paul. I gesture at the ghostly shapes. 'Who did all this?'

He pauses a moment, gazing in. 'Me,' he says.

Next morning, back in Building 15, I'm bent over a borrowed desk, trying to make sense of my notes. The door is half open and I'm aware of someone outside, looking in. It's Amanda Butcher. She's very much part of the command loop. There isn't much she doesn't know.

'How's it going?'

'Fine.' I gesture at the pile of scribble in front of me. 'Help yourself.'

She steps into the office and peers over my shoulder. The word Jumbotron brings a smile to her face. 'Welcome to RIAT,' she says lightly. 'Amazing how they get you on board, isn't it?'

CHAPTER THREE

....

November 1997

Winter has settled on the airfield. It's time to get a secure fix on the geography of RAF Fairford, and the man to help me is Mel James.

Mel spent his twenty-seven years in the RAF as an engineer. He left last year with the rank of Wing Commander, and now works alongside Paul Bowen as the RIAT executive charged with 'Special Projects'. What exactly this means isn't immediately clear but Mel drives a big, comfortable Toyota people-mover and, as we surge off towards the ramp that gives access to the runway, he hands me a detailed map of the airfield, a smaller version of the one I've seen on various office walls.

Engineers tend to be businesslike, hands-on, practical men with a limited interest in small talk, and Mel is no exception. He's been passionate about aircraft for most of his life, and it must be enormously satisfying to have translated that passion into a monthly salary cheque and a successful career. Unlike some of the Fairford team, whose talents might lie in marketing or business sponsorship, Mel has an iron grip on the various mechanical and aerodynamic miracles that get an aircraft airborne and keep it in one piece. He understands a great deal about fatigue monitoring and airframe life. He could probably change a turbine fan single-handed. He doesn't suffer fools gladly.

A solid-looking pair of gates bars access to what Mel terms 'airside'. Airside is the active bit of the airfield, the preserve of the aircraft themselves. Fairford hasn't seen an aeroplane for weeks and the gates are open, but Mel stops none the less to check his tyres for FOD. FOD means Foreign Object Damage, and there are signs everywhere reminding drivers just how easily a shard of glass or a stray pebble can be sucked into a passing jet engine, tearing it apart.

Back in the Toyota, Mel bends to the map. Fairford began life in 1944 as a support airfield for the allied invasion of mainland Europe, and the familiar triangle of three runways is still visible on the easterly end of the map. Stirling bombers towed Horsa gliders out of here on the night of 5 June 1944, heading for the Orne canal on the flank of the Normandy beachhead, and the Stirlings rolled again in September when airborne troops seized the bridges at Arnhem. Post-war, Fairford was handed over to the US Air Force. The east-west runway was lengthened to 10,000ft and the airfield became home for a squadron of B-47 Stratojets. Back under RAF command in 1964, it served as the test centre for the Concorde development programme before being leased once again to the Americans. Activated for specific crises like the Gulf War, Fairford found room for the B-52 Stratofortress, as well as a squadron of KC-135 Stratotankers.

'Here's where we base Eng Ops.'

We've stopped beside a smart, brown, newish-looking building beside the main northside east-west taxiway. Eng Ops is, in Mel's phrase, 'abbrieve-speak' for Engineering Operations. During the week of the show this will become the nerve centre for Mel's empire. Engineering, technical and fuel support for nearly five hundred aircraft will be down to his team of volunteers.

He shows me a root-and-branch diagram establishing who does what in the engineering and fuels operation. There are lots of boxes, lots of names, lots of abbrieve-speak. I notice one box in particular, down towards the right-hand corner. It reads 'Drivers/shotguns'.

Mel shoots me an appraising look. Like so many in RIAT he's proud of what he's done, and it's all-important that everything be framed in the right context. 'You've got to understand how we operate,' he says. 'We put a system in place. It's tested year after year. OK, we may modify it, change things round a little, but fundamentally we *know* it works. And that's what matters.'

'So what about this shotgun?' I gesture at the diagram.

Mel's still looking wary. Engineers aren't that comfortable with writer-types.

'The shotgun is our guy. He's a volunteer. The driver comes with the vehicle. We borrow six 10,000-litre bowsers plus a smaller bowser with diesel for the aerobatic teams' smoke generators. Our guys ride shotgun with the driver. They know the RIAT system. They handle all the chitties and the paperwork. Like I said, the job gets done.'

I begin to make notes. Last year, Mel's volunteers pumped four million litres of fuel into airshow aircraft. They have to buy it in and sell it on, so the paperwork becomes all-important. One lost chitty can make a hefty dent in the Benevolent Fund's income.

Mel swings left on the ramp and we dawdle slowly up the big fat spur of concrete that extends one of the old wartime runways towards the north-east. On my map this is marked as Apron Green and subdivided into three areas: Alpha, Bravo and Charlie. Looking out at the acres and acres of hard-standing, interlaced with fading lines of various colours, all the abbrieve-speak and clipped military acronyms suddenly make sense. How to conjure order out of chaos. How to find room for 486 aeroplanes.

We purr to a halt in the middle of one of the huge parking bays. These, it seems, are called 'spectacles' or 'spots'. Here, in Spot One, Mel plans to park up to ten VIP aircraft. The nearby building that houses Eng Ops also serves as the VIP reception centre, and it makes diplomatic as well as practical sense to minimise the length of the VIP stroll across the ramp. At this point, more relaxed now, Mel strays from the engineering brief.

'The Protocol lot use the front door,' he growl. 'Us oiks have to come in through the back.'

'Why?'

'Because we're the oily rags. All we do is keep the planes in the air.'

Appearances and the pecking order matter a great deal within RIAT. Mel has the fondest memories of his youngest son, in T-shirt and backward-facing baseball cap, bumping by accident into a minister of state. Not the least bit fazed, Mel did the introductions and the minister was graciousness itself, but Paul Bowen – for one – would have been less than amused.

We're out of the Toyota now. A keen wind cuts across the airfield from the north-west. Mel tugs the peak of his own Breitling baseball cap a little lower, then nods at the vast expanse of concrete.

'Aircraft on the ground can be a real pain,' he says. 'They're like incontinent aunts. They're not happy at all.'

The parking plan to berth this medium-sized airforce is in itself a work of art, and Mel borrows my map to explain the broad principles. Individual parking areas, or 'aprons', are colour-coded. Northside are Aprons Green and Red. Southside, to the west and to the east, are eight additional areas including Aprons Brown, Orange, Violet and Blue that together make up the two-mile static display line. Mel's gloved finger darts across the page. Southside is the public area, or 'showground'. He'll be putting fighters here. Training aircraft there. Heavies will be stowed safely away on Brown, Grey, White and Pink, down at the western end.

'Heavies?'

'B-52s. Some of the big Il-76s. The C-5.'

He peers briefly south, across the airfield, shielding his eyes against the sun. Parking the giant C-5 Galaxy, he says, is like having a gorilla as a pet. She sleeps where she likes.

I chuckle, making a note. There's room for laughter, after all, among the organograms and triplicated RIAT fuel chits.

A long yellow line loops in and out of Spot One. This is the nosewheel track line for the pilots of the bigger aircraft. All-important is the angle at which the aircraft parks.

'Why?'

Mel gestures across the airfield again, towards the southside. 'The static line can take more than a hundred aircraft,' he says. 'That's a fantastic photo-opportunity. All those noses, side by side, inch perfect.'

'So what's the angle? Have you worked it out?'

He shoots me that look again. Silly question to ask an engineer. 'It's exactly forty degrees off-set from the taxiway,' he says. 'We give the pilots the bearing and leave them to park on their compasses. Most of them get it right first time.'

He begins to explain how the arrival sequence works during the week of the show, the aircraft flying in from all over the world, calling the tower for clearance to land. At four miles out, Air Traffic Control notifies Eng Ops. The duty Ops Controller confirms the parking location and advises the appropriate Area Controller and Fuel Controller that the aircraft is about to land. A 'Follow-Me' vehicle, one of the Volvo estates I rode in July, escorts the aircraft to its parking position and hands over to one of Mel's marshallers. Mention of the marshallers reminds me of Sir Roger Palin's nightmare. Several hundred tons of strategic bomber – effectively in the hands of a twenty-one-year-old.

'Do you train these guys?'

'Of course we do.'

Mel briskly details the hazards of the job. How the outside trailing edge of a swept-wing fighter can cut a far wider swathe on the turn than you'd ever imagine. How important it is to give highly conservative tolerances on the ramp. How you absolutely must keep an eye on ground equipment. How the wheels of a heavy like the B-52 can literally gouge the tarmac on a hot day.

My pen's racing. 'Not easy then, this parking game.'

'Not at all. We had a Canberra once – it belonged to some German research outfit. It had wingtip tanks, and we were bringing it in on the edge of a taxiway, and until you saw it head-on you didn't realise just how much oscillation those tip tanks induced.'

By oscillation, Mel means that the wings were going up and down. Flapping would be another word for it.

'So what happened?'

Mel, for a moment, has gone quiet. Then he musters a smile. 'The starboard tip tank missed a hot-dog stand by inches,' he says. 'We were bloody lucky.'

We walk across the parking bay. In the middle I spot what looks like a hydrant.

Mel nods. 'But it's fuel,' he says, 'not water.'

We gaze down at the shallow, dome-shaped lid of the hydrant. Back in the days of the Cold War, when the base was truly operational, the big KC-135s – tanker versions of the Boeing 707 – would take on fuel here, pumping 200,000 litres of Avtur in just fifteen minutes. Underneath Fairford, Mel explains, is a huge ring-main system, the biggest in the country outside Heathrow, and this in turn draws fuel from enormous pipes that criss-cross the country. These pipes, buried 100 feet below ground, are fed directly from a handful of oil refineries at various coastal locations.

In thirty years of being nosy, today is the first time I've heard of this network – and the realisation that it exists is slightly sobering. Mel looks pleased with himself. He thinks I'm beginning to learn a thing or two. And he's right.

Our tour of the airfield continues. This is where Mel will be putting some of his operational fighters, a mixed bag of Jaguars, Tornados, a couple of Mirage IIIs, a Starfighter, half a dozen F-16s. Over here, on a strip of newly cut grass, a line of helicopters. Over here, their long tails overhanging the lip of the concrete bay, a couple of 'Fat Alberts', or C-130 Hercules. And just there, once they've confirmed they're coming, the six MiG-29s of the Ukrainian Falcons aerobatic team.

Mention of the MiGs brings the Toyota to a halt. It's more than obvious now that Mel has indeed been crazy about aircraft for probably the whole of his conscious life. As a kid, he fell in love with the lines they scrolled in the sky. As an engineer, he got to know about their insides too, and his association with Paul Bowen has brought him the opportunity to take an intimate look at all kinds of hitherto unreachable aircraft.

'We were in Czechoslovakia in 1990,' he says. 'They wanted us to organise an airshow. The Cold War was over, of course, and we spent some time at Zatec, the fighter base in Bohemia.' Even eight years on, Mel still smiles at the memories: the chance to talk to the pilots, the chance to get a close peek at their training schedules.

'They had a real problem, and that problem was money. These guys were allowed two or three hours' flying a month. Our guys get maybe ten times that and even then we don't think it's enough.'

'Money for what?' I wonder.

'Everything. Fuel. Maintenance. Even maps. From Zatec they'd fly due north, round Berlin, up to the Baltic weapon-training ranges at Peenemunde. They did it all VFR because they had no maps. They shared one big one, pinned to the wall in the Ops Room. Before you went, you had a good hard look and memorised it all. Amazing.'

VFR means flying under visual flight rules, or having to look out of the window to stay on course.

Mel shakes his head. I ask him about the Soviet aircraft he saw in Czechoslovakia.

'Bloody incredible planes.' He grins. 'Tremendous aerodynamics. Outstanding performance. Huge engineering tolerances. Nice clean design. Unlike us, they always build in extra power from the start, which means you can hang all kinds of stuff off them and not pay the price in performance.'

Mel is obviously a fan of the Russian school of aeronautics, and I'm back in July again, watching the Ukrainians haul their *Fulcrums* around incredibly tight turns. Given this amazing performance, why are we bothering with Eurofighter?

'Because there's a downside. Like always. The finish quality on the MiGs is appalling. Go and take a look at some of their complex double curvature structures. They're built to agricultural standards. I kid you not, twenty per cent of the riveting is U/S.'

'U/S?'

'Unserviceable.'

I scribble myself a note, then add another. 'Double curvature structures' is a truly wonderful phrase – and I'm still wondering whether it might apply to one or two of the younger female staff back in Building 15 when the Toyota is abruptly under way again. Mel wants to talk about AGE.

AGE, in plain English, means Aircraft Ground Equipment. Four hundred and eighty aircraft need a great deal of attention, and though the American base commander is more than helpful lots of extra kit has to be begged, borrowed or hired from outside sources. Checked and logged, it's then pre-positioned, ready for the descending armada of incoming planes. Some visitors, especially the larger aircraft, carry their own equipment. The tug and towbar for the Lockheed Galaxy, tucked away in the belly of the giant freighter, is itself bigger than anything available at Fairford. It looks, says Mel, like the Forth Bridge.

At this point it occurs to me to ask about mechanical problems. Mel has assembled an impressive team of nearly a hundred volunteers.

Aircraft sometimes get sick – or, in Mel's phrase, 'go tits up'. Can RIAT engineers deal with *anything*?

Mel shakes his head. 'Small stuff is no problem. Paint scrapes, the odd dent, minor damage, we can deal with all that. But anything bigger we have to leave to the specialists.'

Foreign air forces, especially those providing aerobatic teams, often ship in spare engines and full engineering back-up aboard big transporters, but in practice it's rarer than you might think for an aircraft to develop a major problem. By the end of a typical show, maybe four or five planes will have fallen victim to a bird strike or need structural repair. Seriously ill, they'll remain on the ramp at Fairford until specialist engineering teams arrive from their home bases, and it may be as long as a week before they're well enough to fly home again.

By now we've almost completed a full lap of the airfield. From one end to the other, it's more than two miles – a bare, windswept landscape drenched in a cold winter light. At the easterly threshold to the main runway Mel pulls the Toyota to a halt. He's been going through the sequence of events on the Monday after the public weekend. The flying displays are over. The pilots are keen to get home. Already, the day they arrived, most will have put in bids for an early departure slot, but the launching of outbound aircraft is determined by any number of factors. First, the runway must be meticulously checked for FOD. At the same time, after two days on the ground, each aircraft must be prepped for flight. For some pilots this is a fifteen-minute routine – 'kick the tyres, light the fires' – but for others it can take far longer. Fuel loads must be checked. So-called 'lox pots' – tanks of liquid oxygen for high-altitude flying – must be filled and reinstalled. Aircraft requiring air traffic clearance on to airways must file flight plans – and the queue for the precious airways slots is always long. The big national air traffic control centre at West Drayton will only accept four aircraft an hour from Fairford, and once these airways slots have been agreed the departing pilots have to meet them. Yet another invariable that must be factored into the Monday master plan. Yet more – in Mel's phrase – 'buggeration'.

The departure sequence finally agreed, the lines of aircraft on countless aprons must be carefully broken. It's an interesting choice of verb, heavy with implication. Certain aircraft, by virtue of their size and shape, will lock in an entire line. Without moving one, none of the others can escape. Mel sketches a particular example on my notepad, and it's startling to see just how intricate a jigsaw his team has to put together. They can, of course, move the aircraft by themselves, using a tug and a towbar, but first they must be sure that the brakes are off.

For a moment or two, the implications of this escape me. Mel offers a clue. 'Pilots,' he says, 'live in a world of their own.'

'Meaning?'

'They never leave the bloody key.'

The key? I gaze out at the empty aprons. It's easy to imagine these huge spaces filled with aircraft, but it's the first time I've thought about keys and doorlocks and anything as ordinary as a handbrake. I listen in wonderment while Mel tells me stories about aircrews disappearing for days on end, leaving neither a phone number nor a key, while the Eng Ops team goes half-crazy trying to shift 200 tons of rogue aeroplane so the rest can fly away.

'So what did you do?'

'We changed the system.'

'How?'

'We now insist they leave us a key.'

'Where, exactly?'

Mel looks at me a moment, then shakes his head. 'What do you think I am?' he says. 'Stupid?'

A minute or so later, rounding the threshold of the runway, Mel gestures out to the right. Beyond the wire, across the public road, is a big area that RIAT turn into a coach park for the airshow. Compared to much Mel's already told me, this information is less than exciting and I don't bother to write it down. This makes him smile.

'Ask me about the bunkers,' he suggests.

'What bunkers?'

'The bunkers under the coach park.' He pauses. 'That's where the Americans used to store their buckets of instant sunshine.'

I can't help looking bewildered. After an hour of technical chatter, abbrieve-speak and fascinating stories, he's finally got me.

'Buckets of instant *sunshine*?'

'Yeah,' Mel nods. 'Nuclear bombs.'

A week and a half later, Amanda and Sue take the train to London to launch their two-week blitz on the capital's community of foreign air and defence attachés. These tend to be serving officers seconded to their London embassies to represent the interests of their parent airforce. Charming, attentive, with that special aura of the fast-jet pilot, most of them are only too happy to open their office doors to the likes of the RIAT aircraft procurement team. Be nice to these guys, murmurs Sue, and you can walk away with a sackload of airplanes.

Our day begins outside the Algerian embassy in Holland Park. The Algerians have yet to make an appearance at the show and Amanda in particular is determined that they shall. Up six flights of stairs, we sit on buttoned leather Chesterfields while an aide pours coffee. Colonel Khamri, the attaché, is a slim, courteous, friendly man with soft brown eyes and a ready smile.

While Sue unpacks the contents of the RIAT goodie bag, Amanda describes the success of the last show. Mention of the sheer numbers of aircraft on display – 300 static, 150 operational – draws expressions of amazement from Colonel Khamri, a reaction I judge to be genuine. Neither his English nor our Arabic is up to much, so a lot of our conversation is conducted in a strange *patois* – partly English, partly French – peppered with a ready sprinkling of aircraft designations, which appear to pass from language to language without major damage.

By the time the aide returns with more coffee, we've established that Colonel K learned most of his fighter pilot skills at the hands of the Russians; that London is a truly wonderful city; and that the Algerian airforce, while plentiful enough in terms of numbers, is very definitely ageing. This, to be fair, is no surprise. The Algerians' best piece of kit, a squadron of MiG-25 *Foxbats*, was delivered in 1979, while the status of much of its Soviet-vintage inventory is – in the words of *Air Forces of the World* – 'very much in question'.

Amanda, a born diplomat, insists that this won't be a problem. The

Royal International Air Tattoo, she says, values displaying historical aircraft every bit as much as it likes to showcase the cutting edge of aviation technology. Describing the frontline Algerian interceptor as a museum piece is a brave move, but Colonel Khamri is a man of infinite good humour and pretty soon we're discussing the small print of the RIAT invitation.

The bid, formulated earlier in the taxi, is for five aircraft – two operational, three on the static line. It would be nice, in particular, to see the reconnaissance version of the MiG-25, an aircraft that would fit perfectly with next year's SkyWatch theme.

While Colonel K scribbles himself a note, Sue and Amanda exchange glances. Sue has already baited the RIAT hook with a calendar, a video, a handful of beautifully-produced brochures, and a detailed description of the operational benefits of enrolling Algerian aircrew in the various training exercises. Now, Amanda produces a long white envelope.

'This is a personal invitation to General Mohamed Benslimani,' she explains. 'It comes from our Chairman, Air Chief Marshal Sir Roger Palin. It would be wonderful if General Benslimani could join us next year.'

She goes on to describe the VIP entertainments awaiting the Chief of the Algerian Air Force, should he choose to accept the RIAT invitation. The wining and dining begins on Wednesday evening. On Thursday, there's a House of Commons reception and a dinner in Apsley House (still known in certain circles as Number One, London). On Friday, after a day of inter-aircrew competitions, there's a gala evening hosted by British Aerospace. Over the weekend, after days spent watching the flying display from the comforts of the Patrons' Pavilion, there's a barbecue at a nearby private airfield and a chance to fly in any number of vintage biplanes. Should General Benslimani be interested in golf, the Fairford VIP experience ends with eighteen holes on Monday morning. Back in July, says Amanda, Sir Roger welcomed the chiefs of no less than twenty foreign airforces. To be able to add General Benslimani to the list would be a tremendous pleasure.

The invitation is perfectly pitched. Colonel Khamri is smiling broadly. Life in Algeria just now is pretty grim, and there are worse career moves than pleasing the boss. We get to our feet and reach for our coats, the meeting over. Sue submits to a kiss on the cheek. Thanks to *Air Forces of the World*, she knows the Algerian Airforce by heart.

'Might General Benslimani be coming over in the Falcon or the Gulfstream III?' she enquires.

Colonel K returns her smile. He's still holding the official invitation. 'The Falcon 900,' he nods. '*Sans aucun doute.*'

Next stop is the Danish embassy in Sloane Street. The cool Scandinavian decor is a world away from the rich browns and reds of Colonel Khamri's office. Captain Grooss, the Danish air attaché, is an old friend of the Air Tattoo and for most of the meeting I might as well have been at a family reunion.

Captain Grooss's favourite story, aside from the one about the aircrew who ate an entire Swindon hotel out of breakfasts, concerns the fate of a RIAT trophy awarded a couple of years back to the crew of a Danish Lynx helicopter. The Danes had put up a polished performance in the *Concours d'Elegance*, and were delighted with their Dartington crystal bowl. One of the crew had carefully packed the trophy in bubblewrap inside a black plastic sack and stored it aboard the Lynx for safekeeping. Only on the Monday, 6,000 feet above the North Sea, did he realise that the sack was missing.

The Lynx captain was on the radio back to Fairford within seconds. A search for the sack revealed that cleaners had removed it from the aircraft, thinking it was rubbish. A rummage through umpteen wheelie bins and skips proved fruitless, and in the end Dartington were commissioned to provide a replica bowl. Suitably engraved, it now graces the trophy cabinet in the squadron mess at Vaerloese.

The meeting with Captain Grooss ends early. The Danes are only too happy to tick the aircraft on Sue's wish-list, not least because they keep winning the Friday competitions.

'But you heard about the Swedish this year?' Captain Grooss has escorted us out to the street. 'They collected their trophy at the Friday gala dinner and then dropped the damn thing.'

'Dropped it?' Sue is racking her memory 'What exactly did we give them?'

'A huge piece of glass crystal.' Captain Grooss is laughing. 'They took the biggest bit home.'

At lunchtime we trek to Harvey Nichols for a sandwich and a pause for breath. First call this afternoon will be at the Turkish embassy, and for reasons I don't fully understand we need to discuss tactics.

'So what's the problem?'

We're up in the café bar on the top floor. I'm wedged against a sharp-angled American woman with no sense of humour. The place is heaving.

'It's a couple of things really.' Amanda hands me the menu. 'They owe us money, and that's a pain. But it's mainly the Turkish Stars.'

'Turkish Stars?' I'm looking at the menu. Char-grilled breast of chicken with a light saffron mayonnaise sounds nice.

'Their aerobatic team. They fly F-5 Freedom Fighters. It's a nine-ship display and they kept getting it wrong. Well, not wrong exactly. They just kept breaking the rules.'

A story of Paul's comes back to me. The F-5 was never built for aerobatics. It's a nice-looking little fighter and the Turks paint theirs in a rather fetching red and white colour scheme, but the turning circle's none too tight and as a result the Stars needed a great deal more sky than most of the other aerobatic teams. Fairford happens to lie near the conjunction of Gloucestershire, Somerset and Wiltshire, and the Turkish Stars, in RIAT legend, have become known as the Three Counties Display Team.

'But you're saying they broke the rules?'

'Twice. In fact three times.'

'How?'

'By overflying the crowd.'

This, in RIAT terms, is a cardinal sin. All display-flying at Fairford is subject to regulation by a specially-formed Flying Control Committee, chaired by Geoff Brindle, a steely-eyed Group Captain currently serving in Oman. The committee is very high powered indeed, with a range of experience extending from veterans like Brian Trubshaw, chief test-pilot on the Concorde programme, to Wing Commander Les Garside-Beattie, who spent three seasons as the RAF's Harrier display pilot. Members of the committee discuss each flying display with the pilots, and often insist on a rehearsal to make sure that the version they've seen on the ribbon diagrams accords with reality in the air. Overflying the crowd without a special dispensation is strictly off-limits.

'And the Turks?'

'Over flew the crowd. Not only that, but the two singletons stitched in a couple of extra manoeuvres none of them had ever mentioned before. Real wing-and-a-prayer stuff.'

Singletons are the solo pilots who break out of the main formations and twirl around on their own. I'd watched the Turkish Stars myself back in July, and had thought they were pretty good.

Amanda agrees. 'No one's saying they're useless. They're just not wonderful at obeying the rules.'

'And that matters?'

'Of course it does.'

The sandwiches arrive and I press for more details. Dissuading the Turkish Stars from appearing again is obviously going to be tricky. The Air Tattoo depends on goodwill from participating nations and no one wants to upset the Turks. On the other hand, the list of national aerobatic teams keen to do their stuff at Fairford is growing and growing. This year there were no less than eight of them. At twenty-five minutes per display, that's half the flying programme already filled.

'You see the problem?'

'I do.' I bite into the sandwich. 'So what about the money?'

'They owe us £26,000 in unpaid fuel bills.'

'Ah ...' This afternoon is becoming more interesting by the minute. 'So how do you intend to play it?'

Amanda looks at Sue and grins. 'By ear,' she says. 'How else?'

The Turkish embassy is in Belgrave Square. We ascend in a tiny lift and follow the corridor to the air attaché's office. Colonel Erdogan wears a pink shirt and a big smile. He orders coffee with a flourish. He's very pleased to see us.

Amanda settles into her airshow routine. She's never met Colonel Erdogan before, and she excites him at once with her account of the success of RIAT 97. When she gets to the log-jam created by too many aerobatic teams I can see exactly where she's headed, but Colonel Erdogan beats her to the draw.

'The Turkish Stars are ready and waiting,' he says at once. 'Very keen, very keen. Next year . . .?' His hands rise from the desk. 'Better than ever, I promise you.'

For a split-second Amanda is non-plussed. The obvious conclusion is that Colonel Erdogan has missed the diplomatic nuance – that the Turkish Stars might consider resting for a year or two – but I'm not at all sure that's right. I think Colonel Erdogan knows. And I think that Colonel Erdogan is about to play a blinder.

He waves at a picture above my head. 'Two thousand hours,' he says, 'in the best plane in the world.'

I half-turn in my seat, looking up. Hanging from the picture rail is a battered print of *The Haywain*. I look at Colonel Erdogan again. What on earth has John Constable got to do with military aviation?

He nods at me. 'Two thousand hours,' he confirms.

His right hand is miming movements on an imaginary joystick. Completely lost, I look at Sue. Her eyes tell me I've got the wrong picture. I try again. To the right of *The Haywain* I spot a colour photograph of an F-4 Phantom. Colonel Erdogan, I realise, was a fighter jockey. At last his manoeuvring – so deft, so agile – becomes clear.

Amanda, undaunted, steers the conversation back to the Turkish Stars. Colonel E assures her that next season's display will be better in every way than 1997's. Better in every way is, I realise, code for behaving themselves. The Stars have learned their lesson. They love Fairford. They'll ease back on their wilder excesses. Geoff Brindle and his committee are right to be tough, but from now on they'll have no problems. Not, at least, with the Turkish Stars.

At this point, getting absolutely nowhere, Amanda declares a stand-off and changes tack. One of next year's highlights will be the Berlin Airlift re-enactment. She understands that the Turkish Air Force still operates the C-47 Dakota. Any chance of a couple making an appearance?

Colonel Erdogan looks troubled. 'C-47s?'

'Yes.'

'No.' He shakes his head, frowning.

'You haven't got any?'

'No, not yet.'

Amanda blinks. Not yet? A fifty-year-old aircraft – not *yet*? She tries again. Like me, she's been reading *Air Forces of the World*. According to page 27, Colonel Erdogan's buddies operate forty C-47s. Where on earth have they all gone?

Another change of tack – Sue this time. She outlines next year's operational theme, SkyWatch. She's noticed that the Turkish Air Force flies the RF-4E, the reconnaissance version of the Phantom. Tactically, this is a brilliant move. The very mention of the aircraft brings a wistful gleam to Colonel Erdogan's eye, and this time I swear he's not playing diplomatic games. He wants to be back in the rugged old fighter again. He wants to feel the kick of those two massive J-79s.

'No problem,' he smiles at Sue. 'You've got the rag?'

The rag? I'm back in the world of John Constable and *The Haywain*. What on earth is this man talking about?

Amanda and Sue are deep in discussion. Evidently they had a rag last year. It had to be trucked in on the back of a low-loader, and it cost the earth.

Colonel Erdogan shakes his head, deeply sympathetic. Alas, Turkish Air Force regulations insist on a rag. No rag, no landing. No landing, no RF-4E. He pulls open his desk drawer and consults a small handbook. Then he looks up. 'I can give you a maximum landing speed of 150 knots,' he says.

Sue makes a note. 'What about weight?'

'44,000 pounds.'

Amanda has a calculator. 'That's twenty metric tons.'

'Sure.' Colonel Erdogan spreads his hands again. 'So you have a rag? No problem.'

Rag, it finally turns out, is pilot-speak for Rotary Hydraulic Arrester Gear, or RHAG. In plain English, it means a thick wire cable stretched across the runway, hydraulically buffered to hook and stop a landing aircraft. Without one at Fairford, Colonel Erdogan confirms, the RF-4E will be staying in Turkey.

Amanda makes a careful note while Sue produces yet another invitation from Sir Roger. This one is addressed to the Chief of the Turkish Air Force. Colonel Erdogan opens the envelope and reads it, hugely impressed by the way Sue has managed to insert two dots, Turkish style, above a 'u'. The issue of the Turkish Stars appears to have gone away.

Several cups of coffee later, we get to our feet. Colonel Erdogan will be forwarding Amanda's bid-list of aircraft to Ankara. Sir Roger's letter will go in the same diplomatic bag. We all shake hands. Then Amanda gently enquires about the monies owing for July's fuel.

Colonel Erdogan needs no prompting. He darts behind the desk and pulls open the drawer again. A photocopy of the unpaid invoice lies waiting inside a file. He taps it, beaming. 'I telexed only this morning,' he says. 'Your cheque will be in the post.'

Back outside on Belgrave Square, taxis race past in the thin drizzle. There are still two embassies to come. Tomorrow, there will be six more. By the end of the week, these girls will either be dead of coffee poisoning or walking zombies, eternally pitching the biggest military airshow in the world. After only three performances, my admiration for their stamina, their enthusiasm, and their extraordinary tact is limitless. The least I can do is hold out the promise of a decent drink at the day's end.

They glance at each other. I've forgotten our earlier conversation, last month, about the dashing young air attaché who's resisting a transfer to Washington.

'Tonight's a bit tricky,' Amanda mutters. 'Maybe some other time.'

Five days later, on a blustery November weekend, I'm due to meet Amanda again. She's driven down to the Cotswolds to look at a replacement hotel for next year's VIP programme. The hotel she intends to recce is the Cheltenham Park, an elegant four-star establishment on the southern fringes of the city. With her is Kevin Leeson, the volunteer who co-ordinates the huge protocol operation. It will be

Kevin's job to look after the foreign service chiefs for whom Amanda has been trawling all week. The Swindon hotel they used last year proved less than successful, and Amanda has high hopes of the Cheltenham Park.

I find them both in the corner of a comfortable lounge. Kevin is tall and slim and looks far too young to be an RAF Group Captain. Based at Strike Command headquarters at High Wycombe, he looks after engineering and supply for more than 250 frontline aircraft. This empire of his evidently stretches from the Falkland Islands, through Canada's Goose Bay, to the NATO bases in Turkey, from which Tornado GR1s mount surveillance patrols over Northern Iraq. Quite how a job this vast leaves him any time for Paul Bowen and the insatiable demands of the Air Tattoo is beyond me, but just now he's looking pretty relaxed as he and Amanda run a professional eye over the hotel's facilities.

'What was wrong with the last hotel?'

'Not flexible enough. They wanted to box us in far too early. In the VIP game, you can't do that. Fair, Kevin?'

Kevin is studying the lunchtime menu. For the first time, I notice a slight flicker under one eye. He looks up, nodding. 'Absolutely true. It's the one thing you can rely on. Everything changes. All the time.'

We order coffee. Kevin and Amanda, it turns out, go back years. They met when Amanda herself was in the RAF. Recruited by Paul Bowen to look after a succession of royal children during the early Fairford shows, she'd watched the VIP programme growing and growing and had realised the need to find someone to grip it. In this context – as in so many others at RIAT – the language is all important. 'Grip' is a military term. It means seizing control. It means leaving nothing to chance. It's a wonderful concept, wholly reasonable, but I wonder how exactly it translates into reality. I've listened to enough Fairford stories by now to conclude that organising an air show on the scale of RIAT is a little like going to war. No plan survives contact with the enemy. No matter how good your preparations, things always go wrong.

I'm still watching Kevin. The tiny facial tic would argue that the pressure this man is under is indeed immense. So, given the near-certain traumas of keeping the show on the road, how come he ever volunteered in the first place?

Kevin smiles. 'Face time,' he says.

Face time turns out to mean exactly what it says. Getting yourself in front of the people who matter. Three stars. Four stars. Generals. Air Chief Marshals. VIPs and VVIPs. Even royals. Do the job well, and they'll remember you. No bad thing when the race for promotion is so tight.

I make a note. This is the first time I've ever thought of the Air Tattoo as a career opportunity, but on reflection it makes perfect sense.

'So what does it take?' I wonder. 'To sort it all out?'

Kevin leans forward in his chair. He has an easy manner, the lightest conversational touch. He's funny, perceptive, and nicely self-deprecating – and I understand at once why Amanda thinks he's a bit of a star. Dealing with umpteen foreign air chiefs can't be easy. These, after all, are men well used to getting their own way.

'That's true.' Kevin nods in agreement. 'But it's actually subtler than that. When you're dealing with the guys at the very top, you'll find they always have a PSO and an outer office.'

'PSO?'

'Personal Staff Officer. It's his job to free up the great man, to keep the world at arm's length, to make sure he's not troubled by the small print. That's understandable, of course it is; but the result is that they can become – if anything – *over*-protected. They rely on you completely. For the smallest things.'

'You?'

'Us.' He glances at Amanda. 'We become the outer office. For the duration of the show.'

Kevin sketches a family tree, mapping his own little corner of the Fairford empire. Over the years, he's recruited a staff of nearly forty – men and women he knows he can rely on. A lot of the girls, logically enough, come from the commercial airlines. They've put in hundreds of hours in the first-class cabin and they're already professionals at the business of applying that extra-special coat of gloss.

'We're smoothing, smoothing all the time.' Kevin's hands stroke the air. 'Trimmings Are Us. That's the way we like to think of ourselves.'

He returns to the sketch. The two protocol teams look after the service chiefs, one for incoming VIPs from overseas, the other for UK luminaries including government ministers. A third team devotes itself to VVIPs – very, very, *very* important people, who would include foreign monarchs like King Hussein and members of our own Royal Household.

I'm still looking at the box marked 'Overseas VIPs'. A lot of these people won't speak English. Some of them, conceivably, will be sharing a golf course or a barbecue with former enemies.

'Where do you get the interpreters?'

'The Defence Language School at Beaconsfield. And the Joint Services Intelligence set-up, over at Chicksands. Luvvies, mostly. But they do a bloody good job.'

'And do they have degrees in diplomacy? As well as languages?'

Kevin grins. 'You're right. It can be tricky. If we got the chemistry wrong, then that could be awkward. But that would be a failure. And we're not here to fail.'

It's impossible not to warm to his confidence. In essence, he's running an enormously intricate five-day party, thickly seeded with social events, symposiums, training exercises, and some of the best flying in the world. Most important of all, he's offering the opportunity for fifty or so 'principals', plus their wives, to meet and talk and enjoy each other's company without any intrusions – and that, of course, means privacy. No pressures. No media. No hard sell.

It sounds hopelessly ambitious – impossible, even – but a phrase of Sir Roger's comes back to me. He's heavily involved in the VIP programme – Amanda's invitations to foreign chiefs go out under his name – and he's absolutely determined to protect that very special informality that has made the Air Tattoo such a magnet for the leaders of the world's airforces. 'It's protocol without the robes and silver sticks,' he told me. 'It's there, but you'd never know it.'

That sounds to me like an enormous compliment, and I pass it on to Kevin. The invisible hand. Smoothing and smoothing.

He acknowledges the paradox at once. 'But that's exactly it. You're always there, on hand, but you're never in the picture. You've got the event by the throat but you're the guy they never notice.'

He goes on to talk about the constant judgement calls – how much leeway to take, what assumptions to make – and about his absolute preoccupation with spotting problems before they happen. 'Take the aircraft steps. That's an absolute classic. You're up at Heathrow or Northolt, or even Fairford. The plane's just flown in from eastern Europe or some other corner of the world and you absolutely haven't a clue who's going to appear first. Is that guy at the top of the steps the steward or the principal? You just don't know.'

I'm intrigued. 'So what happens?'

'You probably take a punt and assume it's the principal. Most of the time it works, but even if it doesn't people are happy that someone's got a grip. But that can be a problem too. You absolutely *mustn't* overshadow what's going on.'

I'm writing fast now. This is a dimension to the airshow of which I've been only dimly aware, an absolutely fascinating corner of the Fairford operation. The VIP programme was originally developed as a come-on for the hardware – invite the Chief and ask him to bring a couple of aeroplanes with him – but now it's become an event in its own right, and a key element in the success of the weekend. Invite the right people to the party, work hard to create an aura of relaxed specialness, and remarkable things begin to happen. The ice between Buenos Aires and London began to melt at Fairford. Why? Because the Chief of the Argentinian Air Force accepted an invitation to come to the show.

By the time the waitress arrives with the coffee, Kevin is talking about national stereotypes. His all-time favourite guests are the Scandinavians. They are, he says, an absolute delight: charming, courteous, low-profile, requiring the absolute minimum of attention. Guests from the various parts of the old Soviet Union, on the other hand, can offer a challenge or two. Not because they're rude or over-boisterous or not excellent company, but because they're simply not prepared for the shock of dropping into a very different society.

'They simply don't have any money,' Kevin points out. 'We're all glad the Wall's come down and it's marvellous having them along to the show, but it's a bit of a shock when you realise just how poor they've become.'

The event-costs of the VIP programme are met from commercial sponsorship – next year, Boeing will be picking up the tag – and I spend a moment or two pondering the irony of the western aerospace industry making it possible for their old adversaries to sink pints at the Arkell's VIP night. There is, though, a certain commercial logic to inviting air chiefs from the old Soviet bloc. The aircraft they bring with them – like the MiG-29 and the Sukhoi Su-27 – are proven crowd-pleasers. When the Russians flew in two of their giant *Bear* bombers several years ago, Kevin swears it was worth another ten thousand on the gate.

'Their aircraft are tremendous,' he confirms. 'That's the kind of kit people pay to see.'

All the talk of money leads us to the Middle East. Paul has already told me about King Hussein and the Jordanians, but what about the Omanis and the Saudis? Isn't it especially important to give the Gulf Arabs a good time when they're buying billions of pounds' worth of aircraft from UK factories?

'Ah.' Kevin masks a smile. 'The great god Al Yamamah.'

Al Yamamah is the oil-for-Tornados deal negotiated by the Thatcher government back in the Eighties. Thousands of jobs all over the country still depend on it. I try and push Kevin a bit further. Does Al Yamamah buy the Arabs special favours?

'Not at all.' He offers me a practised smile. 'We treat everyone equally.'

'But don't they have a reputation for ... ah ...' I try and find the right word. '... capriciousness?'

'Not at all,' he says again. 'They're absolutely no problem. It's only food and drink you have to worry about. No alcohol, of course. And plenty of lamb and duck.'

I gaze at him, admiring the perfection of the diplomatic answer, and he neatly sidesteps my next question by returning to King Hussein. The King normally pilots himself from Amman. With him will be an assortment of VVIPs from his royal household – and the real art lies in trying to guess how many Qs, Ps and Cs will emerge from the big TriStar.

'Qs? Ps? Cs?'

'Queens, princes and cousins.' Kevin grins. 'We normally send a fifty-two-seater coach and try and keep track, but there always seems to be one P missing. The King's a gracious man, though. Much loved. Much admired.'

By now, Amanda has declared her hand to the management and departed on a tour of the hotel's facilities. Kevin will catch up later, but for the moment he talks me through the protocol year.

As early as a couple of months ago – nearly a year away from next July's Tattoo – he and Amanda began to shape the VIP programme. The Wednesday evening of show week will find a retired Air Chief Marshal hosting an informal supper at the VIP hotel.

'Here?'

'Very probably.'

On Thursday, while some of the chiefs attend the SkyWatch symposium in Church House, Westminster, the wives will be enjoying what Kevin calls 'the Harvey Nichols experience'. In the evening, after their formal dinner at Apsley House, the VIP party will return to the West Country, where other chiefs have been sampling local brews at the Arkell's pub night. Friday offers the wives a chance to tour Lord Ashcombe's estate at Sudeley Castle, with some gentle shopping in Cheltenham after lunch, while their husbands – back at Fairford – watch the flying rehearsals from the comforts of the Patrons' Pavilion. On Friday evening there's a formal Gala Dinner in one of Fairford's huge hangars – five courses for 600 people – and this function, says Kevin, will serve as a curtain-raiser for the two public days of the Tattoo.

It was this programme – together with vintage flying, an evening barbecue and an eighteen-hole golf tournament – that formed the basis for Amanda's pitch to the London air attachés, but only now do I realise the sheer scale of the thing.

'So how many people will you be looking after?'

'Including the wives? About 120.'

I half-close my eyes, trying to imagine the logistic complications involved in making a discreet fuss of 120 people: saving them from boredom, saving them from each other, saving them from themselves. The scope for disaster seems limitless.

Kevin anticipates my question. 'We design separate programmes.'

'*Individual* programmes?'

'Absolutely. It's the only way. The outer offices insist on getting the plot agreed.'

'So when does that happen? Drawing up all these individual programmes?'

'By June, latest. That gives them six weeks to change it all at least three times. We always build in a bit of flexibility, though. You have to have a buffer. Otherwise the thing goes off the rails.'

I'm still trying to cope with the notion of 120 separate programmes – each one, I'm certain, timed to the last second.

Kevin, modestly, is trying to downplay the challenge. 'I've got bloody good people,' he says, 'and excellent kit too.' He tallies his private transport fleet, on free loan for the duration of the show: half a dozen brand-new air-conditioned XJSs from Jaguar; five big Mercedes from Marshalls of Cambridge ('US Generals love them – it's the leather, I think, and the way the doors go clunk'); two specially air-conditioned minibuses; a couple of luxury coaches. Oh, and a twelve-seat Gulfstream V executive jet.

Kevin's eyes are gleaming now. 'That's the perk,' he admits. 'Not having to drive to London.'

'You take the jet? To *London*?'

'Certainly.' He nods. 'It's all about the use you make of your time. Just think it through. I'm up to my eyes down here. We've got a hiccup or two. But late afternoon, I'm supposed to be up at Heathrow to meet an incoming chief. The Gulfstream's mine for the week. That particular day it might give me an extra hour. What would *you* do?'

The logic is faultless, but that's not the point. The point has to do with millions of pounds' worth of airplane. The ultimate executive toy. Yours for a whole week.

'Tool, not toy.'

'Of course. But nice, eh?'

At my insistence, Kevin relives bits of the Gulfstream experience from last year's show. The interior of the aircraft is equipped with VIP reclining chairs and armchair screens which offer a variety of views for take off and landing. The video pictures are fed from externally mounted cameras – nosewheel, wing, belly, tailfin – and Kevin talks me through the twenty-five-minute hop to the RAF airfield beside the A40 at Northolt, where a chauffeur-driven Jaguar awaits him at the foot of the aircraft steps. Invariably, on the way out to Heathrow, they drive past the reception lounge in the terminal building. And invariably everyone stares out, wondering just who the hell this man is.

'Sometimes I give them a wave,' Kevin laughs. 'They think I'm someone really important.'

I smile, glancing up. Amanda has reappeared. Unknown to Kevin, she's been standing behind his armchair, listening.

'But you are,' she says softly.

Back at Fairford, the talk is of promotions and a degree of re-organisation. It seems that Paul and Tim have announced the creation of a handful of deputy directors, key figures who have been invited to step up and shoulder a bit more responsibility. The new deputy directors include Amanda and Mel James.

I find Paul behind his desk. The building is abuzz with the news. The politics of the place, after four brief weeks, are already fascinating.

'Why have you done it?' I enquire. 'As a matter of interest.'

At first Paul offers a half-hearted rationale, heavily camouflaged in the usual management speak: more accountable structures, a greater degree of flexibility, talk of 'spreading the decision-taking load'. Then he looks me in the eye and tells me to shut the door.

'It's the Board,' he says wonderingly. 'They think Tim and I have acquired too much power. Can you believe that?'

I can, and I tell him so – not acquired, perhaps, but certainly created.

He looks glum for a moment or two, then grins. 'They're worried about the succession. They're thinking of taking out key-person insurance. You should see the premiums. They're enormous.'

Key-person insurance is a way of buffering an organisation against the sudden loss of a vital employee. In this context, sensibly, the board are hedging their bets against Tim and Paul going down in a plane crash, or simply working themselves to death. Creating a raft of deputy directors is, I imagine, part of the same exercise. Either way, Enterprises would continue to stay afloat.

'You think so?' Paul's looking surprised. 'You really think that's it?'

'I'm sure it is.'

'OK.' He glances at his watch. 'I told Wally you wanted to see him. You'd better say well done.'

'Why?'

'He's a deputy director too.'

Wally Armstrong heads the catering operation at Fairford – yet another fiefdom within the RIAT empire, this time blessed with a formal title: Hospitality International Catering Services. Wally's in his fifties, a cheerful, friendly Scot with a passion for rugby and a fund of amazing stories. He joined Enterprises after thirty-one years in the RAF, ending his service days as staff officer in charge of flight catering for Air Transport.

News of the deputy directorships, including his own, has left him unimpressed. 'Giving people titles doesn't solve problems,' he says, 'it creates them.'

'How?'

'Because you make gaps where gaps shouldn't exist. This place has always been a family. You might be in danger of losing that.'

'You think so?'

Wally gives the question some thought. Then the smile returns. 'Maybe, maybe not. Either way, it'll make no difference.' He gestures up the corridor towards the end of the building, where Paul and Tim have their offices. 'They'll still be into everything. They can't help it. It's just the way they're built.'

Wally, this particular afternoon, is mapping out a menu for the staff pre-Christmas dinner. Reading upside-down from his scribbled notes, I suspect that Fairford's finest are in for a treat. Soup. Turkey. Roast beef. Stuffing. Bread sauce. Christmas pudding. Syllabub.

I look up. 'And plenty to drink?'

'Loads. There's free Champagne to start with, thanks to our suppliers.'

'And wines with the meal?'

'Until the table sags.'

'Speeches? Charades? Silly games?'

'The lot.' He nods. 'And a raffle before the taxis arrive.'

It sounds more than festive – and I'm wondering what's involved in knocking out high-quality grub to forty-four hungry souls when it occurs to me that this is the man charged with keeping 4,500 volunteers fed and watered through a traditionally hot midsummer weekend. I enquire, predictably, about the volume of food involved in this operation, and Wally obliges at once with an impeccably typed analysis, detailing exactly what it took to fuel the men and women who marshalled the crowds and parked the aeroplanes and rescued umpteen lost kids this year.

I study the figures. Wally appears to have dished up 42,829 meals.

'Is this right?'

'Of course it's right.'

The figure is beyond my comprehension. How does he manage it? What does it take?

Wally doesn't think much of my questions. In terms of mass catering, feeding the volunteers is pretty straightforward. The South Side Diner served up 2,500 lunches a day. Burgers, it seems, are always in huge demand. And so is wet food.

'Wet food?'

'Curry and rice, that kind of thing. Stuff we can keep hot without a problem.'

On the other side of the runway, two other venues serve breakfast and supper as well as lunch. Wally stifles a yawn. The volunteers, he says, are like any family, only slightly more numerous. I note down the comment, underlining the word 'slightly'.

'Ask me about Hong Kong,' he says suddenly. 'Now that *was* hairy ...'

The Hong Kong Aviation Ball took place back in 1990, a one-off event in aid of the RAF Benevolent Fund, and Paul volunteered Wally for the catering. The Gulf War was on, Wally was just two weeks into his new Air Transport job – and yet there he was, sitting at his desk at RAF Strike Command, gazing at a Cathay Pacific ticket.

Sixteen hours later, a little dazed, he emerged from a 747 at Kai

Tak to learn the worst. The hangar in which the ball was to take place was full of aircraft. There was no staff to wait on table, no refrigeration for the chilled champagne and white wines, and the two big freight containers packed with gilt chairs and tables had inexplicably gone missing. By now, the ball was a sell-out. In a couple of days' time, 1,500 guests would be sitting down in expectation of a wonderful meal.

Wally and Paul set off to look for the containers. A day and a half later, they found them. A visit to a contact on a local dairy farm produced chilled storage for several hundred cases of champagne, and from the RAF mess at Sekkong they managed to blag 1,500 serviettes. Next day, the day of the ball, the champagne and the serviettes were choppered to the apron outside the hangar. Wally and Paul, unloading 1,500 chairs from the freight containers, broke off to welcome the incoming Sikorsky S-76. The champagne posed no problems, but the serviettes got caught in the rotor wash, producing a blizzard of pressed white linen across the helipad.

It's impossible to write fast when you're laughing. Wally pauses for breath.

'It gets worse.'

'It can't.'

'It does. We'd got someone to hire all these local Chinese to wait on table. Someone had to tell them what to do and of course it was muggins. I was standing there in my kilt and my sporran, all dressed up for the party. I gave them the full brief, twenty minutes' spiel, everything you can conceivably think of. At the end of it they just stared at me.'

'Why?'

'None of them spoke a word of English.'

He stares glumly down at his scribbled Christmas menu. Plum duff for forty-four. What a doddle.

'How about the food? How did you cope with that?'

'Swires were doing it. They're the Cathay Pacific people. They had a proper catering set-up so that was no problem, but there was a locked gate between them and us and we couldn't get the bloody thing open.'

'The food was ready?'

'Oh yes, and so were the guests. The food was in those big hot-cupboards, big steel things. We could have taken them round the long way, out on the public road, but the traffic was awful. Best estimate was over an hour and we were late already.'

My pen is poised. 'So what happened?'

'I'm not telling you,' Wally leans back in his chair. 'Ask Brian Hughes.'

Brian Hughes is a legendary RIAT figure. During the air show he acts as Chief of Staff to Paul and Tim, and commands something called SOC – Show Operations Control – but in real life he works as a security consultant for a major city bank.

I wait for a moment, hoping that Wally will cap his story, but he doesn't. Instead, we talk about CIP catering. This, it seems, can also be tricky.

In addition to hosting Kevin Leeson's VIPs, Fairford also sells hospitality packages to a series of corporate customers, who in turn become CIPs, or Commercially Important People. The package includes a small city of specially erected chalets, to which aerospace companies like Boeing, Hughes, Lockheed and Rolls-Royce can invite guests of their choice. Wally's task is to keep them well supplied with food and drink. For this, he has a food budget of £10 per head per day.

'So what does that run to?'

'Danish and coffee in the morning. Then lunch, plus afternoon tea.'

'For ten pounds?'

'No problem.'

In my eyes, Wally is fast acquiring hero status. What kind of magic turns ten quid into a day's wonderful eating?

'The food's not the problem,' he insists. 'It's serving the stuff that gives me the headache.'

In all, Wally's chefs will be preparing more than 1,500 CIP meals a day. Some customers, like Rolls-Royce and Lockheed, insist on silver service, but this skill, in Gloucestershire, is apparently hard to find. Calls to the local catering colleges came to nothing. During the last show, waiters were bussed in daily from South Wales.

'It's the unemployment, you see. The Welsh need the jobs. Round here, you can't find anybody.'

I flip back a page or two, studying my notes. Serving 1,500 high-quality meals – on top of everything else – sounds a nightmare, but I've heard on the Fairford grapevine that something beyond Wally's control, back in July, went disastrously wrong. What was it?

Wally takes his time in answering. Even three months hasn't healed the wounds. This, I sense, was no Hong Kong romp.

'We were let down,' he says at last. 'Badly.'

This turns out to be an understatement. It's Wally's job to kit out the twenty-eight hospitality chalets, each with fifty covers, plus the big patrons' pavilion, which seats 300. A contract that large can only be handled by one firm in the country, and the order was duly despatched. The previous weekend, the suppliers had been engaged in a similar exercise at the British Grand Prix at Silverstone. The tables, chairs, crockery and glasses were due for delivery at Fairford on the Tuesday of show week. At midday, Wally got a phone call. From the suppliers.

'What did they say?'

'They told me there'd been some problem at Silverstone. And the stuff would be late.'

'How late?'

'They wouldn't say.'

'So what happened?'

'I told them eight a.m. Wednesday. Absolute latest.'

'And?'

'Nothing turned up.'

I think back to my conversation with Kevin and Amanda at the Cheltenham Park Hotel. Wednesday sees the arrival of the first VIPs. Thursday is Press Day. By Friday, the corporate guests are arriving in their hundreds, eager to be wined and dined and given a front-row seat for the flying rehearsals. Year by year, corporate hospitality has become more and more important for the financial success of the Air Tattoo, and the thought of Rolls-Royce's guests turning up to a row of empty tents sends a shudder down my spine.

Wally isn't laughing either. 'The first deliveries turned up on the Thursday. All the tables and the catering packages were out of order. It took us most of the day to sort them all out.'

'How were you coping? Personally?'

'I wasn't. I thought the whole thing was going to fail. That had never happened. Ever.'

'But you sorted it?'

'Only just. The glasses didn't arrive until first thing Friday. Most of them were still dirty.'

'No one had washed them?'

'No. You could see the red wine sediment. We had to wash the whole lot.'

I shake my head. This is beyond belief. But it gets worse.

'The water supply failed. I think some clown ran over a pipe. We were getting water the colour of tea.'

'So what did you do?'

'We had to tanker water in. Just to wash the glasses. Truly. I thought my head was going to burst.'

He lapses into silence, brooding. Then he talks, very quietly, about the aftermath. How well the show went. How pleased the sponsors were. And how, afterwards, he handed in his resignation.

'I'd just had enough,' he says. 'We impose this discipline on ourselves because we're a charity. We all cut corners and we all make and mend and we all know it's totally unreasonable and yet we all do it. RIAT has always been unreasonable. We always say we'll never do it again. But this time I meant it.'

There's a long silence. Very gently, I point out that he's still here, still employed, still planning for the next one. Wally nods. He and Paul had a long chat. Wally made various stipulations. Things changed. But he'll never forget the memory of those heart-in-the-mouth July days.

'We've taken lots of risks over the years,' he says softly, 'and we've had lots of luck. But I hated those three days. I really hated them.'

....

CHAPTER FOUR

December 1997

By the turn of the year, plans are beginning to firm up for the key elements in the 1998 Air Tattoo. These will provide the building blocks for the air display, and one of the most important is the celebration of the Berlin Airlift. For thirteen long months the Soviet Army sealed off a city of two and a half million. Fifty years later, the Fairford team intend to pay tribute to the thousands of aircraft and countless aircrew who kept Berlin alive.

To do this with the necessary panache, Paul Bowen and Tim Prince need money. The polite word is sponsorship, but what it boils down is hard cash to fund a gathering of vintage aircraft, to pay for the fuel and the maintenance and the pilots who will fly them, to design a display that will capture the public's imagination, and to put the anniversary into a context that will be both respectful and impressive.

Anniversaries at Fairford don't come cheap, and it's Clive Elliott's job to lay hands on the money. Clive has aviation in his blood. At seventeen he made a nearly-successful bid to win an RAF bursary as a trainee pilot. Nine years later, after a series of adventures around the world, he joined the Fairford team. Now, the sign on his office door reads BUSINESS DEVELOPMENT. Last year, from an impressive range of companies, he raised £532,000 − a sum that underwrote umpteen elements of the July show. This year already he thinks he'll do better.

'It's becoming an easier sell all the time,' he says. 'We took a conscious decision to put ourselves up among the major players. Eventwise, we like to think we're in the same league as Wimbledon and the Rugby Internationals, and Formula One. This year's show was a terrific success. The Americans in particular were amazed.'

It's true. Paul has shown me countless letters from senior aerospace and service figures in the States. The July show, in essence, was a fiftieth birthday party for the USAF and the Americans were not only grateful but impressed.

Clive nods, gesturing at a pile of bulging files. Boeing have just agreed to sponsor Kevin Leeson's VIP programme for '98. The money they're pumping in is a fourfold increase on last year's contribution. Raytheon, another major player in the aerospace industry, will be funding the '98 SkyWatch Club, a specially designed enclosure for the use of visiting aircrew. Clive rattles on, tallying the big corporate fish already hooked on the RIAT experience: British Aerospace, Lockheed Martin, Rolls-Royce, Northrop-Grumman . . .

'I'm given the show crowd,' Clive says cheerfully, 'and my job is to go out and market all those people to the corporate world. The big players don't come here to sell aeroplanes. We're not a trade show like Paris or Farnborough. But they are determined to make an impression. And where better to do it?'

Clive, like Heidi Standfast, is in his early thirties. Tenacious, hard-working, totally committed, he has the same fluency in marketing speak – talk of 'footfall' and 'audience profile' – and the same frank acceptance that he's on board to sell a product. The fact that the show is run on behalf of the Benevolent Fund is certainly a help when he deals with the aerospace industry, but in the general marketplace – talking to big public companies like Breitling or Lloyds Bank – he has to live on his wits. Every product, he says, must have a USP, or Unique Selling Proposition, something that makes it wholly different to anything else in the field – and at Fairford the USP couldn't be simpler.

'It's informality,' he says, 'and spectacle. We're in the wonderful-day business. The best flying in the world. Great food. Great company. We're here to make these guys *happy* and by and large I think we do.'

Put this way it sounds absurdly simple. Who could possibly resist

Wally's profiteroles and a Tornado on re-heat? But marketing directors are notoriously sceptical people, and I suspect that behind Clive's easy confidence lies an eternity of twelve-hour days.

True?

'Of course it's hard work,' he says. 'You have to persuade these people. They don't know anything about what we do. They've probably never been to an airshow. So you invite them along as a guest, and you let the event speak for itself, and when they come back and take a bit of sponsorship on this or that then you make sure you look after them, make sure you grow them, make sure they become *part* of what we're doing.'

This sounds very similar to the way the volunteers are recruited – letting the show work its own magic – but it still feels an implausibly sentimental pitch to risk in the hard-nosed world of commerce. Surely these people eat and sleep the bottom line. They'll want to be able to quantify the gain. They'll need to be sure about what they're getting for their marketing spend.

Clive's beaming. He loves all this. 'You're right,' he says, 'but there's a feel-good factor too. They've made a decision. They want to come on board. From that point on there's just three things that matter: one, how much money do they have? Two, how can I spend it for them? Three, how can I make them really, *really* happy?'

Dimly I begin to understand the shape of Clive's operation. In some respects he's a broker, matching the demands of the show to the needs of a small army of sponsors. This, of course, begins to explain the wild growth of events in the margins of the show weekend and across the days that surround it: sponsored competitions for competing aircrew; Friday night's Gala Dinner; Monday's post-Tattoo golf competition. The list, seemingly endless, would never exist without financial support from a queue of commercial backers.

A thought occurs to me. What would happen if there was nothing left to sponsor?

Clive rocks with laughter. 'There's always something left to sponsor,' he says. 'And if there wasn't we'd invent something. That's the beauty with this event. We can do anything we like with it. The sky's the limit.'

This brings us, rather neatly, to the Berlin Airlift. Later this morning there's a get-together in the staff dining room. Air Marshal Sir John Curtis of the Berlin Airlift Association is driving down to be briefed on Paul's plans. Also due at the meeting, according to the neatly printed agenda, is a Mr Roger Smart.

I look up at Clive. 'Who's Roger Smart?' Clive is grinning again. 'The sponsor,' he says. 'Who else?'

The meeting starts an hour or so later. Sir John Curtis turns out to be an amiable seventy-three-year-old whose interest in the Berlin Airlift goes back to the grim winter of 1948–49. As a young 30 Squadron navigator, he shuttled back and forth to the airfields at Wunstorf and Fassberg, threading his Dakota through week after week of appalling weather. Now, his Berlin Airlift Association numbers nearly 500 members, and it's clear from the start that he's delighted at Paul's invitation to become part of RIAT 98.

'Anything we can do to help,' he murmurs, 'just ask.'

Paul motors briskly through his plans for the Berlin Airlift tribute. At this stage he's thinking of a thirty-minute display slot, ending with a flypast from participating squadrons. The latter may include Australian and Canadian crews, representing their forebears who helped maintain the airbridge. But the real heart of the display will lie in a special re-enactment of the extraordinary round-the-clock shuttle that saw aircraft touching down in Berlin every ninety seconds.

'Ninety seconds.' Paul's cigarette describes a perfect circle in the air. 'That's the key figure.'

He looks round the table, pledging RIAT's determination to come up with something that will do the Airlift justice, if not in scale then certainly in period detail. He conjures up the image of a dozen Dakotas streaming off the runway, six making a left-hand turn-out, six banking sharply to starboard. They stay in the circuit, a choir of piston engines. From base leg on to finals they reconverge as a stream, looser this time, touching down one after the other just ninety seconds apart. Waiting on the edges of the taxiway will be convoys of period trucks, and as the Dakotas wheel to a halt, gangs of volunteers dressed in rough serge will empty the aircraft of coal, flour, medicines, salt – the bare necessities that kept millions of Berliners a calorie or two this side of starvation.

To most of the watching crowd, this tableau will be a series of small black dots in the distance, but hand-held cameras will beam back video pictures to huge Jumbotron screens as the ground crews battle to break the six-minute-fifteen-second record for emptying a fully-laden Dakota.

Paul pauses for effect, trying to catch my eye, but I'm too busy watching Sir John. I'm not sure whether he's trying to reconcile his own memories of Berlin with this flamboyant piece of theatre, but he's plainly impressed. He's already told us rather glumly that no one under twenty-five has ever heard of the Berlin Airlift, but this extravaganza might just put the record straight.

He reaches for a pen, then glances across at Paul. 'How many Dakotas did you say?'

'Twelve. Plus a couple of DC-4s. And maybe a Constellation.'

'And you can actually get them?'

'No question. We're talking to the South Africans and the Turks. And there are still some here, of course.'

It's impossible not to admire Paul's confidence. My trip to the Turkish embassy has given me an insight or two into the realities of aircraft procurement – but here he is, exercising RIAT's global reach, hinting at favours to be called in, promises to be honoured. A dozen Dakotas? No problem. A DC-4 in flying condition? Just a phone-call away.

Sir John, happier than ever, makes a note or two, and Paul hands over to Patti Heady for a word about some of RIAT's other plans for the Berlin Airlift. Patti is Enterprises' press and PR officer, a tall, rather striking Australian with a brief – among other things – to dream up wild ideas for the Fairford Press Day, traditionally held on the Thursday before the show weekend. Among her many past triumphs was the arrival of actor David Jason in a two-seat Harrier jet, and last year – to introduce the Tiger theme – Patti somehow acquired the real thing from the advertising agency responsible for the Esso advertising campaign. Tessa the Tiger obligingly posed with the French pilot of a Mirage 2000, newly arrived from the big Armée de L'Air base at

Cambrai. The pilot had only been tasked for the mission four hours earlier – but that, as they say in showbusiness, is another story.

Patti takes her cue. One of the Americans flying into Berlin was a young aviator called Gail Halvorsen. Appalled at what he could see from the air, he took to arriving with bundles of home-made parachutes. Attached to the tiny parachutes were parcels of sweets, and these he dropped to the huddled kids waiting patiently beneath the glideslope. Gail quickly acquired near-legendary status in the wrecked suburbs around Gatow and Tempelhof, and fifty years later the Candy Bomber has succumbed to Patti's charms. He'll be at the press day, and at the show – as will Mercedes Wild, a native Berliner who was herself a child at the time.

Laying hands on the Candy Bomber is undoubtedly a master-stroke, and I'm thinking hard about the Jumbotrons. Paul is absolutely right – close-ups of the unloading sequence beside the runway will make all the difference to the display – but surely there's room too for an item featuring Gail Halvorsen. With lashings of archive film – smoke-grey Dakotas ghosting down through the fog – a nicely cut interview with the Candy Bomber could add yet another dimension to the golden anniversary tribute. Not just the theatre of the air, but a twitch of the curtains and a glimpse or two of exactly the way it was for the veteran airmen gathered at the show.

I make a note of my own as Patti finishes her briefing. Nationally, the Berlin Airlift indeed appears to have been consigned to the dustbin of history. Sir John has been pressing for a commemorative anniversary postage stamp, but his proposal has been turned down. In favour of Dracula.

Clive Elliott takes up the running. He will be providing a special Berlin Airlift enclosure at the show for the use of Airlift veterans. The enclosure will offer hospitality, a small archive display, and a wonderful view of the flying. This initiative has already met with Sir John's wholehearted approval – but now comes the trickier question of just who's going to pay for it.

Roger Smart comes from a company called Cobham plc. They're based in Dorset and they're big in component and system manu-facturing for the aerospace and defence industries. One of the companies within the Cobham Group is an outfit called Flight Refuelling, and for the 1995 show they sponsored SkyTanker, that year's operational theme. Cobham has a much lower profile than headline companies like British Aerospace or Westland Helicopters, and they're always on the lookout for what Roger Smart calls 'appropriate sponsorship opportunities'. The fact that Flight Refuelling played an important role in the Berlin Airlift, losing a Lancastrian and seven aircrew in the process, has prompted a phone call to Clive Elliott, and now Roger has arrived to talk serious money.

Clive knows exactly how much Cobham have in their budget for the Airlift re-enactment. It's a five-figure sum and, remarkably, Clive has prepared a sponsorship package that will meet it. To the penny.

'The enclosure will have a tented area,' he explains, 'as well as its own garden. There'll be tables and chairs out there, plus a sixty-six-seater grandstand. Inside we've got room for a hundred sitting down. Hospitality-wise, we're thinking morning coffee and danish, a full buffet lunch, plus afternoon tea and stickies. How does that sound?'

Roger Smart's busy with his pad and his calculator. 'How about the entrance ticket?'

'That's included.'

'Drinks?'

'Cash bar.'

'Phones?'

'We can run a line in if you want one. The calls will be down to you. Keep an eye on the South Africans – they're always phoning home.'

Roger looks up, and a longish debate about the tables and chairs ensues. Cobham have their own garden furniture. Maybe it would save a bob or two if they trucked the stuff over.

Clive, sharp as a needle, leans forward. 'Who pays the transport costs?'

'We do.'

'But will that come out of the Airlift spend?'

'No, I've got another budget.'

Clive pauses. He's like an animal, nose in the air, sniffing the wind.

Another budget. More money. Extra sponsorship. 'How much – exactly?'

Roger isn't keen on sharing his figures. He wants to nail down the deal on the Berlin Airlift. He thinks he's still got some money left in that first budget and he wants to know exactly how Clive proposes to spend it. Clive talks persuasively about the Airlift flying display. The Dakotas represent a truly fantastic sponsorship opportunity. Then, on top of that, there's a special two-page historical spread in the souvenir programme. Lots of editorial. Lots of archive photos. A wonderful home for what's left of Roger's Airlift spend.

Roger is happy to agree. It feels right – Flight Refuelling's historical links with the shuttle; Cobham's name all over the programme; corporate mentions during Sean's airshow commentary; the company logo splashed across bannering around the tented enclosure. Nice.

'About this other budget...'

Clive isn't about to give up. These two men know each other. They've been doing sponsorship business for years. Yet the negotiation, move and counter-move, is no less keen for that. They trade figures, push around various sponsorship options. To the outsider it's a fascinating clash of cultures – not just commerce and this curious branch of showbusiness, but other worlds as well. Sir John, for one, looks slightly dazed. Can those long-ago days of white-knuckle flying, of seat-of-the-pants GCA approaches in appalling weather, really have come down to this? To debates about bannering and corporate profiles? To tussles about the impact of promotional spend?

In reality, of course, they can. And one of the beneficiaries is undoubtedly Sir John's Berlin Airlift Association. With Clive still hunting down Roger's second budget, Sir John makes an early departure. A brief conversation by the door confirms that he's delighted with Paul's plans for the Dakota display and deeply grateful to Cobham for their enthusiasm and support. Especially gratifying are their plans to commission research on the period. They've hired a specialist historian to poke around in the archives. His name is Colin Cruddas and, after the show, the fruits of his labours will end up in the RAF Museum at Hendon.

Sir John shakes Paul warmly by the hand and promises to stay in touch.

Shortly afterwards, at lunch, I corner Clive. 'Good result?'

'Excellent.'

'Pin down that second budget?'

'Afraid so.'

'And...'

He takes a mouthful of Wally's excellent lasagne, then tells me about Cobham's extra spend. 'One, a full-page ad in the programme. Two, ten seats in the Trenchard Pavilion. Three, sponsorship for a competition trophy. And four ...' He frowns. 'Oh yeah, sponsorship for Is and Ps.'

I'm lost again. 'Is and Ps?'

'Instructions and Procedures. That's our Op-order. It's a kind of battle-plan we draw up for the show.' He grins. 'Just to make sure nothing slips past.'

A little later the same day, Paul convenes another meeting. Clive Elliott is a hard act to follow, and I'm anticipating a long afternoon among the acronyms, but I couldn't be more wrong. The time has come to expose the more visionary of Paul's flypast plans to the chill kiss of reality. To mark the RAF's eightieth anniversary, Paul wants to press ahead with the notion of a series of vertically stacked fly-bys. It's never been done before, and Paul has decided that David Roome is the man to sort it out.

He's the perfect choice. David Roome is a serving officer at nearby RAF Innsworth, a tall, photogenic Group Captain who might have stepped out of one of those post-war black-and-white movies – *The Dambusters*, perhaps, or *Reach for the Sky*. At Innsworth he has enormous responsibilities, running the training budget for the entire Royal Air Force, but he's also won himself a reputation for organising multi-aircraft flypasts on the grandest scale. An ex-fast jet pilot with 5,000 hours on Lightnings, Phantoms and Hawks, he masterminded the now legendary Battle of Britain fiftieth anniversary flypast, feeding 170 aircraft down the Mall and over Buckingham Palace in a seamless display of close-formation flying. Now, after similar triumphs for the

Heathrow, D-Day and VJ Day anniversaries, David has driven over to listen to what Paul has in mind.

Also at the meeting – along with Amanda, Sue and Tim Prince – are two other key members of the air-display team. One is Sean Maffett, the voice of RIAT, the man whose commentary must weave the individual display slots into a coherent programme. The other is Ian Sheeley, the young wing commander in charge of the radar set-up at nearby RAF Brize Norton. Fairford comes under the jurisdiction of Ian's area controllers, and it's they who will act as sector traffic cops when the show comes round.

The meeting begins. After the briefest of introductions, Paul shares with us his vision for the RAF eightieth. Most of it I've heard before: how he wants to send over packet after packet of aircraft, each spanning eighty years of RAF service, and how – for one unforgettable second – each of these packets will form a perfect vertical stack.

Paul looks round, letting the concept sink in. Bold is too small a word for what he has in mind. If there's a ceiling in the world of air displays, a limit beyond which no formation pilots have yet dared venture, then Paul has just burst through it.

I'm looking at David Roome. His pad carries a line or two of jotted notes. After the word 'vertical' there's nothing but white space.

He clears his throat. In another life, he'll make the perfect diplomat.

'Stacked how, exactly?' he enquires.

'By groupings. By type. Maybe we'll start with fighters. I'd want something like a Camel at the bottom. A Hind next up. Then a Spitfire, a Venom, a Harrier, a Tornado, and, on the top ... a Eurofighter.'

David's pen remains beside his pad. He has a far-away look on his face, richly contemplative. 'Separations?'

'A hundred feet between them.'

'And the Camel? What kind of altitude?'

'As low as possible.'

David nods, aware now that the meeting is effectively his. There's a sub-plot here. David is the country's top choreographer of formation displays and Paul is determined to recruit him to the RIAT cause. What we're watching is courtship, a delicate *pas-de-deux* every bit as

71

complex and challenging as Paul's vision for the RAF tribute.

David stirs. 'So, just how many stacks are we talking about?'

'Eight.'

'*Eight?*'

'Yes. Fighters. Bombers. Heavies. Trainers. Ground attack. Maritime reconnaissance. Tankers. Odds and sods.'

'All stacked vertically?'

'Yes.'

'OK.' David finally picks up the pen, only to put it down again. In the asylum, as any psychiatrist will tell you, it pays to do everything very slowly.

'I can see one or two problems,' he says at last. 'First off, you'll never get any military organisation flying one hundred feet vertical intervals.'

'No?' Paul is feigning surprise.

'No. Just think about it. The guy at the top sees nothing beneath his nose. He's flying blind. So is the bloke underneath. And underneath him. And so on, down. The stack's inherently unsafe. That's number one.' David glances round, softening the bad news with a smile. 'Secondly, there's the speed differential. The guy at the bottom, the Camel, is flying at four miles a fortnight. He probably launched the previous day. Your Eurofighter at the top? He might be making 360 knots. That's four miles a minute closure. A huge differential when all these guys have got to stack at the datum.'

Datum is pilot-speak for the focal point of the display – eighty RAF veterans taking the salute on some kind of podium in front of the crowd.

Paul is looking troubled. I hear the word 'rehearsal'. David shakes his head, emphatic now.

'Wouldn't solve it,' he says, 'even if you could organise all the kit.'

'Why not?'

'Because the guys get blasé. What we're after in any display is one hundred per cent concentration. You go for it once and once only. That's the way I've always played it, and so far . . .' He looks down at his pad, letting our memories of the Battle of Britain fiftieth speak for themselves. This man knows. He's been there. He's done it.

Paul frowns. Twenty-seven years of Air Tattoos tell him that David Roome is bluffing. If you think about it hard enough, if you really *want* it to happen, then anything's possible. 'Maybe there's another way,' he says slowly. 'We can't just keep flying the same old displays.'

'No, quite.'

David is nodding. He agrees. Paul scents an opening. He leans forward, his third cigarette as yet unlit.

'So what do you suggest?'

'Maybe lateral separation as well.'

'You mean sideways *and* up?'

'Yes, maybe some kind of rotor formation. Fast guys high and wide. Slow guys tight and down low in the orbit. Everyone flying very positive tracks.' His right arm, raised, sweeps round. At the end of his fingers, the Eurofighter. Around his elbow, the Spitfire. Up by his shoulder, the Camel.

I hear the scrape of a match. Paul sucks hard on the Superking, then his eyes narrow as he watches David through a fog of blue smoke. This, at last, is looking good. Maybe better than good. 'You think that might do it?' he asks.

David says he doesn't know. Stepping up the aircraft laterally will solve the safety problem – every pilot should be aware of everyone else – but the speed differentials are still a problem.

David reaches for an empty glass. 'This is the datum,' he says. 'Upwind, here, you've got the aircraft dribbling all over the sky. Downwind, here, you've got the same rat's nest. Only here ...' – his hand returns to the glass – '... is there any semblance of order.'

We all look at Paul. David Roome, wittingly or otherwise, has just summed up RIAT. Order, ever so briefly, out of chaos.

Paul treats himself to another lungful of Superking. 'You think we've got too many stacks?'

'To be candid, yes. The airspace won't take it.'

'How about seven?'

'How about four?'

'Four?' Paul, for the first time, looks wounded. There's a long silence. Then he perks up again.

'But you think it's a nice idea?'

'I think it's a lovely idea. Don't get me wrong. The concept's wonderful. It's just the reality I worry about.'

'But you think you can come up with something?'

'Oh, I'll try . . .' David grins. 'Of course I will.'

Paul looks at him long enough to be sure that he means it, then nods. From defeat, victory. From David Roome, the first real indication that RIAT may have recruited the Busby Berkeley of the air display business.

Sensibly, Paul moves the discussion on to other elements of the programme. How the Red Arrows may be persuaded to fly an RAF fin-flash, sky-painted in multi-coloured smoke. How an assortment of black Tucanos will burst through the white bit in the middle. How a swarm of Tiger Moths will formate on each other to spell the figure 80 against the blue Gloucestershire sky.

This latter challenge provokes an in-depth debate about the numbers of aircraft required. Paul, ever optimistic, opens the bidding at eleven. David, with great gentleness, reminds him that he needed no less than twenty Hawks for the figure 50 in the Battle of Britain flypast. We all put pen to paper, trying to configure an 8 on the basis of David's 5. Watching the crosses take shape on the pads around the table, it reminds me of one of those Christmas party games.

Eventually Sean Maffett thinks that twenty-one Tiger Moths might do the trick. Tim wonders whether he can find twenty-one qualified pilots who'd be up for this kind of display. Paul looks at him in astonishment, but Tim makes the sensible point that civilian pilots are governed by CAA rules. Most of the Moth boys hold commercial licences – flying 747s for a living – and the last thing they want to do is upset the regulators.

Paul grunts something I don't quite catch and suddenly we're talking about the last item on the agenda. The operational theme next year will be SkyWatch – the enormously hi-tech and often secret world of airborne surveillance – and Paul is briskly touting for ideas. What can you download from an AWACS-E3D? Does the recce Jaguar record pictures on wet film? How much sense would a J-Stars real-time battlefield radar picture make, beamed down to the Jumboscreens? What might be available in terms of heli-telly? Might the Israelis volunteer one of their unmanned UAVs? What if we laid hands on a Tornado GR1A with the Vicon Pod – the kit the RAF are currently using to keep an eye on both ends of Iraq?

The conversation swirls back and forth, most of it beyond my comprehension, but as the minutes tick by it begins to dawn on me that this is yet another RIAT fishing expedition. The need, as Sean points out, is to build the SkyWatch event – to theme it somehow so that it ceases to be, in Sean's phrase, 'just snapping'. There might be mileage in some kind of chronological pageant, starting with a spotter in a balloon basket, unrolling the narrative through World War Two – Spitfires in reconnaissance blue, Lysanders chucking out message streamers ('BT could sponsor them') – and then maybe ending with a state-of-the-art aircraft like the SR-71 Blackbird. Mention of the Blackbird prompts a discussion about whether or not Fairford would be able to supply the right kind of specialised fuel, and I'm still trying to figure out just what might take this monster to 80,000ft when Tim Prince reminds us that this debate is academic because the Blackbird – thanks to an edict from President Clinton – is no longer flying.

The problem with a hi-tech subject like surveillance is that no one really knows what's possible and what isn't. The need is for a 'tekkie', an electronics buff with hands-on experience – and Tim volunteers to pursue some contacts in the Defence Evaluation and Research Agency, someone who's up to speed on the latest kit, someone who, in an unguarded moment, has expressed a casual interest in helping out the RIAT team. I make a note of the phrase, imagining the phone ringing tomorrow morning on some far-flung desk. *Hi, how are you? Tim Prince here. Just wondering whether you might fancy popping over for a spot of lunch...*

Late afternoon, with David Roome on his way back to Innsworth, I drift into Paul's office. His PA, Sarah Taylor, is already typing up the minutes of this afternoon's get-together, and I can hear her in the outer office, checking a detail with Amanda.

Paul motions me to shut the door. For a minute or two we discuss the way the meeting went, but I can tell that Paul's heart isn't in it. He lapses into silence, staring at the pile of letters awaiting his signature. Then, at length, he looks up. The problem isn't David Roome. As far as Paul can tell, he's happy to be on board. No, the problem is the fate of Paul's babies, his precious vertical stacks.

'You know, I'm not sure David's totally convinced,' he says glumly. 'What do you think?'

A couple of days later I track down Sean Maffett for a chat. For years, Sean's has been the voice the public associate with the show, and for my money he does a very fine job indeed. I listened to his commentary a great deal over this year's show, and his balance of wit, warmth and unparaded knowledge is near-perfect. Sean knows how to let the action – and the sound effects – speak for themselves. And that, believe me, is a rare talent.

'It's a monster. It's got far too big. Sometimes it just drives me insane.'

We're sitting in a pub in Bourton-on-the-Water. In the hall outside, a lurcher curls up beside a blazing log fire. Sean's love affair with aircraft goes way back. His father, a Lysander pilot, disappeared without trace over the Mediterranean during the war when Sean was eleven months old. Years later Sean himself joined the RAF, becoming a navigator on the big old Short Belfast transport before ending his flying days as a Squadron Leader. Saturday mornings at Radio Oxford – the closest station to RAF Brize Norton – gave him a real taste for the media, but he resisted joining the BBC's staff management organisation because he wanted to become a sharp-end broadcaster, staying as close as he could to the action. This, of course, is deeply in tune with the RIAT can-do spirit, and with the benefit of hindsight I suggest that it's no surprise that he, Paul and Tim would one day get together.

'I suppose not. Whatever you think of the end result at Fairford, you have to admire their sheer enterprise. They're the most amazing fixers in the world. They keep their cards pretty close to their chests and they gamble like crazy, but most of the time it comes off. Just occasionally, I wonder whether they might find it easier to be more straightforward, but I guess it's just their style. They love doing deals. And they love proving everyone wrong.'

I'm thinking about the B-2, back in July. Sean agrees at once that tempting the stealth bomber to Fairford was a classic RIAT coup.

'They nearly didn't get it, you know.'

I nod. Since October, fuelled by the memory of that black manta ray swimming over the airfield, I've made it my business to find out a little more about exactly how the aircraft came to feature in the flying programme, and I know that Sean's right. With the crowds pouring through the gate, word had come from the Pentagon of a sudden change of plan. Within minutes Tim was working the phones, applying pressure, pulling strings. Even now I'm not sure what it took to bring the B-2 ghosting towards the perimeter fence, but when Paul hints darkly of help from the highest reaches of the establishment, I've no reason to doubt him.

Sean and I talk about the profile of the show, how big it's got, and how important.

'It's unique,' Sean nods. 'In fact it's got so popular on the international military circuit that the air attachés are falling over themselves trying to get here. This year, Prince and Bowen had more aerobatic teams than you can shake a stick at. It's in danger of getting ridiculous.'

Sean frowns. Like some of the other sharp-end people I've begun to meet, he sometimes worries where the show may be headed. The iron laws of capitalism seem to insist on successful events becoming ever larger, ever more ambitious – but there's a downside too.

'It can become *too* big and I think that's begun to happen. There's just so much hassle, so many complications. This thing might disappear up its own backside, and that would be a pity.'

We fall to discussing Paul's plans for vertically-stacked tribute fly pasts, toasting his ambition with freshly charged pints of Saddlers, and mention of David Roome prompts a story from Sean. For twenty years now he's been a freelance radio presenter, voicing and shaping his own material, and one of his commissions took him back to the RAF as part of the team reporting on David Roome's Battle of Britain anniversary fly past. For Sean, it was the dream assignment. For most of his life he'd wanted to fly in a Lancaster bomber, and here he was, in the Battle of Britain Memorial Flight's Lanc, droning south to join the torrent of aircraft streaming in towards London. Sean was voicing live into the BBC's coverage, but his assigned position in the Lancaster was back in the fuselage of the aircraft, bent over a microphone with no view forward. The high spot of the flypast lay at the end of the Mall. The royal family had assembled on the balcony at Buckingham Palace to watch the waves of aircraft breaking over London, and it was Sean's job to record the exact moment when the big old bomber shadowed the watching royals. With only landmarks abeam the aircraft to go on, Sean was driven to make an inspired guess – and only later, watching a recording of the TV coverage, did he learn that he'd got the moment the Lancaster flew over the palace spot on.

'Dead reckoning,' he murmurs. 'Once a nav, always a nav.'

We return to RIAT. What makes it so special? And so different? Sean, along with his co-producer Graeme Bowd, tours all the major summer airshows and puts together a three-hour video at the season's end. Some of the events, like the Shuttleworth gathering at Old Warden, are small, almost intimate in scale. Others, like Paris, offer a glitzy international marketplace for the major players in the aerospace industry. But RIAT sets out to be neither of those things. Small-scale it most certainly isn't – though I know Sir Roger would defend the intimacy of the team's VIP operation to the death. Equally, unlike Paris or Farnborough, it's never set out to be a trade fair. If you want the hard sell and the billion dollar deals, then Fairford isn't for you. That, though, leaves the question unanswered. What exactly *is* RIAT?

Sean ponders the riddle. Like many who've lived with it through the Seventies and Eighties, he's watched it change. Already this evening he's voiced an anxiety about the direction that change may take.

'Well, number one, it's undoubtedly successful,' he says at last. 'You don't get to hand over all that cash to the Ben Fund without pulling a fair few people through the gate. And they wouldn't be there, wouldn't be paying all that money, if they didn't think it was worth it.'

So a good day out, then?

'Yes, definitely. The attendance speaks for itself.'

'And the formula? The flying display? The way it's all bolted together? You're happy with that too?'

The question prompts a silence. I know that Sean has views on what's possible at Fairford. I know he worries about the quality of the public address system, about the obvious truth that aircraft noise and poor loudspeakers can rob the commentary of most of its potential.

'What I'm trying to supply is the glue,' he says at last. 'It's my job to stick the thing together.'

He's right, of course. The show's commentary is immensely important in turning a procession of aircraft into something infinitely more satisfying. But what else can be done?

This is a tricky question to put to any commentator, but an hour's conversation has more than established his seriousness. He cares deeply about radio, about the challenge of involving a huge audience with nothing more than the human voice and a handful of sound effects and maybe some music. That recipe describes pretty much what he has at his disposal in the Fairford commentary booth – and as the evening unwinds we both agree that technology can give him a helping hand.

Introducing the Jumbotron screens would be an obvious advance but I'm acutely aware by now that RIAT is a delicate jigsaw of interlocking empires and the last thing I want to do is stand accused of trespass. Should I suggest that live pictures might add an exciting new dimension to next year's show? Or should I keep my mouth shut?

'I used to be in telly,' I say lightly. 'And Paul's asked me to lend a hand.'

Sean looks at me a moment, and then smiles. 'That's what all the girls say,' he murmurs.

....

CHAPTER FIVE

January 1998

The first week of the New Year, oddly enough, brings an invitation from Paul to join a RIAT negotiation with Central Television about the purchase of the broadcast rights of the 1998 show. I suspect that the summons is serious, because Paul's letter is accompanied by a RIAT tie, a stylish confection in dark-blue polyester. Paul's attitude to my dress sense varies between exasperation and bewilderment. When I point out that writers tend to wear pretty much what they like, he says that's no excuse for scruffiness. On this particular outing, I shall be representing RIAT. Hence the tie.

I meet the other two members of the RIAT posse at Euston station and we take the train to Birmingham. Tony Webb holds the Public Affairs brief for RIAT. Tall, shrewd, watchful, Tony spent his years with the RAF flying a variety of aircraft including the C-130 Hercules. His affection for 'Fat Albert', as the phone is dubbed, is matched only by a fund of wildly improbable stories, but his airborne involvement with special forces won him the AFC. Paul plainly regards him as an enormous asset and has recently appointed him a Deputy Director. I suspect that Tony, like so many other volunteers, has found a strange kind of comfort among the ups and downs of the Fairford year. His feet may rarely leave the ground these days, but he's still flying by the seat of his pants.

Also joining us is a media consultant recommended to Tony, whom I happen to know. His name is Peter Urie, and ten years ago he was a programme manager in the factuals wing of Television South, where we both worked. Now he heads his own company, providing specialist advice to programme-makers in both broadcast and non-broadcast fields. Peter has an intimate knowledge of the black arts of independent production, and Tony is keen to be briefed ahead of the meeting in Birmingham. In particular, he wants to know exactly how the ITV commissioning process works.

The train rattles north. Overshadowing everything in Tony Webb's empire is Paul's determination to lay hands on the Jumbotron screens. He's begun to talk to major public companies about the possibilities of sponsorship, but the sums involved are daunting. The bill for the whole operation – screens, cameras, control room, production staff – could indeed climb to £120,000. Is there really anyone out there willing to sign a cheque that large?

Tony Webb, for one, has his doubts, but by the time we get to Milton Keynes an alternative deal has begun to take shape. What we really need is serious network interest from a major broadcaster. Over the years, television and video rights to the airshow have been sold to a small independent production company called Onyx. They in turn have sold on the broadcast rights to Central TV and HTV West in a complicated deal that gave Onyx access to the rushes. During the show itself, both Central and HTV mounted coverage for their regional audiences, and Onyx later edited the pictures from their cameras into an eighty-minute video, which RIAT were only too happy to sell through their gift catalogue for a hefty profit. This deal gave Tony Webb both money up-front and an ongoing stream of revenue from the videos.

Now, though, Peter Urie thinks Tony Webb can do better.

'It should be a seller's market,' he says. 'What you're offering is the biggest military airshow in the world. Amazing planes. Sexy pictures. Hunky pilots. It's *made* for broadcast. It's absolutely perfect.'

Tony, unsurprisingly, warms to Peter's enthusiasm, but he wants to know a great deal more about the way the system works. Paul Bowen's primary contact is with Central, Fairford's local broadcaster. Recently, over a lunch in Abingdon, the managing director has indicated that the company want a deeper involvement with the show. There's talk of a three-year deal. Is this something Tony Webb should run with?

Peter shakes his head. 'Central are small-time,' he says. 'Central belongs to Carlton now. That's where the power lies. They're the people we should really be talking to.'

This sounds like bad news. Why are we bothering to get up early, put on ties and take the train to Birmingham when the real conversations should be happening elsewhere?

Peter steadies his coffee as we hit points outside Northampton. 'That's not what I meant,' he says. 'In the first place, of course we have to talk to Central. But we – and they – should be thinking network. That's where the money is. That's how you'll get to feed your video screens.'

Carlton, with Granada and United Media, are the key players on the ITV network. The way Peter sees it, they need to buy into RIAT with serious money. Major outside broadcast. Twenty-four-channel scanner. At least a dozen cameras. Downlinked pictures from solo and team aerobatic displays. Archival packages to plump out the Berlin Airlift and RAF eightieth anniversaries. Lots of colour. Lots of noise. Lots of big, hairy aeroplanes whazzing around. All thanks to a six-figure budget.

Peter mops up his coffee with a wad of tissues. He's a pilot himself – he recently acquired a PPL – and it shows.

Tony is still trying to work out where all this involvement might lead. 'You're saying they'd bring in a scanner? All the stuff we'd need to feed the video screens?'

'Absolutely. They'd have to.'

'And we could take our own feed?'

'Of course. We'd structure the deal that way.'

'And you think they'll bite? At network level?'

'They'd be mad not to.'

Tony sits back, impressed. I have a problem with the notion of sharing a scanner. The scanner is TV-speak for the mobile control room, the nerve centre for any live outside broadcast. In my experience, no TV director is happy serving two masters. On the day, the crew and equipment would be there to service the programme. RIAT would be queuing for scraps.

Tony sees the logic at once. 'How about two scanners?'

'We'd be back where we started. You'd have to pay for it.'

'How about us just taking their feed?'

It's an interesting proposal, but it doesn't bear examination. A lot of production time is spent in rehearsal – getting the to-camera links right, sorting out the timings, pre-recording packages for later use. Is that really the kind of material to grace Paul's Jumbo screens?

The suburbs of Coventry are slipping past the window. Regardless of the small print, our mood is upbeat. What we're selling is a major event. So far the television audience has been strictly regional, but Peter's surely right. It's time to think big. It's time to go network. Two hundred thousand spectators can't be wrong. RIAT is irresistible.

A taxi ships us from New Street station to Central's Birmingham studios. The executive we are to meet is Laurie Upshon, Controller of News and Operations – and he too is someone I've known before. At TVS, he ran the Maidstone newsroom. It'll be interesting to see what a decade in the upper reaches of regional television has done to him.

We meet in a glass-walled corner of a big open-plan production area. Laurie is more guarded than I remember, more businessman than programme-maker, and contrary to Paul's impressions at the earlier meeting I detect no great enthusiasm for the airshow. It's a big event – of course it is – but Central's attempts to market an airshow video abroad have come to absolutely nothing, and Laurie's plans for the coverage of this year's show are, to be frank, modest. Three two-man camera crews and a satellite link in the event of a major disaster doesn't somehow match the vision that Peter has shared with us.

It's Tony Webb who broaches the N-word. He and Laurie are already wrangling about a split between the video and broadcast rights, and Tony doesn't think much of Laurie's offer of £2,500 for the latter.

'What about the network?' he enquires.

Laurie shakes his head. 'Unlikely.'

'Really?'

'Yes. We're trying to package it as an event, like Formula One, and we've got a proposal in with Network Centre – but I'd say you're looking at 30:70. Against.'

'Why?'

'Because it's fringy.'

I'm not at all sure what 'fringy' means. Big audiences have been watching the Farnborough show for years, thanks to the BBC. The flying at Fairford is better still. Fringy? Is Laurie serious?

'I'm afraid so. We might be able to do something with the Spy in the Sky thing ... you know, some kind of mini-*Horizon*. That might be interesting if we could stand it up.'

'And this would be based around the show?'

'Probably not. You'd get a mention, of course, but we'd do the programme for the science.'

Big deal. I'm looking at Tony. Tony is looking at his notes. Peter takes up the running, arguing for free access to the video rushes should Tony decide to offer the broadcast rights to Laurie, and I listen to the talk of front-end splits, NAR percentages and secondary broadcast rights, marvelling at the gap between our giddy expectations on the train and this infinitely depressing display of near-indifference. I once worked in the same organisation as Laurie Upshon. I thought I understood the kind of culture he came from. But there appears, just now, to be absolutely no desire to seize this extraordinary event and shape it, pass it on to a huge national audience. Maybe it's just me. Maybe I've spent too long at Fairford. Maybe going native clouds your better judgement.

The discussion peters out, and I decide to play our wild card. An outfit called Double Exposure – a London production company – has come up with a proposal to make a fly-on-the-wall documentary about this year's show. A similar series they did on the backstage ructions at Covent Garden, *The House*, has been a huge critical success, and they want to apply the same treatment to Fairford. As far as I can judge the concept is a near-certain network sell – probably to the BBC – but the Benevolent Fund's board have reservations, and Sir Roger for one is far from convinced. That, though, isn't something I need necessarily mention.

'You remember that series about the Royal Opera?' I begin. 'The one that walked off with all the prizes?'

Laurie hears me out. Documentary soaps are hot just now, and I think I detect a quickening of interest. Maybe he was a little harsh with the odds against a network commission. Maybe he ought to put in a phone-call or two. We all agree that might be a good idea, and the meeting comes to an end.

Half an hour later, tucked into the corner of a pub across the road, the three of us take stock. Disappointment isn't quite the word to describe the way we feel. Disbelief would be closer. Are we kidding ourselves about the airshow? Doesn't *every* red-blooded male warm to the howl of a MiG-29 on re-heat? Or the silhouette of a looping Spitfire? Or the sight of the Red Arrows' final, unforgettable, Vixen Break? We pick over the bones of the meeting, wondering what we've missed, telling each other that Laurie's probably playing the long game, feigning disinterest in a bid to drive the price down, but none of us really believes it. On the train, we'd figured a production spend of perhaps £250,000. Central, on the basis of the meeting we've just attended, would be committing less than a tenth of that.

I gather up the empty glasses and step across to the bar for refills. The barmaid says she's worked here for years. I enquire about trade. Having the studios across the road can't do business any harm. She looks up at me, then pulls a face.

'There's nobody there any more,' she says. 'The place is dead compared to the old days.'

Several days later, another invitation arrives from Paul. After our trip to Birmingham I'm a bit luke-warm about a re-match with Central, but Paul has something very different in mind. The Air Display Association – a Europe-wide body representing the organisers of major airshows and airshow participants – is having one of its periodic get-togethers. The weekend will centre on a symposium. The subject under discussion will be safety. RIAT will be mounting the first presentation in the morning session, and Paul thinks it might be fun if I come along.

'Yes?'

'I'm not sure. Where is it?'

'Reims.'

The Fairford minibus picks me up from a Reading hotel off the M4. On board are Paul, Tim, Sue Allen, Heidi Standfast, Amanda

Butcher and Tim Cairns. Tim has recently joined Enterprises as Paul's staff officer, but is now in charge of co-ordinating all the emergency and security arrangements for this year's show. An ex-Royal Navy Lieutenant Commander, with service afloat as an Air Traffic Controller, Tim brings his own brand of dry wit to the travelling party that is RIAT at play.

Half a day of gossip, scandal and sheep jokes gets us to Reims. By the time we locate the hotel it's nearly seven, and delegates are beginning to appear for the pre-dinner champagne. Before we can join them, though, there's the small matter of a rehearsal.

Between them, Paul and Tim Cairns will be presenting an account of a mid-air collision during the 1993 International Air Tattoo. The incident itself, together with an analysis of what happened afterwards, will be illustrated by video footage, slides and overhead projections. Paul and Tim have never used the hotel's equipment before, and they want to be certain that the images will mesh with what they want to say. A roomful of their peers – airshow organisers and display pilots from every corner of Europe – is the last place on earth to make a cock-up.

The rehearsal is a shambles. More or less everything goes wrong. The power sources are unreliable, the cueing system doesn't work properly, and the pictures on the screen – once projected – are either ahead of or behind the narrative. Try as I might, I can foresee nothing but disaster come tomorrow, but that – in a sense – is academic. What rivets me to my seat, time and time again, is the video footage.

It comes from someone with a camera in the crowd. I've heard about this collision before, of course, and I have a dim memory of once seeing something about two Russian MiG-29s on the evening news, but nothing prepares me for the impact of what I'm watching, up there on the screen.

The camera is tracking a MiG-29 flown by a Russian pilot called Sergei Tresvyatsky. The big jet fighter, codenamed *Fulcrum*, is one of a pair from the Russian Flight Research Institute at Zhukovsky. The MiG is pulling out of a loop. There's little cloud about, and the bright July sunshine does justice to the blue, yellow and black of the *Fulcrum*'s colour scheme.

Abruptly, from the bottom right hand corner of the frame, comes another MiG-29, flown by Tresvyatsky's partner, Alexander Beschastnov. His airplane slices through the first MiG, just aft of the cockpit. For a brief, unforgettable second the crippled fighter folds in two. Bits fall off. Then the cameraman pans on, tracking a patch of empty sky, wondering what on earth has happened to that lovely MiG.

By the time the camera is stable again, the remains of Tresvyatsky's *Fulcrum* is a fireball scorching earthwards. It explodes behind the bulk of a parked C-130, sending a huge tumble of smoke and flame billowing upwards. Half a mile away, plainly visible, the other MiG spins gracefully down. Another column of smoke.

I'm thinking of the airfield tour I took with Mel James. The MiGs must have come down beyond Apron Green Alpha. Definitely.

Up on the screen, there are shouts on the soundtrack. People can't believe what they've just seen. Then, from the public address system, comes the voice of the show commentator. It's Sean Maffett. He sounds breathless, shocked: 'The incident you have just seen is not an exercise,' he says. 'The emergency services are responding.'

A hundred thousand people hold their breath. Behind the racing firetenders, two parachutes are drifting downwind. Both pilots, improbably, are intact. No one on the ground has been seriously hurt. And even as the drama unfolds – the swirling flames, the wailing sirens, the nearby Sea King scrambling with emergency equipment – the next display team, the *Patrouille Suisse*, are taxiing past in the background in preparation for take-off.

The images flicker and die. Sue, at the video machine, respools the tape and we watch the whole episode again while Paul and Tim adjust their commentary. Transfixed, I can only scribble the odd note. The way the second MiG flutters gently to earth. The deep crimson heart of the fireball. The extraordinary fact that everyone – including the pilots – walked away. I shake my head. Truly incredible.

The rehearsal goes from bad to worse. A couple of hours later, at dinner with Heidi, I tell her I've got my fingers crossed for tomorrow. In telly I've often sweated through hours of shambolic dry-runs, but I confess in all truth that I've never seen anything as ominous as that.

Heidi looks surprised. 'It'll be fine,' she says, 'I guarantee it.'

*

The Saturday programme starts at half past nine. Seven hours earlier, most of us were still in the bar. The association's president opens proceedings with a flourish and then hands over to Paul and Tim. There's a ripple of applause. Paul has their respect as well as their attention. RIAT is a giant among airshows. It's one of the things the Brits happen to do well.

Paul launches into a brisk guide to the show itself: the way it's developed, what it's tried to achieve, the sheer scale of the event. He then details a menu for the coming hour and bounces the presentation across to Tim Cairns. Tim is equally businesslike, offering a profile of the emergency services on call over the show weekend. So far, the visual aids have behaved themselves perfectly. I steal a glance at Heidi. She winks.

Paul again: 'Saturday twenty-fourth of July. Two eighths cloud at three thousand feet. A hot, sunny day. On the south side of the airfield, a crowd of 96,000. By half past three, the two MiGs are spooling up for the display. Elsewhere, the Duke of Kent is getting ready to depart. Oh yes, and we'd just had a major cardiac arrest over on Apron Orange...'

Paul is good at this. He lets the bare facts speak for themselves, building the tension, and when he makes a tiny gesture with his left hand the video pictures suddenly blossom on the screen behind him. No one moves a muscle. Once again, Tresvyatsky's MiG soars into shot. Once again, the camera tracks with the big *Fulcrum*. And once again, in the blink of an eye, something big and blurred and extremely violent chops it in half. Even Paul, who must have seen this footage a million times, can't take his eyes off it. Billions of roubles of airplane. Wrecked.

The video comes to an end. Paul details the mix of luck, courage, and meticulous advance planning that pulled the organisation through. The air show's emergency plan emerged from the subsequent board of inquiry with a clean sheet – but in front of this audience, fellow professionals, it's important to be candid. He describes in detail what went wrong. How the various elements within Emergency Control might have been better integrated. How the Fireball emergency response helicopter lifted off without a fireman. How the column of firetrucks racing to the wreckage of the second MiG – burning in a field off-base – couldn't find a way across an encircling ditch. How the emergency services' net was jeopardised by the lack of R/T discipline. How the public phone system in and out of the airbase was simply overwhelmed.

At this point, Paul looks up from his script. 'On the Monday night we always have a wind-down party,' he says. 'In 1993 some people got especially excitable.'

Excitable? Most of the delegates here speak pretty good English, but even in my native tongue I'm not entirely clear what he means. Someone calls for clarification and Paul obliges with a description of how professional and how cool everyone had been throughout the public days of the show, and how the real impact of the crash had been tucked away until there was a chance to properly relive it all. That opportunity came on the Monday night. People got angry. People got upset. 'Excitable' was perhaps too weak a word.

I think I can picture more or less the way it was – Fairford's finest getting one or two things off their collective chest – and while the delegates debate media strategies and the importance of clear chains of command, I begin to ponder the central conundrum at the heart of every airshow. RIAT's emergency orders – the bible for every volunteer associated with the emergency services – runs to nearly a hundred pages. I've seen it. It's thick, and pink, and much-thumbed. But the all-too-evident truth is that no amount of planning, and no amount of post-incident reappraisal, can ever entirely remove the risk of – in that deceptively dry phrase – an incident.

Air displays are inherently dangerous. No one comes to watch people die or get hurt, but pilots love to stack the odds against themselves, and that's what brings people in through the gates. Flight itself is absurd, a defiance of gravity. Add low-altitude displays, multi-aircraft displays and head-to-head closing speeds in excess of 800 m.p.h., and the resulting spectacle acquires an almost Roman dimension. Mess with gravity once too often, like Tresvyatsky and Beschastnov, and the consequences can be on television screens all over the world within minutes. That's why Laurie Upshon sets up his satellite link. That's why airshows happen.

This same point is neatly made that same afternoon. Second in the presentation batting order after lunch is a display pilot called Rod Dean. Rod was a fast-jet pilot in the RAF, and he's become an Air Tattoo regular ever since. He won the first Embassy solo display trophy back in 1971, and his hands-on talents run from warbirds like the Spitfire and the Mustang to classic jets like the Vampire and the Hunter. As it happens, I've got to know Rod reasonably well over the last year or so because he's given me a lot of background research on a novel. Now he's offering the pilot's perspective on the perils of the international display circuit.

He makes a series of pithy points about the need for thorough preparation. You can never iron out all the wrinkles, and you're a fool if you think you can. But above all, he says, give yourself *time*. He nods, making the point again, then launches into a story about his first ever display. He was flying a Hunter from RAF Chivenor. The display site, a West Midlands public school, was barely twenty minutes away from North Devon but he was already late. By the time he clambered into the cockpit, his ground crew had already gone through the start-up checks. Strapping himself in, he waved the chocks away and taxied out.

Half an hour later he was upside-down over the school cricket pitch, displaying the Hunter for all he was worth. The programme, as far as he could judge, went well. Back on the ground at Chivenor, pleased with himself, he shut down the engine and reached down for the pin to make safe the ejector seat. The stowage was empty. The pin had gone. Very carefully, he began to search the cockpit. Only minutes later did he find it, still seated in the safety mechanism – where it prevents the seat from being fired.

He looks at the rows of watching faces. 'Had I wanted to punch out ...' He nods, then draws a finger across his throat.

A couple of weeks later the story draws a wry smile from David Roome. Towards the end of the month I've driven over to Innsworth, the big RAF station near Gloucester where David works. I want to know how he's going to deal with Paul's vision of vertically stacked flypasts. In the light of the Reims weekend, this has suddenly acquired a new importance.

Innsworth has turned out to be much bigger than I'd ever imagined, a cluster of modern-looking office blocks looming behind a series of wire fences. David offers me coffee and asks me to hang on in his office for a couple of minutes while he finishes a meeting elsewhere in the building.

There's a copy of the latest edition of *RAF News* lying on top of the bookcase, and I pick it up. The lead story is headlined ANNIVERSARY SPECTACULAR, and previews the delights to be offered at this summer's Royal International Air Tattoo. In the third paragraph, RIAT Director Paul Bowen is waxing lyrical about the specially choreographed tribute flypast, six groups of aircraft 'stacked above each other'. It's official. It's in print. It's going to happen.

David Roome returns minutes later. I show him the story. He reads it, then shakes his head.

'Regretfully not,' he says. 'No can do.'

'Too dangerous?'

'To be frank, yes.'

'But a nice idea?'

'A lovely idea.' He pauses, choosing his words carefully. 'I've tried to work it every way I can. I know what Paul wants. I know it's got to be new and I know it's got to be safe. But those two things don't necessarily go together.'

He pulls a sheet of paper from a drawer and reaches for a pencil, quickly sketching the essentials. Crowd line. Display line. Wind direction.

He looks up. 'The problem is this,' he says. 'Let's say the pilots get it dead right. Let's say it's a complete mess on the run-in and they're all over the sky afterwards, but for that one split second, in front of the veterans, they're all stacked up. Now, who's going to see that? The veterans? Just here? Of course. But stand anywhere else in the crowd – say here, or here – and it'll *still* look a mess.'

I'm watching the pencil. He's definitely got a point. Why didn't anyone think of this before?

'How about lateral separation? Stacking them up sideways? Can you do that?'

'Yes we can, but would Paul want it? Think it through. The guy at the bottom's reasonably close to the crowd, but the guy at the top, way over here to the north, he'll be a dot in the distance. No.' He shakes his head. 'Paul wants impact, novelty, something different. Lateral separation simply won't do it for him.'

I return *RAF News* to the bookcase. Now that the stacks are officially dead and buried, I wonder what alternative David has up his sleeve. At the next Fairford meeting he's due to share his thoughts with the Flying Control Committee, men well used to translating Paul's wilder fantasies into flyable lines in the sky.

David starts a new page on the pad. 'This is what I've come up with,' he says. 'We start, say, with fighters. First over would be three World War One biplanes. I'm thinking of an SE5, a Camel and a Bristol Fighter. Now, here's the clever bit.' He quickly sketches a loose triangle, three pencilled arrows heading across the page. 'We fly them in the period formation, a loose vic. It's a gaggle really, but that's the way they'd have done it then. OK?' He looks up.

I nod. 'And then what?'

'We go for the inter-war years and do it Hendon-style. Say a four-ship this time. A Tiger Moth. A Hind. A Tutor. And a Gladiator. All four of them tied together.'

'*Tied?* You mean literally?'

'Yes. With ribbon. That's the way they used to do it. Here . . .'

More pencilled lines. More little arrows. Hendon, in North London, was the home of the famous RAF pageants, extravaganzas designed to boost the profile of the RAF while raising money for its infant Benevolent Fund. It's a nice idea, Fairford tipping its cap to the men and women who blazed a trail for today's airshows. Paul will love it, and I suspect David Roome knows that.

We're on to the Second World War now, a finger-four formation, a Spitfire, a Mustang, a Hurricane and a Thunderbolt roaring past the watching veterans. David turns another page. Time for the early jets. The Venom, the Meteor, the Vampire and the Hunter.

'Formation?'

'Low-level battle. A loose four.'

'And today's planes?'

'I'd go for a Harrier, a Jaguar, a Hawk and a Tornado. Card Four formation.'

'Card Four?'

'Yeah ... like this.'

Four crosses appear on the pad in the shape of the four of spades on the face of a playing card. David hesitates a moment then flicks back through the earlier formations.

'OK, nineteen aircraft in all. The speeds are going to vary, of course. The biplanes might be making a mile a minute. We could whistle the Card Four through at 540 knots. But that doesn't matter. I can plan out the nasties. I can give Paul an absolute assurance that it will happen. Fly this thing accurately, and it'll look really nice.'

I believe him. The vertical stacks are history now, but I can think of at least four reasons why Paul will jump at David's replacement. Number one, it's historically accurate. Number two, it'll look good. Number three, it's feasible. And number four, it's safe. Fair?

David nods. 'Absolutely. But there's something else too. It's not weather-dependent. If we settle for this we won't be looking for oodles of sky. And that, on the day, might be important.'

My eyes return to the pencilled patterns on David's notepad. I'm fascinated by the notion of choreography, of designing an aerial ballet in three dimensions. Paul's demands for the Fairford programme are never less than ambitious, but here is a man who cut his teeth on a 170-ship flypast for the Battle of Britain tribute. Given the fact that he'd never designed a flypast in his life, the learning curve must have been steep.

'It was vertical.' David shakes his head, 'And the worst of it was that my boss was leading the whole damn thing. There he was up front, piloting a Spitfire with a map on his knee. If I'd got it wrong, then he'd get it wrong. And if he got it wrong, then the consequences might have been tricky.'

David Roome's brief, back in 1990, was to have the aircraft overfly the capital in no more than ten minutes. On the day, with split-second timing, they did it in six. The aircraft came from RAF bases all over the UK. They flew big racetrack patterns over six separate locations and then merged into one long stream of aeroplanes. The key was to fly the compass heading that would take the aircraft to the gates of Buckingham Palace. Draw a line northeast from the Mall and you end up off the coast of Suffolk, close to the town of Southwold. That's where the racetracks began to converge. That's where the aerial column formed up.

'Were you up there with them?'

'No, I watched them from the ground.'

'And what did you think?'

'I was pleased. It looked OK.'

This sounds less than a yelp of excitement, but David's very moderation masks something infinitely more emotional. After the flypast had cleared to the west he found himself in Trafalgar Square, trying to collect film from a cameraman. The square was packed with spectators and parking was out of the question. Spotting a policeman, David asked his advice. The policeman looked at his RAF uniform and enquired whether he was on business. David nodded, indicating the last of the black dots, away to the west.

'I am,' he said. 'In fact I organised that bloody thing.'

The policeman smiled and then stepped back onto the pavement. 'Leave the car here, sir,' he said, 'I'll make sure it's looked after.'

It's a lovely story, and it must have been a nice moment. Proof – if an ex-Lightning pilot ever needed it – that mounting something so challenging could bring a very special reward. After that first display came many others, all of them tricky, and all of them – by definition – wide open to the public gaze.

In 1993, at RAF Marham, David designed a seventy-fifth anniversary display around the notion of spokes in a wheel, four generations of aircraft closing the airfield on different radials. In a way, it was the mirror image of the Fairford problem – huge variations of speed coupled with the need to compress the action into a reasonable period. David planned the radials with thirty-degree separation, the slowest aircraft lowest, the fastest thundering over the top. The Queen was to be there, together with other members of the Royal Household, and by all accounts the display would have been an immense success – had torrential rain not grounded all the aircraft.

Two years later, David found himself in a Hawk over London, acting as 'whipper-in' for a sixty-ship VJ-Day flypast, an experience that lives with him still. 'For the best part of an hour I had *carte blanche* to go anywhere, low level. Can you imagine that? Can you imagine whistling around over London with no one to get in your way? Absolute magic.'

The phrase 'whipper-in' is wonderful. It means exactly what it says – the choreographer up aloft in his sleek Hawk jet trainer, eagle-eyed for the slightest breach of formation discipline. Given the infinite range of things that can go wrong – from wind to lack of concentration – how on earth do you get these guys to stick to the script?

'With military pilots it's very easy. They're used to taking orders and they appreciate accuracy. That's the way they're taught to fly. They take great pride in getting it exactly right.'

'And civilian pilots?'

'Civvie pilots can be different. They don't always appreciate this need for accuracy. My nightmare is the guy who's looking out of the window and doesn't realise he's just lost a hundred feet in altitude or drifted off-heading.'

He goes on to answer my unvoiced question, describing the way he plans any display, making it his business to clamber – mentally – into each and every cockpit and thus view the shape of the formation through every pilot's eyes. What he ends up with is a comprehensive plan, easily broken down into individual briefs. The burden of responsibility is immense – David resists rehearsals, and once airborne the display formations are never controlled from the ground – but so far he's yet to get it wrong.

'It may happen one day,' he admits, 'because there are rogue factors you simply can't plan out. There might be wind shear. Some light aircraft might wander through the formation. A pilot might have a heart attack. It's all pretty unlikely, but it could happen.'

'And if it does?'

'Then I guess it's my fault.'

'Is that fair?'

'No, but that's not the point, is it?'

He smiles, talking about the buzz he gets from a well-flown display, that very special marriage of airmanship, showbusiness, and a meticulous concern for safety. The coupling is nicely appropriate, and takes us back to Fairford and the future of the Royal International Air Tattoo. In the shape of both manpower and hardware, the RAF already offers a great deal of hidden support for RIAT. In return, they've been offered a unique opportunity to build bridges to a small army of foreign air chiefs – and as MoD resources dwindle, David Roome believes that RAF involvement may become more and more visible. Indeed, given how few Air Days remain, RIAT may one day be adopted as the RAF's official air show, putting all the air force's display eggs in Fairford's basket.

Whether or not this would marry happily with the plans that Paul and Tim are hatching is anyone's guess, but for now David Roome appears to have finessed Paul's vertical stacks. After the fighters will come the bombers. Then the heavies. Then the trainers and the recce boys and the ground attack aircraft in any number of appropriate formations. The crowd will have lots to look at. Sean Maffett will have lots to talk about. And, who knows, maybe even Paul will be happy.

David leans back in his chair, pleased by the thought, and we talk for a while about that strange, almost Masonic process whereby serving officers – busy, pressured, capable men – find themselves co-opted to the Fairford cause. Is it sleight of hand? Is it a moment's weakness? Are they doing it for the Benevolent Fund? Or is it simply another job?

The latter notion broadens David's smile. He's looking at the patterns on his pad. 'My job's simple,' he says. 'My job's to stand between Paul and disaster.'

'To save him from himself?'

He shakes his head and frowns for a moment. Then the grin returns. 'I didn't say that.' He folds his arms. 'Did I?'

The month ends with a progress meeting at Fairford for all the airshow managers, a central corps of more than a hundred volunteers who will be responsible for every aspect of RIAT 98. The briefing takes place on a Saturday morning, and on the evening before Paul convenes a small dinner for key staff in Building 15.

Wally Armstrong decides on an Italian theme for the occasion, and after pre-dinner drinks we settle into *Pollo Alla Cacciatori* and *Scalopping Alla Bisteca Fiorentina* with all the trimmings. The wine is excellent and the conversation even better. The Fairford year, I've discovered, is dotted with stepping stones like these, generously mounted social occasions when stories are told, good times remembered, and legs pulled. It's also, I suspect, a wonderful moment for Paul to sound out the men and women who make and shape the airshow. If there ever was an opportunity for people to step back from the clamour of the telephones and take stock, then this is surely it.

After helpings of Gorgonzola and Pecorino Romano, Paul launches a discussion about the way the Tattoo has developed. He's aware of grumblings about 'remoteness' and an absence of fun, and it worries him that the sheer size of the event may have doused what he calls 'the old spirit'. The air show has always depended crucially on volunteers, and it's important to try and define exactly what it is that keeps them fuelled.

The depth of the collective RIAT memory is immense and many of the people around this table go back decades. They bring with them a natural tendency towards nostalgia, a belief that – in event terms – size and self-importance are generally the enemies of goodwill. But it's a policeman, Peter Williams, who offers the alternative view.

Peter has been with RIAT for more years than he cares to remember. He encountered it first down at Bournemouth. He was the Dorset Divisional Commander on whose patch the event was being held, and he was sufficiently hooked to return in subsequent years. As a superintendent, the RIAT commitment takes a substantial bite out of his annual leave, and he's now the co-ordinator in charge of all admissions during the two public days of the show, a job that makes him gate-keeper to hundreds of thousands of incoming spectators.

Paul is still fretting that something is missing, that something has been irretrievably lost.

Peter shakes his head. 'I think you're wrong,' he says. 'I think the truth is that most of the blokes who volunteer today don't go that far back.'

Peter is talking from hard experience. The volunteers in his own team number 300 plus, and like everyone else over that hot July weekend, he has plenty of chances to talk to more. So why do these guys volunteer in the first place?

'Because it turns them on.'

'But why?'

'Because it's something different. Think about it. The show gives them several days of incredibly hard work, an extraordinary *esprit de corps*, and a chance at the end of it all to pour limitless amounts of alcohol down their necks. That's a good result. By the Monday they're wrecked, but they've had a bloody excellent couple of days. Next year, same time, same place.'

Paul is beaming. None of this has much to do with nostalgia, but he and Tim were the original architects of the Sunday-night hangar party – RIAT's thank you to the troops and the aircrew – and it's good to hear that new recruits are as robust and as thirsty as the old campaigners. Should the organisation do more to foster this spirit? Might an official Christmas card to each volunteer be a nice idea?

Peter doesn't think so. A formal card is all well and good, but gestures like that get easily lost at Christmas. Much better that each volunteer gets a post-show note from his or her team leader. RIAT, like many organisations, is cellular. It's broken up into individual fiefdoms – like Kevin Leeson's protocol team or Mel James' Eng Ops – and it's at that level, Peter thinks, that the volunteer spirit is best kindled.

There are murmurs of agreement around the table and Paul, looking relieved, moves the discussion week on.

Next week, the London production company Double Exposure are to make a formal presentation to Sir Roger Palin and the board of the RAF Benevolent Fund. Paul and Tim sit on that board, and Paul wants to canvas opinion ahead of the presentation. After the triumph of *The House*, the BBC are currently transmitting the latest Double Exposure documentary soap. Entitled *Pleasure Beach*, it draws a bead on the huge amusements-and-rides operation up in Blackpool. In terms of visitors through the gate, Heidi's precious footfall, this state-of-the-art funfair is Britain's biggest attraction – and after the first couple of episodes it's not difficult to understand why Double Exposure are keen to bring their cameras to Fairford. But should RIAT say yes?

Paul looks around. He's worried, again, about the volunteers. The programme can never do justice to all 4,500. What about the thousands who'd never get a mention?

The discussion is remarkably brief. No one in his right mind would expect any programme to be comprehensive. The production team is bound to select. That's what film-making's all about. Paul nods. But what if they select the wrong story? What if they show nothing but traffic jams? Or Patti Heady going ballistic as the pressures mount?

The latter thought warms the conversation up. Television, especially this kind of television, is irresistibly attracted to pressure and conflict and people losing their rag. The demands of the show weekend practically guarantee all three – and that, presumably, is why Double Exposure are so keen to come. But who cares, when the potential is there for three hours of national network exposure? What Paul and Tim have always preached is the need to get bigger and better. That means raising the show's public profile – and what better way than stepping aside and letting the likes of Double Exposure do it for you?

The discussion ends with a vote. With a couple of exceptions, every hand around the table rises to support the Double Exposure bid. Paul, who is personally in favour, is grinning again. Only Peter Williams sounds a warning note.

'You say they'll be transmitting this time next year,' he groans. 'Just think of the traffic jams in 1999.'

The progress meeting for the managers takes place next morning. It's a cold, still, grey day with fog blanketing the airfield. The only venue big enough to hold the hundred plus volunteers is the base cinema, and the first cars roll in through the gate at half past eight. Some of these people have driven hundreds of miles to be here. With a wary eye on the weather, they've been on the road for hours.

The briefing starts at ten o'clock. The volunteers settle into the rows of cinema seats and there's a comfortable hum of conversation. These men and women are the lifeblood of RIAT. They've survived the rigours of previous airshows and doubtless have the scars to prove it. Every year they turn the impossible into sixteen hours of unforgettable entertainment, and every year they swear never to do it again. Yet here they are, back for an update and a chat, and as Paul mounts the stage and calls for silence there's a collective growl of welcome. Even with six months to go to July, you can scent the faintest whiff of grapeshot in the air. RIAT is war. And these men and women are the officers who will win it.

The agenda for the briefing runs to fifty-six items. Paul, in a rather fetching denim shirt, stands at a lectern on one side of the stage, while Tim, in a sports jacket and open-necked shirt, awaits his cue at a similar lectern on the other side.

Opening the proceedings, Sir Roger Palin treats us to five minutes of brisk exhortation. He salutes 'the best event team in the world'. He congratulates Paul and Tim and everyone else in the cinema on last year's spectacular. And he reveals, with a flourish, that RIAT 97 has poured nearly half a million pounds into the Benevolent Fund's coffers.

'You should all be proud of yourselves,' he says, 'because you're the best.'

With Sir Roger back in his seat in the front row, Paul takes up the running, mapping the outlines of RIAT 98. He explains why ticket prices have had to go up (from £20 to £24 for a single full-price ticket on the gate). He announces how many aerobatic teams have already been booked and what SkyWatch might contain, and why a South African 747 pilot called Flippie Vermeulin may well be arriving with a beautifully restored DC-4.

When he gets to Item 11, Traffic and Admissions, Paul pauses. His tone is sombre. Last year, he says, we got as close to the wire as we'd ever done. The stealth bomber sucked in traffic from hundreds of miles away and it was nearly dark by the time the queues of departing cars began to thin. No one was amused, least of all the drivers, and so this year an invitation has gone to the RAF Central Band to provide an evening open-air concert in a bid to stem the rush for the car parks.

He pauses for a moment to list the route designations to channel the huge crowd out of Fairford. The airfield is cradled in a web of minor country roads, all of them built for the horse and cart, and I wonder how much difference the military-style route designations will really make. The Red route zig-zags down from the north. The Blue route, everyone's favourite, feeds in from Swindon. The Green route sweeps across from Cirencester. The Purple route is dedicated to bus traffic. While the Orange route is the low-key preserve of visiting VIPs. The latter concept sets me thinking. Do you plan it for the best views? The prettiest villages? Or is it a really cunning confection of short-cuts, bolted together for speed of access and minimum visibility?

The meeting goes on. There's good news for Barney Bruce and his ATC volunteers in the shape of a bronze Tornado trophy for the best cadet. Reg Bloomfield is once again in charge of photobuses. Pete Busby has great plans for dressing the rear of the evening concert stage with hot air balloons. Ray Dixon is returning from the Falklands to mastermind operations at the flight centre. Sylvia Quayle will be on site again, troubleshooting on behalf of the medics, while Dave Ineson and Dave Fraley are trying to rationalise the comms set-up.

Paul pauses for breath, and Tim takes up the running. Over last year's show there was a problem with unreported minor damage to borrowed vehicles. RIAT accountants have been doing the sums. With no recourse to insurance, every little scratch costs £200. With seven affected vehicles, that's nearly one and a half thousand pounds. Tim repeats the figure then draws the necessary lesson.

'Brief down that we need to protect the bottom line,' he says. 'Every penny matters.'

On the subject of alcohol, another gripe. Certain teams on the airfield have been setting up mini-bars to raise what he delicately calls 'mess funds'. As a piece of private enterprise, it's impeccable. As a cut-price alternative to the authorised booze outlets, it's a pain in the arse.

'So no more mini-bars,' he says sternly. 'End of bollocking.'

Paul again. The addition of a discreet crown to the IAT logo, the grant of the royal warrant for the show, has resulted in all kinds of variations. For the purposes of stationery, product sales, advertising, and pretty much everything else, he's spearheading a drive to standardise the RIAT corporate look. Templates will be circulated and the exact Pantone colours agreed. 'It's called branding,' he growls, 'and believe me, it matters.'

The meeting finishes with good news. Sponsorship for RIAT '98 is already past £700,000, and Caroline Rogers and Clive Elliott are shooting for more. Lockheed Martin and British Aerospace are committed until the turn of the century, with Boeing now pledged to come in at the same level. Last year's show was the best ever with a flood of plaudits from the Americans, and this year – with luck – should be equally memorable. All in all, it's looking good, maybe better than good – and after Sir Roger winds up with another pep talk, the meeting comes to an end.

As the volunteers head for lunch I'm left in the empty cinema, gazing rather glumly at my notes, numbed by the sheer scale of the event. The rows and rows of faces around me represented just the tip of the volunteer iceberg. Behind these men and women are thousands of others, equally dedicated, equally vital. I flip back through the pages of pencilled scribble, looking for lifelines, finding only fresh bits of the puzzle. Who is Reg Bloomfield? What does Barney Bruce do? Where will I find Pete Busby? Why does everyone speak so warmly of Sylvia Quayle? And why does it really matter about non-standard stationery and flogging the odd tinnie?

I'm still in a trance minutes later, when I feel a tap on my shoulder. It's Paul. He's come back to find me.

'Any the wiser now?' he asks.

....

CHAPTER SIX

February 1998

The beginning of February sees David Higham taking the M5 north, towards the National Exhibition Centre alongside Birmingham Airport. There, he's planning to spend a couple of days at the International Spring Fair, trawling for items for his pride and joy, the new-look catalogue.

David's corner of the Fairford operation might be half a world away from nine-ship aerobatic teams and the tang of unburned Avtur, but last year the Benevolent Fund catalogues sold £250,000 worth of merchandise. Add the revenue from the Skyhigh Village – the sales outlet at the show itself – and the trading arm of Enterprises will be contributing more than £350,000 to Enterprises' operating revenues.

For anyone with even the mildest aversion to shopping, the Spring Fair is a nightmare. Each of the twelve exhibition halls houses hundreds of display stands offering everything from desk accessories to collectible spoons, and if you've ever wondered who supplies some of the hundreds of catalogues that thump in through the letterbox, then look no further. In a consumer society, this is choice gone mad.

David, though, adores shopping – which is probably just as well. An accountant by training, he joined Enterprises nine months ago as Deputy Financial Controller. A month later, the Trading Division became leaderless. David had never run a catalogue in his life, but he had curiosity, enthusiasm and a resilient sense of humour – and Paul Bowen needed all three. David's brief was simple. Get a grip on the

Trading Division. Make whatever changes you like. And double the turnover.

Away from the comforts of the spreadsheet, the dazed newcomer took stock. 'When I first arrived it was a really hard place to come to terms with, a really unique organisation. For one thing, it takes on so much. There's the airshow, of course. Then you've got the concerts in the autumn, and the RAF Year Book to produce, and the rest of the publishing titles, and the videos, and all the other merchandise, and on top of that lot you've got all these military acronyms. Everything's in capital letters. It's a kind of code. If you've got a military background, there isn't a problem. For someone like me, you either sink or swim . . .'

He shakes his head. He's looking at the Avia stand. Avia make watches. Getting a grip on the catalogue means a fundamental change of image. He wants to update the look of the thing, make the merchandising operation classier by taking it more up-market. He also wants to theme it, offering the kind of quality giftware inside the catalogue that will make good the promise of the new cover. Even the title will change. No longer *Skyhigh* but *The AvIATion Collection*. Cool.

'But why Avia?'

David shoots me a look. 'Haven't you heard about the link-up with the Falcons?'

I shake my head. The Falcons are the RAF's Parachute Display Team, and it seems that they're lending their name to a new range of Avia watches. In exchange, Avia have agreed to hand over a cheque for at least £3,000 to the RAF Benevolent Fund. This three-way association between Avia, the Falcons and the Benevolent Fund excites David, not least because he thinks the product might sit nicely in the new-look catalogue.

'Number one, it's got the association with the Falcons,' he says. 'Number two, it's a quality product. And number three, it'll come as a package.'

'Containing what?'

'A gift box, a Falcons baseball cap, a certificate . . .' He frowns, 'And a poster. Now that's excellent value. You've got to admit it.'

I have no choice but to nod. If RIAT are into the business of changing lives, then David Higham is one of their showpiece converts.

This accountant-turned-marketing man pitches with real fervour.

I nod at the display of watches. 'So they're definitely for the catalogue?'

'Very probably, yes.'

I catch the hesitation in his voice – not one of David's usual characteristics – and when I probe a little further it turns out that there may, after all, be a hitch. Over the last couple of years, Paul has built an important bridge between RIAT and the Breitling organisation, over in Switzerland. Breitling also make up-market watches, and they've decided that state-of-the-art military aviation offers perfect branding. Last year they put serious money into the show, sponsoring the Aircrew Enclosure; Paul afterwards volunteered Mel James to help co-ordinate the bid to fly the Breitling balloon – *Breitling Orbiter II* – around the world. Mel James and Paul are also researching the possibility of a Breitling fast-jet display team, an enormous project that could ensure extra revenue for the Benevolent Fund. Given the possibility of a seven-figure investment, how will Herr Breitling view the appearance of a rival watch in David Higham's new-look catalogue?

David, for once, looks uncertain. 'I don't know,' he admits. 'That'll have to be Paul's call.'

Paul's shadow lies across the catalogue. I know from my own conversations with him that he wants to expand the publishing operation. He's looking for wider markets for the titles that already exist, and among his bolder initiatives is the book I'm writing now. But when I suggest that Paul's hand is rarely far from the tiller, David shakes his head.

'I've not found that at all,' he says. 'He definitely has a vision and he makes sure you share it, but when it comes down to the small print he leaves you pretty much alone.'

The small print is all around us. Stand C14: hot-water bottles and car mats. Stand D10: whisky flagons and ceramic containers. As David gets out his pocket calculator and punches in the numbers I remember a comment of Heidi Standfast's. When it came to dealing with Paul and Tim, she had exactly the same story: 'They're not really interested in problems,' she told me, 'only solutions.'

Our tour of Exhibition Hall 7 continues. By lunchtime, I'm footsore and brain dead. If I see another novelty candlestick I'll scream. We head for the bar. Mercifully, there isn't a candlestick in sight.

'So you really enjoy it – all this?'

'I love it, yes.'

'You don't find it . . .' – I struggle to find the right word – '. . . daunting?'

David thinks about the question.

'It's bloody hard work,' he says at last, 'and the responsibility, if I ever stop to think about it, is awesome. But that's the thing about this lot. They take you at your word. If you're silly enough to say you'll do something then – bang – that's it. At first I thought the show itself would be the real crunch time – and it was, of course. You don't just hire the pavilion and stock it and banner it and all the rest, you probably end up painting the thing as well. That actually happened. There we were, Friday night, the last of the light, paint brushes in hand, everything behind schedule. It scares you half to death, but somehow you cope.'

'And enjoy it?'

'Enormously. It was incredibly exhilarating.'

'And now?'

'Now's just the same. It never stops. Ever. There's always another deadline. The catalogue re-design. The special anniversary concert we're doing at the Barbican. The RAF Yearbook. You know when we start mailing out the Christmas catalogue? August.'

The AvIATion Collection catalogue, as it will be known, mails to a database of 210,000 twice a year. A quarter of those names will belong to serving or retired RAF personnel. The rest will be people who've attended the airshow, or one of the other events organised out of Fairford. Given the absolute necessity of trying to visualise the kind of market you're selling into, doesn't that leave lots of questions unanswered?

David's looking thoughtful. The table between us is littered with brochures and giveaways. Heidi Standfast's analysis of the airshow crowd – fifty-eight per cent ABC1s – would argue for a relatively up-market database but that still leaves plenty of room for error. Isn't this whole exercise terrifyingly subjective? Isn't David Higham putting an awful lot of faith in his own taste?

He agrees at once. 'I am. But that's the challenge. The database gives me a foot in 210,000 doors. But from that point on – the moment when the catalogue hits the doormat – I've tried to rethink the whole process. Should we wrap it in RAF blue polyfilm – in which case you can't see what's inside – or should the polyfilm be clear? Should we stay with 80 gsm paper, or should we trade up to 110 gsm? Will the new themed approach work? Or should we have stayed with the old layout?'

He raises his hands, not in surrender but simply to illustrate the sheer number of decisions he has to take. Get any of them wrong and the consequences will, in marketing parlance, flow straight through to the bottom line. Mention of the bottom line takes us back to Paul Bowen and Tim Prince and the strange tides that swirl around Building 15. Paul and Tim talk the language of results. People who don't deliver don't stay.

'That's true. They expect an awful lot of you. I've not been with them a year yet but already I know that there are some people who have been broken by an organisation like this. It eats you up. If you're not careful, it can become all-consuming.'

At this point, I make my excuses and leave. Half a day at the International Spring Fair has done more damage to my nervous system than anything else I've seen or done since October. Invisible among the crowd of browsers I look back at David, bent over his calculator and his pile of brochures. Gold-backed photo albums. Ronson lighters. Specialist Christmas wrap. Novelty fridge magnets. Stealth underwear.

Who says there isn't glamour in military aviation?

Three days later I'm back at the Benevolent Fund offices in Portland Place. The board room is at the front of the building on the first floor. There are fifteen faces around the table, including Tim Prince – who is a board member – and Tony Webb, who piloted our abortive strike on Central Television. In the chair is Sir Roger Palin, and facing him across the table is Andy Bethel, who is the moving force behind Double

Exposure, the independent TV production company bidding to take its documentary crews to RIAT 98.

Andy comes to this presentation with a substantial track record as a successful producer. He's a big man who walks with a slight stoop. He wears a rather striking burgundy jacket, and when he begins his pitch he betrays not the slightest trace of nervousness. His voice is strong and he marshals the arguments with enormous self-confidence. Within a minute or two we know that his father was a wartime M jor General who walked the length of Italy after escaping from the Germans. The sub-text is plain: this man understands the ways of the military. Fairford – and the Ben Fund – will be safe in his hands.

I know a bit about fly-on-the-wall observational documentaries because I've made a couple myself. I know that they're extremely difficult to get right because no producer can ever guarantee that enough will actually happen to warrant the making of a programme. The trick is to find an event that is itself bigger than the presence of the camera. At the Royal Opera House Andy Bethel struck gold because the institution was in deep and self-evident crisis. At Blackpool Pleasure Beach, on the evidence of two episodes, the reverse is true. The place runs like clockwork. And there's very little for Andy's video crews to get their teeth into.

The Royal International Air Tattoo? Andy talks persuasively about the fascination of the event. About reaching *beyond* the aviation buffs. About establishing a broad audience appeal. It's escaped no one's attention that the first episode of *Pleasure Beach* won more than seven million viewers, and if this morning's debate is to be about public profile then surely the battle's almost over. In half an hour of airtime, this man can deliver more spectators than have – collectively – watched every airshow in the history of RIAT. That's a lot of potential converts to the cause, would-be fans who'd do no damage to Sir Roger's treasured bottom line.

Andy, warming to his theme, talks about the mysteries of the network commissioning process. How he has to sell the event to another tier of broadcasters. How their views will inevitably play a part in what goes on the screen. This is a clever, if necessary, move. For one thing, it's literally true. The network will pay the bills and will therefore become the client. For another, it may help keep the board at arm's length if the project gets under way and Andy encounters turbulence at the editing stage. With the best intentions in the world, fly-on-the-wall cameras are drawn irresistibly to things going awry. Given the perceived public appetite for disaster – in either the major or minor key – Andy Bethel will find it extremely difficult to resist network pressure to include 'friction'. Friction, in both Clausewitz and television, is code for conflict. And that, as Andy knows only too well, is what the board fears most.

He glances around the table. He's just reminded us again about the potential size of the TV audience. 'These kinds of figures don't come for free,' he warns, 'and I have to say that this kind of television does carry a modicum of risk. But it's risk that can be very, very carefully managed. For both our sakes.'

He goes on to predict the outcome, should the project proceed. Seventy-five per cent of what appears on the screen, he says, will be pure joy for both parties, while twenty per cent might not, at first viewing, be entirely palatable.

And the other five?

'Well ...' He looks regretfully at his notes. 'There may be one or two bits that might just cause you a twinge of aggravation.'

There's no reaction around the table. Board members are still watching, still listening, still trying to come to some kind of judgement. Television, especially this kind of television, remains a black art. Like a powerful drug, it can do you an awful lot of good, but it can also have side-effects.

Andy stirs. It's time for a little reassurance. The Fairford show, he believes, is tailor-made for television. And he hopes that it will be his privilege to make it available to a huge national audience. 'You have a great spectacle. You have an organisational operation of great complexity compressed into a short space of time. You have – I'm sure – some wonderful characters. You have the public in very large numbers. And you have, on top of all that, some of the sexiest aircraft in the world.'

I smile, noting down the phrases. I was there, last July, at the very heart of it – and he's dead right. That's why I'm writing this book. That's why I'm here.

Andy is talking small print now. What he's proposing is a series of six half-hour programmes charting the lead-in to the show and then the show itself. In production terms that will boil down to two or three two-men video crews operating under his own personal control. He pauses to emphasise this point. He understands the mind-set of the people around this table. The military is in his blood. What he's after is collaboration, not conflict.

'We're not in the business of prowling around, spying on people,' he repeats. 'We'll be in this together.'

For this project, as with others, he intends to draw up what he calls 'terms of engagement'. These will establish the ground rules for disputed bits of territory, areas of possible disagreement during and after the location work. Individuals or areas off-limits to the video crews. Dos and don'ts in terms of show protocol. Safety issues . . .

He pauses again. The crux of this subtle, complex negotiation has yet to come and everyone knows it.

Andy looks around the table. 'Editorial control, I'm afraid, must rest with us. You're not paying anything, so we must retain the right to make the final decisions. On issues of commercial sensitivity we're always willing to compromise, but what we can't allow is the power of veto over individual shots. You *will* see the film at rough-cut stage, when it can be changed. That I guarantee. And if there's anything that really gets up your nose then we'll listen very, very carefully to your views. But if I was to leave you with the impression that you have the power to order changes, then I'm afraid you'd be mistaken.'

Put this way the shape of the deal couldn't be less ambiguous, and around me I can sense a mute approval of Andy's candour. He could have fudged it. He could have left the impression that everything in the cutting room would be up for negotiation. Instead, he's made the nature of this prospective marriage absolutely clear. In return for access and co-operation, I can build you an enormous audience – but the right to decide exactly what that audience will be watching will, I'm afraid, be mine. We'll listen. We'll talk. But if, in the end, we still disagree, too bad.

Like any marriage, courtship is all-important, and before Andy brings his pitch to an end he takes a moment or two to sugar the pill. In the series about the Royal Opera House, no cuts were asked for at all. After watching *Pleasure Beach*, the Blackpool management requested a couple of minor changes to the commentary, willingly conceded.

Andy looks Sir Roger in the eye. 'No institution I have filmed has ever felt that they've been ripped off or in any way tricked. My reputation as a film-maker is what matters to me, and that I intend to keep.'

There's a long silence, then the questions begin. Would the series concern itself with other Benevolent Fund activities? How would Andy fend off pressure from the network for sensation and controversy? What about all the volunteers who would – inevitably – never get their faces on screen? What if a particular individual – through no fault of his own – was made to look a fool? TV's collective memory is short but these men and women will be living with the consequences of Andy's editorial judgement for a very long time indeed.

Issue by issue, the shape of the board's anxieties become clear. Television adores making mischief. It wants to be looked at. It'll do anything to keep people glued to the screen. That, of course, is why it delivers such a tempting audience, but the board are worried about controlling this boisterous infant, and despite all Andy's warm assurances they're not entirely sure it can be done.

Andy obviously understands this. He talks of this being a 'feel-good' series, of there being so much to watch that there'll never be a need – in his phrase – to 'hit the controversy button'. He'll have cameras in cockpits. He'll do lots of air-to-air. He might even send a crew to Kiev to profile the Ukrainian MiG-29 display team before they fly west. All these elements will be part of the narrative, a compelling story that will build and build. The last thing on his mind is stooping to some of the rough tricks that have given 'reality television' such a coloured reputation.

The board hear him out. The memories of *Pleasure Beach* are very fresh indeed, and some of them speak louder than this polished, articulate film-maker-turned-entrepreneur. After he and his development executive have left the room, the board begin to debate a decision. Some members have been impressed. Others still have misgivings. But what is oddly comforting is a very real preparedness to show television the door. There may, in the end, be more important things in life than a seven-million-strong audience, and the paradox at the heart of this whole episode is that one of them may be the show itself.

Back outside, Portland Place is bathed in early spring sunshine. I borrow a mobile phone and call Simon Spanton, my editor at Orion. A great deal hangs on the board's decision, and one of them is the commercial success of this book. A TV tie-in would do its sales prospects no harm at all. So what's the news?

I explain that a decision has been deferred. The board want to watch a bit more of *Pleasure Beach*. There's to be another meeting.

Simon can't believe his ears. 'You mean they might turn it *down*? A prime-time series?'

I smile. I'm back in the world of marketing decisions, audience build and tough commercial realities. 'I rather fancy they might.'

A week later, they do. The decision is far from unanimous, but Sir Roger, in particular, is unconvinced that Andy's style of coverage would be good for the show. He's worried about what he's seen in *Pleasure Beach*. He's fearful that a series of minor eruptions – personality clashes caught on camera – might overshadow everything else on offer. And he's determined, above all, to protect Paul and Tim's baby, the show itself.

Paul and Tim, oddly enough, have no qualms at all. An audience of seven million is all the justification they'll ever need.

'Strange decision,' Paul grunts, shaking his head.

Some days later, in mid-February, David Roome returns to Fairford. In his attaché case are the fruits of two months' hard thinking. After front-page stories about vertically stacked flypasts, the time has come to ease Paul Bowen back into the real world.

The meeting begins with some gossip about the aerobatic teams. To Sue Allen's alarm, the menu for July is suddenly looking a bit thin. The Brazilians – who would have been a RIAT first – have pulled out. The Austrians have also said no. The *Patrouille Suisse* appear to be unavailable, while the cream of the French Air Force – The *Patrouille de France* – are still insisting that they must depart at nine thirty on the Sunday morning, effectively limiting themselves to a single display in Saturday's show. Far from boxing herself in with too many display teams, Sue is now wondering whether she has enough. An obvious replacement for The *Patrouille de France* would be the Italians. The *Frecce Tricolori* are old show favourites, and Paul suggests a call to a favoured Italian colonel, only too happy to apply a little gentle pressure on RIAT's behalf. This is thought to be a good wheeze, but Sue disagrees. If the plan is to elbow the French and install the *Frecce* for the whole weekend, she's certain the Italians will say no.

Paul looks astonished. 'Why?'

'Because they're friends,' she says sweetly.

I'm about to lobby for the Turkish Stars when Paul decides that enough is enough. David has come to explain how he's managed to fly the vertical stacks. The meeting must press on.

David Roome refuses to rise to the bait. As I know from our meeting in his office at Innsworth, he's invested a great deal of time and effort proving to himself that vertical stacks with aircraft as various as the Camel and the Eurofighter are simply unflyable. More than that, they're unsafe.

'It ain't a goer, I'm afraid,' he says, 'even with lateral separation. It swallows height. It's weather-dependent. And it would be a nightmare for the pilots. What you'd get is same way, same day. It would look a complete pig's ear. You want a gaggle formation? Vertical stacks is the way to do it.'

Paul looks briefly startled. He's never been keen on coming down to earth, and this represents a fair-sized bump. He mutters something about GPS. GPS stands for global positioning system – a small, hand-held device that will tell any pilot exactly where he is at any given moment. Might this not help?

David is merciless. Once a fighter pilot, always a fighter pilot. 'GPS will only get you to the right place,' he says. 'After that, it's a percentage game. Working up the stack, we're talking sixty-knot speed differentials. That's mile-a-minute overtakes on the run-in. Down the bottom you've got something from Shuttleworth tacking across the wind to get there in time. Up at the top there's Eurofighter practically falling out of the sky trying to slow down. And they've all got to stack up precisely, *precisely*, in front of the veterans. You're talking a split second. You'd hardly see it. You're shooting for the moon.'

I'm already convinced by David's quiet common sense, but the image of some priceless antique biplane from the Shuttleworth collection adopting dinghy tactics to make it to the airfield in time is priceless.

Paul, to no one's surprise, refuses to give in. He's seen practically every flypast there's ever been, and he's absolutely determined to come up with something different. That's his job. That's what RIAT's *for*.

A flurry of ideas hits the table, everyone piling in. Opposition flypasts at different heights. A slow four-ship box with a fast one through the middle. Some kind of rotational sweep with the slowest aircraft on the tightest tracks. David gives each new suggestion due thought. Opposition flypasts? No problem. Would we need to rehearse? Only with the element leaders. Sue makes notes. Tim smiles. David wants to make it work every bit as much as Paul. And that, in itself, is good news.

Paul stirs. 'What about a three-ship stack?' He's looking at David. 'Wouldn't that be easier than a six-ship?'

'Easier to plan, yes. But there's still no guarantee of a result.'

'So it's definitely not going to work?'

'No.'

This, I sense, is the moment when Paul's wheels finally hit the runway. He's back on planet earth. The vertical stacks, at last, are history.

'But how else do we produce this cavalcade of aviation?' He frowns, reaching for the Superkings. 'It's got to be unique, something really different.'

Discussion begins about the little grass strip out at Rendcomb, home for some of the veteran aircraft. Many elements in the eightieth tribute could be launched from there. Talk of sequenced take-offs brings Paul to life again.

'Hey ...' Smoke curls from the cigarette. 'I'm getting an idea here. How about we bring in some of the early stuff from Rendcomb and also launch from here? That way we could roll time-right formations off the runway and mesh them in with the Rendcomb fly-bys.'

'Mesh them in how?' David's watching him carefully.

Paul gives the problem a moment's thought, then solves it. 'We fly them between the runway and the southside.'

Tim reminds him about the display regulations. Flying the Rendcomb aircraft on Paul's track would bring them too close to the crowd.

'No it wouldn't. It would be like using the hard shoulder. It's OK, but you shouldn't do it too often.'

The hard shoulder. Wonderful. I make a note of the phrase, underlining it twice, Paul at his buccaneering best. Every organisation, for its own good, should always be pushing the envelope outwards. The hard shoulder is for emergencies only. Unless you happen to be Paul Bowen.

David, ever-sane, heads Paul off. His pen is sweeping across a clean sheet of paper. 'If you *do* want to generate something like this, then – yes, it's easy to control.'

'How many aircraft?'

'Depends. How many would you want? For each launch?'

'At least twelve.'

'No problem. You want to recover them too?'

'We have to, David. Getting them back next day would be a nightmare. We just don't have the landing slots. Or the airspace.'

'OK.' David shrugs. 'Then you recover them.'

'Not a problem?'

'No.'

'What about putting it all together? Who's in the chair?'

'Me. I design it. I brief them. Then it's the green light and off they go.'

'Phenomenal.' Paul leans back, a huge smile on his face. 'David, you've got eighty minutes to fill. Here are the ingredients. Type flypasts. Missing-men formations. Singleton displays in between. Plus the Arrows at the end. The Arrows will take twenty-four minutes. The rest is down to you. It's got to be different and it's got to be busy,

busy, busy. Things happening all the time. Everywhere.'

There's a silence. David is tidying his notes. Paul's grin, if anything, is an inch or so wider – and it's a second or two before I realise what's happened. RIAT has won. David Roome has just become a volunteer.

The rest of the day breaks into smaller meetings, each exploring aspects of the RAF tribute. Why the Tiger Moths opening the display will have to be stepped in altitude to make the figure 80 more legible from the ground. How a para-drop from the RAF Falcons might neatly buffer the main display from the Red Arrows at the end. Whether or not the Tucanos bursting through the painted roundel in the sky will have enough endurance if they're flying down from Linton-on-Ouse. The latter, says David, doesn't begin to be a problem. The Tucano, the RAF's primary trainer, has masses of gas. They could spend half a day over Fairford and still make it back to Lincolnshire.

By late afternoon the talking is over. David, RIAT's new cho-reographer, has agreed to come up with a cast list of aircraft within a week. It will then be time to go shopping for prices, trying to shoehorn David's script into the confines of the show's budget. That, I suspect, will be a constraint every bit as important as gravity or the safety regulations, and I wonder how many of those boldly pencilled strokes on David's pad will survive.

Outside, in the car park, David and I say goodbye. I've no idea whether a week is long enough to choreograph eighty minutes of unforgettable flying, but David doesn't seem perturbed. He's got a vast chunk of the RAF's budget to look after, plus a million and a half other things to do. But deadlines are deadlines.

He opens his car door, then pauses. 'Besides,' he says, 'the heavies will be there.'

'Heavies?'

'The Flying Control Committee.' He tosses his attaché case on the passenger seat. 'See you there?'

'How many cans of drink?'

'About half a million.'

'Pints of beer?'

'Fifty thousand, plus or minus.'

'Teas? Coffees?'

'Impossible to count.'

Tom Watts is exhibition manager at Fairford. After thirty-two years in the RAF Police, he's salting his retirement with a three-day-week contract with Enterprises. In Building 16, he shares an office with Catherine Iddon.

Catherine – young, blonde, leather-booted – looks after the many demands of the showground site, the vast acreage to the south of the runway which becomes the public area throughout the show. This morning, for my benefit, we're trying to compute a relationship between the ocean of hot and cold drinks bought over the show weekend and the tricky issue of exactly how many portable toilets should be on site to cope with the consequences.

Tom's calculator is running out of noughts. It's part of his job to manage the hundreds of trading sites available across the showground. Of these, ninety will be selling food and drink. Add seven huge bars, plus whatever drinks people bring in through the gate, and you're looking at what Tom terms 'serious throughput'.

Catherine and Tom compare calculators. The call, finally, is Catherine's.

'Last year we brought in forty blocks of portaloos,' she says. 'That's literally hundreds of individual stalls. In fact it's so many that there isn't a single supplier big enough to cope, so we have to split the contract.'

But is it enough?

She and Tom exchange looks. Five years at Fairford has taught Tom a number of lessons, and this is one of them.

'It's never enough,' he says. 'Whatever figures you dream up, it'll never be enough.'

Catherine agrees. 'Sometimes you get close – but Tom's right. Last year we more or less cracked it, but it's trial and error really. You can be as rational as you like but what it boils down to is an inspired guess. This year?' She glances up at the rows of neatly labelled files. 'We'll order forty again and keep our fingers crossed.'

'Legs?'

'Hopefully not.'

Catherine has been with Enterprises for just over a year. Barely twenty-four, she made her airshow debut as Paul Bowen's gopher, and the memories of that exhausting July weekend are still with her.

'I've never come across people who work so physically hard. They were a great bunch, but I couldn't believe how much they had to get through. No one ever stopped. No one ever walked. It was incredibly exciting, the sheer pace of it all, but it was different too.'

Like Tom, Catherine is now part of the full-time staff. As Site Manager she must ensure that everything will be in place on the showground, ready for July. In this sense, she must brace herself for two invasions. First, the small army of contractors, sponsors, exhibitors, food concessionaires and sundry tradesfolk, who gather up their wares and descend on the airfield ahead of the public display days. These people will already have paid a great deal of money to Tom Watts for the right to do business at the show, and they will expect the airfield to be ready for them.

Come Saturday morning, the second invasion arrives – a tidal wave of spectators. Airfields, by definition, are huge spaces, but the sheer volume of aircraft movements feeding the eight-hour display means that most of the airfield is off-limits to the general public. That, in turn, demands miles of roping and staking, of metal crowd barriers and security fencing, to keep spectators safely corralled within the showground. Does it work?

Catherine nods. 'Yes it does – but you have to keep at it. The key thing is information, letting people know where they are, telling them where to go next. We have an entire building full of signs, and I have a special team who do nothing but put the signs up.'

'How long does it take them?'

'Three weeks.'

Three *weeks*? I'm trying to relate figures like these to what I saw last July. The ropes and stakes, as I recall, reached miles out into the surrounding villages, sealing off verges where you might be tempted to park the car, or tiny access tracks that might – at first sight – look like a short cut. Crawling towards the airfield at something less than three m.p.h., the operation had a D-Day feel to it: gigantic in conception, unimaginably chaotic should things go wrong. Given the sheer scale of RIAT, does the weight of responsibility rest heavily on Catherine's young shoulders?

The question makes her laugh. It's Paul, of course, who draws up the final masterplan for the showground, carefully cross-hatching this area and that; and it's Catherine's job to translate all those multi-coloured squiggles into ropes and stakes and chalets and tentage and endless supplies of clean water. The nightmare, understandably, is not getting it ready in time, but Catherine has a young team, and with them she shares a positive relish for what might seem to most of us an impossible challenge.

'The great thing about the show is the experience it gives you. It's just phenomenal. It stretches you and it stretches you, and just when you think you've got it cracked, something else happens. At the end of it all you're completely knackered, but that doesn't matter because the fact is that you've done it. It's worked. All those people have come and they've had a great time and they've gone again. Being part of all that, helping make it happen, gives you an incredible independence, an incredible feeling that you can do *anything*. You never thought it was in you. But it was.'

This is the other half of Tim Prince's equation, proof positive that impossible challenges trigger impossible responses, that people can find within themselves undreamed-of depths of resourcefulness, stamina, and low cunning. Catherine Iddon, like a number of other people I've met at Fairford, has an almost religious relationship with the airshow, a body-and-soul commitment she'd never dream of questioning.

I ask her, out of curiosity, whether aircraft turn her on, but she shakes her head.

'To be frank, I don't know much about them. There's something called the B-1. It's big and black and it's got four engines and it makes an incredible noise when it takes off. I like watching that one. It makes the hairs on the back of my neck stand up. But the rest?' She shrugs. 'We never get time to watch. Maybe that's it.'

The B-1 is an American supersonic swing-wing bomber. I've watched them myself, and Catherine's right – it's a big, well-muscled, hunky aeroplane, and once it starts to roll you get the feeling that nothing in the world could ever stop it. Isn't the show itself a bit like that? Isn't it reality on re-heat?

Catherine gives me a funny look. There are limits to all this writerly chatter, and I get the feeling that I've just crossed them.

'All I'm saying is that it takes an enormous amount of your life.' She nods at the paperwork cluttering her desk. 'It's only February, but already I'm thinking about the grass-cutting schedules and the grandstand contracts. Come the summer, June, and the pace just quickens and quickens. It gets unreal sometimes ... but is it like the B-1 bomber?' She frowns, gazing down at the figures she scribbled earlier on her pad.

'I think I got the beerage wrong,' Tom volunteers. 'I think it's nearer 60,000 pints, not 50,000.'

We're back in the world of portaloos, and we go through the usual repertoire of jokes about the Fairford evacuation plan. Portaloos form something of a running gag at IAT. Paul has treasured memories of a Lockheed senior manager helping unblock a particularly troublesome unit at one of the early Greenham Common shows, and I suspect that Clive Elliott will die and go to heaven the day he sells all forty blocks as a sponsorship opportunity. Tom nods. If I think Clive's joking, I'd be wrong. Challenges at Fairford, as Catherine's just pointed out, are part of the job description.

Tom Watts fits neatly into Catherine's carefully nurtured masterplan. While she provides the ropes and the stakes and umpteen other bits of kit to shape and define the public areas south of the runway, it's Tom's job to turn those precious acres into profits for the Benevolent Fund. Part policeman, part entrepreneur, he sells and supervises the 650 sites that chequerboard the showground. Last year, Tom's self-styled 'Trading Emporium' raised £115,000. This year Paul's set him a target of £120,000. Challenge again – and reward.

Tom leans back in his chair. He's a big, weathered man who plainly loves his job. Patrolling the bottom line of his little empire, he's learned a great deal about the traders, big and small, who queue at dawn on the Friday before the show weekend, eager to take possession of their precious squares of Fairford turf.

'Most of them come back year after year,' he says. 'There are fewer and fewer airshows, and most of the little guys are having a thin old time. What we deliver is 100,000 punters a day. If they can't hack it here, they won't hack it anywhere.'

Booking a pitch at RIAT doesn't come cheap. The standard ten-metre frontage will cost you £1100 for the weekend, regardless of how much you make. If the sun shines and you happen to be selling ice creams or cold drinks, you'll make a fortune. If it tips down with rain and the crowds don't turn up, you might be out of pocket. Either way, it's a gamble. Tom demands half the money up front with the completed application form, while the rest is payable by 12 June. Sadly for the traders, the Met Office doesn't yet extend to six-week forecasts.

'And they pay it? These traders?'

'On the nail. Otherwise they're out.'

'And you're taking money already?'

'Of course.' Tom reaches for a long computer printout. 'Sixty-three thousand pounds, as of yesterday.'

I make a note of the figure, remembering Sir Roger Palin up in Portland Place, explaining how Enterprises must pay for itself, underwriting its own risks. With money already flooding in from sponsorship and on-site traders, I'm beginning to sense how it works.

Tom's attention has been caught by another printout. This one details the sheer range of products available in what he calls the 'overnight city'. His finger wanders down the list of traders: people selling hand-embroidered tablecloths, fur-lined leather boots, insurance, garden gnomes, fashion accessories, Devon cider, country fudge, £3 rides on a Hawk simulator, fancy doughnuts, pick-a-winner competitions...

Mention of the latter produces a story or two. A lot of the traders have been selling from site to site all their working lives, part of the travelling fairground community, and there's very little that life can teach them about keeping the 'billies' (Billy Bunters – punters) happy. Rumours in the early days about winning lucky-dip tickets glued to the bottom of the bucket alarmed the detective in Tom Watts, and he's now devised a system that is, he believes, as con-proof as humanly possible. When I ask for details he gets a little coy, but more

121

conversation unearths some gems. An 'arrival pack' is sent to contracted traders in early July. The pack contains passes and permits worth a small fortune on the black market – and an alarming number used to go missing 'in the post'. At first, Tom obliged with replacements, but for the last few years he's mailed everything by recorded delivery.

'It's pricier postage-wise,' he says, 'but it saves us a fortune on the day.'

Once inside, traders had a habit of abandoning allotted pitches for something more promising. This naturally caused untold grief, with pitched battles for fancied sites – so now all passes are colour-coded by area, with the invoice and site numbers prominently displayed. Trespass still happens – 'a rush of blood to the wallet' – but Tom has a small army of patrolling stewards to keep the peace, and if all else fails he has a forklift truck at his disposal to return a stroppy trader to the gate.

'And you'd do that?'

'Happily,' he nods. 'And they know I'd drive it myself.'

Within Catherine's site plan, Tom himself decides the jigsaw of trading stalls that will tout for business. The turf at his disposal is limited by the presence of hundreds of aircraft on static display, and he knows only too well that Paul's search for extras is never-ending. The surprise arrival of a Belorussian freighter or an Italian Atlantique can play havoc with Tom's jigsaw, but he's long learned not to make a fuss. Least of all to Paul.

'There'd be no point,' he says. 'He'd never listen anyway.'

'So what do you do?'

'I always have a couple of pitches up my sleeve. Just in case.'

The image makes me laugh. Blessed with a fine weekend, this man could make me several thousand pounds the richer. Given his long experience, what should I go into? Garden gnomes? New-age jewellery? Cartons of chilled mango juice? Burgers?

Tom shakes his head. The guy's name has slipped his mind, but the figures he'll never forget: 'Bloke bought a three-metre frontage. Cost him £250 for the weekend. You know how much he took?'

'Tell me.'

'Five and a half thousand quid.'

'But what was he selling?'

Tom pauses a moment, relishing the story. Catherine is listening too. 'Little plastic aeroplanes,' he says at last. 'What do you think?'

The end of the month brings a soft spring day with a fluffy eiderdown of broken cloud and a splash or two of early daffodils beside the road in from the main gate. This morning sees the year's first meeting of the Flying Control Committee, a cadre of aviation's finest recruited by Tim and Paul to make sure that every element in July's flying display meets the Ministry of Defence's safety regulations.

The committee is chaired by Geoff Brindle, an RAF Group Captain currently posted on loan service to the Royal Air Force of Oman. As it happens, I've met Geoff a couple of times before. He's a small, wiry man with a mischievous smile. The moustache and the blue eyes give him a slightly Forties look, and I've always wondered whether this fantasy of mine extends to black Labradors and moist-eyed WAAFs. As a frontline fighter pilot, Geoff flew Lightnings and Phantoms, and Paul has a number of impressive stories about his solo display performances at IAT during the Seventies.

With Geoff at the meeting are four other members of the committee. Brian Trubshaw I recognise from countless photographs and TV documentaries. He piloted Concorde through the test and development programmes and earned a CBE in the process. Roger Beazley, another fast-jet man, ended his service career as the RAF's Director of Test Flying, while Mike Chapple won honours as an international helicopter display pilot. Les Garside-Beattie, last to the meeting, is a tall, quietly-spoken Wing Commander. An ex-display pilot in the Harrier, he recently moved to RAF Wittering after a spell as Team Manager with the Red Arrows. In terms of the treasure trove of collective experience around the table, his is probably the most current.

The meeting takes place, as ever, in the staff dining room. Paul is away but Tim Prince begins with an update on the preparations for the July show. His style is altogether quieter than Paul's. He favours consensus rather than confrontation, and in meetings like this he has the talents of a good chairman, fashioning a party line from a broad range of forcefully expressed opinions.

The event, he says, is selling well. The big sponsors are all locked in, much to Sir Roger's delight, and public support is building nicely. As far as the hardware is concerned, it's still early days, but the news here is less promising. For the SkyWatch operational theme he and Paul have been hoping for an Israeli UAV, but the chances of acquiring permission to fly one of these pilotless aircraft in front of a six-figure crowd appear to be thin. The effectiveness of SkyWatch, too, is partially dependent on downlinking pictures to the big Jumbo screens, and these – alas – are proving difficult to finance. They depend on a big helping of extra production kit, and the jury's out on whether or not this package can attract a sponsor.

There are nods around the table. It occurs to me that Tim's talking about my little corner of the wood, and I make a note to check with Tony Webb about the latest developments. Has Laurie Upshon had a rush of blood to the head? Are Central Television going to lend us an outside broadcast scanner? I rather doubt it.

Tim, meanwhile, has moved on to the aerobatic teams. It's official now that the Italians are refusing to replace the French, which leaves Sue Allen with just three definites; the Red Arrows, the Jordanian Falcons and the Blue Eagles have all said yes, and the Ukrainians look like turning up as well. The Spanish have already been told that it isn't their year, and the Swedes haven't been invited. There's word from Lisbon that the Portuguese have reformed their display team, flying Alpha Jets, and they're certainly a possibility. The Irish Silver Swallows, after their triumph at last year's show, have sadly had to pack it in.

'Why?'

'No money.'

There are murmurs around the table. Fewer aerobatic teams, in theory, will free up precious display time – but clearly there comes a point when they'll be obvious by their absence. Tim agrees, but repeats that time is on our side. The show is a living thing. It's changing all the time. Who knows which phone may ring next – bringing with it the offer of untold delights?

Tim looks round the table, brimful of confidence. There are certain elements in the July show that will very definitely go ahead, he says, and the time has come for David Roome, 'our man in the pink tights', to share his masterplan for the Berlin Airlift and RAF anniversary displays. David has brought with him a map and a pile of printed schedules, timetabling each display. He has copies of the paperwork, and he hands them round. The detail is impressive. For the Berlin Airlift, David has predicated a series of twelve take-offs on runway 09 into an imaginary east wind. A flypast by a Falcon 20 of Flight Refuelling opens this segment of the display at 1400. Thirty seconds later the first of the DC-3s rolls for take-off. One minute and forty-five seconds later this aircraft is one nautical mile upwind at a thousand feet, maintaining a speed of 120 knots. For the next two minutes it levels off, flying the same track. At 1404 plus fifteen seconds, for one minute, it completes a rate-one turn to the reciprocal heading, taking it back on the parallel track. After two and a half minutes, it is abeam the upwind end of the runway.

Adjusting the track by ten degrees, it continues downwind for another ten nautical miles before turning on to base leg, still at 120 knots. One minute fifty-five seconds later, after a base-leg adjustment, the DC-3 makes a final turn on to the centreline at six and a half nautical miles out. At 1420 precisely, nineteen and a half minutes after take off, the lead aircraft touches down.

Behind it, airborne, are eleven other aircraft, beads on David Roome's string. At ninety-second intervals they too will land, roll along the runway, and then take off again, completing the second twirl of the aerial roundabout.

I study David's map with its carefully marked tracklines, remembering Roger Smart and Clive Elliott at their pre-Christmas meeting around this same table. At that point the Berlin Airlift tribute had been a gleam in Paul Bowen's eye. Barely two months later, thanks to some inspired courtship of David Roome, it's become a series of compass headings and split-second turns, now subject to the attentions of some very experienced airmen indeed.

Geoff Brindle is the first to voice the obvious query. 'Is ninety seconds between touchdowns a safe clearance? Will Julie Morrissey be happy?'

Julie Morrissey, RIAT's ATC supremo based at Manchester International Airport, sequences flying operations from the Fairford tower during the July show. Today she's represented by Ian Sheeley, himself the radar chief over at RAF Brize Norton. As Flying Display Manager he's already working closely with David Roome, and sees no problem with the closely spaced landings.

'We'll give the green light to the crews and leave it to them,' he says.

I look at David. From our meeting at Innsworth I know this is the way he likes to play it. Write the masterplan, brief the crews, press the button, then settle back and watch the display.

Brian Trubshaw isn't convinced. He's still looking at David's map. 'A roller puts a pretty big scatter into this,' he says.

A roller is the touch-and-go in the middle of the display. David scribbles himself a note but points out that the plan leaves a margin for mid-air adjustments.

Brian's still frowning at the map. 'Why use 09?' he queries. 'When the wind's normally from the west?'

David gently explains that he prefers to plan for the worst option. At the easterly end of the runway there's plenty of room for twelve aircraft to await their turn for take-off, because the parallel taxiways and a wide ramp connect directly to the threshold. Up at the westerly end of the runway, the nearest taxiway feeds in well short of the threshold, forcing aircraft to backtrack for hundreds of metres along the runway before turning 180 degrees prior to their take-off run. With a dozen DC-3s in the queue this, to say the least, would add a complication.

Brian Trubshaw nods. This man must know the skies around Fairford by heart. For years he flew Concorde here, circuit after circuit, ironing out the wrinkles in the test programme. 'What about wake turbulence?' he asks. 'Aircraft this close?'

'We'll check it out.'

There's a pause. Then more questions. Finally, all anxieties met, David briefs on the RAF display. To Geoff Brindle's immense relief, the vertical stacks have gone. In their place, a brand new masterplan.

'Take the Moth 80 formation,' David begins. 'From a visual point of view the best way of keeping the thing coherent is to fly stepped-up towards the crowd. But civvie pilots won't do that because the CAA might not like it so we're stuck with the display line, flying along the crowd. Now that can be a problem. For a minute or so you might see a perfect figure 80. Thirty seconds later it would appear to be a shambles. These are inherently less stable aircraft. Do we really want to ask some of these people to fly in line abreast?'

It's a question the committee can't avoid. If David Roome is looking for support in his bid to accident-proof the flying displays, then he's just made a brilliant move.

Geoff Brindle stirs. 'I've got lots of reservations,' he confesses. 'We'd be asking these guys to fly exact but not commonplace formations. They won't have done this kind of thing too often. What about turbulence? What about a crosswind? What happens if some guy goes sick and they have to field a late replacement? No.' He shakes his head. 'I don't like it at all.'

There are murmurs of agreement around the table. Someone enquires about the Roman numeral for eighty. Suggestions wing in from all quarters, but when we finally sort out the answer we all know that the possibilities of translating LXXX into several dozen Tiger Moths look even more remote.

At this point, Tim attempts a finesse. 'Let's talk to the Tiger leaders,' he suggests, 'and see what's possible.'

David shakes his head. 'I think we need something neat and tidy. Maybe a diamond-nine formation. Something the guys can feel comfortable with.'

Geoff agrees with an emphatic nod of the head. The Moth 80 – like the vertical stacks – is off the airshow agenda.

David directs our attention to the second schedule. He's applied his flypast experience to Paul's demand for something eyecatching and original, and he's come up with a series of staggered take-offs, circuits, and then a final turn on the display line.

The first batch of aircraft, timed once again to the second, are fighters – and I catch the ghost of a smile on Tim's face when he realises that David Roome has indeed squared Paul Bowen's circle. There are six aeroplanes in the circuit – a Bristol Fighter, a Gladiator, a Spitfire, a Meteor, a Hunter and a Tornado F3 – and if the pilots manage to translate David's schedule into accurate tracks, then on the second circuit all six aircraft should thunder past the eighty veterans at exactly the same moment.

On the face of it this appears to achieve exactly what David himself has said was impossible – but I'm only too aware of the flying experience around this table, and I'm certain that their analysis will be infinitely more painstaking than mine. For a minute or two, while David's hands sweep persuasively across his map, people watch and nod. Clearly they can tease out the individual strands in David's knitting, translating these climb-and-turn timings and downwind tracks into pathways in the sky. Whatever the outcome they seem pretty content, and as the debate moves on to the show's climax I'm left with the tiniest suspicion that their approval is based not on the small print of David's plan but on the knowledge that he's very definitely gripped it. This man knows his stuff. Both the Berlin Airlift and the RAF anniversary display will be safe in his very capable hands.

We're discussing the *coup de théâtre* which will close the display. The Eurofighter will lead the Reds in one full circuit, then turn and head for the crowd. At the display line, the Eurofighter will climb vertically while the attendant Reds perform a vixen break, fanning out to either side. As a spectacle, this sounds pretty amazing – the biggest firework in the world – but the committee are already addressing themselves to the small print: how will the Reds reform with the Eurofighter after the fan-burst? Will they 'sniff and go', like a pack of hounds? Or will the Eurofighter 'back into' the formation? The latter sounds like something from a goods yard or a car park, and I'm still trying to figure it out on paper when the meeting begins to wind up. As far as Geoff's concerned, David has done a pretty thorough job. To everyone's relief he's managed to thread Paul's cotton through the eye of the regulatory needle, and the results – on paper – look more than promising.

'Any other business?'

There's a long silence. Behind the servery, John – Wally's chef – is laying out trays of breaded escalopes for lunch. From the kitchens next door comes the scent of fresh coriander.

Across the table, someone enquires whether it might be an idea to find room for a rehearsal of each of David's displays within the Friday schedule.

Roger Beazley, packing his briefcase, looks amused. 'Rehearsal?' he snorts. 'God, no! You'll uncover all kinds of problems.'

CHAPTER SEVEN

March 1998

Spring sees the first stirring of the RIAT Emergency Services organisation. The video pictures from the Reims symposium weekend, coupled with a series of conversations about the 1993 MiG collision, have left me in no doubt about the importance of guarding against disaster. The possibility of something going dramatically wrong is one of the excitements that bring people in through the gate. A failure to cope with the aftermath could close the show for ever.

The Emergency Services planning meeting is scheduled for 11 March. Co-ordinating everything in this corner of the Fairford empire is Tim Cairns, co-presenter at the Reims symposium. Ahead of the meeting, Tim thinks it might be a good idea for me to take a look at last year's Emergency Orders. Expecting a couple of sheets of nicely-typed A4, I find myself tucked up with an eighty-seven-page book, printed on pink paper, complete with maps, diagrams, exhaustive appendices and – guess what – a thick top dressing of acronyms and call signs.

At the front, sensibly, there's a three-page explanatory list of the latter, and I browse through it, trying to resist the thought that these are the first rough notes for some wide-screen Hollywood epic. Mention FIREBALL on the radio net and you'd be talking about the big fire/rescue helicopter, the show's first response to a major incident. BRONZE ONE is comms shorthand for the police officer taking command at the site of a crash off the airfield. He will be reporting back to

SILVER COMMANDER, the lead policeman back in the Emergency Control Centre, who in turn will be talking to all kinds of folk from CAROUSEL (RIAT Emergency Services Co-ordinator) to CHARLIE LEADER (the NCO in charge of the third of the emergency crash crews), to PEDRO TWO (second of the casevac helicopters), to EMBASSY TWO (Director of Operations, Royal International Air Tattoo, or – rather more simply – Tim Prince).

The kind of incident prefigured in Tim Cairns's Emergency Orders isn't small-scale. Fires are doused. Crash sites cordoned off. Bodies laid out. Relatives comforted. The media briefed. And the injured patched up in the 100-bed field hospital, prior to being choppered out to pre-alerted hospitals as far away as Portsmouth and South Wales. Rather worryingly, the radio call-sign for the Army Colonel in charge of the Casualty Clearing Station is STARLIGHT.

Beyond the acronyms and call signs I plunge into the structure of the emergency services organisation, determined to keep my bearings. The way the bits of the emergency jigsaw fit together is evidently too complex for one of RIAT's beloved organograms, but as I wade deeper and deeper into the woods, the shape of the thing becomes evident.

If the organisation resembles a body, then its brain is the control room, shared by the police, the RIAT emergency control team, the fire chiefs, the ambulance controllers, and representatives from the medical services. From here, in Building 1223, the organisation's nervous system reaches out to every one of its many limbs.

On the airfield itself are the two Mobile Response Columns (RED and GREEN). Each column comprises more than a dozen vehicles with room for more than 100 personnel – doctors, paramedics, firemasters, plus a twenty-two-strong cordon party to seal off the crash site. On permanent stand-by north of the runway, these columns will follow the three fire/rescue combines (ALPHA LEADER, BRAVO LEADER, CHARLIE LEADER) as they speed to the scene of the incident. Should an aircraft – like one of the two MiGs in the 1993 crash – come down beyond the perimeter fence, then 'off field suppression tasks' will fall in the first place to FIREBALL, a big, fat Sea King helicopter loaded with firemen, a doctor and paramedics. Should the incident warrant it, a second helicopter, FIREBALL TWO, is also on standby.

On the heels of the three crash crews will come the civilian appliances from Gloucestershire County Fire Services. Back in Building 1205, a huge hangar on the north side of the runway, a fully equipped RAMC field hospital awaits the first of the incoming casualties, with a fleet of ambulances and helicopters on stand-by for emergency evacuation. Tim's contingency plans even extend to the provision of three C-130 Hercules heavy-lift aircraft, part of the airshow display fleet, 'selected and briefed on arrival'. Between them, the aircraft and the helicopters have a lift capacity for hundreds of stretchered casualties – and I begin to wonder exactly what kind of nightmare catastrophe Tim has tried to imagine. He doesn't strike me as an especially gloomy man. I guess the key to this kind of exercise is to plan for the worst and thank God when it doesn't happen.

I leaf on through the orders, marvelling at the sheer volume of detail. On one level it reads like a set of rules for an extravagantly complex board game. There are carefully itemised responses and counter-responses for every player on the board and the more I read, the more I'm reminded of David Roome and his design philosophy for multi-aircraft fly-bys. Think yourself into every cockpit. Plan for every contingency. Then leave it to the guys at the sharp end. Tim's approach. Exactly.

At the end of the orders I flick back through the pages, trying to arrive at a sensible figure that will include all the individuals involved in this operation. Totalling up the firemen, paramedics, crash-site doctors, helicopter pilots, cordon parties, police officers, surgeons, nurses and padres, my figure comes to something over 300. This turns out to be an under-estimate (the real figure is 680), but when Tim tells me that the show sucks in more emergency resources than exist in the whole of Gloucestershire, I have no reason to disbelieve him. If you're next on the list for a heart attack, there'd be no better place to have it than Fairford. Struck down by a coronary, you'd be in an air-conditioned resuscitation tent within minutes.

The meeting begins at eleven. There are sixteen faces around the table and it's obvious at once that these people have knocked about together –

show-wise – for quite a while. The atmosphere is cheerful, relaxed; the chatter is peppered with jokes, and digs, and nicknames. These are people who have been through it all before; ambulance directors, fire chiefs and medical officers by profession, they've all made room in their busy working lives for the five days of madness that is RIAT.

The volunteer in charge of the Emergency Services operation is Jack Taylor. A retired Chief Superintendent with Hampshire Police, he first encountered Paul and Tim back in 1982, when they were organising an airshow for the Army Air Corps at Middle Wallop. Two years later he worked alongside them again, and when they enquired whether he'd like to run one of the Mobile Response Columns as a volunteer, he was foolish enough to agree.

'It seemed pretty straightforward at the time,' he says ruefully. 'Greenham Common was fifteen miles away from where I lived and we were talking a weekend at the most. They weren't after an arm and a leg. Just a bit of help.'

'And now?'

'Now's different. Fairford's fifty miles away, and calling it a weekend is a joke. God knows how much time I put in.'

For the last three years Jack has been heading the entire operation and chairmanship of this morning's meeting belongs to him. At Jack's invitation, Tim opens with an update on current developments within the flying programme. He talks of 'sneaky-beaky' SkyWatch aircraft, 'rollers' and 'turn-arounds' for the Berlin Airlift, and 'rumours about some humungous flypast' for the RAF anniversary tribute.

I think at once of David Roome's meticulous schedules, and wonder just how much spin Paul is still imparting to the remnants of his original vision. 'Humungous' isn't a word I'd associate with David's plans, but the briefing has already progressed to confirmation that this year the B-2 stealth bomber will *not* be making an appearance at Fairford, and this, for once, appears to be good news. The emergency teams must be the only bit of RIAT to welcome a reduction in the expected crowd. Last year the B-2 brought huge numbers of spectators flooding in and there was real concern about overcrowding on and off the airfield. That this is unlikely to happen again brings a collective sigh of relief.

The briefing zips along. There's discussion about stand-down times for the Mobile Response Columns, about getting shifts adjusted to fit in with helicopter pilots' permitted hours, about the on-stream availability of the show's field hospital. Mention of the latter brings in Brian Robertson, a colonel with the TAVR and an Aldershot GP. He commands 306 Field Hospital, this year's occupants of Building 1205, and he appears to have an impressive grip on the potential for disaster locked into every major airshow.

'It may not be an aircraft,' he warns. 'It could be the LPG fuel cylinder in the concessionary burger bar.'

Suggestions pour in about stand-down times in Building 1205. There are dozens of medical personnel in there; it would be unreasonable to keep them at it longer than strictly necessary.

Brian Robertson shrugs these qualms aside. 'We'll be there as long as you need us,' he says quietly. 'If the wheel comes off we'll be sorted and ready. And that's an absolute guarantee.'

The gesture goes down well. Brian is also the manager of medical services for the Farnborough Air Show. He was hands-on at the Clapham rail disaster, at the Purley crash, and on the night the *Marchioness* went down. This man is big in trauma management. He's been there, he's done it. I make a note to talk to him later. If emergency planning is a mix of hard experience and inspired foresight then there are worse places to start than Brian Robertson.

The discussion has come round to the provision of stretcher helicopters for casualty evacuation. Laying hands on the choppers themselves is relatively simple, but installation of the right equipment is a great deal trickier.

Eventually, Tony Twiggs of Gloucester Ambulance makes the inevitable offer. His own organisation can lay hands on spare resuscitation gear, and he's also got a promise up his sleeve from another county HQ. 'We'll kit one,' he says, 'and Cornwall will kit the other.'

Tim Cairns adds a note to the lengthening list on his pad, and it dawns on me that this is truly RIAT in action, the cashing-in of saved-up promises, favours owed and honoured. The support comes in kind, not in cash – but every precious loan of kit frees up another pound or two that either can be spent elsewhere or will flow straight through to the Benevolent Fund coffers. In this sense, RIAT volunteers at every level become inspired blaggers, adept at chiselling endless help from resource-rich organisations for whom they work, or with whom they have some kind of leverage.

The biggest, of course, is the RAF itself. As far as aircraft are concerned, money only changes hands for the Red Arrows, and the Spitfire, Hurricane and Lancaster of the Battle of Britain Memorial Flight – but the spirit of beg, borrow and steal affects every corner of RIAT, and this meeting is no exception. Hills the chemist, for instance, have yesterday confirmed that they'll be returning to the showground this year to man a pharmaceuticals stall.

This turns out to be excellent news. Hills sell thousands of pounds' worth of pain-killers, sunblock and 35mm film over the show weekend, and Tom Watts's specially negotiated commission neatly covers Tim Cairns's expenditure on what he calls 'medical consumables'. This might seem to be the smallest of small print – infinitely less sexy than the Red Arrows or the B-2 stealth bomber – but the showground medical tents are on call throughout the weekend, and the fact that one tiny chemist's stall can pay for the bandages, drugs, splints and all the other bits and pieces needed to patch up the show's walking wounded is a perfect example of deft management. In my head I can hear Tim Prince desperately defending the bottom line. 'There's always a better way,' he says. By better, he means cheaper. And he's right.

The morning meeting ends with a wrangle about the Emergency Control Centre, the inner sanctum at the heart of this huge operation. It's already obvious that Tim Cairns's inspired staff-work hides some pretty substantial turf wars, and as the discussion moves to talk of 'evacuation cells' and 'incident tote boards' I begin to wonder about the clash of cultures when two very different bodies of men come together.

Around this table are the volunteers – highly experienced pro-fessionals, mostly still employed but emphatically infected with the can-do spirit of RIAT. Locked into the organisation with them are seconded contingents of serving personnel from Gloucestershire ambulance, fire and police services. The latter may not share the enthusiasm of the RIAT managers in the room; indeed, some of them might even resent this wearing spell of extra duty. So how wide is the gap between the two cultures? When push comes to shove, might one get in the other's way?

Debate is now centred on provision for this year's Emergency Services Control Centre, and the big issues couldn't be more pertinent. It was only last year, after two and a half decades of airshows, that the police finally agreed to share the same control room as RIAT. Previously they'd occupied separate premises, with liaison officers in each offering a token bridge between them. During the 1993 emergency, with the remains of two MiGs still smoking in the long grass, this arrangement was less than perfect, yet it took three more shows before Paul's argument for a shared facility bore fruit. In terms of primacy, it falls to a police officer – SILVER COMMANDER – to take charge should anything happen; yet the emergency plans are of RIAT's design, and it would seem sensible to have guys on hand who know every inch of the airfield and who put those plans together.

This year's shared Emergency Control will be sited in Building 1223, and already there are signs of friction. The police have certain operational procedures – tried and tested – and their early submission of a seating plan hasn't gone down at all well. Jack Taylor's team has been allocated certain desks without any prior discussion, and the atmosphere has been further soured by the news that – like last year – the police planners are insisting on including the traffic controllers within the emergency set-up. This seems to me to be pretty logical – surely traffic control would be essential to getting resources in and out of the airfield? – but Jack Taylor doesn't see it that way at all.

'The traffic blokes are bloody noisy,' he says. 'It's a full-time operation in its own right. Putting them in with us is a pain in the arse. You can't hear yourself think.'

Across the table there are nods of agreement, and as the debate extends to cable runs, aerial arrays, and the crucial importance of restricting control-room access to key personnel, I ask myself again just how serious this cultural clash might become. Around this table there's plainly an awareness that the divide exists, and further up the organisation – at Paul's level – there's another frustration.

In 1992, Gloucestershire and Wiltshire Police began making a charge for the man-hours they expend on the air show. The first bill was for £6,000. Six years later it had climbed to £160,000, and this year it'll be even higher. In principle Paul has no quarrel with paying a contribution towards the costs of the emergency services. Last year, cheques for £3,000 and £1,500 went to the fire and ambulance headquarters. But £160,000 is a huge sum, and there's inevitably a suspicion that RIAT are being overcharged.

Superintendent Adrian Grimmitt of Gloucestershire Police points out that precious resources have to be paid for. He'll be Silver Commander this year, the police officer in charge should an incident occur, and he insists that the costs they pass on are in line with a nationally agreed scale. But Paul isn't entirely convinced. Does the bill include all the extra traffic cops on the roads around Fairford? Does the emergency set-up really need all the uniformed officers who appear to man Silver Control?

The talk around the table has returned to the seating plan. Last year, no one could get a proper look at the incident board. Worse still, Jack Taylor's deputy didn't even have a desk. Is this set-up to continue this year? Or will the police planners consent to sit down and thrash the whole thing out? Jack Taylor, for one, certainly hopes so – and I'm still trying to envisage what might happen if they don't when the meeting breaks up.

As we queue for lunch, Jack nudges my elbow. He's seen me scribbling away, and he thinks I might have taken the political in-fighting just a little too seriously. On the day, he says, everyone just gets down to it.

But what about the incident board? And the traffic desks? And, most important of all, the seating plan?

Jack shakes his head. He's eyeing a dishful of lamb chops. 'Don't worry about it too much,' he says. 'As soon as anything happens, everyone stands up.'

RAF Brize Norton is 8.6 nautical miles north-east of Fairford. I know that because I'm nursing a coffee in Radar Approach Control, a long, darkened room beneath the tower on the south side of the runway. Brize is a Strike Command airfield, and operates most of the long-haul trooping and VIP flights to destinations like Calgary, Cyprus and the Falklands. Brize's radar coverage extends to Fairford, and during the show week all aircraft movements in and out of the airfield are handled from this room.

Ian Sheeley is in charge of the radar set-up at Brize. He's a tall, dark-haired, friendly Wing Commander with a passion for aircraft and airshows that dates back to his youth. Brize Radar is the vital link in the chain that brings hundreds of aircraft funnelling into Fairford from all over the world, and without this man's goodwill airshow operations would be a nightmare. Fortunately, Ian is a signed-up fan.

'I've been to lots of IATs over the years and I've watched it develop. What I love is the way they keep pushing and pushing. They try and theme it. They try and ring the changes. They're always thinking about the history. It's not just a queue of aircraft whazzing around the place.'

There are nine consoles in the Radar Approach room, four dedicated to arrivals and departures in and out of Brize, the rest servicing aircraft *en route* through the surrounding Flight Information Region (FIR). On the Wednesday of the show week Ian reconfigures these consoles, dedicating three to movements in and around Fairford. For six hectic days, the air traffic control workload will be immense, and a team of elite controllers ('simply the best') are hand-picked to man the Fairford consoles.

I'm gazing at the console screen in front of me. The orange sweep of the radar beam paints the aircraft in transit, each tagged with a special code. Even today, the sky seems ominously cluttered. What on earth is it like in July?

Ian reaches forward and adjusts the luminance. 'It's busy,' he concedes. 'The Wednesday is favourite for the heavies. They're difficult to park up, so Mel and Sue tend to ask for them early. You get a sprinkling of fighters too, but they don't need the long approach. You just point them at the airfield and leave them to it. They don't carry much fuel either, so you don't leave them hanging around.'

I'm thinking of Geoff Brindle and David Roome, both fast-jet men. Neither, I fancy, ever wasted much time on long, straight approaches. I nod at the screen, the blizzard of dots, and wonder about the hazards of Fairford's inbounds conflicting with traffic being handled by the other controllers. Ian says it's no problem.

'Everyone else on the shift has the picture too. They know what's going on over at Fairford and they make sure there's no friction. It's a really whazzy week. Everyone pitches in.'

I reach for my pen. The image is irresistible: all the passers-by crossing the road and keeping their distance while the six-day Fairford party gets under way.

What about the complications of language? Most of the twenty-odd daily entries on the Brize movements schedule are RAF pilots, while the Fairford jamboree is open to all comers. Do Ian's controllers ever have trouble making themselves understood?

I can see Ian nodding in the reflection on the screen. 'They do,' he admits. 'The Eastern bloc guys can be a bit challenging. If it gets desperate, Fairford send out a couple of Tornados to escort them in. It costs a bit in fuel but if you're dealing with big formations – say a six-ship display team – they can take up an awful lot of sky.'

He goes on to tell me about the now legendary near-miss during last year's show week. An Il-76 with an escort of two Su-30 fighters, *en route* to Fairford, got in a muddle over Henley-on-Thames. Air traffic controllers from the joint civil and military ATC centre at West Drayton tried to establish contact as the Il-76 drifted lower than its assigned flight level, and only a hard turn to port avoided catastrophe for the startled occupants of a domestic BA flight, inbound to Gatwick. The controllers at Brize had nothing to do with any element of this drama, and telling the story now provokes a wry grin, but I make a mental note to avoid the London Terminal Manoeuvring Area towards the end of next July.

Ian is describing the Thursday and Friday at Fairford. From where we're sitting now, his controllers must mix incoming aircraft with display rehearsal slots. Geoff Brindle and the Flying Control Committee are understandably determined to check out many of the display pilots, and it's Sue Allen's job to liaise with Ian and agree the twenty-five-minute chunks of flying time the FCC will need to put their tick in the box. If one of these rehearsal slots happens to coincide with the arrival of an Su-27, low on fuel, then the phones start ringing. But by and large, Ian says, the system works.

'It's one of the things that's really impressed me about the RIAT operation. The Friday can be a real nightmare, but they're very effective and very efficient. If you think of the Saturday and Sunday displays, they always seem to end within a couple of minutes of the announced times – and believe me, that takes some doing. Watching them, it's obvious they've been at it for a while. They have a lot of experience. And they keep it on a very tight rein.'

On the Saturday and Sunday, during the show itself, the pressure on the Brize controllers slackens. All the display flying is handled by Julie Morrissey's team in the Fairford tower, and pilots only contact Brize if they're told to fly away and await their display cues. There are two holds – or aerial parking lots – for Fairford. One is to the north-east, 3,000ft over Brize, while the other lies to the west, over the water park at South Cerney.

'What about Monday? Getting the planes away?'

Ian pulls a face. Monday is Mel James's nightmare, a succession of pilots pushing to be first off the parking ramps. For Ian's controllers, too, the workload is heavy, feeding aircraft out of Fairford and designating paths back to their home airfields. The so-called 'outbound plot' has been agreed for days, a strict sequencing of 450 aircraft, but among them will be the pilots who have filed for airways. The Air Traffic Control Centre at West Drayton will accept only four aircraft an hour from Fairford, and these departures must be timed to the minute to meet their airways slots. The big oceanic and trans-continental airways start at One Zero Zero (10,000ft), and the controllers beside me must launch outbound aircraft to the north-west of Fairford before turning them south to enter the big Golf One east-west airway five miles NNW of Lyneham. Ian demonstrates the track on the console, and I watch as his finger curves out of the rectangle of airspace that is Fairford and then drifts down towards the bottom left-hand corner of the screen.

This is a fascinating perspective on RIAT, not least because Ian Sheeley, in addition to all his Brize responsibilities, has recently himself become a volunteer. For this year's show he is to be Flying Display

Manager, a huge job that makes him responsible for each of the building blocks in the eight-hour display programme. No wonder he's been attending all those David Roome meetings. And no wonder he's starting to look just the slightest bit knackered.

'So why did you do it?'

'Do it?'

'Volunteer?'

Ian thinks about the question for a moment or two. It's not that he's uncertain, but he's keen for me to understand the context. He has only one RIAT left before he's due for another posting. He loves airshows. He admires the Tim Prince operation. While Fairford is still so close, he can't resist a real, hands-on involvement.

'But Flying Display Manager ...?'

'I wanted something sharp-end. I didn't want to be tucked away somewhere. I have to bite the bullet.'

He's certainly done that. In my mind's eye I can see the list of confirmed aircraft slowly building on the boards in Sue Allen's office, as the results of the pre-Christmas embassy trawl come through. Already she's had dozens of acceptances. By the end of next month the board will be solid with fighters, trainers, ground attack, heavies and maritime reconnaissance, and all the other odds and sods that will – in Ian's phrase – be whazzing in from God knows where. It'll be his job to knit all these strands together into a seamless sequence of displays. Will bottomless enthusiasm and an intimate knowledge of the world of air traffic control be enough? Is he really prepared for the impossible world of Messrs Bowen and Prince?

As it turns out, he is.

'Remember, I've watched these guys for a couple of years. I know the way they operate. I know they load and load and load you until you have the sense to say stop. But I've told Tim already, don't give me too much hassle because I've got the letter of resignation typed out.' He nods, patting his jacket pocket.

I'm sure it's a wise precaution, but so far, according to the rumours I've heard, Ian is playing a blinder. Working with David Roome and Sue Allen, he's currently calling the specialist operators for prices to put alongside the aircraft on David's wish-list. His £40,000 budget, as much as David's concern for safety, will be a key factor in shaping the Berlin and RAF displays and to date – in this new world of aerial choreography – he's loving it.

'Am I nervous? Of course I am. It's a huge job, a huge challenge. But it's defined by assets, and by what you can do with them – and that bit I especially like. It's my job to shape the masterplan, and then keep it in shape by juggling those assets. So far, touch wood, it's working.'

There'll come a time, of course, when Ian will have to hand over his masterplan to Julie Morrissey, the Fairford air traffic controller, and to the pilots – and from that point on the entire display programme will be out of his hands. Does that scare him?

'Not really. It's a strange organisation. If problems arise – and they will – then you just have to solve them. RIAT has always attracted can-do people. They don't want graduates. They don't want a thesis. They just want a solution.' He shakes his head, staring at the screen. 'There's such a determination to make things happen. That's the ratchet that Tim and Paul turn.'

We fall to talking about the dangers involved in the very concept of air shows.

Ian's recently been to a flying display symposium at Linton-on-Ouse, and he returned more than ever convinced that risk lies at the heart of it all. 'It's obvious really. You're pushing the aircraft and the pilots to the limits, and you're doing it at very low level. There *are* no more demanding kinds of flying. Against this, of course, you should take into account the training and the regulations and the checks and all the rest of it, but the fact is that you can never get rid of the risk, and – if you're honest – you'd never want to.'

'So what do you do?'

'You manage it. You try and make it acceptable. You go in for planning and briefing and rehearsals and you try and minimise it. But don't ever kid yourself that the risk disappears. It doesn't. It's still there.'

The thought takes us back to Fairford. We're both looking at the screen. An old VC10 is doing training circuits around the airfield. A Tristar is out to the east at 4,000ft, inbound from Ascension. It's another quiet day at Brize, but I can't rid my mind of the traffic jam of arriving aircraft that is the Friday of show week.

Ian nods. He's still watching the descending Tristar. 'They're born gamblers, Paul and Tim, and they always push it to the limit. That Friday arrival plan is weather-dependent. To recover that volume of traffic you need reasonable cloudbase and reasonable viz. To tell you the truth, I've often wondered about the back-up plan.'

'What back-up plan?'

He looks up at me a moment, then his eyes return to the screen. 'Good question,' he says softly. 'There isn't one.'

....

CHAPTER EIGHT

April 1998

April the First. Paul has chosen April Fool's Day to stage a press conference to launch the Benevolent Fund's menu of public events for the spring and summer. They include, of course, the July air tattoo – but the *hors d'oeuvre* is to be served tomorrow evening in the shape of a special commemorative concert to celebrate the RAF's eightieth birthday. Preparations for this lavish black-tie spectacular haven't figured heavily in my research, but it's impossible not to have picked up the odd tremors of excitement and apprehension on the Fairford net. Not the least of these has been a conversation with Sean Maffett.

A couple of months ago, Paul approached him with news of the concert. He'd been having a quiet think about trying to pull off something new and had come up with the idea of projecting film and video footage as a backdrop to the music. The bandmasters were putting together a programme to illustrate various phases in the RAF's development. Perhaps Sean could do the same in pictures?

Sean, who is a radio man, was slightly awed by the invitation. The concert would be one of the gala highlights of the Benevolent Fund's year. The Barbican, complete with an audience of Air Marshals, government ministers, and assorted VIPs, was hardly the place to launch one's career as a live director. None the less, there were bits of the challenge that fascinated him. One was the chance to blend archive film with live music, a potent, emotional mix. A second was the fact that Paul himself obviously thought it was in him. And the third, I suspect, was the opportunity to say a small and very personal thank you to the service he'd loved.

Preliminary research turned up a number of problems. Laying hands on the right calibre of archival film wasn't easy, but a trawl through Bruce Vigar's *Battle for the Skies* netted some fine sequences, and material from other sources, including the generous donation of some wonderful search and rescue footage from Scottish Television, worked beautifully against the music. In the hands of a gifted editor, Nick Elborough, each chronological package took shape until Sean was able to phone Paul and confirm that the pictures would cover the bulk of the two-hour programme.

That was the good news. Sean is still word-perfect on the rest of the conversation.

'What's the bad news?'

'We'll need special projectors. They're called Barcos.'

'How much?'

'A thousand each. Per day. And these people aren't into sponsorship.'

'How many of these things do you need?'

'Two.'

Sean paused, waiting for the explosion. It didn't happen.

'You've got them,' Paul growled. 'But it'd better be bloody good.'

The press launch is to take place in the RAF Club on Piccadilly, and Paul has asked me to turn up to say a few words about this book. *Airshow* is to be formally launched at the Royal International Air Tattoo 1998, and will be in the bookshops – deadlines permitting – in November.

I take the train to London and walk across Green Park to Piccadilly. I've never been to the RAF Club before, and it makes a strange impression. The corridors are lined with squadron badges, seemingly hundreds of them. Intermixed are dozens of paintings, impressively framed, softly lit, depicting cherished moments from the RAF's past. A flurry of SE5s over the Western Front. Spitfires taxiing out at Tangmere. A pair of Meteors in a golden sky. This, of course, is the stuff of history – but with the RAF down to 55,000 serving personnel, this version of the airforce already belongs to another age. Bomber

Command alone lost almost exactly the same number of aircrew in four brief years.

I meet Paul upstairs. He's relieved to see the tie again. I enquire about the prospects for tomorrow night's Barbican concert and he says it's shaping well. When I ask about the Barco projectors and the lump they've taken out of this year's budget, he seems surprised.

'Presentation Services aren't making a charge,' he says.

'How come?'

'I put Clive Elliott on to them.'

The briefing begins shortly afterwards. Patti Heady, the Fairford press chief, has invited two veterans to attend as special guests. Phillip Bristow joined the newly formed RAF in 1918. That same year, Edith Pearce signed up with the Women's Auxiliary Air Force. Both are now seated on the left of the stage and both – aged respectively ninety-eight and 100 – will be among the eighty veterans taking the salute at the tribute flypast in July. Quite what shape that display will take is still anybody's guess, and as Sir Roger gets to his feet and opens the proceedings I find myself wondering what Edith and Phillip would make of a candid peep behind the Fairford curtains. In all probability, I decide that quite a lot of it might well be familiar. Flair, bullheadedness and the positive enjoyment of risk aren't entirely confined to theatres of war.

After his introductory remarks, Sir Roger hands over to Kevin Leeson. Kevin is to talk us through the goodies on offer at RIAT 98, and Amanda is perched on a seat beside me, cueing the sequence of slides and video excerpts that garnish his presentation. His address is carefully scripted, and as the Tattoo takes shape in front of our eyes I become aware of a curious formality in his choice of language. In a sense, of course, it's entirely appropriate; this is, after all, a fairly high-powered audience. Air Vice-Marshal Ron Elder is on the platform alongside Sir Roger, and there are several important sponsors in the audience. But the measured rise and fall of Kevin's sentences don't begin to match the witty irreverence of the private conversations I've enjoyed with him, and for the first time I begin to wonder whether the tone of the book I'm writing will be quite what the upper reaches of the aerospace establishment expect.

Graham Hurley

Paul Bowen (left) and Tim Prince. Before the Storm.

After the '98 show, Air Chief Marshal Sir Roger Palin congratulates Flying Officer Tonya Glover on weathering the Storm.

Catherine Moubray

Saturday 24th July 1993. Sergei Tresvyatsky's MiG-29 plunges earthwards.

Saturday 25th July 1998. After four years of accident free flying, another full house.

Engineering Services Co-ordinator, Mel James, with a MiG-29, his favourite Russian aircraft …

… complex double curvature structures notwithstanding.

Graham Hurley

Caroline Rogers, Deputy Director for Business Development,
a Very Important Person in the VIP business.

Business Development Manager Clive Elliott plots another raid on the corporate world.

Catherine Moubray

Catherine Moubray

Amanda Butcher,
putting the gloss
on the big picture.

Wally Armstrong,
king of the caterers.

Catherine Moubray

Heidi Standfast, Marketing Co-ordinator, shepherding in the crowds.

Tony Webb, Deputy Director for Public Affairs ... the meetings go on and on.

Commentator
Sean Maffett, the
voice of RIAT.

Graham Hurley

Graham Hurley

Tim Cairns, Events Services Manager, in Show Operations Control (SOC).

Graham Hurley

A room with a view. On the flight deck of the C-130 Hercules
rehearsing the Tac Demo.

Graham Hurley

The Tac Demo C-130 back on the ground. Landrover off. Ramp up. Away again.

Gp Capt David Roome,
master of the aerial ballet,
eyes up his stage.

Graham Hurley

Paul Bowen, Tim Prince and Deputy
Director Air Operations,
Gp Capt John Thorpe at work
behind the scenes.

Graham Hurley

Gp Capt Geoff Brindle,
Chairman Flying Control
Committee.

'What do you mean the
Slovak team's caught
in traffic?'

Graham Hurley

Flying Display Manager, Ian Sheeley, has another hole to repair in his programme.

Graham Hurley

Aircraft Participation Manager, Sue Allen, counting the aircrew in.

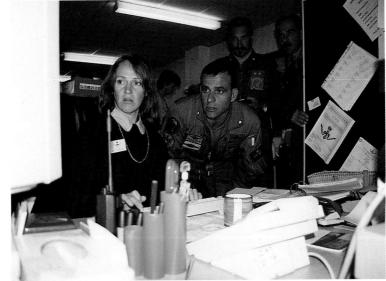

Graham Hurley

Deputy Director Aviation Trading, David Higham, counting the customers in.

Graham Hurley

Graham Hurley

Comms Line Supervisor, Mike White.
Badgering Air Traffic Control.

Col Brian Robertson, OC 306 Field Hospital (V)
in conversation with Col Sylvia Quayle.

Graham Hurley

Graham Hurley

Fuel bowser driver Andy Chapman, call sign Jaffa ...

And shotgun Dave Jeffreys, pumping in the juice.

Graham Hurley

One airfield, 400+ aircraft ... the parking meet in session.

'Room for a little one?' A Boeing C-17A Globemaster III about to squeeze in.

The show weekend approaches. Tim Prince works the phone …

Graham Hurley

… while for Paul Bowen the meetings go on and on and on.

Graham Hurley

The point of it all 1. A Hungarian MiG-29 on Apron Green.

The point of it all 2. A Ukranian TU-22M *Backfire* newly arrived from Poltrava.

In a moment or two Kevin will invite me to get to my feet and explain exactly what I'm up to. I've planned a few helpful remarks, altogether in keeping with the nature of this occasion, but on a whim I decide to be a little bolder. There's a truish story that launched these pages, and it's suddenly very important to know whether that story – or my interpretation of it – works.

Amanda's projector delivers a mocked-up front cover of *Airshow* to the big screen behind the platform, and Kevin calls me up from the audience. Like many others in the RIAT organisation, he's genuinely curious about the contents of my little red notebooks, and I fancy that the remark about 'the spy on the wall' is only partly in jest.

I begin by taking the audience back to last year's show. I write novels for a living. In the hunt for background to my latest tome, I'd seized Paul's offer of a couple of days backstage at RIAT. There, in the Flight Centre, I'd happened on the Ukrainian Air Force display team, newly arrived from Kiev. They were going through the reporting procedures – immigration, accommodation, food vouchers – but their most important conversation was with Geoff Brindle, Chairman of the Flying Control Committee.

The Ukrainians had brought with them a certain reputation, and Geoff was keen to find out exactly what they intended to do with their six MiG-29s. Rumour, of course, had preceded the Ukrainian Falcons, and not all of it was reassuring. What would happen to the singleton when the rest of the team were upside-down over the display line? Was the opening six-ship barrel-roll really intended to be supersonic?

The team was headed by a character called Colonel Viktor. He had the eyes and the loose-limbed stance of a gunfighter, and he talked to Geoff through a pretty young interpreter. When Geoff got down to detail, Colonel Viktor produced a series of beautifully drawn ribbon diagrams, each featuring one of the manoeuvres to be performed by his precious MiGs.

I'm looking at the audience, trying to recreate the feeling of that extraordinary encounter. Here were two fast-jet men. Neither spoke the other's language and, while I expect the translation was faultless, I very quickly realised that neither English nor Russian was ever designed to catch the nuances of life at 600 knots. The issue, in essence, was minimum height. The colonel was a veteran of countless displays, and the big MiG was plainly the love of his life. As ever, he felt honour-bound to do his precious machine full justice, and he therefore opened the bidding at thirty metres.

There's a gladdening rumble of laughter from the very middle of the audience. These people know about military aviation. About display flying. About the remorseless battle between gravity and showmanship. Thirty metres is absurd. There isn't a military display team in the West with a manoeuvring minimum below 150 metres.

I plunge deeper into the story, describing how Geoff and the colonel got themselves into a serious bidding war, how Geoff did his best to explain the display regulations, how the colonel waxed lyrical about the importance of aesthetic integrity and the beauties of the hammerhead stall, his lean frame bent over the diagrams, his big hands translating the twisting blue ribbons into three dimensions.

Kevin has given me exactly five minutes. These occasions are, in the parlance, time-sensitive, so I begin to wind up, explaining how Geoff finally made his point. Regulations, sadly, were regulations, and the colonel – with enormous regret – had agreed to reconfigure his display. The conversation over, a nice hotel in Swindon awaited the Ukrainian Falcons, but before the team left for the transfer bus, Colonel Viktor muttered something to the interpreter.

He'd been aware of me writing the odd note. He wanted to know what I was up to.

'I'm the base novelist,' I explained, gesturing at my open notepad.

The interpreter, ever-literal, assumed that 'base' meant 'common' or 'low'. She therefore translated my little joke.

Colonel Viktor looked thoughtful for a moment or two, then favoured me with a huge grin. 'Ah, my friend.' He patted me on the shoulder. 'So you write dirty books?'

I'm still looking out at the audience. Some are laughing already. Double punch-lines aren't always a good idea, but I see no point in not going the whole way.

'The book's called *Low and Dirty*,' I announce. 'And it's on sale from November.'

There's more laughter, then a round of applause. Mightily relieved,

I resume my seat alongside Amanda. She's looking less than amused.

'It's called *what?*' she says.

Next morning, I'm back on the road. Boscombe Down is world famous as the home of the Empire Test Pilots' School. The airfield is clearly visible from the A303, the big trunk road down to Exeter, and like the rest of the defence establishment it's an organisation that has had to bend itself to a new and more entrepreneurial Britain. Boscombe Down now belongs to the Defence Evaluation and Research Agency (DERA), and one of its roles is to acquire each new military aircraft and expose it to the most searching tests.

It's a lovely spring day with broken cloud bubbling into the Wiltshire sky. I've driven down to talk to John Thorpe, the Ministry of Defence's Director of Flying, and his secretary meets me at the gate. She drives an ancient Morris Minor estate, even older than my 1974 VW camper, and we bucket down through a tangle of roads to Building 419, a flat-roofed office block that houses the Directorate of Flying. Overhead, all too briefly, is the shadow of a Tornado GR4, flying carefully calibrated circuits around the airfield.

Upstairs, John Thorpe emerges from his office. He's a tall man, with that businesslike cheerfulness you so often meet in professional pilots. I first came across him at last year's show – John was the man who lent me the binoculars to view the B-2 stealth bomber – and since then I've learned a good deal more about him, chiefly from Paul Bowen.

In an organisation that prides itself on hooking big fish, RIAT rates John very highly indeed. For three busy years he was the RAF's Chief Test Pilot, taking delivery of early models of new aircraft and exploring every corner of the flight envelope prior to their formal acceptance into operational service. Now, as a Group Captain, he regulates all military test flying, both here at Boscombe Down and at all other MoD test establishments. John has been involved in aircraft evaluation for more than twenty years. Park ten aircraft types up on the Boscombe ramp – from the TriStar to the Bulldog – and he's probably flown all of them.

'So what do you do for Paul and Tim?'

'Pretty much anything. I'm not choosy.'

Strictly speaking, this isn't true. John Thorpe is now Deputy Director of RIAT with special responsibility for Air Operations. As such, he has the authority to take so-called 'primary decisions' with regard to air ops during the show. This kind of gold-plated delegation – parting with real power – isn't something I've so far associated with the upper reaches of the Fairford organisation, and I wonder what prompted it.

John looks amused. He's as much fascinated by the holes that Tim and Paul have blasted in the management textbooks as I am. 'I think it's rather a question of their time,' he says. 'Airshow weekends are getting busier and busier on the commercial front. They need to be able to concentrate a bit more on that.'

'And you?'

'I'm the guy with the bricks.'

'Brick' is RAF-speak for a hand-held two-way radio. I know from last year that John manages the bulk of his empire from one of a fleet of brand-new Volvo estate cars on loan from a local dealership. This enables him to keep physically abreast of problems on the airfield as they arise, and as he speeds from brushfire to brushfire he carries with him an impressive array of communications equipment: two management bricks, one ATC brick, one mobile phone, one pager, plus one built-in ATC set, already installed in the car. Ogling the B-2 last year, I was always aware of John in the background. His ability to conduct three conversations simultaneously impressed me no end.

We settle in John's office. On the floor beside his chair sprawl two enormous German shepherd dogs. On the wall behind the desk, a framed photo of a Kawasaki 1100 cc superbike. Here, very clearly, is a man with an interest in the bigger end of the scale. So what did he make of IAT when it first crossed his path?

'Interesting question. It was 1979 and I was doing Hawk displays out of Brawdy. That summer I did twenty. Mildenhall, Ramstein, all the biggies.'

'And IAT?'

'They were still at Greenham. You noticed the difference from the start. For one thing, they sent you a whole packet of stuff months beforehand. Information, briefing, car hire forms, stuff like that. There's a questionnaire, too, an enormous thing, umpteen pages – what kind of aircraft, display profile, the lot. Then, closer to the day, you got another bunch of goodies: allocated display times, rehearsal slots, airfield maps, guidance on surrounding airspace. Good stuff. Useful stuff. And then, of course, you arrived.' John's smile, reflective, betrays his fondness for getting the small print right. That, I guess, is what turns a good pilot into a test pilot. No wonder it was love at first sight at Greenham Common.

'They were marvellous,' he says. 'Most of those summer shows were a pain. You'd set down at some far-flung RAF base and it was just wall-to-wall apologies. They'd never geared up for it properly. Whether it was ground transport or accommodation, or simple items like gate passes, they'd never thought the thing through. Now that can be a nightmare, especially when you're displaying every weekend. But IAT were in a different league. For a start, you were met on arrival. The engine would be spooling down and the moment the canopy went up there'd be a can of cold beer in your hand. Just like that. Then there'd be a car to take you to crew reception, and a proper briefing from someone who knew what he was talking about, and a decent hotel where you could get your head down. It was amazing. That first time I remember looking round and thinking, My God, someone's really gripped this.' He shakes his head as if he still doesn't quite believe it, then leans forward, determined that I grasp the central point. 'They're professionals,' he says. 'From the air cadet who shows you where to get on the transfer bus to the briefer who gives you the big plot, they're all completely on top of it.'

'But volunteers.'

'Sure, but *professional* volunteers. Not amateurs. Not people who've signed up for the ride.'

This is a nice distinction, and applying it to the volunteers I've already met I understand exactly what he means. Over the years, Tim and Paul have managed to fine-tune a very special talent. To be able to persuade hard-pressed men and women of exceptional ability to give up weeks of their precious free time for no financial reward whatsoever should, on the face of it, be impossible. But somehow, time and time again, they manage it.

For John Thorpe, the call came in 1981. He'd flown a couple of displays at the 1979 show, and he'd been impressed enough to write a thank you letter. At the end, as you do, he'd included a casual offer of help, should help ever be required.

'That was my big mistake,' he says ruefully, 'because they never throw anything away.'

Press-ganged for the 1981 show, John found himself heading something called the Northside Co-ordination Cell. It sounded impressive enough, but behind the military mumbo-jumbo there lurked a darker purpose.

'They test you. There's no two ways about it. They want to see if you're serious – and I don't blame them. They don't want posers. They're not interested in the gin and tonic brigade. If you want to prop up a bar, there are perfectly good pubs around. If you want to help run an airshow, there's work to be done. They can't afford to carry passengers. You *have* to put the effort in.'

Put this way, volunteering sounds rather daunting, an exercise in sleeplessness and self-denial, but I know from last year that Fairford's finest party as hard as they work. John has a point, though. The pace of the weekend is unrelenting. Things are forever going wrong. So, if you don't have the wit and the willingness to put them right, forget it.

'That first year, I was basically part of a troubleshooting team. There were ten of us. We did everything from unblocking toilets to hosting VIP visits. The sheer range of stuff was incredible, and by the Monday evening I was totally whacked.'

'Did you enjoy it?'

'I don't know that I ever had a chance to stop and think. In fact the greatest emotion I can remember was on the Monday. By that time I'd been there a whole week. The weekend – the public days – had gone by in a flash, and I was standing there in the middle of the airfield, watching it all literally disappear. The aircraft had gone. The buildings – all the temporary structures – were going. It was just another empty airfield. That, and a huge feeling of anticlimax.'

'You *missed* it?'

'Yes.' He nods. 'Yes, I did.'

John passed the initiation test. After the Northside Co-ordination

Cell he was persuaded to put on his posh frock and take up a front-of-house role, glad-handing visiting dignitaries. He didn't much like it and, because a volunteer – unpaid – has more leverage than a wage slave, he managed to crab sideways through the jungle of interlocking empires until he found a job that suited him perfectly.

'Actually, I created it. And I did that because Paul and Tim arranged it that way. That's very typical. If your face fits, if they like you, if you give them what they want, then they allow you enormous leeway.'

The command post John furnished for himself was out in the no-man's-land between the rival IAT fiefdoms of Air Traffic Control, Engineering Operations, Parking, and Exhibitions. Ever the gypsy, it kept him free of a desk and pile of paperwork and the odd glimpse of a passing jet through some Portacabin window.

'I never wanted that. What I wanted was to be out there, doing it. They called the job airfield manager, and that sounded pretty grand – but ninety per cent of it boiled down to straightforward co-ordination. The only assets I directly controlled were the Follow-Me cars and the FOD sweepers. The rest of it was nosing around, troubleshooting, cajoling, making sure that everything was on-line.'

Troubleshooting. Cajoling. Making sure that everything's on-line. Isn't this exactly what test pilots are for? And isn't that, in turn, a tribute to the IAT organisation?

'In what sense?'

'In the sense that they were flexible enough to define the job around you, rather than just slot you into a vacancy.'

John stirs one of the dogs with his foot. He's been with the RAF through a period of profound organisational change, and as a result he's developed a more than professional interest in the all-important arts of management. For a while, we discuss the rival merits of 'flat' management structures, weighed against the more traditional hierarchies within which he's spent most of his working life. The former, we both agree, are all too often an excuse for cutting costs, despite the management gurus advancing all kinds of fancy theories about 'interlocking matrices' and 'the horizontal spread of decision-taking'. In reality, without clear lines of responsibility upwards, every-one passes the buck sideways, a sure recipe for inertia. Apply the same logic to an airshow – split-second timing, hundreds of tons of fast jet, tens of thousands of people – and you have, it would seem to me, a problem.

'Too damn right,' John nods. 'And that's why Paul and Tim keep such a tight grip. RIAT is *very* hierarchical because it has to be. If a problem crops up – and they do all the time – then you have to identify it, allocate it, then get it sorted. There's no other option. Running an airshow is like running a war. Unless you get on top of it, it'll swamp you.'

This is powerful stuff, evidence enough of the sheer scale of what Paul and Tim have achieved. John offers another vigorous nod.

'I think what they've put together is just amazing. I can't think of any other event with the same degree of success. Here we have a couple of civvie air traffic controllers, just out of college, who put on an impromptu show for themselves and their mates. And then they grow it and grow it until it becomes the biggest in the world. And they do it inside a charity culture that simply isn't tuned in to that kind of hard-nosed commercialism. They have to make their own luck. They have to go out and beg each year, for money and for hands-on help. Without the sponsors and the worker bees they'd be nowhere.'

'Worker bees?'

'Volunteers. People like me. Without the volunteers and the sponsorship they'd be dead in the water. Now that's remarkable. In fact I can't think of anything quite like it anywhere else in the world.'

From a man used to asking the harder questions – of aeroplanes, of pilots – this is praise indeed, and for a moment or two I ponder the downside of all this high-profile success. The airshow world can be as bitchy and vicious as any other corner of the planet, and there are certainly people who mutter darkly about the Fairford culture.

John shrugs. 'That's bound to happen. Bound to. Wherever you find true excellence, you'll get the knockers. That's one of the things the English do really well. Think of the Arrows. Their flying is second to none. Does everyone agree? Sadly, no.'

This is interesting. Both Paul and Tim are aware that their very success is, in some quarters, less than welcome. To achieve it, they drive themselves and their core team very hard indeed. Some break under the pressure, and the danger, I suppose, is that every casualty becomes a potential subversive.

John, plainly, thinks that's daft. If you elect to do something well, then you also elect to pay the price in time and sheer hard graft. The lead comes from the top. 'Take Paul. He's single-minded to the point of tunnel-vision. I've never known him not to address a difficulty, but if he can't solve it then he just ignores it. The B-2? Everyone said it was impossible but he persevered and – guess what – there it was. Tim? On the face of it he's much gentler, much less abrasive, but believe me he's tough as hell and just as determined. That's what you need. I suppose in a way they're very old fashioned. These are wartime attitudes. It's got to be done? Do it. End of story.'

Odd, this. Other people I respect have already talked of the airshow in terms of war, and now John – for the second time this morning – is doing it too. Is this just fanciful? Or are the parallels real?

John gives the question some thought. He's never been in a shooting war so in one sense the issue is academic. But that's not the point. The point is the *people*, and the kind of demands the event makes upon them.

'It can certainly be a killer. Not literally, of course, but serious enough to put you off for life. But the guys who stick with it, the men and women who make it happen year after year, they'd be exactly the people I'd choose to go to war with.'

'Why?'

'Because they think on their feet. Because they know how to fix things. Because they're not easily put off. We've had fifty years of peace by and large, thank God, and it's good to have been part of keeping that peace. But if you were ever to get frustrated at missing out on the real thing, then, yes ... you're right.' He nods at the phone at his elbow. 'Give Fairford a ring and volunteer.'

I frown for a moment, aware of John watching me, aware of the smile on his face. Then my eyes stray to the open window. The Tornado is back, thundering overhead.

Four days later I return to Fairford. After a flirtation with late spring the weather has clamped down again, and the flat Gloucestershire fields are shrouded in gloom. In the words of a Met Office forecaster on this morning's radio, the southern half of the UK has become a parking lot for used frontal systems – and I suspect that one of them has been abandoned over Fairford. Ian Sheeley's car is here already. Parking the camper van, I remember his comment about the Friday fly-in. If the weather hasn't cheered up by July, Ian's air traffic controllers over at Brize will be wrestling with a nightmare.

This morning's get-together features yet another brainstorming session on the evolution of the two centrepiece displays for the July show, the Berlin Airlift and the RAF's eightieth anniversary tribute. By lunchtime, if we're lucky, a more definite shape will have emerged from the endless complications that must, I'm beginning to realise, haunt every airshow.

David Roome and Ian Sheeley have got together before the meeting begins to compare figures, and the paperwork they bring to the staff dining room is impressive. David hands round timing charts for the latest version of the anniversary finale, and to this Ian adds a cost breakdown for the aircraft on David's shopping list.

By now, this tight little group – David, Ian, Tim Prince, Paul Bowen and Sue Allen – has acquired a life of its own, and while the coffees are organised the first couple of minutes pass in a pleasant fug of gossip and those little snippets of passed-on conversation which serve as brushwood to fire the meeting proper. Are the Kinloss guys playing ball over the bid for a three-ship Nimrod fly-past? Is it true that the Reds have abandoned their lump-in-the-throat Vixen Break? Does it really make sense to spend a hefty chunk of the budget on securing the Project Thrust land speed record-breaker when the money might better be spent on buying the Connie for the weekend?

The Connie is an old post-war Constellation, a four-engined trans-Atlantic passenger airliner with the growl of a tiger and the lines of a swan. I happen to know that it's one of Paul Bowen's favourite aeroplanes, and I have no doubts whatsoever that Project Thrust's days are numbered.

The coffee on the table, David confirms that his plans for the Berlin flypast are complete. Two DC-4s will be coming from South Africa and Holland. The Dutch Dakota Association are also supplying a DC-

3. From the Battle of Britain Memorial Flight, David expects another DC-3, plus their much-loved Lancaster. The balance of the Dakotas – probably seven – are still in service with Air Atlantique and South Coast Airlines. For a payment of £2,000 each, these aircraft will be spending the whole weekend at Fairford.

David's Berlin display has been shifted to the morning, and it will launch with a flypast by a Falcon 20 at 11.34. The Falcon belongs to Flight Refuelling, one of the companies in the Cobham Group, and will give Sean Maffett the chance to stamp the display sponsor's name over the following fifty-five minutes. After the Falcon, David plans the stream take-offs, thirteen-minute circuits, and ninety-second interval landings we've already discussed at the last meeting. After a couple of these, punctuated by unloading sequences on the ground, the display will end with a four-minute flypast from participating squadrons. In this impressive stream of aircraft, David has cast roles for a Chinook, a Puma, a pair of C-130s, a Nimrod, a VC10, a C-5 and a C-17. There's a brief discussion about whether or not Freddie Laker – himself a veteran of the Berlin Airlift – will ever deign to answer the two formal invitations that have so far been sent, before Paul Bowen signals his approval of David's latest masterplan.

'Tick in the box?'

There's a general murmur of agreement. Then a polite cough from Ian Sheeley.

'I have some difficulty with these ninety-second landings,' he says. 'First time round they might be OK, but having them go on for an *hour* ...?'

'You think there's a problem?' Paul's looking slightly shocked.

'Yes.'

'Why?'

'I think it'll be boring.'

'Boring? The sound of those engines? *Boring?*'

'Yes.' Ian isn't about to be bounced. 'I think you'll be filling the beer tent after the first couple of minutes.'

Paul's looking to David for help. I know, in his mind's eye, what he sees. He sees the Gloucestershire sky full of Dakotas – the unmistakable spread of the wings, the lovely bluntness of the nose, the wondrous drumbeat of those Pratt & Whitney engines. It won't quite be post-war Berlin, but with luck and a bit of imagination it might come bloody close.

David Roome clears his throat. 'Actually, I wasn't planning on a visual circuit,' he says.

'You weren't?'

'No. These guys have got to be airborne for at least thirteen minutes. That puts them well to the north.'

Given this alarming news – the Dakotas largely invisible – we're left with the sound of those fabulous piston engines. But what happens if the wind's in the wrong direction? What happens if we're left with the world's first stealth Dakotas?

Paul takes the implications on the chin. Maybe David could somehow mesh take-offs with landings. David isn't impressed. He calls this 'concertinaring'. Even to me, the air traffic implications sound ominous.

Ian Sheeley intervenes again. Nights alone with the responsibility of producing eight hours of unforgettable flying have clearly concentrated his mind. The Berlin aircraft will be landing up one end of the two-mile runway. He's worried about the crowd down the other end.

'They won't be able to see anything,' he says. 'For them, it'll be a complete no-no.'

This, of course, holds equally true for the ninety-nine per cent of the crowd who don't happen to be in the front row. The beauty of air displays is that anyone can look up and watch the action. Entertainment at ground level, no matter how wonderfully choreographed, will be largely invisible.

'What about the Jumbo screens?' I enquire.

Paul shakes his head. No signs, yet, of a sponsor.

Tim Prince agrees with Ian. Somehow the flying has to be com-pressed. More going on in the air. More action. More variety.

Paul clambers back into his trench. 'But you'll lose the history,' he complains. 'It's *got* to be every ninety seconds. Just like it was in Berlin.'

There's the briefest silence, but even a couple of seconds can seem like an eternity. Which is exactly the point that Ian is determined to make.

'A minute and a half is for ever these days,' he points out. 'People have different expectations. They want it all and they want it now. Planes droning in every ninety seconds will bore them to death.'

'Ninety seconds is bloody tight,' Paul reminds him, 'in ATC terms.'

'Of course it is. We know that, but they don't. All they're seeing is another plane. Then another plane. Then another plane. On and on and on. Bor-ing.'

Paul looks grumpy. The pile of butts in the ashtray beside him is steadily mounting. 'OK,' he says at last. 'So maybe we ask David to reconfigure.'

'Reconfigure how?'

'Make it more exciting. Break it up a bit.'

David's magic pencil gets to work. In seconds, the display has changed shape.

'How about this?' He looks up. 'Some of the Daks take off and go to the hold. The DC-4 displays. Maybe the Connie displays. Then the Daks wheel in for a landing and all the unloading business.'

Paul nods. 'OK, but how about interspersing solos with the DC-3s on launch?'

'That's possible. It depends how you want to slice it.'

'How about three separate displays – DC-4, Connie, Lancaster – but somehow interleaved?'

'Dodgy. All three guys will have individual routines. What's fast for one might be a dawdle for another. Best to keep them apart, give them their own slots.' He studies his pencil. 'Frankly, I'm with Ian. The question we have to ask ourselves is whether or not the Berlin Airlift is really a crowd-puller. To tell you the truth, I've got some doubts.'

For the second time in ten minutes, Paul's looking shocked. 'Mr Cobham's giving us quite a lot of money,' he points out. 'We *have* to make it work.'

David bends to his pad again. Sue circulates with more coffee. I'm watching the racing pencil. Finally, David tables a solution.

Twelve aircraft are to take off at seventy-five-second intervals. The first aircraft to land is on short finals as the last aircraft gets airborne. Aircraft one to eight touch down and go into the unloading sequence, leaving the airspace above for the remaining four aircraft each to do a six-minute display. This, says David, will burn the fifty-five minutes and give the crowd a chance to see the DC-3, DC-4, Connie and Lancaster each go through their paces. For the sake of brevity, David labels this latest version Plan B.

Paul looks across at him. 'You can make it work?'

'Yes.'

'OK, let's go firm.'

'Fine.' Tim Prince shuffles his papers. 'Plan A's a bin then.'

After Berlin, the RAF display. David invites us to imagine the opening flypast, nine Tiger Moths in formation. After the excitements of the last meeting – trying to calculate how many dozen aircraft we'd need to sketch the figure 80 in the sky – Paul braces himself for another bumpy landing.

'Only *nine*?' he queries.

'That's what the guys say they want to do. Ian?'

Ian Sheeley's been talking to one of the Moth pilots. It seems they all did a turn at Fairford a couple of years back and they aren't desperately keen to repeat the experience.

'Apparently this guy had a mare,' Ian says.

This is a new one on me. By now I've more or less mastered the acronyms, but what on earth does 'mare' mean? Is Gloucestershire even more rural than I've been led to believe? Have the Moth pilots grown tired of sheep? I make a discreet inquiry while an argument rages about the roots of their grievance. Sue says she has a file an inch thick on the affair. The pilots, among other things, objected to having to break CAA display rules.

Tim Prince moves quickly to squash this falsehood. RIAT operates under military regulations, not civil, and the Tiger Moths always stayed well this side of the law.

My neighbour bends towards me. 'Mare' means nightmare. We're lucky to get the Moths back at all.

Paul is still wrestling with his beloved 80. One way or another, he's determined that the magic figure shall somehow appear.

'Lecomber,' he says at last. 'He'll do it.'

'Do what?'

'David ...' Paul, ignoring the question, tosses a challenge across the table. 'As a pilot, could you paint an 80 in smoke?'

'You mean a flat 80?'

'No, vertical.'

'Ah ...' David's head goes back. He's looking at the ceiling. 'Yes,' he says at last, 'you could. You'd do the 8 first, then a big loop would give you the zero, and you'd just hope to hell the wind didn't blow the one into the other. You'd need to be precise, of course. And you'd need the right kind of aircraft. A Sukhoi, a Pitts, something like that.'

'Lecomber,' Paul repeats. 'He'd definitely be up for it.'

As an author, I need no introduction to Brian Lecomber. I've been reading his novels for years – an unmatchable blend of break-neck prose and wonderful airmanship. In these respects he's the airborne equivalent of Dick Francis – a hell of a read – but to my shame this is the first time I've realised just what a reputation he's won for himself in the upper reaches of the air display world. I make a note of his name while debate continues about raising the curtain for the anniversary tribute with a big tall 80.

David, as ever, has seized Paul's vision and translated it into speeds and times and carefully pencilled tracks. Two figure-writing planes will be better than one. They'll fly parallel tracks to the Moths, crossing the threshold abeam the Diamond Nine formation. Their airspeed will be exactly twice that of the Moths. In line astern, they'll climb together, the lead plane painting the 8, his partner flying an elongated loop to produce a zero. By 1,500 feet they should be through it. At 60 knots, the Moths will take two minutes to flutter the length of the runway. By then, towering above them in blue smoke, Paul's beloved 80.

Paul's looking pleased. The chemistry's working well. Not for the first time, David's hands-on good sense, coupled with Paul's showmanship, have produced a result.

Ian Sheeley turns to money. To me, his carefully typed quotes in the boxes alongside David's aircraft look pretty daunting. The Bristol Fighter is going to cost £4,500. Four classic aircraft from the Shuttleworth Collection (a Gladiator, a Hind, a Tutor and a Magister), another £10,000. A Fury from the Old Flying Machine Company, £4,500. The total bill for twenty aeroplanes comes to nearly £40,000, and that's without VAT, fuel, and aircrew accommodations. Rolls-Royce have agreed to pitch in £20,000. What about the rest of it?

Paul shrugs the question aside. A shuffling of budgets, plus the prospect of extra sponsorship, mean that the shortfall is covered. More important just now is the troubling absence of any representative aircraft from the RAF's transport fleet in David's carefully choreographed flypasts.

David shakes his head. 'No can do, I'm afraid. Number one, they don't suit this kind of flying. Plus we're very tight on time.' He gestures down at the brief he's circulated – grid after grid of timings, each flypast buffered from the next by individual solos and missing-men formations.

Paul's spotted another problem. The RAF have something called the Participation Committee. Every year they take in bids for service aircraft for the forthcoming display season and duly allot each airshow a quota of airplanes. Should space not be found for some of these aircraft within the flying display programme, the consequences could be ugly. This year the Participation Committee have given RIAT a total of 120 planes.

Paul's looking at David. 'I don't see any mention of the Bulldog,' he complains, 'nor the Jetstream.'

'That's because they're not there.'

'Why not?'

'Because we haven't got the time. We're chocka. Full up.'

Tim Prince steps in, ever diplomatic. 'Maybe we fit them into the Berlin display. Do we know which squadron they belong to?'

Heads shake around the table. Only if the aircraft belong to squadrons that flew into Berlin can they have a place in the Airlift display.

Paul shrugs. 'How about the quiet period, then? Over lunch? Sue?'

Sue Allen makes a note. One way or another every aircraft on the PC list must get airborne over the weekend. Tim, meanwhile, is busy coming up with a total for the aircraft guesting in David's flypasts.

Paul looks bemused. 'Why?' he asks. 'Who's counting?'

'Some sad man will.'

'You really think so?'

'I know so. I guarantee it. We've announced eighty. Eighty it must be.' The list on his pad grows and grows. At length, it comes to eighty-two. Take away the two Lecomber figure-writers, and it is − in Tim's phrase − a bullseye.

Paul isn't listening. He wants David Roome to start thinking in terms of reserve aircraft, spares he can use to plug up sudden holes in his carefully crafted flypasts.

David frowns. 'What did you have in mind − exactly?'

Paul gestures at David's list. 'Say you get hold of a Lysander. For stand-by.'

'In place of what?'

'I don't know. A Blenheim?'

'You mean a straight swap?'

'Yes. Could a Lysander hack it? Speed-wise?'

'No way. It might hack a hundred, but that's hot planning in my book, back-of-the-fag-packet stuff. Give me a week and it's feasible. Forty-eight hours out, we just leave a gap.'

'Really?'

David looks him in the eye, totally merciless. 'Really,' he confirms. 'And I'm afraid I mean it.'

Paul still studying the figures. He hasn't finished yet. He and Tim have been weaving airshows together for years. They know how critical time can be, how quickly it can be eaten up. He goes through David's choreography again. The concepts delight him, but time-wise he thinks there might well be slippage.

David offers a guarded nod. The wind direction, as ever, will be all important. 'It's very tight on 27,' he agrees. 'On 09 it's critical.'

Using 09 means taking off towards the east, a proposition complicated by the need for aircraft to backtrack nearly a mile along the runway to get to the threshold.

In planning terms, the RAF display is scheduled to end at 1800. Paul, now, has second thoughts. 'It's looking like 1815 to me,' he says.

David has faith in his timings. He's not sure an extra fifteen minutes will help.

Paul reaches for another cigarette. 'Then we'll start early if we have to.'

'*What?*' David is staring at his beautifully typed timings, aghast. Starting early is even worse than finishing late. He's asking pilots to fly strictly by the clock. Vary the pattern and the knitting will unravel.

Tim interrupts. He, too, doesn't think an earlier start will help. The RAF flypast is the climax of the show. Sean Maffett will need a chance to build it up, to offer a proper introduction. David's eighty minutes is like the dowager aunt. She's an extra-special guest. You don't just drag her into the drawing room and plonk her down. There's a certain etiquette to these things. It has to be done nicely. Tastefully. With a little decorum.

David Roome has been having a think. This sounds very much like his last offer. 'We could delay,' he concedes, 'but only in five-minute chunks. On no account could we bring it forward.'

'OK.' Paul shrugs. 'I just wanted to make the point that you have absolute precedence, that's all. If you think the timings will work ... let's go for it.'

'Fine.'

'You agree?'

'Of course.'

The meeting ends minutes later. Discussion of the Israeli unmanned reconnaissance vehicle, the pilotless spyplane designated for SkyWatch, has prompted a story from David.

Flying an F-4 Phantom at a Bilbao airshow, his Nav in the back cockpit had access to an adapted tank periscope that gave a magnified view forward. Awaiting take-off clearance, the Phantom was pointing at the walls of a nearby nunnery. As his hand closed on the throttles, David suddenly heard a wild yell from the back seat. Alarmed, he checked quickly across the dials. FOD ingest? Something fallen off? Conflicting traffic?

A second later, the Nav came through from the back.

'They're all out sunbathing,' he gasped, 'topless.'

'Who are?'

'The nuns!'

The following day I take the train to London. Behind me, at Fairford, I've read a pile of letters heaping congratulations on the team responsible for the Barbican concert. The evening was a sell-out. Sean Maffett's pictures worked beautifully with the music and the Benevolent

Fund Council were delighted by the flood of plaudits afterwards. In a letter to Paul, Sir Roger has talked of 'a magnificent achievement' and 'justifiable pride'. For the hard-pressed occupants of Buildings 15 and 16, it was another triumph.

In London, I'm to have lunch with Fred Crawley. I've met him a couple of times now – once at Portland Place on the morning of the Double Exposure pitch, and again at the RAF Club only last week. After some initial reservations, Fred has warmed to the idea of the book. He serves as the honorary treasurer on the Benevolent Fund Council, and is also Deputy Chairman of Enterprises, and he thinks it might be useful for us to chat over lunch.

We meet, once again, at the RAF Club. Fred is seventy-one years old, a city banker with a distinguished career in the upper reaches of the financial world. He rose to be chief executive of Lloyds Bank and he still sits on the board of Legal & General. Four years' service with the RAF took him to post-war India and he emerged as a Flight Sergeant Met Assistant, barred from flying by poor eyesight. It amuses him still that he should now spend so much time hobnobbing with Air Chief Marshals and their ilk.

The restaurant at the RAF Club is a big, high-ceilinged room on the ground floor, and we settle at a table near the window. In person, Fred is trim and courtly, a man who chooses his words with some care, but beneath the banker's natural reserve it isn't hard to detect yet another aviation nut. Fred finally learned to fly fifteen years ago. His Cessna 172 is hangared with the Army Air Corps down at Middle Wallop, and he regularly makes the cross-Channel hop to Northern France.

We're talking about the PPL course. I've always somehow assumed that becoming a pilot is a real challenge, but Fred shakes his head.

'Learning to fly isn't that difficult,' he says. 'I'm not a natural pilot – I plod around – but it's nothing that most people couldn't handle.'

'Do you wish you'd started earlier?'

'Yes, very much. It's been in my blood. Always.'

Fred first ran into Paul and Tim at Greenham Common in 1977. At that stage in his career he was assistant chief general manager at Lloyds Bank, and after he'd watched his first IAT he was only too happy to dip the bank's toe in the sponsorship pond. A decade later he joined the Benevolent Fund's Council, and shortly afterwards became chairman of the Alliance & Leicester Building Society, who agreed to take title sponsorship for the 1991 show.

From Paul's point of view, I know how much the relationship with Fred Crawley matters. This wise, thoughtful, immensely experienced financier has been a kind of mentor to both himself and Tim, offering advice, brokering board-room decisions, and prompting the odd change of course with the subtlest touch on the Fairford tiller. He brought a lifetime's knowledge of commercial organisations to Portland Place, and even now the shape and style of the Benevolent Fund's trading arm – Enterprises – seems to surprise him.

'It's Paul and Tim's baby. There's no question of that. They built this huge airshow. They built it from nothing and now it's the biggest in the world. Don't get me wrong – plenty of people helped them along the way. But essentially it's theirs. Their doing.'

Before Fred became deputy chairman, Paul and Tim were still consultants, driving Enterprises forward yet strictly speaking not part of it. Not, at least, in the salaried sense.

'It was my idea to regularise all that. It was simply unacceptable to have an organisation with these kinds of responsibilities, headed by a couple of chaps with no proper stake in the place. We had to appoint them both as co-directors, and that's exactly what we did.'

This tandem approach to top management seems to fly in the face of conventional business-school theory. Is it really best practice to have two in the pilot's seat?

'No, it's most unusual, but I think what we've found is that these things sort themselves out. Paul and Tim are very different characters. You'll have seen that yourself. Paul is very punchy, very pushy. Tim has a completely different approach. They mesh very well together. From our point of view it's an expensive solution, having the two of them, but it undoubtedly works.'

'*Our* point of view?'

'The board's.'

Over dover sole and breast of duck I pursue this tack a little further. My experience of life at board level is non-existent, and I'm curious to know how a board member as experienced as Fred Crawley views his role. Within a plc it must occasionally be delicate. Within a hybrid like the Benevolent Fund – part charity, part commercial enterprise – isn't striking the right balance even more challenging?

Fred shakes his head. 'In my view it's fundamentally the same job,' he says. 'Board members are there to take the broad view. We like to set the strategy. It's our job to ensure the succession, to monitor developments, to make sure the ship stays on course.'

'Ensure the succession?'

'Yes. Paul and Tim won't be there for ever. We have to accept that fact, and we'd be remiss if we didn't somehow make certain that the organisation would survive if they weren't around any more.'

The light begins to dawn. This, then, is where the new company structure came from – the raft of deputy directors on which RIAT would float, should Paul and Tim depart for pastures new. Fred is watching me carefully. He doesn't want me – or Paul or Tim – to get the wrong idea.

'Don't misunderstand me,' he says. 'We're talking absolutely standard commercial practice. It's a tribute to Paul and Tim that they should have created something so successful that we'd even have to have a conversation like this. The watchwords on any board of directors are *No Surprises*. We have to be on our guard against every eventuality. Tim and Paul often fly together. What would happen if – God forbid – they went down in a plane crash? We have to know. We have to make provision.'

This is indeed taking the long view, and it sparks my curiosity. For months I've prowled around the Fairford organisation, building a view of the way the place works. Without doubt it's driven from the top. And that drive, I'm equally sure, is as red in tooth and claw as any mainstream commercial organisation. Paul and Tim are entrepreneurs. They take risks. They have a vision. How comfortably does all of that sit with the charitable articles which govern the activities of the RAF Benevolent Fund?

Fred permits himself a quiet smile. Paul, we both agree, has a completely black and white view of the world. That kind of total conviction can be a very real commercial strength, but it can also provoke difficulties. 'You're right about the two cultures,' Fred says. 'And it's my job to build a bridge between them. It's absolutely Paul's nature to take all the decisions himself, to knock the ball into the long grass and hope we never find it. But in an organisation like ours you simply can't do that. You have, on occasions, to take direction from above. That's just a fact of life.'

'Does Paul see it that way?'

'No, of course he doesn't. That's why he can be such a damn good negotiator. He never listens.'

'So what do you do – as deputy chairman?'

'I rein him in. I keep him on track. He and Tim have immense energy, and immense experience as well. We need both those things. We mustn't lose them. But we need, as well, to understand that what we do – together – remains ... ah ... appropriate.'

Appropriate is a very carefully judged term to use in this context. Worries about what Enterprises should or shouldn't do seem to me to be the inevitable consequence of straddling two cultures.

Fred agrees. 'There's no management book on earth that will tell you about RIAT, because elsewhere it simply doesn't exist. What other organisation depends so wholly on volunteers? Where else will you find so much goodwill, so much loyalty, among thousands, yes *thousands* of people? It's an extraordinary formula, but it doesn't travel well. They've tried to export it but they've failed. We have to be careful about that. There are substantial risks here, and we have to make sure they're containable.'

I've heard this from other sources. Over the past decade or so, Paul and Tim have accepted challenges abroad. Some, like the Hong Kong Aviation Ball, were an acknowledged success. Others, like an aborted airshow in Holland, never got off the ground. The latter resulted in a £100,000 write-off, making a hefty dent in Enterprises' annual accounts. There may still be some prospect of compensation, but it's beyond dispute that a great deal of Fairford time and effort was squandered on the project.

'Enterprises handed over more than £400,000 this year,' I point out. 'That's a substantial sum of money.'

'Of course it is. It's excellent news. The place is well run. The team are well led. It's just that we operate in a very sensitive corner of the marketplace. We need people like Paul and Tim. But we have to take great care where we tread.'

This seems to me to be at once entirely fair and entirely predictable. Paul and Tim bring both passion and self-belief to what they do. Caging them can't be easy.

'It isn't. But let's keep this thing in perspective. Paul and Tim are both people who pay fanatical attention to detail. Get the small things right and the chances are the big picture will be fine. Get the smallest things right – as they do – and believe me, you'll come up with something fantastic. I've got nothing but admiration for them both. They've built something unique that we should all be proud of.'

'All?'

'The country. We do it – they do it – as well, maybe better, than anyone else in the world.'

I think of the press cuttings after last year's show – *'The number one airshow of the year'*, *'One of the best airshows staged in the UK in recent years, if not the world'*. Fred is right. And because he, too, is part of the team, he's justly proud. Our conversation continues long into the afternoon. Finally, after a tour of the building, he escorts me back to reception. While I wait to reclaim my rucksack, Fred is spotted by another club member who knows Fred is a key part of the Fairford team and wants to shake him by the hand.

'Wonderful concert the other night,' he says. 'Absolutely unforgettable.'

I leave shortly afterwards. Fred is still beaming.

A week later comes a call from Sue Allen. She's been busy fielding the flood of confirmations from foreign airforces, pledges of aircraft to join the July show, and she's just put the phone down after a conversation with the British embassy in Kiev. The defence attaché has had some news from the office of General Antonets, chief of the Ukrainian Air Force. He's sending over a total of six aircraft, including a Tu-22 and a Su-24 MR. Sue pauses, awaiting my reaction. I'm doing my best to run through my mental filing cabinet of Soviet hardware. It's obviously good news.

Sue's a busy lady. 'A *Backfire*,' she reminds me. 'And a *Fencer*.'

'Of course.'

A *Backfire* is the current Russian nuclear bomber. Like the American F-111, it's swing-wing and supersonic. A *Fencer* also flies in the strike role. Both figure prominently on any list of must-see Soviet aircraft.

'Are they displaying?'

'Yes.'

'Does Paul know?'

'I just told him.'

A thought occurs to me. What about the Ukrainian Falcons, Colonel Viktor's six-ship MiG-29 display team? Aren't they coming too?

There's another pause on the line. This time Sue doesn't sound quite so euphoric. 'There seems to be some problem,' she says.

'Like what?'

'I'm not sure. It might be something to do with last year.'

I think back to July. As far as I can remember, Colonel Viktor's boys were the toast of Fairford.

'They were,' Sue says, 'once they arrived. It was getting there. There was a problem with Dutch airspace. I don't know the details.'

I press her a little harder. Eventually, the story spills out. The Ukrainians routed west from Kiev. They landed at RAF Bruggen in Germany to refuel, then took off again. Sadly, someone had neglected to clear their path over Holland.

'So what happened?'

'The Dutch scrambled some F-16s.'

'And?'

'Intercepted them. They were really quite hostile. General Antonets wasn't amused.' She giggles. 'I suppose you can't really blame him.'

The following day, another call – this time from Heidi Standfast in Marketing. The seventeenth of April has seen the final despatch of all the artwork for the 1998 leaflets, posters, and stickers. I reach for my pen, ticking off another waymark on the journey to the July show. Are we talking volume here? Or a couple of boxes of A4?

'Depends.' Heidi sounds icy. 'Do you want the figures?'

'Please.'

'Leaflets first?'

'OK.'

'Over half a million.'

Half a *million?* The view from my office window blurs for a second or two while Heidi rattles briskly through the rest of the order. 40,000 posters. 50,000 stickers. The numbers climb and climb. I'm still thinking about the artwork. Who goes through it all to check for typos? Who makes sure the dates are right? And the spelling? And the marked-up choice of typeface?'

'Me,' she says sweetly.

'You and who else?'

'No one.'

Towards the end of the wettest April since the French Revolution, I take our trusty VW Camper up through the Cotswolds to Nailsworth. The sky, once again, is boiling with thunderheads. The weather forecasters are promising a dramatically wet afternoon, and looking at the towering cloudscape, I believe them.

Nailsworth is the home of William's Kitchen. The premises lie on one corner of a busy intersection and there's a delicatessen at the front, the fish slab piled high with glistening halibut, wild salmon, and a small mountain of lobsters. Up the stairs behind the shop is a bistro. The walls and the low ceiling are a deep, rich terracotta, and five tables have been pushed together at the back of the room to await the morning's guests.

I stand in the gloom for a moment or two, counting the place settings. In all there are sixteen. The knives and forks indicate at least five courses. Three wine glasses await each guest. The smells from the kitchen are already heavy with ginger and lemon grass. For a man who got up too early to face breakfast, this is looking very promising indeed.

William's Kitchen is the brainchild of a gifted chef called William Beeston. The business has been prospering for more than twenty years, sustained above all by an ambitious outside catering operation. William Beeston and his events manager, Louise Grant, cook for hundreds at Berkeley Castle, Painswick House, Badminton Horse Trials and the

Bristol Balloon Festival. Every July, over at Fairford, they mastermind the RIAT Gala Dinner.

At Paul Bowen's insistence I attended last year's Gala Dinner, and in my portfolio of memories from those extraordinary four days it ranks second only to the B-2 stealth bomber. Imagine the biggest aircraft hangar you've ever seen. Drape the walls and the ceiling with black cloth spangled with tiny star-like bulbs. Carpet the floor, provide a platform for a small musical ensemble, and then wheel in four state-of-the-art USAF fighters, each guarding one corner of this enormous cave. Get the lighting just right – subtle spots for the sixty-eight tables, ice-blue colour gels for the aircraft – add 560 black-tie guests and, hey presto, you have an experience that none of those guests will ever forget. Last year's dinner was designed as a fiftieth anniversary tribute to the USAF, and the news that Lockheed had paid £90,000 to sponsor the event came as no surprise. I've never eaten a five-course meal under the nose of an F-117 stealth fighter before, and in my judgement it was worth every last cent.

The food last year came from William's Kitchen, and before I succumbed to the 1995 Sancerre and the 1984 Château Grand Puy Lacoste, I have a very clear memory of a small army of waitresses emerging from a fold in the drapes, each toting an enormous silver salver. The food was delicious, wonderfully judged and piping hot. Given the sheer scale of the operation, how on earth does William do it?

This morning's get-together at Nailsworth is strictly for the benefit of British Aerospace. They're sponsoring the 1998 Gala Dinner, and a small delegation from their head office in Farnborough is due any minute. Amanda Butcher, Kevin Leeson and an accompanying posse from Fairford are also on the road, and another big table in the bistro has been readied for the inevitable meeting. According to the agenda, we have twenty-seven items to wade through before we're allowed to abandon the coffee and move to the other table. Only then can we get stuck in. On the phone, Amanda has described the event as 'a tasting'. To me, hungrier by the minute, it has all the makings of a five-course meal.

Waiting for the troops to arrive, I quiz William on the secrets of

VIP catering. The Cotswolds ooze money, and it must be a nice business if you can get the formula right – but the penalties of failure don't bear contemplation. Last year's top table at the Gala Dinner included HRH Prince Andrew, General Fogelman, Chief of the US Air Force, plus a covey of assorted VVIPs. Get even the tiniest details wrong and Paul Bowen – for one – would be less than forgiving.

William acknowledges the pressure, but seems curiously nerveless. 'It's a world of its own,' he admits, 'and it certainly isn't to everyone's taste. The one thing you can't be is a pop-star telly chef. There's absolutely no scope for that kind of showbiz stuff. No, it's all about culinary logistics, about getting the right things in the right order. It's a hundred metres from the service tent to the farthest table. I've actually paced it out. It's a silly statistic, I know, but it's that kind of thing that governs what you do.'

I'm still thinking about last year's event. The memory of the roast saddle of lamb, sweetly pink, stays with me still. There were three of these miraculous little chops on my plate. Multiply that by 600 and William's right, you're looking at a serious logistic challenge. How many ovens does it take to convert nearly 2,000 lamb chops into the centrepiece dish?

'Twelve,' William says at once. 'We use portable fan-assisted ovens, plus ten sets of those multi-ring boilers you fuel with propane.'

'Staff?'

'Fifteen chefs and sixty-five waitresses. They insist on one per table.'

He reels off more statistics. Trillions of langouste for the fish course. Umpteen individual syllabubs. Like any successful general he knows that victory is a consequence of meticulous preparation, of constantly narrowing the odds against the unforeseen and the unexpected. The possibility of disaster, though, must be written into the job description. True?

'Yes,' he nods, 'very definitely.'

'So how close have you been? At RIAT?'

William glances at his watch. He's got a little behind with the potatoes he's preparing for the beef fillet. 'A couple of years ago it was pretty hairy,' he admits. 'We'd just served the fish course when all the power went. We work in this big, big service tent and there's an ample supply laid on, but suddenly – *phut* – it all went dead.'

I try to picture the scene. Once again, he was serving English lamb. With lamb, timing can be all-important. The ovens were full. The cooking was underway. Six hundred guests were polishing off the last of their little parcels of langouste. How on earth did he cope without power?

'I sent for Amanda,' he says promptly. 'I'm there to do the cooking. The power supply isn't my responsibility.'

Amanda, it seems, sorted the problem, and the power was restored in time for William to rescue the main course. But the memory has stayed with him – the culinary equivalent of a mid-air near-miss. Six hundred VIPs easing seamlessly from the fish course to the pudding would not, I suspect, have done the reputation of William's Kitchen any good at all.

Amanda herself arrives shortly afterwards. William has retreated to the kitchen, but mention of the power supply raises a smile.

'Shame,' she says, 'I never did get to finish those langouste.'

There are four expected from British Aerospace, and the meeting's due to begin at half past ten. By eleven o'clock, still waiting for Michelle Moore, one of the Aerospace delegation, Amanda elects to start without her. Attempts to raise Michelle on any of a dozen mobiles have come to nothing. She's been working alongside the Fairford team for a number of airshows and her map-reading skills are legendary. Driving down from Windsor, she's probably in South Wales by now.

For the first half-hour or so Amanda offers an update on the latest developments. She and Caroline Rogers, Deputy Director for Business Development, have been looking after British Aerospace for a number of years. Keeping the sponsor happy means keeping the sponsor informed, and she briskly tidies up the small print while we await Michelle's arrival.

Price Waterhouse, she announces, have agreed to sponsor the RAF Veterans' Enclosure. Raytheon, the American aerospace giant, are on the brink of underwriting £25,000 worth of Jumbotron screen. It looks, after all, as though the SkyWatch planes will be able to downlink their spooky-dooky surveillance pictures for public consumption.

Mention of SkyWatch takes us to the Thursday symposium, a day-long exploration of the world of hi-tech reconnaissance, also sponsored by British Aerospace. The symposium is to take place in Church House, Westminster, a stone's throw from the Houses of Parliament. Amanda lists an impressive cast of speakers, including the USAF's Director of Airborne Reconnaissance and a top-level team from the Israeli Air Force, who will be addressing the operation of UAVs, or Unmanned Aerial Vehicles. There are nods around the table, and sheets of photocopied A4 pass to and fro among the forest of mineral water bottles in response to queries about the seating plan.

It's at this point that Michelle arrives. She's tall, striking, blonde and lost for words. Her map gave out in one of the council estates that ring Stroud. She sinks into the remaining chair, eyeing the coffee pot.

'*Stroud?*' One of the locals is having difficulty with Michelle's choice of route.

She gives him a withering look. 'Don't even ask,' she says.

The meeting gets under way again – more small print. A new plastic clip for the symposium ID badges, kinder on lapels than the old pins. Discussion of an upgrade for the 400 standard-issue RIAT folders and pens, distributed to symposium delegates. A gentle enquiry from Amanda about the propriety of Lockheed Martin – a rival aerospace company – having some kind of display presence in the Church House foyer. The latter is regretfully turned down by Robert Gardner, British Aerospace Vice-President for exhibitions and promotions.

I'm beginning to have serious fantasies about lunch when Kevin Leeson offers his thoughts on what he calls 'the VIP plot'. We're discussing the schedule for the Thursday evening. The symposium is over. Julie Kirkbride, a friend of Amanda who happens to be an MP, is hosting a reception for RIAT invitees at the House of Commons. The reception over, the foreign air chiefs will move on to Apsley House for a formal dinner. The key to the evening's success is, as ever, timing: who goes where when.

In response to a question from Robert Gardner, Kevin eases into gear. 'The intention is to move Sir Roger and CAS together,' he says, 'but there's a luggage issue here. The Palace of Westminster get a bit tedious about cars going in.'

Kevin broods about the Westminster authorities for a moment or two. CAS is short-hand for Chief of the Air Staff, the RAF's top serving officer. In an ideal world, Kevin would doubtless teleport him the mile and a half to Apsley House.

The plot moves on. 'At Apsley House there'll be a receiving line, of course. Our guests may wish to have a look round before dinner. We'll have the appropriate people with guide books posted. It's an exquisite venue.'

'What time into dinner?'

'2015.'

'What time away?'

'2230.'

This conversation has the feel of a catechism, prompt and response, the programme fine-tuned to the last second. The trick, of course, is to create a little bubble of conviviality within this unyielding schedule, and listening to Kevin I haven't a moment's doubt that the evening will be an immense success.

On the Thursday afternoon, sponsored by Boeing, it will be the VIP ladies' programme. Kevin, once again, is word-perfect. He's looking across at Robert Gardner. 'You may be able to help us here. Thursday afternoon tends to turn into a bit of a Lockheed feast. The husbands are all in the symposium. Their wives all meet up at the Lanesborough or some such. It might be nice to leaven it a bit, throw in the odd chiefie's wife. We can tea them separately, of course, and then feed them into the Commons but socially . . .' He shrugs. 'What do you think?'

There's a brief discussion about the social chemistry at the Lanesborough and I'm still wondering what it must be like to play ringmeister at an event like this when Kevin moves the schedule on to Friday. The ladies are to begin their day at Sudeley Castle, a famed Gloucestershire attraction, once the residence of one of Henry VIII's queens, Catherine Parr.

'Ten o'clock to one.' Kevin glances up from his brief. 'A twirl around the gardens followed by a finger buffet lunch. We'll pitch in Lady Ashcombe for that. Then it's back on the Cheltenham radial to freshen up at the hotel, followed by a windscreen shopping opportunity in the city.'

I'm losing track again. Cheltenham radial? Windscreen shopping opportunity? But Kevin pauses for no man. It's late afternoon. The ladies, shopped out, are back in their hotel awaiting their 1800 transfer to Oxford. By now I've worked out that windscreen, in Kevin-speak, means coach-borne.

'We're planning for a brief windscreen tour of collegiate Oxford,' he's explaining, 'followed by an evening event at Balliol. We're going to kick off in the chapel with an organ recital followed by a champagne reception in the Fellows' Garden. We'll be taking dinner in hall – styled very much as "Dinner in Hall" – and there'll be a string quartet in the background. The good news here is that it's *not* numbers-sensitive like last year. In fact the ceiling's 150.'

He turns to Michelle. He wants to know how many British Aerospace wives she can feed into the Balliol event. By now, Michelle has got her bearings. 'Five,' she says.

Kevin looks faintly disappointed. Boeing, he points out, are picking up the tab.

Robert Gardner stirs. 'Excellent,' he murmurs. 'Then we shall eat their declining profits with glee.'

Preparations for lunch are gathering pace. Bread rolls have appeared on the table behind me. I weigh my chances of taking an early nibble while Amanda directs our attention to Item 18, the Gala Dinner. In keeping with the theme of the RAF's anniversary, she's planning on incorporating five aircraft into the seating plan. She hands round various configurations. The aircraft involved are an SE5, a Gloster Gladiator, a Spitfire, a Hawk and a Eurofighter. Three of these aircraft can be replicas. Only the SE5 and the Gladiator have to be for real.

Robert Gardner voices the question I'm itching to ask. 'Is that an issue?'

Amanda nods. 'I'm afraid it is. With replicas, we can allow smoking. If the aircraft are real, we can't.'

It's true. Military regulations forbid smoking in the vicinity of live aircraft. As a non-smoker I love this little irony, but assume there'll be some way round it. Swap the SE5 and the Gladiator for something else. Keep the whole fleet strictly replica. To my surprise, though, the veteran aircraft win the day. Robert Gardner thinks they're irreplaceable. We absolutely must have them. This year's Gala Dinner, like last year's, will be a smoke-free zone.

'What about outside?' Amanda's still looking at Robert, 'Would you like something parked by the flagpole? A Tornado, say, and a Harrier?'

Both aircraft are made, at least in part, by British Aerospace, and I can see Robert visibly warming to the proposal. The apron in front of the hangar is where the guests gather before the dinner to sip champagne and listen to the RAF Band Beating The Retreat. There'll be a tribute flypast – probably a Spitfire – and Amanda thinks it might be nice to have the company's credentials on display. So far, the British Aerospace corporate presence has been pretty low-key, and this might go some way towards redressing the balance.

Robert has a thought. 'But where will you get them?' he queries 'Would that be down to us?'

'Absolutely not.' Amanda beams at him. 'We've got hundreds on static. We'll just pop across and borrow a couple.'

Mention of specific aircraft prompts a question about Eurofighter. This, too, is partly made by British Aerospace, and so far only two prototypes are flying in the UK. Eurofighter will be Strike Command's mainstay well into the new millennium. The aircraft is a headline attraction for the July show and one of them is the main feature of Heidi Standfast's 40,000 posters. But as the debate picks up speed it begins to occur to me that no one's actually got round to confirming that one of these precious prototypes can actually appear.

Amanda is gently floating the issue past Robert Gardner. What kind of approach might he favour? Would a formal letter be best?

Robert shakes his head. 'Use the pilot's net,' he says at once. 'Talk to Chris Yeo. He'd be favourite.'

Chris Yeo was the lead test pilot on the Eurofighter development programme. He's now left British Aerospace for Flight Refuelling but he still sits on Geoff Brindle's Flying Control Committee. Amanda, sensibly, is wondering quite how the pilots' net can deliver £20m worth of state-of-the-art jet fighter.

Robert shrugs the question aside. 'They'll simply extend a training flight,' he says. 'Believe me, it's the best way to tackle it. Otherwise the paperwork will be horrendous.'

I'm scribbling all this down. The thought of a pilot on a training flight just happening to stray over an airfield in front of a crowd of 100,000 is irresistible. How low profile can you get?

The meeting breaks up shortly afterwards. Discussion about a speaker for the top table has resulted in a decision to bid for George Robertson, Secretary of State for Defence. He's gone down very well indeed among the service chiefs and is thought to be an excellent after-dinner speaker. Kevin makes a note to tackle his outer office.

I'm still wondering about the Eurofighter. Have I really got this right? Do RIAT's gambles extend to giving top billing to an aircraft that may never turn up?

Lunch, mercifully, takes us to the other table, and I manoeuvre myself to sit opposite Wally Armstrong. We all have our views about food and drink, but if anyone brings a professional eye to William Beeston's offerings, then it's surely Wally, RIAT's catering chief.

The first course is already waiting for us, a confit of duck with leaves on a Cumberland sauce. Mine lasts about three minutes. Even the leaves are delicious. Around me, I begin to sense a certain curiosity. It's Penny Telling, from British Aerospace, who voices the key question.

'Hungry?'

'Starving.'

I'm eyeing her plate. After the first mouthful, she's plainly saving herself. With a smile, bless her, she swaps her plate with mine.

Wally can't believe his eyes. 'Doesn't your wife feed you?'

I mutter something about the shame of wasting good food when it dawns on me that another dozen parcels of duck are heading my way. And all this with four courses to go.

William arrives from the kitchen. He wants a verdict on the confit, and there are voices from all sides only too happy to oblige. Too meaty. Too heavy. Too greasy. Too solid. Looks like a blob.

I'm staring down at Penny's empty plate. Too meaty? *Duck*? What on earth are these people talking about? Aren't they hungry? Wasn't it just delicious?

William's obviously been through all this before, and takes the criticisms on the chin. He'll come up with an alternative. Someone suggests stripping off the meat and cross-hatching it on a bed of rocket. Someone else mentions the word 'terrine'. After our introductory glasses of champagne, we've all become master-chefs.

The news, for William, improves on the second course. The fillet of sole pané with lemon grass and ginger meets with almost unanimous approval. It's light. It's beautifully flavoured. It's an ideal partner for the 1996 Pouilly-Fuissé. The latter, along with umpteen other wines, is being served by Nick Arkell. After each course we're invited to vote for a particular wine, an exercise that begins to do untold damage to our vocabularies. A '96 Gewurztraminer is 'very low on surprises'. A '94 Sauternes is 'a touch treacly'. An '88 vintage port 'is, to be frank, an impostor'. For little me, a veteran of countless Sainsbury's wine boxes, this is the purest fantasy. Lunchtime at William's Kitchen has parted company with real life. Someone is wondering whether I mind having another go at the Chablis. *Mind?*

The tasting ends an hour or so later. Thanks to Nick Arkell's wines, each of the beautifully presented courses has been analysed to death, and William Beeston has retreated to the kitchen to lick his wounds and conduct a post-mortem. I've never seen sixteen adults devote quite so much energy to a discussion about vegetables, but the centrepiece dish − a deliciously rare fillet of beef nestling on a roundel of roast potato − is now to be accompanied by a mountain of assorted *légumes*. In the majority view, this will satisfy the traditional service yearning for meat and two veg, though personally I can't see much point in hiring a chef of William's obvious qualities and then playing safe.

As ever, Kevin Leeson has the last word. It comes as we're saying goodbye in the car park.

'I thought the spareness of the dish was divine,' he says wistfully. 'Why are we trying to cater for tastes we don't understand?'

....

CHAPTER NINE

May 1998

May brings Sean Maffett back into the planning loop. David Roome is to appear for yet another session on the Berlin Airlift and RAF eightieth anniversary elements of the flying display, and this will be Sean's opportunity to gauge what progress David has made with the goodies in store for July. Much of the inspiration for the Berlin pageant came originally from Sean, and his contribution on the day will be critical, especially for the success of David's meticulously choreographed anniversary tribute. His commentary, relayed through the PA system and broadcast live on Wings FM, the airshow's own local radio station, should turn a formidable feat of airmanship into an unforgettable piece of theatre.

The meeting begins with some bad news from Ian Sheeley. In the hunt for aircraft for the Berlin tribute he's been able to lay hands on only eleven vintage machines, one short of David Roome's dozen. This smacks to me of disaster, but David is pretty sanguine about the sudden hole in his line-up. He gestures at his carefully typed masterplan.

'They'll just have to close up,' he says cheerfully. 'It's not a problem.'

Paul, of course, has other ideas. He's sure there's an extra DC-3 on charter to Racal from Air Atlantique. Sue Allen, distributing coffee, thinks there might be another Dakota still operational in Helsinki. Either way, David isn't to worry. Come what may, the long arm of RIAT will deliver the raw material for his fifty-five-minute spectacular.

David scribbles a note to himself, then briefs on the latest adjustments to his master plan. Wary of boring the watching crowd, he's tightened the interval between take-offs to a bare seventy-five seconds. Airborne on runway 27, the aircraft will climb out at 120 knots. One mile upwind, compressing the circuit, each of the long line of Dakotas will commence a rate-one turn. By the time aircraft number five is lifting off, the leader will be one mile north of the airfield, clearly visible, heading in the opposite direction. Abeam the downwind end of the runway the DC-3s will turn out forty degrees, taking them virtually due south of neighbouring Brize Norton before dipping a wing for another rate-one turn to bring them back in towards the airfield.

David glances up, pencil in hand. 'Then it's checks and down the slope,' he says. 'By the time number twelve is taking off, number one is one and a half miles to land.'

Sean is visibly impressed. It's a nice marriage of airmanship, history and showbusiness, an aerial merry-go-round which will gladden watching veterans while providing a clue or two to those tens of thousands of spectators for whom the Berlin Airlift is the faintest of historical footnotes.

The first eight aircraft will land back at Fairford, taxiing to pre-designated positions on the ramp, where a dozen vintage trucks will be waiting for ground crews to re-enact the furious bustle of Tempelhof, Tegel and Gatow. In the air meanwhile, the four remaining aircraft – a DC-3, a DC-4, a Lancaster and a Constellation – will each perform a six-minute display. RIAT's tribute to the fliers of the Berlin Airlift will end with a flypast of nine aircraft representing the UK, US and Commonwealth squadrons which shipped vital food and fuel into the beleaguered city. Ian Sheeley, as Flying Display Manager, has been bidding for present-day transport aircraft. Among the finale cavalcade will be a VC10, followed by a trio of the big maritime recce Nimrods from RAF Kinloss.

A thought occurs to David Roome. 'Does the VC10 know he's leading a box?' he asks.

Ian shakes his head. 'Not really,' he says. 'I did mention it in the bar at Brize the other night but I don't think it stuck.'

David grins, then makes a technical point about the four-ship formation. We're still discussing the exact degree of visual separation when Paul interrupts. He, Tim Prince and Mel James have just returned from yet another foreign adventure, this time to South Africa. The Breitling organisation have commissioned RIAT to pull together the elements of a three-ship display team to showcase Breitling chronographs at venues around the globe, and Mel has been running an engineer's eye over two SAAF Cheetah supersonic jets, plus a Rooivalk attack helicopter. Paul, meanwhile, has been furiously networking and, between guest sorties in various classic aircraft, he's managed to lay hands on a SAAF C-130. This aircraft, he now suggests, might find a place in Ian Sheeley's finale flypast.

The suggestion has the force of an order, and Ian has been with RIAT long enough to know it. He pencils in the South African Hercules, adding it to the list of aircraft flying in from a nearby RAF base.

Paul shakes his head. 'The SAAF Herc will be here.' He taps the table. 'We'll launch it locally.'

'Not from Lyneham?'

'No, here. Definitely here. He'll need slots. Make a note of that, Ian.'

I watch Ian's racing pencil, wondering exactly what kind of promises Paul has been making in South Africa. Take-off and landing slots during the show itself are immeasurably valuable, but Paul's is the voice that count in meetings like these, and the system – in the shape of Ian Sheeley – must somehow accommodate him.

Ian is staring at his three-page running order for the Saturday display. 'We could launch the SAAF Herc at 11.00,' he suggests at last, 'just before the Falcon runs in.'

The Falcon 20 executive jet is to start the Berlin segment of the flying programme. It belongs to FR Aviation at Bournemouth, who are paying for this part of the display.

Sean frowns. As commentator, he's keen to keep the odd rogue take-off separate from the Berlin Airlift tribute. Otherwise, he says, the punters get confused.

David Roome again, with yet more good news: 'We're talking endurance aircraft,' he points out. 'They could take off before breakfast if you want.'

Paul is looking alarmed. His conversations with the South African Herc crew clearly didn't extend to early-morning wake-up calls. 'A ten minute buffer will be fine,' he growls. 'I'm sure Ian will sort it out.'

Ian offers a wry smile. Finding a hole for the SAAF Herc is the least of his problems. At Paul and Tim's suggestion, he's taken his first tentative stab at a properly timed running order for the eight-hour flying display, and according to my copy, the programme is running nearly an hour over length. The RAF band's concert is scheduled to start at 18.15. By that time, if draft one is an accurate guide, David Roome's eightieth anniversary tribute will still be forty-five minutes short of its grand finale.

Ian talks us through the programme. In broad terms, he's tried to pack the five national aerobatic teams around the show's four major themes. Four? I tally the themes on the fingers of one hand. SkyWatch, Berlin and the RAF eightieth make three. How come four?

Tim Prince directs my attention to page two of Ian's running order. Half-way down, at 14.31, there's a billing for something called *The Sounds of Freedom*. Beneath, at eight minute intervals, come a succession of aircraft, occasionally in twos but mostly solo. They vary from Concorde and the huge B-52 bomber to the Swedish Gripen fighter and a pair of French Mirages. In all, *The Sounds of Freedom* provides a home for seventeen aircraft. By 16.18, anyone who isn't deaf will be looking forward to the Royal Jordanian Falcons, and then, at last, David Roome's anniversary finale.

I catch Tim's eye. 'Why do you call it *The Sounds of Freedom?*'

'Because it's sexy.'

'But what does it mean?'

There's a silence, an exchange of glances, then the admission that these two hours, at the height of the afternoon, serve as a kind of airshow lucky dip. Get yourself to Fairford between two and four and there's bound to be something to take your fancy.

'You mean it's a rag bag?'

'Not at all. It's a showcase.'

'For stuff you couldn't put anywhere else?'

'For aircraft that stand alone.'

Wonderful. The perfect rationale. I'm thinking back to last year and the sequence of earsplitting solo performances that bludgeoned the crowd into a post-lunch trance. *The Sounds of Freedom.* Democracy on re-heat.

Ian directs our attention to SkyWatch, the first of the show's major themes. Despite the dozen aircraft billed to appear, Ian thinks it's looking a bit thin.

Paul, sucking on a brand-new Superking, agrees. 'We'll pull out the B-52 from *The Sounds of Freedom,*' he says. 'That should cheer it up.'

A B-52 eight-engined bomber in the reconnaissance role appears to be news to Ian Sheeley. From the other end of the table I can hear him muttering darkly about artistic licence. With a curl of smoke, Paul waves his reservations away. These days, B-52s do all kinds of things: deep penetration, mine laying, interdiction. Why not recce? This answers Ian's qualms, not least because he's been bidding for the B-52 to fly in a three-ship with a pair of supersonic B-1B bombers, and the pilots have turned him down. Better, on reflection, to separate the bombers and do as Paul says. At a stroke of his pencil, the B-52 joins the SkyWatch club.

Someone else raises a query about the Gulfstream. Gulfstream Aerospace are funding this year's Flight Centre – a five-figure hello to visiting aircrew – but flying one of their executive jets in a surveillance display is surely pushing commercial favours just a little too far?

Paul shakes his head. The Gulfstream, he says, is the lead contender for the multi-billion-pound ASTOR project. Should it win, Gulfstream's pride and joy will become the RAF's mainstay in the airborne command and control role.

We move on through the list of SkyWatch aircraft, Paul spading in yet more extras. A Hawk. A Spanish F-18. A Czech recce MiG-21. The line-up fattens, becoming ever more exotic. Finally even Sean, a veteran of umpteen air displays, admits that it's got a promising feel. In commentary terms, he can make these aircraft work. It's a shame that the Israeli UAV hasn't materialised, but even so there'll be lots for him to say.

'And see.'

Paul's looking meaningfully at me. For a moment, I haven't a clue what he's talking about.

'Haven't you heard about the Jumbotrons?'

'No.'

'We've got the sponsorship.'

The Jumbotrons are the giant TV screens Paul has been trying to acquire for the July show. They cost £25,000 each for the weekend's hire, and the bid is for four. Raising £100,000 in sponsorship isn't easy, and over the last couple of months, with various deadlines fast approaching, I've somehow assumed that the idea has withered on the vine. Far from it.

'How much are you getting,' I enquire, 'in sponsorship?'

Paul doesn't answer. Instead, he outlines the difference the screen will make. Downlinked pictures from the SkyWatch aircraft. Archive pictures to garnish the Berlin Airlift. Live coverage of the rest of the show. Adverts for David Higham's Aviation Collection. Crowd information. Live relays from the evening concert. In other words, the works.

As the flood of possibilities washes over me, I'm still clinging on to the key word. 'You said screen.'

'That's right.'

'Not screens? Plural?'

'No – screen, singular.'

The sponsorship, it turns out, isn't quite six figures. In fact it's just enough for one screen. Plus some extras.

'Extras?'

'Whatever you'll need.'

'Me?'

Paul nods, grins, then pushes smoothly on to the final item, David's RAF anniversary tribute. Sean Maffett has always been keen on vertically stacked flypasts, but he knows that translating this concept into any kind of reality has been fraught. Now, thanks to David Roome, Paul's original cartoon doodle has become a five-page masterplan, timed to the second, mapped to the last degree.

Sean listens to David's quiet exposition, envisioning the four swirls of aircraft, slowly untangling into a perfect vertical stack. It's never been tried before. There'll be no rehearsal. But David has absolutely no doubts that, accurately flown, his masterplan will work.

Paul is waxing lyrical about the community singing, the eighty veterans taking the salute, and the grand finale with the black Tucanos bursting through the multi-coloured RAF flash, painted in the sky by the Red Arrows, but Sean is still looking at David. When Paul asks him what he thinks, Sean shakes his head in admiration.

'I love it,' he says quietly. 'I love it. I think it's absolutely super.'

David seizes his moment. He's rather planning to be in one of the twin-boom Vampire jets towards the end of the tribute. The Vampires come from Source Aviation down in Bournemouth, and David regularly flies with them.

Paul and Tim are both shaking their heads. 'No can do,' Tim says. 'Against regulations, I'm afraid.'

Paul nods. 'We'll need you in the tower, David. It's your display, your baby.'

For the first time in more than four months, I sense a certain quickening in David's voice. He's disappointed, sure, but he's angry too. 'OK,' he says briskly, 'but let's clear one thing up. Ian Sheeley is in charge of this thing. I choreographed this bit but he's the guy who calls the shots. I'm sorry, but I will *not* have two people in charge.'

Paul tries to edge in, but David waves him off. 'No, hear me out. This isn't about the Vampire. That's fine. That's OK. I'll be up there in the tower if that's really where you want me, but I promise you I won't say a word. Once it starts, it starts. The guys will have been briefed. The timings are all down there on paper. Ian's in charge. End of story.'

There's a brief silence. The unspoken consensus is that David has made his point. Then Sean clears his throat.

'I still think it's bloody wonderful,' he says softly.

Several days later, I'm talking to Sean on the phone. Paul, all too obviously, wasn't joking about the Jumbotron screen, and yours truly has been volunteered to join Tony Webb – Deputy Director for Public Affairs – to troubleshoot the problems. The money coming from Raytheon, the sponsor, might just stretch to a half-decent production operation, but it's clear from the start that Sean Maffett will be vital to the pre-planning. To have the show commentary and our single screen pulling in opposite directions would be less than perfect.

After agreeing a strategy for use of the screen, Sean and I go back to the meeting with David Roome. Sean, if anything, is even more enthusiastic about the stacks. 'It's a brilliant piece of work,' he says. 'Everyone said it couldn't be done, and he's done it. Or at least planned it. I suppose we should wait and see how it works on the day, but from where I sit it's a very big step forward.'

The latter thought provokes a rather wider discussion. The previous day I'd been over to Rendcomb, a tiny grass strip eight miles north-west of Fairford. The private airfield is co-owned by a character called Vic Norman, something of a legend in the airshow world. Vic is making the airfield available as the venue for RIAT's Saturday-night barbecue, one of the highlights of Amanda's VIP programme, and the chiefs of a dozen of the world's airforces will have the chance to fly in one of his superb collection of vintage aircraft. Vic, on first acquaintance, isn't short of an opinion or two, and some of his judgements on RIAT have been brutal.

Sean says he knows Vic well. The man is extremely shrewd. He runs the Cadbury's Crunchie wing-walking three-ship flying circus. He flies the world's biggest single-engined biplane for St Ivel. He put together the act that launches the world's smallest twin from the top of a Mitsubishi Shogun. A born entertainer, he has a real flair for making things work and then finding commercial sponsors to pay for them.

'He's not wild about RIAT,' I point out. 'He thinks Tim and Paul are great at the politics and the fundraising, but he's pretty rude about the content.'

'It's too big,' Sean agrees. 'That's not Vic's scene at all.'

He's right. Vic had lectured me for half an hour about the limitations of RAF display pilots. The Red Arrows are the exception, but the solo pilots only display for a single season, and in his view they find it difficult to escape the corset of the standard routines.

'That's exactly right,' Sean says, 'which is why David Roome's plan is so exciting. He's got a different mindset. He wants to push the envelope out. The RAF guys are operationally minded. RIAT reflects a lot of that. What Vic Norman's after is entertainment. And so, I suspect, is David.'

'And Paul?'

'The same. He's an entertainer, just like Vic – but Paul's in the numbers game too. He wants to grow it and grow it and grow it. More aircraft. More airforces. More promotion. More media. Bigger crowds. More revenue. That's fine, but at some point you're going to be in danger of killing what you started with. It's a monster.'

'Out of control?'

'Definitely.'

A week later, I drive to Aldershot to meet Col Brian Robertson. Brian will be commanding the field hospital at this year's show. The field hospital, a Territorial Army unit, will be occupying the bulk of Hangar 1205, providing a 100-bed capability plus full surgical and resuscitation facilities in the event of a major incident.

In civilian life Brian Robertson is a GP, and among the clutter of his tiny consulting room I'm keen to grasp exactly what kind of provision it's possible to make against the unthinkable – not because Sean is talking literally of events unspooling out of control, but because airshows, by their very nature, can be dangerous.

Middle-aged and portly, Brian has an intensity that smacks of mild obsession. Some doctors become fascinated by circulatory problems or pediatric care. Brian's bag is disaster management. As one of the handful of doctors belonging to the BASICS scheme, he's on twenty-four-hour call-out for major emergencies. Over the last ten years he's attended the Hungerford massacre, the Clapham and Purley rail disasters, the sinking of the *Marchioness* and the City of London's Bishopsgate bombing. The last accusation you'd level at Brian Robertson is lack of experience. Just what has it taught him?

He gives the question some thought. 'This might sound a bit arrogant,' he says at last, 'but it's given me a great belief in command structures. I've been with the military most of my life and the thinking rubs off. Someone has to take over. Someone has to make a plan. There has to be an agreed place where the buck stops. If we're talking civilian disasters, that's not always possible. The buzzword there is co-ordination. But in the military it's much more clear-cut. When it comes to 306, I'm the guy who'll be facing the public inquiry.'

306 is shorthand for Brian's pride and joy – 306 Field Hospital RAMC (V), one of a number of similar outfits which rotate around major UK public events. This year, it's 306's turn to stand watch over Fairford. Brian has never been to Fairford before, but his knowledge of airshows is extensive. Since 1996 he's been medical director at the Farnborough International Air Show and he's proud of the work he's done there, bonding nine different agencies into a single comprehensive medical plan. This plan, he says, is designed to cover not only a major incident but the demands of mass-gathering medicine as well.

The latter phrase defeats me.

Brian leans forward. 'Mass-gathering medicine is Joe Public,' he explains. 'Take Fairford. You've got a huge crowd. People are bound to want attention from time to time, and you provide that through the South Side Medical Centre. Get sunburn or a headache, and that's where you go. The other element is the major disaster, a totally different scale of event. That's my lot. Northside, Hangar 1205.'

306 is staffed entirely by volunteer army reservists, and next weekend a couple of hundred members of Brian's field hospital will be getting together at the Royal Army Medical Corps' field training centre, up at Saighton Camp near Chester. The bulk of Brian's team come from the healthcare world – surgeons, doctors, nurses – and Brian will launch the weekend with a detailed brief for his twenty-five or so key players. The trick, he says, is to tailor 306's standard operational procedures to the special demands of the Fairford airshow. Level by level, these will translate into hands-on training exercises, and by Sunday night – fingers crossed – his little family of frontline medics will, in his phrase, have 'signed-on'.

The nightmare scenario at any airshow is the direct impact of an aircraft into the crowd. The UK's worst-ever disaster occurred back in 1952, when John Derry's DH110 crashed at Farnborough. Twenty-nine spectators were killed and sixty-three injured among a crowd of 120,000. Thirty years later, at Ramstein in West Germany, there was another hideous crash. This time three aircraft were involved in a mid-air collision, a trio of Aermacchi MB 339s from the Italian *Frecce Tricolori*. Seventy-four spectators were killed, with another 530 seriously injured. From Brian Robertson's point of view it's the latter statistic that truly concentrates the mind.

'If you look at the ratio of fatalities to the size of the crowd, it's almost exactly the same. If you want the figures, it's 0.02% of the total number present. But that's not the point. It's the rest, the injured, that matter. Fuel is the key. Avtur is so volatile. Put an exploding jet into a densely packed crowd and you've got a helluva burns problem.'

Brian beckons me forward to inspect the preliminary layout for Hangar 1205. The plane – or planes – have crashed. While the rapid intervention vehicles and foam tenders fight the conflagration, the injured and the dying are ferried across the runway to the east door of the Hangar 1205. A triage doctor makes an immediate decision on the seriousness of the injuries. The walking wounded are led to a treatment area on the right. The stretcher cases are carried to one of ten resus teams – a doctor, three nurses and an operating theatre technician – each occupying a cubicle on the left. Those in need of immediate surgery go to a fully equipped operating theatre where a senior consultant surgeon – a veteran of the Gulf War – will staunch bleeding, clear airways, and repair major wounds. The emphasis here, says Brian, is on stabilisation. The field hospital is merely one link in the evacuation chain, and the job of the medical teams is to prepare casualties for transfer to nearby NHS hospitals.

Brian fingers the diagram, following the arrows towards the west door and the waiting helicopters on the ramp outside. Every casualty will have a number. Their relatives and friends, flooding in for news, will be counselled by a welfare cell and a psychological support team. Padres are as important as surgeons, he reminds me. TLC as important as the waiting phials of morphine and adrenaline.

I'm trying to imagine this scene – a pall of smoke drifting across the airfield, the blare of the emergency two-tones, the crowds milling about beyond the runway, the chatter of the casevac helicopters preparing to lift off for hospitals in Swindon and Bristol, and God knows where else. Five hundred and thirty casualties, many of them critical, sounds an enormous challenge. Is Brian sure his team can cope?

Brian looks briefly troubled. Then he offers a vigorous nod. 'It's my job to think the unthinkable,' he says. 'It's not just aircraft. We've got car parks, tanks full of petrol, burger stands, LPG tanks. Anything can happen, in any combination. Air displays are implicitly dangerous. That's why people turn up. That's why they're so popular. I'm not saying they shouldn't happen, but I am saying we should be able to cope. From point zero, from the moment it happens, we're in a coping situation. And it's not just the injured, either.'

'It's not?'

'No.' He pauses, eyeing me. 'People will die, and the way they die – the way they're permitted to die – is equally important. My team knows that. They know about dignity, about the need to hold a hand, once it's obvious that someone has no chance.'

I nod. I'm thinking about the weekend's forthcoming exercise. Is this kind of terminal reassurance all part of the package? Is that something you can rehearse?

Brian shakes his head. 'Of course not,' he says. 'But we care very much, and it's important to say that.'

Sobered, I return to Fairford for an end-of-month update. Sue Allen's office now boasts a three-board wall display, colour-coded, keeping tags of the 1800 hotel rooms she's managed to pre-book for the visiting aircrew.

I browse through the T-cards. The American B-1B bomber crews have landed the plush De Vere in Swindon, while the Nimrod guys have been booked into the Goddard's Arms. Three Dutch fighter pilots riding F-16s are down for the Swindon Post House while Gail Halvorsen, the fabled Candy Bomber from the Berlin Airlift, is nicely tucked up in the Crown at Ampney Crucis.

With eight weeks to go, the white T-cards are already creeping across the three boards. This operation smacks of foresight and meticulous planning, but fighter pilots are rarely less than assertive – and Sue Allen has ten years' combat experience in coping with their endless lists of demands.

'The aerobatic teams are the worst,' she says ruefully. 'They expect the earth.'

She tells me about the *Frecce Tricolori*, the Italian national team. Last year, their manager opened negotiations about accommodation a full five months before the show, and his guideline brief ran to twenty pages. No hotel below a four-star classification. A gourmet restaurant within walking distance. A car for the squadron commander. Four more for the officers. Plus four minibuses with drivers for the technical support team. The list goes on and on.

'So how do you cope?'

Sue pulls a face. Experience and charm smooth out most of the wrinkles in her programme, and a budget of £78,000 for aircrew accommodation certainly helps. But it would be nice, none the less, if some of Fairford's more arrogant heroes occasionally had the grace to say thank you.

I'm looking at the latest Aircraft Participation list. From March onwards, Sue updates the list every three weeks. As of late May, RIAT is expecting upward of 400 aircraft, from thirty-eight participating air arms. The Ukrainian Falcons, sadly, are not coming, but in their place General Antonets is sending various pieces of Russian hardware including a Tu-22 *Backfire*. Rumours about the appearance of a Tu-160 *Blackjack* have sadly proved unfounded. The *Blackjack* is the most advanced of the Russian Cold War bombers, the Soviet equivalent of the American B-1B, but none of the *Blackjacks* operated by the Ukrainians are airworthy, thanks to a spares problem and a general lack of funds.

There's better news, though, from the Eastern Mediterranean. For the first time in years the Greeks and the Turks will be sharing ramp space. Mention of the Turks takes me back to November and our trawl through the foreign air attachés. Colonel Erdogan at the Turkish Belgrave Square embassy had been only too willing to send his beloved F-4 Phantoms. Has he now delivered?

Sue nods, consulting her list. 'We've got two,' she says, 'both for SkyWatch.'

'And is he still insisting on the arrester gear? The RHAG?'

Sue's eyes stray to her file of correspondence. 'That isn't clear,' she says. 'I think he may have forgotten.'

The phone rings. It's a pilot called Des Biggs. He flies a replica SE-5 out of Boscombe Down. The SE-5 is a vintage World War One biplane and features on Amanda's list as a prop for the Friday-night

RAF anniversary Gala Dinner in Hangar 1200. Des's problem is landing. The SE-5 has a wooden tail skid which hates tarmac. Touching down on the main runway is therefore out of the question. What he's after is a couple of hundred metres of grass plus a gang of engineers to shoulder the aircraft's tail while he's taxiing. The outfield at Fairford is pockmarked with rabbit holes, but Sue assures Des that a solution will be found. Maybe Eng Ops will mow him a special landing strip. Maybe Mel James will come up with some other bright idea. Either way, it'll all be sorted. See you in July. Take care.

Sue puts the phone down. She looks bewildered. 'He says the plane's got no brakes.' She frowns. 'How can that be?'

My end-of-month brief continues, department by department. Clive Elliott's just emerged from Renault with the promise of fifteen brand new Grand Espace people-movers, adding yet more freebie vehicles to his fleet of Jaguars, Daimlers and Mercedes saloons on loan from the Marshall Group. Renault are intrigued by the social mix that descends on Fairford, and view it as a welcome change from Formula One Grand Prix race meetings. Paul, scenting money, is determined to sell them a package of seats on the DC-4 charter, and in Clive's view their response is a foregone conclusion.

'Smoked salmon and champagne on that old bird?' He chortles. 'They'll love it.'

Back in Building 15, David Higham is monitoring the sales performance of his new-look catalogue, and the smile on his face tells me everything I want to know. His twelve-hour days at the Birmingham Spring Fair have paid off in spades. After a month and a half out in the marketplace, with seven weeks still in hand, he's already ahead of last year's sales figures. He's now two-thirds of the way towards meeting Paul Bowen's sales target, and he sees every prospect of going beyond that figure.

'Beats accountancy any day,' he says, tapping the catalogue page marked *Feel the Power*.

Heidi Standfast, meanwhile, is a blur between telephones. She's just organised the new RIAT website. It runs to forty-eight pages, and in the first week alone it's attracted 31,500 visits. Over four hundred and fifty of these web browsers stayed for more than seven minutes and read more than four pages. These figures mean absolutely nothing to me, but Heidi is wildly enthused.

'The web people say we've got a monster on our hands,' she says gleefully. 'Isn't that great?'

I nod, making a note. A monster. Sean Maffett used exactly the same expression, but in Heidi's little corner of the empire this phrase signals nothing but good news. She races on, telling me about the promotional programme (bigger than ever) and about her assistant Emma's success in acquiring twelve extra sites for high street banners. Those sites, multiplied by the period of time the banners are permitted to remain there, evidently result in forty-two additional 'hanging weeks'. This unit of measurement is a new one on me, but for Heidi it's yet another cause for celebration.

'Every extra hanging week means more footfall,' she says. 'And that, in the end, is what Paul's after.'

It's at this point that I realise just how intimately one bit of RIAT dovetails into the next. Paul and Tim dream up the entertainment. David Roome and Ian Sheeley make it happen. Sue Allen sorts out the aircraft. Mel James and John Thorpe keep them in one piece. While Heidi, eternally optimistic, gets out there and sells the event.

'It's building nicely,' she says. 'In fact it's better than ever.'

That same evening, local councillors arrive for a formal brief. Since the MiG crash, which could so easily have brought RIAT to an end, a great deal of time and energy has gone into a hearts-and-minds campaign to reassure this picturesque little corner of Gloucestershire that RIAT is the best of neighbours. In charge of the evening is Tim Cairns. He's sent invitations to more than seventy local figures, and the evening begins with coffee and soft drinks, with the promise of something more substantial after the briefing.

Sir Roger is on hand to chair the proceedings. He launches the brief with a passionate account of just how important a cause the RAF Benevolent Fund has become. It operates two residential homes of its own. With RAFA, it jointly runs two others. And it currently has a welfare spend of £14.4 million, a sum that has doubled over the last six years. As an introduction to RIAT 98, this is beautifully judged. The Air Tattoo is the biggest single event in the Benevolent Fund's portfolio of fundraising activities. Last year, it contributed over £400,000. This year, according to Sir Roger, this figure could climb even higher. 'Thank you for your support. Thank you for bearing with us. God Bless.'

Paul Bowen takes the stand. The sell is much softer than usual. There's still a flag to wave but he does it in slow motion, with none of his trademark gusto. When he outlines the special items on this year's display programme, the emphasis is on compassion and patriotism, on the Cold War's most vulnerable city saved, and on the world's oldest airforce honoured. Eighty veterans will be taking the salute. A hundred thousand voices will be singing 'Land of Hope and Glory.' The sun will beat down, pockets will empty, and the crowd's precious pennies will ensure the softest of landings for airmen in their twilight years.

The audience stir. These are decent country folk, middle-aged and older, tweedy, serious-minded, most of them veterans of countless earlier shows. There's no antagonism here, no digging in for peace and quiet, and their concern is mostly for the small print. They want to know about the traffic, and they want some modest assurance that the incoming hordes will leave their villages the way they found them. On both counts, Paul and his team play a blinder.

Traffic, Paul admits at once, is the real bugbear. Last year, to be frank, there were lessons to be learned. The heavily advertised appearance of the B-2 stealth bomber sucked in cars from every corner of the UK. There were queues on arrival and a nightmare at exit time. Some drivers were still stuck in traffic jams as darkness fell. This year, Paul promises, changes have been made. In response to heavy flak from a spectator called Roy Denning – who just happened to be a retired police Superintendent – a brand-new Exit Team has been appointed. They'll be taking over from the Admissions Team at 3 p.m. Their leader? Roy Denning.

There's a ripple of laughter. Paul rides the wave. At 6.30, another innovation: a two-hour concert hosted by Robin Boyle and featuring RAF bands. This, thinks Paul, will attract a sizeable audience and thus stagger departure times. I can see heads nodding. I can hear murmurs of approval. This is another master-stroke – not simply the staging of the concert, but the choice of Robin Boyle as compere. These people, one sense, are very Radio Two. Robin Boyle is reassurance personified.

The briefing goes on. How early-bird car parks will free up the incoming traffic flow. How residents stickers will give the locals priority over show traffic. How miles of chestnut fences will protect verges and keep pedestrians out of the road. How visiting pilots are being briefed to avoid over-flying sensitive areas. How the helpline especially welcomes suggestions from local people. And how the souvenir programme will, this year, include a special Cotswold promotion. This last curl of icing on the RIAT cake is, for Paul, almost subtle. Stick with us, goes the message. We're bringing in people. And they're bringing in money.

The meeting ends with two police officers fielding questions. One is from the Gloucestershire force, the other from Wiltshire, and they both control traffic operations. Predictably enough, the handful of questions all want clarification over this bottleneck or that. Will the Red overspill route be one way? What happens if the traffic backs up to the Crown at Crucis? Are there any plans to use the Latton bridge? The police officers – Chief Inspector Ian Jones and Chief Inspector Craig Mackey – quieten concerns with practised ease. These men have the same soft country accents as the audience. They know their patch. They care about the area. They'll be on hand to manage the situation, not play catch-up. The locals, once again, nod.

Before we break for drinks and a buffet supper, Tim Cairns's powerpoint presentation throws one last image on to the screen. It shows a handful of graduates from RIAT's flying scholarships for the disabled scheme. Every year, a handful of disabled students are flown to America and taught to fly. Back in 1985, when the scheme started, just six earned their wings. This year, the figure will be eighteen. We gaze at the beaming faces on the screen. The meeting has come full circle. All this noise, all this upset, all this anxiety, leads only to one outcome: other people's welfare.

Minutes later, over chicken chasseur and a glass of wine, I'm talking to a local schoolteacher called Tony Williams. Last year he was one of the team manning the admission gates. Mid-morning, he stooped to talk to a particularly flustered driver trapped in the long queue of arriving cars. The man didn't appear to have a ticket, and when Tony asked why he got even more upset.

'I only came out to go to Tesco's,' he complained. 'I hate bloody aeroplanes!'

At the very end of the month, another progress meeting. The weather is glorious and the small army of volunteer managers demolishes coffee and Danish in the sunshine before trooping into the base cinema for the formal brief. Last time, back in January, there was a great deal of laughter. Now, with barely seven weeks to go, the mood is altogether quieter.

The briefing lasts three and a half hours. Tim Cairns's projector supplies a bullet-point analysis as Paul and Tim address each item on the agenda. The sheer volume of detail is overwhelming: everything from Eurofighter and the Arrows' Vixen Break to new goldfoil blocks on the tickets to prevent home-computer fraud, from emergency procedures in the event of a disaster to the provision of jugglers and stilt-walkers to amuse the punters queueing for the loo.

My awareness of the vast scale of this event is sharpened by a series of references to the Jumbo screens. Already, in much smaller meetings, Paul has locked me into delivering the pictures. Now, he sketches the real challenge. The screen, he announces, will be on line from half past seven in the morning to half past eight at night. Thirteen daily hours of continuous live feed is a huge undertaking, and listening to Paul going through the menu of goodies I'm only too aware of how easy it is to become a volunteer.

The briefing over, I encounter Heidi out in the sunshine.

'I thought you were here to write a book,' she queries.

I nod. 'Me too,' I say glumly.

....

TEN

June 1998

By early June the pressure is on. Orders have gone out from site manager Catherine Iddon for fifty-one toilet units and 1500 patio chairs. Amanda Butcher is busy re-configuring the interior of Hangar 1200 – venue for the Gala Dinner – for the third time. And Sue Allen, at the very heart of Flight Operations, must spend this first weekend of the month putting together the masterplan that will sequence aircraft from every corner of the globe into a seamless flow of arrivals arrowing into Fairford.

These aircraft *are* the Royal International Air Tattoo. The first will be touching down on the Wednesday of show week. A trickle will become a flood. By dusk on Friday, weather permitting, the two-mile static display line, plus countless parking ramps, will be full to bursting.

While this extraordinary arrivals jigsaw is Sue's responsibility, she can call on specialised help from RIAT campaigners old and new. This will be Mike Sweeney's second year in charge of air traffic control during the show. In real life, he's one of Ian Sheeley's team in the radar set-up at nearby RAF Brize Norton, but today – as the bidding gets under way in Sue's office – it'll be his job to take the wider view as arrival slots are allocated to aircraft after aircraft. Guarding Brize's corner, he must somehow ensure that the Fairford carousel doesn't bring operations to a halt elsewhere. Both RAF Brize Norton and RAF Lyneham are only minutes away from Fairford, and both have busy schedules of their own to maintain.

The key word here is *deconfliction*. Airspace is finite, as is time. Already Sue has had a list of must-happen demands from Paul Bowen's office. The Thursday of show week is Press Day, while Friday sees the corporate chalets filling with hundreds of 'A'-list guests. It's Paul's job to make sure that both the journalists and the corporate big hitters get their money's worth in terms of live aircraft, and this – inevitably – will ring-fence big chunks of time.

Paul wants the press to see the Nimrods and the big VC10 rehearse their flypast. He wants the Tucanos in action. He's soppy about the beautiful old Constellation, and so that too must make an appearance. Then there's Lockheed Martin's new Hercules variant, the C-130J. RIAT has bagged the first one to display at a UK airshow, and so there's a rehearsal and demo flight to lever into Sue's schedule. Gulfstream Aerospace, too, have an aircraft they want to show off – the Gulfstream V – and as important show sponsors, they have a great deal of leverage.

The list goes on: the Israeli C-130 tactical take-off demo – a rocket strapped to the fuselage of a C-130; the arrival of the *Patrouille Suisse* and the Polish Air Force Aerobatic team; an ear-shattering display from the French Mirage; plus something from the SkyWatch programme and two hourly pleasure flights on Flippie Vermeulen's lustrous DC-4. Every one of these aircraft generates excitement, and excitement in turn generates both copy and a certain corporate buzz. Before Sue can timetable a single arrival, she must therefore bow to a year's worth of carefully brokered deals.

'It's a compromise,' she says diplomatically. 'Paul gets what he wants, the sponsors and the press boys are happy, and we spend the weekend fitting everyone else in.'

Today's session starts at nine. The computers are off-line for some software adjustments before next weekend's mammoth mail-out, and it's mid-morning before Iain Bell begins to type in the first of RIAT 98's allocated arrivals. As the senior air traffic controller at Boscombe Down, he's another of Sue's right-hand men. He's spent years dealing with fast-jet men, and the news that only sixty per cent of visiting aircrew have so far returned Sue's detailed questionnaire comes as no surprise. Their replies, neatly filed, specify preferred arrival and rehearsal times, and so these provide the first pieces in the weekend's jigsaw. Aircrew who have not so far been in touch will be allocated slots on the basis of availability and inspired guesswork.

Iain bends to his keyboard. Two Mirage F1s from Reims want to turn up on Friday at 14.00. One of Colonel Erdogan's Phantom RF-4s is flying in from his home base at Konya. His preference is for a Thursday touch-down at 12.00, and a Friday 10.00 rehearsal. Both flight plans get the thumbs-up from Mike Sweeney, and Ian Beadle – the fourth member of Sue's team – can likewise see no problems. Ian is an ex-RAF air traffic controller, now based at Bristol International Airport over at Lulsgate, but today he'll be double-checking each arrival slot against the ever-changing situation on the airfield, balancing arrival flows against marshalling pressures, doing his best to maintain a steady supply of aircraft to the parking ramps. The buzz word, once again, is deconfliction – anticipating choke-points in the air and on the ground, exposing Paul's wilder ambitions to the cold eye of experience.

The morning races past. From Wednesday to Friday, each daylight hour is divided into thirty two-minute slots. Two minutes is time enough to land a solo aircraft, or a formation pair, or an entire display team before eyes turn once again to the glide slope. With a schedule this tight, landing slots should be available in their hundreds – but as well as Paul Bowen's demands, there's also the question of rehearsals. Geoff Brindle's flying control committee is mandated to check out certain categories of display pilot – those from non-NATO countries, for instance – but other pilots themselves insist on the chance to get airborne in this unfamiliar setting before the show weekend begins. Rehearsal times vary from display to display. The big teams, like the *Patrouille de France*, need thirty minutes to run through their full programme, but the minimum slot-time for a solo rehearsal is never less than eight minutes. Multiply that by forty or so, and precious hours of airtime simply disappear.

I'm discussing this with Mike Sweeney. Slot allocation has come to a halt while Tim Prince appears with coffee and chocolate biscuits.

'It's not just the length of the rehearsals,' Mike points out, 'it's the way Paul likes to stack them back to back. Mid-afternoon on the

Friday is the favourite. The corporates have filled their guests with champagne and a huge lunch. Now they're all out in their deckchairs, wanting a piece of the action. So, naturally, we oblige.'

I smile at the memories. I was here last year on the Friday, and that's exactly what happened. Lunch was beef Wellington with an exceptionally smooth claret. My deckchair in the enclosure outside was in the front row. The sky was cloudless, the sun was hot, and the moment I lost touch with planet earth was the moment an American B-1B bomber pilot hit the re-heat button, just two hundred metres away, tearing the afternoon into shreds. It's a sound and a sight I'll never forget. The corporate sponsors must have been delighted. Isn't that what airshows are *for*?

Mike is a patient man. The problem with back-to-back rehearsals, he explains, is the sheer length of time they lock away. As a professional air traffic controller he knows only too well that pilots can be less than perfect. A P-3 Orion can stage up from New Zealand and take great pride in hitting the arrival slot bang on the nose, but the guy you have to plan for is the Tornado pilot winging over from Germany. He's ten minutes late getting airborne, he's dawdled en route, and by the time he's letting down for Fairford he's missed his slot. The airspace ahead is occupied by ten Aermacchis of the *Frecce Tricolori* rehearsing their display. After that, a couple of French Mirages. And after that, a Swedish SAAB Gripen. The Tornado, by now, is low on fuel and the flying programme has neglected to provide a window for stragglers like him.

'He diverts. He has to. He says he's an Su-27 out of Kiev, or a Hungarian MiG-29, and say he has to divert to a US air base. That's not a diplomatic incident any more, but there are still security implications, believe me – and that means phone calls and more phone calls and maybe a problem over fuel ... hassle we don't need.' He pauses, eyeing Sue's file. 'We can plan for the straggler in the Tornado by punching in little windows among the team rehearsals. That way, we can make sure he doesn't divert.'

After the last of the chocolate biscuits has gone, we resume. I'm no expert, but it seems to me that the available slots are disappearing fast. Iain Bell's computer screen is laddered with little strips of data.

At 0900 on Wednesday, a Harrier from 1 Squadron will be nosing into Fairford. Two minutes later, the sky will darken with the arrival of an eight-engined B-52, dropping down from one of the trans-Atlantic airways. All times are in Zulu – aviation speak for GMT. GMT, just now, happens to be one hour behind local time. More scope for confusion.

The thought falls on deaf ears. Sue's trying to find a berth for a German navy Tornado flying in on the Wednesday. He's routing out of his home base at Tarp, north of Hamburg, and he's looking for a slot around zero niner – Zed. In plain English, I think that means he wants to land around ten o'clock in the morning, local time.

Iain Bell half-turns from the computer. 'What about rehearsal?'

Sue consults her file. 'He's requesting 1450 Zulu. How would that be?'

Ian scrolls down. 1450 is free. 'How long does he want?'

'Eight minutes.'

'No problem.'

Beside me, Mike Sweeney stirs. There's a Falcons para-drop at RAF Brize Norton that same afternoon. Checks confirm that it's scheduled for 1450. The RAF parachute display team is rehearsing for a royal visit. The times are set in stone.

Sue looks anxious. 'Is that a problem?'

'Not at all. As long as he keeps his rehearsal within the five-mile radius, the para guys know exactly where he is. Putting arrivals through a para drop wouldn't be favourite.'

Iain returns to the keyboard, grinning. Seconds later, the German Tornado pilot has his precious rehearsal slot, 1446–1454. Confirmed.

The bids, and the negotiations, go on. A Spanish F-18 Hornet, shooting for the popular pre-lunch arrival slot. An Italian F-104 Starfighter with something very similar in mind. Healthy continental appetites, just waiting to get stuck in to all that yummy RIAT hospitality. Progress stalls for a minute or so over a Russian three-ship arrival. Sue hasn't a clue when they're due. With the Russians in particular, this appears to come as no surprise. They fly like angels but their interest in the small print is non-existent. This whole exercise – this entire weekend – is a bid to conjure order out of chaos. With 400-

plus aircraft converging on RAF Fairford, there's no other way. Yet the Russians, bless them, have a style of their own.

Meaning?

The men exchange glances, then Mike recalls a previous year. The Russians appeared on the Thursday with a pair of Su-27 interceptors, plus an Il-76 support plane. They, like everyone else, had two minutes to land and sort themselves out. Instead, they roared over at zero feet and flew three miles downwind before circling back. On the second pass, one Su-27 peeled off. On the third pass, the second. In all, they took ten minutes – or five landing slots – to get down, and the arrivals team spent the rest of the afternoon repairing the hole in their masterplan. It was, says Mike glumly, a nightmare.

I'm thinking about the big Su-27, sex with wings.

'So what did you do after they'd landed?'

'We bollocked them.'

'And?'

'They claimed they didn't speak English.'

'Was that true?'

'Of course not.' He offers me a rueful grin. 'Their English was bloody wonderful.'

Three days later I'm back at the RAF Club in Piccadilly for a meeting about feeding Paul's treasured Jumbotron screen with pictures. On this occasion, and I suspect on many more, my role has become a little blurred. Not simply the dispassionate observer lurking in the shadows, but an active volunteer, as harassed by pressure and deadlines as everybody else.

The broadcast and video coverage of the show is a dog's breakfast. Since our visit to Birmingham to see Central's Laurie Upshon back in January, the broadcast rights to the RIAT weekend have bounced around from bidder to bidder. Double Exposure wanted to make a six-part fly-on-the-wall series. Sir Roger turned them down. Peter Hylton-Cleaver, on behalf of the BBC, expressed a strong interest. Nothing materialised. Finally, with a bare month and a half to go, Paul Bowen has contacted Central again. His waking nightmare is to end up with no television coverage at all. Paul has therefore resumed negotiations with Laurie Upshon. Laurie's production budget comes out at £24,000. If he can split this with HTV and an outfit called Onyx, then he's happy to turn up.

HTV is the ITV contractor for Wales and the west of England. They have a long-standing interest in RIAT, and have produced memorable coverage. Onyx is a small Farnham-based production company specialising in aviation-related events. Headed by Jonathan McNicholas, Onyx has been responsible for a successful series of show videos, and over the years the Benevolent Fund have done very nicely from retail sales.

Jonathan is one of the players at today's meeting. He's still smarting from the small print of the deal that Paul Bowen has stitched up with Laurie Upshon. For a five-figure sum he's bought the video rights to the show. In addition to this, he must now pay an extra whack to Central for access to their rushes. 'Rushes' is media-speak for the pictures that Central cameramen gather at Fairford. Last year, these pictures supplied a hefty percentage of Jonathan's show video.

This facilities and budget split is complex enough, but the Jumbo-screen operation adds to the tangle. It works like this. To feed the Jumboscreen, I need access to pictures. Live, they can only come from cameras, and my minimum bid is three. Two of these will be on tripods on a scaffolding tower in front of the Control Tower. One will give me a wide shot of the flying display. The other, with a 50:1 lens, will take the punters into the heart of the action. In addition to this grandstand coverage I need a roaming camera on the other side of the runway. For important items like the Berlin Airlift, this will give me hand-held close-ups of the unloading sequences, planned for the ramp on the other side of the runway. Elsewhere in the eight-hour display, this same camera will offer me other excitements to spice the pictures on the Jumboscreen: ground crews strapping in pilots, minutes ahead of their displays; aerobatic teams – like the *Patrouille de France* – wheeling on to the taxiways; returning aircraft powering down after eight minutes of raw excitement, our camera closing on the pilot as he opens his canopy and clambers out.

I've already had a preliminary meeting with Jonathan – a snatched coffee the previous Sunday morning – and we quickly arrived at a meeting of minds. To make best use of the screen, we need to link back these pictures live to our outside broadcast control room (or 'scanner'). Intermixed with archival coverage of the Airlift itself – black-and-white footage of DC-3s ghosting into Gatow and Tempelhof – this will gladden the hearts of watching spectators for whom the ground components of Paul's Berlin Airlift will be nothing more than a series of specks across the runway.

Jonathan has already quoted me a price for the facilities we need to feed the screen. £25,000 is coming from Raytheon to sponsor the Jumbotron, but this is small change in the voracious world of outside broadcasts and Jonathan has done well to shoehorn our production requirements into the Raytheon budget. Alas, it now turns out that his quote isn't quite the miracle it seemed. For one thing, we'll have to share two of Central's cameras. And for another, it doesn't include provision for a microwave link to feed pictures from our precious roaming camera.

'Who's spoken to Central about sharing cameras?'

'No one.'

'What happens if they say no?'

There's the beginnings of a silence. Then Jonathan points out that we all, surely, have an interest in pooling our resources. He's right, of course – but Central's coverage is likely to be in the hands of a producer called Graeme Bowd, and he and Jonathan are keen commercial rivals.

We agree that I'll talk to Graeme about sharing cameras. More important just now is the sudden absence of live pictures from the other side of the runway.

'That's crazy,' I announce. 'Without the link we're dead. That's why we got the screen in the first place. We're there to supply the close-ups, the stuff that people can't possibly see for themselves. Otherwise, there's no point.'

Jonathan is looking bewildered. A live link will have dramatic budgetary consequences. He was rather thinking in terms of pre-recorded material.

Tony Webb is chairing the meeting. 'When would you record this stuff?'

'Over the rehearsal days.'

'How does that work?'

'We shoot the pictures Graham wants on the Friday. Pre-cut them. Pump it out on the day.'

'What about the weather?'

'You'll never spot the difference.'

Jonathan is looking to me for confirmation. I nod. He's right. With a good cameraman, Friday's pre-recorded sequences should exactly match Saturday's live coverage.

Sean Maffett, hot off the train from Bourton-on-the-Water, shakes his head. It's about the Berlin display. Tony spots him at once.

'Problem?'

'Yes.'

'What?'

'There isn't a rehearsal.'

We go back to the provision of a live link. As well as the money, there may well be technical glitches. The airfield is buzzing with radar and other high-frequency emissions. These can cause havoc with the pictures. The receiving dish will have to be elevated – a potential no-no with the air traffic control people. I'm thinking hard about Jonathan's preference for pre-recording. Peddling old pictures as new is, of course, a cheat, but in production terms it gets us around a lot of problems. As we speak, Sue Allen is printing out her minute-by-minute masterplan for Wednesday, Thursday and Friday. By the end of the week, I'll be in a position to hand Jonathan a list of rehearsal sequences we'll be needing. He'll shoot them, edit them, package them, and hand them back to me on nicely labelled BETA cassettes. No chance of link breakdowns. No chance of our roving camera not making it to the next location in time. Everything, in short, glitch-proof.

I table my little suggestion. Tony Webb reminds me again that there's no rehearsal for the Berlin Airlift, and therefore no pictures. In best RIAT style, I busk it. We'll talk to Paul. We'll sort something out for Press Day. A single DC-3 and a couple of old lorries will give us everything we'll need.

Beside me, Jonathan McNicholas is grinning. 'No call for the link, then?' he says.

The meeting ends a couple of hours later. We've sorted out potential clashes between the Jumbotron screen and Sean Maffett's commentary. At the suggestion of his audio producer, Jonathan Ruffle, we've agreed that there's no point in moving the Jumbotron at 1730 to the concert venue. Paul thinks that adding the screen to the two-hour concert will pull a bigger crowd – thus staggering the rush for the exits – but the logistics are formidable, and in any case the screen should attract a fair few people where it is.

Another talking point has been the downlinking of pictures from the surveillance and recce aircraft in the SkyWatch segment of the show. Paul has been promising these pictures on the Jumbotron, but the technical problems are formidable and the RAF's best brains have yet to come up with a cost-effective answer. At the very least, though, we seem to have access to a police helicopter, and the video camera slung beneath should give us an ample feed of pictures for the screen. With luck, the punters should be able to wave to themselves. Another RIAT first.

The meeting ends at 1.30. We retreat to a pub round the corner to staunch the deeper wounds. With Jonathan McNicholas and his producer, Colin Webb, I talk about telly, and film scripts, and the associated debris of twenty years at the coalface. We drink lots of beer. At around half past four, only Sean, Tony Webb and myself are still there, and we've got to the stage where these two old campaigners are marvelling at the damage that RIAT inflicts. Every year, Sean and Tony agree, the thing gets bigger and more impossible. And every year the determination to call it a day becomes that more irresistible. After three brutal hours, I concede that they have a point. Deadlines are needlessly tight. Stuff should have been sorted out months ago.

Sean sighs. 'But that's their talent,' he says. 'First they break you. Then you come back for more.'

It's a wonderful image, the long file of heavily-bandaged volunteers, cresting the hill, limping back for yet another pounding. Masking a smile, I get uncertainly to my feet.

'Another pint, then?' I enquire.

Next morning, with some difficulty, I'm up at eight. Minutes later, the phone rings. It's Tony Webb.

'I've been talking to Paul,' he says, 'about laying hands on a DC-3 for press day.'

'And?'

'It's totally out of the question.'

Our discomforts on the media front are overtaken by the howl of turboprops. The second week of June sees the arrival of a delegation from the Swedish Air Force, aboard a pretty little SAAB 340. The Swedes have come over to check out arrangements for the show. They're contributing an S100B – an airborne radar aircraft – and three Gripen fighters. The latter belong to the new breed of composite high-tech interceptors. Sales prospects are extremely bright and the marketing push is being heavily supported by British Aerospace, who are of course already underwriting key elements of the show.

The SAAB 340 settles daintily on Fairford's 10,000ft runway, and for the first time in months the scent of Avtur drifts across Fairford's empty green spaces. Mel James is hosting this visit, and he pumps the Colonel's hand. The Swedes, for reasons best known to themselves, have insisted on re-designating aircraft recognised by common names elsewhere. They call the C-130 Hercules the Tp-84. The Puma helicopter has become the Hkp-9. The colonel's name is Jan Wahlgren, and in the spirit of re-designation I suggest we call him Nils Smut-tenkopf – but Mel doesn't think this is a good idea at all.

The Swedes, in their smart, dark-blue uniforms, file into the staff dining room for the inevitable meeting. The party includes a tense-looking security officer who has ruled that during show week the Swedes themselves shall tuck up their aircraft every night, mounting a guard until dawn. Mel thinks this is a bit over the top, and the debate is settled when he mentions the dogs. Alsatians roam the static line at night. The Swedes are welcome to throw a home-grown picket around their precious Gripens, but fending off the dogs will be strictly their responsibility.

Before returning to Satenas, the Swedes descend on the American BX for their helping of duty-frees, leaving Mel to cope with another series of phone-calls. The parking plan, every bit as complex and important as Sue Allen's arrivals jigsaw, is beginning to take shape.

Umpteen factors govern which space each aircraft shall occupy, but whenever possible Mel tries to accommodate what he delicately terms 'special requests'.

One such bid has come in from the Movements squadron of the Royal Auxiliary Air Force. They're keen to lay hands on one of the giant Boeing C-17 Globemaster III transport aircraft. Their exhibition has been sited next to the control tower, and the 'Movers' want to show off their loading skills with a variety of heavy kit. In principle Mel has no problem with this, but warns them that he must, at all costs, keep the aircraft's weight down. If the crew over-fuel the beast, the C-17 will sink into the tarmac. If the movements people get ideas about loading, say, a bulldozer, then the aircraft will tip up on its tail. The parking ramp is close to the corporate hospitality tents.

'Boeing would love that,' Mel says drily. 'Their precious Globemaster up on its arse.'

Elsewhere in Building 15, a small crisis is rapidly brewing into something more serious.

Communications over the week of the show are all-important, and the hard-wired network that Telephones Manager Capt Dave Frayley and his volunteer team from 37 Signals Regt (V) are already installing will become RIAT's nervous system. Without reliable comms, the command and control structure will be under threat. Decisions will slow. At the worst, should the system fall over completely, the organisation will be paralysed.

Two years ago, permission from the Americans to use a brand-new fibre-optic cable buried beneath the runway gave Dave an enormous boost to his comms capacity. To his delight, he was able to route comms traffic between the north and south side of the airfield, and thanks to a windfall piece of kit from the MoD, messages and data flowed back and forth. For once, the hard-pressed telephones manager was spoiled for equipment.

This year, anticipating the same set-up, Dave has discovered that the fibre-optic cable no longer works. No one knows why but it's now down to Dave and Lesley O'Brien – Tim Prince's personal assistant –

to troubleshoot their way out of it. Dave has a full-time job with Cellnet. That leaves Lesley.

When I finally pin Lesley down, she's close to despair. Locating the fault in this hi-tech network requires not only a degree in electronics but a talent for diplomacy that would, under different circumstances, lead straight to a job with the UN. In order to move forward at all, she has to sweet-talk and co-ordinate five separate agencies – RIAT itself, the US Air Force, British Telecom, an obscure troop of signals experts with the army at Bulford Camp, plus representatives from a company called Mitel who manufacture the vital ancillary equipment that allows Dave Frayley to make maximum use of the fibre-optic cable. None of these agencies is keen to take individual responsibility, and talking to anyone about the inner secrets of the USAF's comms set-up is complicated by a fog of security restrictions.

I make as much sense of all this as my feeble brain permits. One question keeps nagging at me. 'So what happens if you can't get the cable working?' I ask at last.

Lesley pales at the thought. It will, she says, be a disaster. Six months' comms work wasted. Huge expense in replacement BT circuits. All kinds of promises under threat.

She shakes her head, trying to dismiss it all. 'We have to find the answer,' she says. 'There's no other way.'

The Swedes have gone by five o'clock. Fifteen hours later a squadron of supersonic B-1B swing-wing bombers joins the circuit after a trans-Atlantic crossing from their base in Texas. Together with half a dozen B-52s, they're here to take part in a two-week NATO exercise. Quite whom the bomber crews will be rehearsing to fight isn't immediately clear, but week one of the scenario calls for the B-52s to practise mine-laying in the Baltic Sea so a wild guess might suggest that Russia's recent conversion to capitalism is less secure than we assumed. Either that or the White House is having second thoughts about Swedish neutrality.

I stand in the car park outside Building 15, watching the incoming B-1Bs. Their wings are extended for maximum lift, and as they bank on to base leg over the distant smudge of Kempsford, I'm suddenly back in the boiling heat of last July, the Gloucestershire sky alive with sinister black silhouettes like these. The B-1B bomber is the one aircraft that can raise Catherine Iddon's blood pressure – I remember her talking about it with a strange, almost feral expression on her face – and I listen for the tell-tale change in the engine note as the lead aircraft slips in, settling nose-high on the tarmac.

After the pilot chops the throttles I brace for the roar of reverse thrust, but the B-1B disappears behind a nearby hangar with scarcely a whisper. I'm still wondering quite what will bring 110 tons of heavy bomber to a halt when I'm joined by Mel James. The B-1B, he informs me, has neither reverse thrust nor a drag parachute.

I'm watching the rest of the squadron nosing down the glideslope. 'How do they stop, then?' I ask him.

Mel says nothing for a moment. Little puffs of blue smoke signal the second touchdown. 'Rockwell came up with this marvellous system,' he says at last. 'They call them brakes.'

The B-52 crews – already landed – are due to be briefed at eight o'clock the following morning, and a call from Tim Prince to the USAF airfield manager secures me an invitation. I report, as instructed, at 07.45. The briefing room lies deep in a complex of buildings at the very heart of the base, and by the time I arrive the bomber crews are already wandering in.

This, at last, is the real thing. No more meetings about the revamped gift catalogue and the tribulations of on-site sanitation. No more wrestling with the small print of Heidi Standfast's marketing plan. These are the guys at the sharp end. By noon, they'll be airborne, thundering north in their B-52s for a brief familiarisation recce over Scotland. Already, the scene has the feel of one of those wonderful World War Two movies. The accents and the setting are perfect. Move over David Higham. Cue Jimmy Stewart.

The B-52 is one of the oldest aircraft in the USAF inventory. The eight-engined strategic bomber was America's biggest stick in the Sixties and Seventies, dropping millions of tons of high explosive into the jungles of Vietnam. Twenty years later, from here at Fairford, eight of them flew bombing missions to Iraq throughout the three weeks of Desert Storm, but at a bare 390 knots, each sortie took seventeen hours to complete. With a mixture of what I take to be patience and pride, the crews call the B-52s 'BUFF's. BUFF stands for Big Ugly Fat Fella. Or something very similar.

I find myself a seat at the back of the briefing room, watching the swirl of aircrew. The men are wearing olive green one-piece flying suits, with rows of silver pens tucked into the little pockets stitched on to the suits' upper arms, and most of them are sucking coffee from huge polystyrene cups. The briefing will feature a power-point presentation and the curtains have been pulled against the morning sun yet many of these men are wearing aviator sunglasses. Quite how they'll ever see the screen defeats me. But they have an indefinable ease – with themselves and with each other – and while they wait for the briefer to begin they josh about the flight over.

One of the base personnel asks whether they had any problems getting in yesterday. The weather has been stormy all week, a series of ever-deepening frontal troughs sweeping in from the Atlantic. A pilot lounging against the desk beside the podium shakes his head.

'Nope,' he says. 'Bit sporty maybe, but nothing heavy.'

'I thought it was a crosswind?'

'You're right,' he grins. 'It was.'

The thought of landing a B-52 in a crosswind defies imagination. The huge wings, heavy with fuel and underslung jet engines, flap in the slightest breeze. Are these guys real? Is 'sporty' American for 'suicidal'?

The room is full. Every B-52 has a crew of six. I count thirty-six heads. The briefer calls for attention. Dominating the room is a pull-down map of Europe. The UK, on the far left, looks curiously adrift, while the continental mainland is almost invisible beneath multi-coloured blocks of airspace. Each colour designates a long list of flying restrictions. Negotiating your way anywhere is clearly going to be a nightmare.

The briefer peers at the rows of watching faces. I can smell the minty tang of newly-chewed gum.

'OK, guys, listen up. We go to the power-point in a moment. This is like an overview.' He gestures over his shoulder at the map. 'Don't fly over anything pink, white, green or blue.'

A voice calls from the half-darkness.

'Gee, you're serious?'

'Sure. You see that big bunch of pink? That's pretty much Germany.'

'Russia?'

'Russia's yellow.'

'That's a go, then?'

'Sure.'

There's a ripple of laughter. I'm not quite sure whether the briefer's joking or not. He returns to the podium as the lights dip.

'Welcome to Fairford,' he growls.

With the aid of the images on the screen, he quickly details the airfield. The runway measures out at 10,000 ft. It's three per cent uphill to the west, part porous asphalt, part concrete. This seems to me to be a pretty arcane distinction, but for each of these dry, technical asides there's a pay-off.

'So no one-eighties on the asphalt, guys. You wanna turn around, you use the concrete hammerheads. Otherwise, it's tow-time.'

The hammerheads are the big turning bays at the end of the taxiways. Burden the asphalt with 180 tons of B-52 in a tight turn and you're courting disaster.

The briefing goes on: radio frequencies, lighting patterns, the tricky little dips and hummocks in the airfield where even a B-52 can disappear from sight ... I'm scribbling furiously in the darkness. Throughout the winter and spring RAF Fairford has been a series of maps on office walls. Now, in this over-heated briefing room, the place is at last coming alive.

The briefer is talking about local glider activity. To the west, he lists half a dozen disused grass airstrips where the soaring fraternity gather. Next week, guess what, there's to be a major competition. The BUFF crews should expect hundreds of gliders. Everywhere.

'These guys lurk under major cumulus,' he warns. 'So you heavy drivers keep those heads swivelling.' He punches up a map on the screen. Sure enough, a semi-circle of gliding sites lies in wait for the newly-launched B-52s. From the left, in the darkness, comes a muttered exclamation, very soft: 'Jesus.'

I'm trying to imagine the sight of a flock of gliders from the cockpit of a B-52, climbing under full power. Even more terrifying is the glider pilot's view. B-52s like to fly in threes. A trio of BUFFS could seriously jeopardise your day.

'Bird strikes,' the briefer announces. 'The birds around here aren't used to loud aeroplanes. That's because the field's mainly out of use. So the good news is that, week one at least, you get a freebie. They'll scatter. They'll dive. One way or another, they'll get out of your way.' He pauses to blow his nose, then resumes. 'The bad news is the lakes to the west. We got twenty Canada geese out there. You hit one of those guys, believe me, they'll get your attention. Any questions?'

In the silence that follows, he hands over to Mike Sweeney, the RAF air traffic controller from Brize Norton who's just donated half his weekend to Sue Allen's arrival plan. His role this morning is to brief on local air traffic control procedures. I suspect he's really here to offer comfort, but there's simply no way of unpicking the tangle that is UK airspace. The first of Mike's images flickers on the screen. A lattice of air corridors covers most of the UK. Unrestricted airspace is coloured green, and there's precious little of it.

Mike zips through his presentation. His tone is defiantly upbeat. He talks about minimum separation and absolute no-go areas. He warns the crews about the savagery of the West Drayton civvie controllers, guarding the London Terminal Manoeuvring Area. He promises to tell them about conflicting traffic, offering them vectors around impending hazards. And he counsels extreme caution at all times.

A barrel-chested major gets to his feet and reinforces the message. 'OK, guys, best behaviour. No showboating. No short-cuts. No dirty dives to get into the Daventry Corridor. There's way, way too much civilian traffic for any of that horseshit.'

He looks out at the shadowed faces, expecting reaction, but there isn't any. These men are from the USAF Reserve. They operate out of a base at Barksdale, Louisiana, on a part-time basis, and most of their working lives are spent flying big, fat, comfortable 747s with the airlines, doodling tracks across the empty reaches of the mid-West and the Pacific Ocean. European skies, by contrast, are hopelessly crowded, column after column of restricted airspace over major cities and airports, endless lists of mandatory do's and don'ts, the entire muddle parcelled with ribbons of tightly controlled civilian airways. For these fliers, the nightmare is something called a Filed Airspace Violation, the blackest of black marks. Beyond that lies a near-miss, and beyond that, a mid-air collision.

At last, someone stirs. 'Can we go ahead and just type that apology letter now, sir?'

The laughter swells, then dies away. The major isn't smiling.

'No problem,' he says. 'But you guys get the message: just because you're all out there, don't think a man and a dog ain't out there too.'

The voice pipes up again.

'Sure, sir. Trouble is, he's faster than us.'

The following day, a Saturday, Fairford staffers flock into Building 15 for the annual mail-out. This, an entirely typical piece of RIAT folklore, boils down to eight hours of intensive envelope-stuffing.

Out there, the length and breadth of the UK, are thousands of volunteers awaiting their orders. In various corners of Buildings 15 and 16 lie piles and piles of the various bits of paper they'll need to sign on, bed down, and do their jobs. The Staff Handbook. The Security Op Order. The Emergency Op Order. The Air Op Order. The Admissions and Exits Op Order. The Evacuation and Search Op Order. The Exhibitors, Contractors and Traders Handbook. Plus a wealth of special-offer leaflets, complimentary tickets, and the all-important reporting T-card. Everything colour-coded. Everything specially bound. Getting hundreds of pages of detailed brief to the small army of volunteers is a job that would occupy the Fairford post room for the best part of a month. Why not lure in the entire staff and turn it into a game?

The hook is baited with iced buns, lollies, teas, coffees, and endless other goodies. Trestle tables piled high with briefs line the main central corridor. The staff divides into three teams, a whistle blows, and off they go. By lunchtime, the first 1400 envelopes are ready for posting. By half past five Tim Prince's team – heavily fancied – have scored another famous victory.

The total postage bill is close to £3000. It takes three vans to cart the envelopes and jiffy bags away. But the Mail-Out is over for another year. And the show weekend suddenly seems a great deal closer.

*

Two days later, I brace myself for another assault on the media tangle. Last week's get-together at the RAF Club with Sean Maffett and Jonathan McNicholas of Onyx resulted in a stand-off on the critical issue of whether or not we could feed live pictures from the other side of the airfield for our voracious Jumbotron screen. Jonathan thought it was impossible within the price. I was persuaded that pre-recording a rehearsal would be an effective solution. Then Tony Webb talked to Paul Bowen and announced that a rehearsal of the all-important Berlin Airlift was a non-starter.

In six busy days since then, both Jonathan and the Central TV producer, Graeme Bowd, have come up with new initiatives. Graeme is happy to offer us the microwave link we'd need to send the live pictures. Delighted with this news, I've invited him to tender for the whole operation. A call to Jonathan to tell him this has prompted a rapid re-think on his part. Maybe, after all, a live link might be possible. He'll talk to some contacts, call in the odd favour or two. Then we'll have another of those nice meetings.

The chemistry of RIAT can be volatile. Event management attracts some powerful personalities and Graeme and Jonathan are two of them. Graeme is a successful freelance producer, specialising in aviation. Jonathan has a substantial track record in exactly the same field. I know neither of them well, but I suspect that they rarely swap Christmas cards.

One of the less helpful consequences of this year's contractual split on the media and video rights to the show is that everything depends on these two characters working together. Without a big fee from Jonathan, Central won't mount their programme. Without a good deal of hands-on control, Jonathan won't part with the fee. The word on the street suggests that Graeme isn't in the business of ceding control.

This impasse seems to me to be the prelude for disaster – no broadcast coverage, no video, no Big Screen – but on the phone during the week Sean Maffett has counselled patience. It is, he suggests rather drily, an entirely typical piece of RIAT business: a mix of good intentions, bullheadedness, on/off negotiation, plus the wildly optimistic assumption that everything will work itself out on the day. I'm not so sure. I've been fielding phone calls all week from various players in this tangled sub-plot and I can see precious little room for manoeuvre. Sean, once again, suggests a couple of deep breaths. That the meeting is important is beyond dispute. He even decides to attend it himself, despite a crowded diary. Nice man.

We convene at Tony Webb's house in Kingsclere. England's first World Cup game, against Tunisia, kicks off at half past one. We therefore have three and a half hours to hammer out a solution.

Tony Webb, as chairman, outlines progress to date. Alas, it's one of his shorter speeches. Graeme then tables his bid. For a modest five-figure sum he can give us everything we want in terms of live coverage: three cameras cabled to the outside broadcast scanner, a prowling camera on the north side of the airfield pumping back live pictures of the aircraft, even the possibility of a fifth live camera, way out on the upwind threshold of the runway. These pictures, plus recorded archival material played in from a video recorder, will look a treat on the Jumbotron screen, and I say as much.

Jonathan, who's obviously seen this coming, trumps Graeme with a new offer of his own. Cabled cameras, linked cameras, plus editing, plus access to his own ample archive of coverage of previous shows. Tony Webb and I exchange glances. Our precious production budget is suddenly buying us rather more than we thought.

While Colin Webb, Jonathan's producer, and Gary Bates, Graeme's technical supervisor, bury themselves in talk of gigabytes and mega-hertz, Tony and I ponder the rival bids. There are two bottom lines here. One is the importance of Jonathan's video, sales of which generate a lot of money for the Benevolent Fund. The other is Central's TV coverage, which gives the show a great deal of profile. Losing either will be unacceptable, but I suspect that Central hold the whip hand. Much of the equipment on Graeme's list belongs to them. They use it every day. They rely on it. Ditto the personnel he intends to use. If the bids are roughly equal, and Jonathan gets the RIAT nod, are Central really going to trust part of their operation to equipment and personnel they don't know.

It's at this point, around noon, that Jonathan asks for a private word in the kitchen. Talk of another pot of coffee fools nobody. These have become hardball, to-the-wire, proxy negotiations with Tony Webb and I holding the ring. First Bosnia, now Fairford.

Jonathan is an angry man. An hour or so before England kick off against Tunisia he sees his own game slipping away. He goes through his new tender again. When we refuse to commit, he plays his trump card.

'The way I see it, they're taking control,' he says. 'If you go with Central, we're left with nothing.'

We try and reassure him. They'll come up with great pictures. Those pictures will be his as well as ours. We'll all be pulling in the same direction. It doesn't work.

'There's no point,' he says.

'No point in what?'

'In me giving them the dosh they want.'

'You mean you'll withdraw it?'

'Yes.'

'But then they'll pull out.'

'Exactly.'

The kettle's boiling. Tony scalds the Colombian roast. We plod back to the chill of the conservatory. I'm hopeless at confrontations except when the circumstances truly demand it.

'OK,' I say, 'this is where we are.'

I outline the impasse. Tony picks up the running. Jonathan is investing oodles in this thing – five figures to the Benevolent Fund, the rest to Central. Understandably, as the client, he's feeling aggrieved.

There's a silence. I reach for the coffee pot. Then Graeme, to my astonishment, turns to Jonathan.

'So how can we help you?' he enquires. 'What do you need?'

Jonathan's list is surprisingly modest. It boils down to a roving camera under his control, plus first dip at the rushes and editing facilities over the weekend. This isn't the solution that he'd like, but he's prepared to live with it. I pour the coffee. Tony is volunteering a guarded smile. From the jaws of disaster, a kind of victory.

An hour or so later, Alan Shearer rises from a ruck of Tunisian shirts and gets his head to a delightful Graham Le Saux cross. As we

all celebrate England's first goal, I feel a touch on my arm. It's Sean.
He's been thinking about the morning's work, out in the conservatory,
and he too is grinning.

'Who'd have thought it?' he says. 'A result.'

The following Thursday, for the second time this year, Geoff Brindle
flies in from Oman to chair a meeting of the Flying Control Committee.
By now, Enterprises' modest accommodation is filling to bursting point.
Twelve young holding officers have arrived – neat, eager young pilots,
navigators, and secretarial officers seconded by the RAF for the six
weeks leading up to and including the show weekend. There are also
a number of new faces on short-term contracts. These extra bodies,
vital if the Fairford juggernaut is to stay on the road, have obliged
Geoff Brindle and his men to find another venue for their meeting.

We convene in a remote conference room, borrowed from the
Americans. There are places for eleven around the long table. Rather
garish colour photos of the B-1B bomber and the Lockheed SR-71
Blackbird hang from the walls.

Tim Prince opens the proceedings.

There are faces here that I don't recognise from our last get-
together, back in February. Air Commodore Rick Peacock-Edwards is
Geoff's deputy chairman. Like Geoff, he launched his operational
career at the controls of a Lightning. Later he converted on to
Phantoms, before soaring through the ranks to a number of impressive-
sounding staff jobs. The Gulf War gave him detachment command at
Dhahran, and seven years later he still remains current on the Tornado
F3.

Ken Robertson, across the table, is another pilot with immense
hands-on experience. He spent four years at Boscombe Down, test-
flying helicopters, Harriers, and oodles of fixed-wing aircraft before
serving Rolls-Royce as Chief Test Pilot. Beside him sits Chris Yeo.
Slim, shirtsleeved, watchful, Chris has recently left British Aerospace
after a number of years directing and piloting Eurofighter through its
development programme. Of all the aviators around this table Chris
is probably the youngest, but he has a steadiness of gaze and a knack
for shaping the killer question that I, for one, find slightly unsettling.

The collective experience of the men around this table is awesome. Between them I count two CBEs, four AFCs, two OBEs and God knows how many thousands of flying hours. Their job over the next six weeks is to ensure that Ian Sheeley's flying programme, and David Roome's specials, remain as safe and glitch-proof as airmanship, prudence and good sense permit. They're not here to hose down Paul Bowen's wilder fantasies. On the contrary, their commitment to the airshow as a source of entertainment is as total as any of the fast-jet men on Ian Sheeley's event-schedule. But they understand the limits of the possible, and they serve as a kind of earthwork between 100,000 spectators and the ever-present possibility of disaster. Should anything go wrong in the air, their invitations to the board of inquiry will be in the post.

Tim Prince is outlining the latest developments in the run-up to the '98 spectacular. As ever, RIAT is a moving target, and Tim's quiet optimism is infectious. The Americans are promising a couple of U-2 spy planes for SkyWatch. The big sponsors are weighing in with pledges extending beyond 2000. The World Cup has caused a temporary blip in ticket sales but the USAF may be helping out with a couple of F-117 Nighthawks – stealth aircraft – and the sales curve is already climbing again.

Tim hands over to Ian Sheeley, ringmaster for the flying display over the two public days of the show. He begins to detail each item in the eight-hour programme, and pretty soon we've got to the first of David Roome's specials. This is going to be interesting. I've been following the steady evolution of David's two set-pieces – Berlin and the RAF eightieth – since Paul Bowen tabled his initial thoughts back before Christmas. The story so far has, to me at least, been a triumph of airmanship, self-confidence and meticulous planning. Everyone acknowledges that David has done a fine job, turning Paul's instinctive need for something different into the overriding requirement for something flyable. The Berlin tribute, scored for piston engines and warm gusts of nostalgia, will be a treat for those with long memories. The RAF eightieth pageant, now running no less than two hours forty-one minutes, will be exploring new corners in the air display envelope. So far, so good. But now comes the moment when David's choreography must submit itself to intense scrutiny. Group Captain Roome is here to sit a kind of examination. Will his specials work? And will they, above all else, be safe?

First comes the simpler of the two tributes. David runs briskly through his masterplan. Sue Allen has been unable to find a replacement for the no-show Air Atlantique DC-3, and so David has adjusted his timings for eleven aircraft, rather than twelve. They roll at seventy-five-second intervals, climbing to 1000ft before commencing a timed radar circuit. Back they come, six landing and the seventh overshooting, while numbers eight to eleven – DC-3, DC-4, Lancaster and Constellation – thrill the crowd with individual displays. The singleton DC-3 will be coming from the Battle of Britain Memorial Flight.

The hot news from Sean Maffett is that Squadron Leader Paul Day, the BBMF Flight CO, has profound doubts about the whole thing, but David Roome doesn't appear to be aware of this and his presentation, as always, is seamless.

The silence after he's finished is broken by Geoff Brindle. 'What happens if another aircraft drops out?'

'Every pilot has his own copy of the brief, and his own timings.'

'You'll leave a gap?'

'Absolutely.'

Les Garside-Beattie, in charge of the Harrier operations wing at RAF Wittering, is still studying David's masterplan. 'What about pilot's individual limits – weather-wise, for instance?'

'They'll be at 1000ft downwind. If it's flyable, they'll all fly. I'm not anticipating different weather limits.' He frowns. 'If the clag's below 800ft we'll scrub the lot.'

Roger Beazley, beside me, stirs. He wants to know what an easterly wind would do to David's cavalcade.

'You've planned this for 27,' he says. 'Is it reversible on the day?'

'Totally.'

Roger nods, then grins. 'A crosswind might be your biggest problem,' he muses. 'They'll be all arms and legs. Great fun to watch.'

Laughter warms the room. If this is an ordeal for David, he's not showing it.

Geoff Brindle is also impressed by David's paperwork. 'I think it's an excellent package,' he says. 'We'll have to talk to air traffic, though.'

'No we bloody well won't,' Roger tells him. 'We have to talk air traffic *out* of it. Tell them to lock up and throw the keys away. Cup of tea time.'

'Absolutely.' Geoff taps the masterplan. 'That's what I meant. It's all here. It's self-steering. It'll fly on automatic.'

Other voices are raised around the table. David's plan must be validated by the RAF. There's a bit of a puzzle about what exactly to call it. Within the strict definition of the term, it's not a display. There are no aerobatics. So maybe the best plan is to submit the whole thing to the Air Commodore Ops up at High Wycombe, in the hope that he'll re-delegate authority to the Flying Control Committee. I'm still trying to slow this dizzying roundabout of top-level validations when Les Garside-Beattie returns David to his masterplan.

'Have you thought of designating a formation leader?'

David gives him a firm shake of the head. 'No way. Because it's *not* a formation. The minute it becomes a formation, the guys will be looking for a leader. I want them to fly as per the briefing and as per the timing.' His hand settles on the paperwork. 'It's a parade, not a formation.'

Geoff Brindle spots another problem. 'This unloading business for the cameras over on the north side. Aren't we going to get coal all over the taxiway?'

'FOD, you mean?'

'Yes.'

'No.' Another shake of the head. 'The coal's binned. They're going to mock something up.'

Are they? I'm thinking about my precious Jumbo screen. The whole point of the live link from the camera on the northside is to pump in pictures of the guys re-enacting those desperate days at Gatow and Tempelhof. No coal? Is David serious?

It seems he is. His Berlin Airlift has passed the exam with flying colours – perfectly safe, wonderfully evocative – and already we're into the second of David's spectaculars: the marathon tribute to eighty years of the RAF.

David is talking us through the introduction. The smoke-scrolled

'80' in the sky is, he understands, under threat. If it doesn't materialise, the tribute will begin with a couple of helicopters – a Sea King and a Puma – running in from the north before splitting laterally in front of the crowd. They'll both be tailing big RAF ensigns.

Roger Beazley spots a problem at once. His years co-writing the bible of military airshows – a dryish publication entitled *JSP 318* – has left him with a passion for the small print. This man is a loss to the legal profession.

'No can do,' he says. 'The ensign qualifies as an underslung load. The guys have to fly down the runway.'

David makes a note. He's still resolutely businesslike, but I fancy I'm beginning to detect just a hint of weariness in his voice. He's already circulated copies of his third draft of the five-page script. Scored for no less than ninety-one aeroplanes, it's now won the singleminded attention of every member of the examination board. The stacks of aircraft will appear in four separate batches – three in a six-ship, the last in a five-ship. Each batch will fly two circuits, stacked diagonally upwards on an ascending line away from the crowd. The first lap will be a positioning circuit. Only abeam the saluting veterans on the second lap will each stack sort itself out into a perfect line. To me, all this still sounds like sleight-of-hand, or perhaps plain magic. To the men around the table it's a very neat – if ambitious – piece of airmanship.

Brian Trubshaw, veteran test pilot, is listening especially hard. He nods at David's grid of timings. He knows the airfield intimately from his days on the Concorde development programme.

'How far out does this put the most northerly fella?'

David's pencil finds a map of the airfield.

'The furthest one will be over the most northerly hangars ... here. Then the southerly hangar. Then the taxiway.'

'The northerly hangar.' Brian is frowning. 'Does that give us a problem?'

'I don't think so.'

Don't *think* so? I make a note of the phrase. For once it seems horribly imprecise.

Les Garside-Beattie is worrying about the possibility of the Bristol

Fighter on the first stack meeting another aircraft on the downwind leg. David explains why this won't happen.

Geoff Brindle is listening carefully. 'What's Plan B?' he asks. 'What happens if something goes wrong?'

David blinks. 'It won't,' he says. 'Not if they fly their tracks accurately. That's the whole point.'

'But say something *does* go wrong. What then?'

David pauses for a second or two, aware of the watching faces around the table.

'It won't,' he repeats. 'But if it did then they'd climb out of it. They have engines. They're adults. They'll sort it.'

I'm scribbling fast now. David, like Paul, has designed a train set. His layout isn't as huge as Paul's but it's every bit as ambitious and – like Paul – he has total faith that it will work. Get the timings right, and the heights, and the angles of bank, and everything else will slot sweetly into place. The trains will run on time. The punters will love it. And there'll be absolutely no possibility of what these men call 'a confliction'.

We're on to the first of the buffer displays between the circling stacks. At 15.58, three Spitfires take off to position themselves for Serial 11. After the second two-lap stack – six trainers – the three Spits join the single Spit from the first stack and fly a missing-man formation.

David holds up a hand. 'They're in a finger-four. Number three pulls up abeam 23 threshold. If the weather is OK they'll be flying at 700ft. The number-three guy should top at around a thousand.'

Heads are bent over the airfield maps that Tim has supplied. Number 23 is one of the old wartime runways. It points south-west. Directly at the crowd.

Les Garside-Beattie is frowning again. 'Number three pulls up,' he says slowly. 'So what happens to the rest of them?'

'They overfly the crowd.'

Les glances around the table. Heads shake. Regulation of airshows is getting tighter and tighter. Since March the Red Arrows have been forbidden to fly over the crowd. Even the RAF's own aerobatic team –

arguably the best in the world – must now restrict their performances to crowd-front.

Les again. He taps the map.

'Why not fly the missing-man along the display line?'

'Because it's so much more effective head-on. What you'll see, looking up, is the hole where the missing man should be. We want maximum impact. For maximum effect.'

Les is looking dubious. So is Geoff Brindle. Has David Roome gone native? Has he spent too long in the company of Tim Prince and Paul Bowen? Has showbusiness gone to his head?

Brian Trubshaw lays it on the line. 'We shouldn't be encouraging people to overfly the crowd,' he says.

David responds at once. He's finding it hard to disguise his irritation. 'What about the Queen's birthday fly-past? That was over central *London,* for heaven's sake.'

He has a point. Only last Saturday, in atrocious weather, the RAF mounted a fly-past over Buckingham Palace. The aircraft were briefly visible in low cloud. Hardly ideal conditions.

Roger has seized *JSP 318* again. The man with his finger on the legal pulse. 'That was a fly-past,' he says firmly. 'This is an air display. Different rules.'

David looks briefly despairing. Roger this time comes to his aid. He's been sneaking a look at the rest of David's RAF eightieth brief. At the bottom of page four there's a glorious moment when twenty-one Tucanos burst through multi-coloured smoke and power straight over the crowd. There is, he points out, no point spilling blood over four Spitfires when – an hour later – twenty-one Tucanos will be breaking all the rules.

Geoff Brindle, as Chairman, is having second thoughts. 'Roger's got a point,' he admits. 'I don't think there's any inherent danger with the Spits. It's a loose formation. There are plenty of escape paths. They've got a bit of height on their side.' He looks across at David. 'What about references?'

'They'll see the old runway, 23, out to their left.'

Geoff nods. Maybe, after all, the FCC can give David a dispensation. It's not that they distrust his calculations. It's just the rules.

Roger again. Yet another change of course: 'Geoff's right. It's not a safety problem, it's a political problem. We can justify the Tucanos. They're a single unit. They're flying modern aircraft. We have some control there. But the Spits? For one thing the engines are less reliable. For another, we're dealing with a group that's been glued together for the occasion.' He looks round, letting the silence reinforce his point. Can this prestigious committee, in the current climate, really condone the breaking of an important rule?

Someone asks David how many other missing-men formations he's planning for the tribute.

'Two. One with Vampires for the early jets. Another with Tornados for the present day.'

'Both over the crowd?'

'Yes.'

There's more debate. David points out that the Vampires are from Source Aviation down in Bournemouth and regularly fly together, and that the Tornados will be coming from a frontline RAF squadron. But this fails to answer the committee's concerns.

Wearily, David concedes defeat. 'You make the decision,' he says. 'If you want them down the display line, so be it.'

There's a sympathetic murmur around the table, but the consensus is beyond doubt: no overflying the crowd with the missing-men formations. Re-jig the display to put them crowd-front. Sorry, David.

David scribbles himself a note, then talks the committee through the rest of his masterplan. When we get to the bottom of page four and the onrushing Tucanos, Geoff Brindle quickly pre-empts objections.

'I know it sounds anomalous but I have no problem with this. Single operator. No deviation. It think it's perfectly safe.'

David looks up. 'Fly it down the display line,' he warns, 'and it'll look absolute rubbish.'

'Quite. I absolutely believe you, David. What height will they be by the time they cross the display line?'

'1000ft.'

'There we are then.'

The Tucanos have made it. The crowd is safe. Roger, meanwhile, has worries about the show's climax: the Red Arrows running in towards the crowd in an extended 'V'. Within that nestles Chris Yeo's Eurofighter, symbol of the RAF's stake in the next millennium. On a cue from the leader, Red One, the Arrows pull up into their famed 'Vixen Break', fanning out across the sky. Eurofighter, meanwhile, goes vertical.

Roger points out that Eurofighter will be blind to Red One. They're both in the vertical. They're both in the same patch of sky.

Tim puts him right. Red One, in fact, will go up and left. The Reds have foreseen the confliction and adjusted accordingly. Eurofighter, one of only four currently flying, will be safe.

Another voice intervenes. Since Eurofighter has turned up to join the Reds, why doesn't it do a solo display? Heads turns to Chris Yeo. He knows the development budget inside out. It's a question of money, he says. There just isn't enough to pay for a display.

Geoff Brindle nods, as resigned as everyone else to the brutal stringencies of the defence procurement programme. He wants to get back to David's choreography. He leafs though the five-page plan, choosing his words with care.

'It's a very brave and complicated finale, David. Could you just give us an overview of the administration?'

David, for a moment, is lost. 'How do you mean?'

'Well ...' Geoff gestures at the masterplan. '... I imagine you'll be breaking it into packages. Some you'll rehearse, some you won't. Could you just talk us through that?'

'Ah,' David nods. 'I see. Well, in actual fact I don't anticipate rehearsing any of the elements.'

'You don't?' It's Geoff's turn to look surprised.

'No.' David shakes his head. 'Each pilot will be receiving his brief and a briefing pack. On top of that, I'll brief them individually, face to face. Here, I imagine.'

'So no rehearsal at all?'

Tim, heading off trouble, intervenes. 'We'll bus the off-base guys in,' he says smoothly.

'On the day?'

'Yes.'

'What about the traffic?'

'We'll use the quiet routes.'

'The what?'

'Don't be mischievous.'

David picks up his masterplan. He has a point to make here and he's not going to be deflected. 'It's down in black and white,' he says. 'Part of my brief is to say to the guys, this is flyable, all you have to do is to stick to the script. So think it through. Imagine where you'll be, and then imagine what's happening to everyone else. Isn't that reasonable?'

Heads nod around the table and Les Garside-Beattie weighs in with a personal endorsement. In his opinion, David's plan will need lots of briefing and lots of concentration on the day, but in essence he thinks it's pretty straightforward. It's flyable. It'll work.

Roger nods. 'Do you think it's the most complex we've done?' he asks Tim.

Tim glances across at David. 'It's the most thoroughly planned,' he says. 'And it'll definitely be the most spectacular.'

This, to me, sounds like a bid to bring the discussion to an end, but Brian Trubshaw has been watching David Roome very carefully and he's come to the conclusion that by sticking so closely to the safety brief, the committee may well have landed David with potentially dangerous complications.

David, going back through the plan, has been jotting notes on his pad. He agrees at once. 'There's going to be a real confliction problem,' he warns. 'By pushing the missing-men formation away to the south, I've cleared the runway. Now the runway's active again. Take Serial 32 at 17.36. I'm trying to land the Blenheim and the Lanc, and now I've got five Tornados three miles out on the same heading. At 300 knots, that's thirty seconds. I'll cuff it somehow or other, but it's not looking wonderful.'

Geoff Brindle eyes David's racing pencil, then decides to leave him to it. With lunch approaching, we begin to work through a long list of participating aircraft, deciding which displays need a closer look. Les Garside-Beattie has recently watched a pair of French Jaguars at an airshow in the north and doesn't like the way they organise their routine. There are also rumours that pilots from the old Eastern Bloc have had their annual flying cut from 50 hours, itself a worry. Roger tables a problem with Lockheed's brand-new version of the best-selling Hercules, the C-130J. The aircraft is currently uncertified. Will the certifications come through in time? There's a debate about a Jaguar GR1A display. The pilot's bidding for something called a 'high-alpha pass', a manoeuvre which rakes the aircraft backwards in a nose-up attitude. Is it a dirty fly-by, with the undercarriage extended, or will he have the gear up? The question is important because, in Chris Yeo's opinion, an engine failure will leave the pilot with nowhere to go but down. On this and other issues, debate rages to and fro, the committee forever juggling safety factors against Tim and Paul's commitment to keeping the crowd on their toes.

At last, after lunch, we get to item 46 on the agenda, the Slovak White Albatros display team. Ian Sheeley has the paperwork. He's looking at the questionnaire they've just returned.

'They've asked for a dispensation to overfly the crowd,' he announces innocently. 'Twice.'

By now, David Roome is on the way back to his office at RAF Innsworth. While Roger and Geoff seek clarification on exactly why the Slovaks want to fly their L-39s over the crowd, Chris Yeo is looking thoughtful. He, like Brian Trubshaw, is acutely aware of the problems their mandated re-jig will be giving David Roome. The last thing this committee should be doing is making this birthday tribute *more* hazardous.

Roger looks up. He thinks the Slovaks should have their dispensation. They're a national display team. They know what they're doing. They're up at 1000ft, for God's sake.

Chris Yeo interrupts. 'Then I think we should give David a dispensation too,' he suggests quietly. 'On the one condition that the Spits get together for a rehearsal. Let's make this thing safer, not play politics.'

There are nods of approval around the table and an agreement that Geoff will talk to David. If it's really a problem, then let's go with Chris.

I sit back in my chair. I feel like applauding. David Roome has passed his exam. With flying colours.

*

Back in the depths of Building 15, there's more good news. The indefatigable Lesley O'Brien, troubleshooter extraordinaire, has just resolved the telecommunications crisis. A cracked connection on the South Side fibre-optic terminal has been fixed. She's re-connected the terminals on the North Side, nipped across the runway, and completed the circuit. Four green lights on the panel in the Frame Room would signal success.

'And?'

'Four greens,' she beams. 'Can you believe that?'

I wander into Paul Bowen's office with the news. He's studying a letter from the Dutch Ministry of Defence. They want to send over a handful of squaddies with the Stinger Battery for a spot of hands-on training.

'What's a Stinger?'

'It's an anti-aircraft missile. It's shoulder mounted. You point it at the target and press a button and the thing homes on various emissions.'

'When do they want to come?'

'End of July.'

'You mean for the show?'

'Of course.'

I reach for my pad. The thought of a troop of Dutch squaddies plodding around with anti-aircraft missiles sounds like entertainment gone mad. Is the Benevolent Fund this desperate for cash?

Paul hides a grin. The airfield, he explains, will be bursting with NATO and non-NATO aircraft, a gourmet feast for the target-acquisition guys. Scoring a kill these days involves a knowledge of all kinds of aircraft signatures – the pattern of electronic emissions special to each aircraft – and past shows have been dogged by unannounced visits from various intelligence agencies. Modern aircraft have alarm systems to warn the pilots when electronic eyes turn their way, and last year protests from American aircrew nearly led to the last-minute withdrawal of the all-important F-117 Nighthawks. A great deal of trans-Atlantic string-pulling resolved the problem with literally hours to spare but the wound is still open and Paul is in no way disposed to saying yes to this latest Dutch request.

I'm still thinking about the Americans. Someone was targeting their aircraft. Was this surveillance interpreted as a positive threat?

Paul nods. 'It was,' he confirms. 'They were going to ground all their aircraft.'

'So who was it? Did you ever find out?'

Paul looks at me for a long moment, then shakes his head. Even now, nearly a year later, the answer to my question defies belief. 'It turned out to be the Americans themselves,' he says. 'Some bunch from one of the intelligence outfits sent in a covert surveillance team. Never told a soul.'

'They were snooping on *themselves*?'

'And others,' he nods. 'You've got it.'

....

CHAPTER ELEVEN

July 1998

Prior commitments keep me away from Fairford for nearly a fortnight. By the time I return, towards the end of the first week in July, the place is undergoing a transformation. Both inside and outside the airfield, a rash of yellow AA signs have appeared. Drop-off points. Collection points. Arrows to the Gulfstream Flight Centre and the Casualty Clearing Station. Plus a big hallo on the main gate from the USAF Base Commander, Lt Col Frank Robinson, wishing everyone a very special day.

The acre or so of tarmac outside Buildings 15 and 16 is now full of parked cars. Beyond the runway, a distant blur of white signals the new reception complex at Gate F. This is where RIAT's army of volunteers will be reporting to pick up their passes and meal vouchers, and already the lavishness of the new arrangements has attracted a certain degree of gleeful attention. Spies in the camp report that the interior of the tented area looks like a cross between a Marriott Hotel and an upmarket Balti House. Within days, Gate F has become known as the Taj Mahal.

My first call is to Sue Allen, at the heart of Flight Operations. After months of careful preparation, her battle plan has suffered a volley of direct hits and she's sitting behind her desk trying to assess the damage. The Russian navy has just dropped off the plot, cancelling a couple of Sukhois and an Il-76. One of the two American U-2s – the aircraft due to fly at the show – has also had second thoughts and it's now certain that the Israelis won't be putting their UAV through its paces. These withdrawals have blasted an ugly hole in the thirty-minute SkyWatch display and Tim Prince's decision to draft in a couple of American fighters from elsewhere in the flying programme is, at best, a cosmetic repair. Back before Christmas, he and Paul had the highest hopes for SkyWatch. Now, even the downlinked pictures to the Jumbotron screens seem to be in jeopardy. Technology of this sophistication is no friend to mass entertainment and if the pictures appear at all they will be pre-recorded.

I linger in Sue's office while she fields a call from the manager of the *Patrouille de France*, the French national display team. She's handed me a letter from our old friends at the Turkish embassy and this, too, brings bad news. Due to operational demands, Colonel Erdogan regrets that his beloved F-4 Phantoms will no longer be available. The letter ends with a flourish. 'I am very deeply sorry for this decision,' he writes, 'because it is most unlikely.'

Sue at last puts the phone down, rolling her eyes. The manager of the *Patrouille* is demanding an itinerary for every member of his thirty-six strong team. They'll be arriving on Friday and leaving on Sunday morning and he wants a minute-by-minute account of exactly what RIAT will be arranging in between.

I console her as best I can. She's eyeing Col Erdogan's letter.

'Shame,' she says wistfully. 'We got the RHAG in specially.'

RHAG is tekkie-speak for the arrester-gear on which the Turks were insisting for their recce Phantoms. Installing it for the show weekend has cost a great deal of money. Tim will be putting pressure on the Turks to think again about their cancellation but Sue is convinced they won't be coming.

'Why not?'

'Because they'll have got our op order by now and they'll know about the Greeks.'

Bringing the Turks and the Greeks together within the same airshow has the makings of a real coup – another feather in RIAT's cap – but for the Turks this is perhaps a diplomatic step too far.

'And the Greeks? Have they cancelled too?'

Sue shakes her head, reaching for the file. The Greeks are still sending a couple of A-7 Corsairs but even this isn't as straightforward as it might sound. Their radios evidently haven't got the bandwidth necessary to change to certain frequencies and they're having some difficulty deciding which way to come. After a heroic exchange of faxes, Sue has established that they only have 50 kHz channel spacing on their UHF radios and carry no VHF radios at all. The relevance of all this is beyond me but it seems that they're now planning to arrive and depart on the OAT system. 'What's the OAT system?'

Sue shrugs.

'You tell me,' she says. 'As long as they get here in one piece, I don't care what system they use.'

The phone rings again. Better news this time, from the Italian *Aviazione dell'Escercito Italiano*. These army aviators are bringing in two helicopters, an A-129 Mangusta and an AB-412. Sue's eyeing the wall board, column after column of T-cards, tucked under dozens of hotels and pubs. The Italian party numbers fifteen. Where will they sleep? How will she organise ground transport? Sue scribbles herself a note while I try and think of a tactful way of framing the obvious question. With this sudden rash of no-shows, aren't aircraft getting … well … a bit thin on the ground?

Sue gives me a withering look.

'If only,' she says.

She opens a drawer and produces a multi-folded computer print-out. It's still a bit early for dramatic gestures but she stands on her chair and lets the print-out unfold. This is the latest update on the expected arrivals. The print is tiny. At the top of page one is a Danish F-16 from 723 Squadron, due to land at 13.04 Zulu on Wednesday. At the bottom of page eight is Lockheed Martin's precious C-130J. I try and focus on the tiny figure underneath.

'Four hundred and fifty-nine? Is that the total?'

'Yes,' Sue nods. 'I don't think there's a problem with aircraft.'

From Sue's office in Building 15, I pick my way past towering stacks of newly-delivered briefing packs, out to the car park. This last week or so, the weather has been positively autumnal – a queue of deep frontal systems rolling in from the Atlantic – and clouds are massing again away to the west, heavy with the promise of rain. Whether summer will return in time for the show is anyone's guess but the clock is ticking fast now and the possibility of a wash-out is the last thing on Tim Prince's mind.

'It'll be brilliant weather,' he says at once. 'It always is.'

He's giving me a lift across the base to the USAF's Community Activity Centre, an R&R facility which is this morning's venue for something called the RIAT Table Top. Tim wants to talk about one of David Roome's tribute pageants but, as the first drops of rain flatten against the windscreen, I'm more interested in the weather. 'Just say it *is* dreadful. Say it pours all weekend. What happens then?'

Tim gives me one of his speciality sideways looks. Optimism is part of the RIAT house style. Assuming the worst gets nobody anywhere.

I ask the question again. It's raining quite hard now.

'OK,' Tim concedes, 'let's pretend it chucks it down. Number one, we know people will still turn up. Most of the tickets are pre-sales. Number two, people actually *want* to come. The Brits are amazingly resilient. A bit of rain ... who's complaining?'

Tim has a point. I grew up by the seaside and memories of childhood summers are stitched through with sodden families tramping cheerfully along the prom. But this is an airshow. What happens if the cloud-base is near ground-level?

'We go to Plan B.'

Plan B is code for so-called wet-weather displays. Every team and every singleton prepare full displays and something with a little less of the third dimension. A cloud-base of, say, 800 feet would rule out anything but a simple fly-by; but weather that dire is rarer than you might think, and a more normal cloud-base of 2,000 feet would still leave room for a modest display.

'Modest?'

'Flattened.'

I'm thinking of all the wonderful ribbon diagrams that aerobatic teams supply with their returned questionnaires – rolls, loops and bunts, and soaring hammerhead stalls expressed in twists and twirls of thick felt-tip marker pen. Take out the highlights – anything over 1,000 feet – and what's left?

Tim adjusts the wipers to rapid.

'Hang around,' he says, 'and you might find out.'

'Meaning?'

'Meaning that of course we take it seriously but you'd be wrong if you thought people only come for the flying. They don't. We've got loads going on. Displays. Exhibitions. Jugglers. Live music. Hundreds of aircraft in the static line. People love all that. If it's really looking dodgy then we'll pull in more breakdown trucks because people get stuck in the mud. We'll get the traders to stock up with umbrellas and rain capes. Oh yes, and I might nip out and buy a couple of thousand galoshes for the volunteers.'

This is heartening news, evidence of RIAT's concern for the welfare of its unpaid frontline troops, and I say so. That look again, curiosity warmed by amusement.

'Of course we care,' he says, 'but it's self-interest, too.'

He describes one of the earlier shows, over at Greenham Common. After a night of driving rain a number of the volunteers manning the admission gates went home. Without wet weather gear, they were chilled to the bone.

'So what happened?'

'The gates were wide open. Everyone got in free.' He frowns, slowing for a puddle. 'And guess what? We lost thousands of pounds in revenue.'

The Table Top is Tim Cairns' first chance to exercise this year's emergency teams. Scheduled to last six hours, it pulls in no less than 127 men and women, a reassuring mix of doctors, para-medics, policemen, firefighters, security personnel and air traffic controllers, each with their allotted place within Tim's masterplan, the 126-page Emergency Operations Order.

This mill of emergency front-liners has been sub-divided into ten syndicates, each with its own table, and I sit in one of the observer's chairs, listening to the buzz of conversation. With the coffee circulating, now is the time to renew old friendships, introduce strangers to each other, and begin that process of team-building to which today's exercise is dedicated. I watch while the syndicates settle around their allotted tables, studying briefs, snapping open attaché cases, arranging pens beside pads, powering up laptops, or simply eyeing the big doors that open on to the patio, wondering whether there's enough time left for a fag.

There isn't. Today's two sessions, morning and afternoon, are to be led by Peter Atkinson, an ex-British Transport Police Chief Inspector and a veteran of the King's Cross tube fire. The latter experience convinced him of the value of disaster planning and he's brought along some impressive inter-active software to illustrate the various scenarios he'll be using to seed debate.

He begins by sketching in the anatomy of Tim's emergency plans, the bare bones on which so much will hang. How the airfield is divided into four colour-coded zones – yellow for the showground, red for the operational areas, green for the base area, blue for the rest – and then further sub-divided into thirteen evacuation sectors. At the flick of a switch, the familiar shape of the airfield appears once again, this time covered with a matrix of letters (A–K) and numbers (1–7). This is known as the crash grid, and each square is sub-divided once again into four – a–b–c–d. The system, in essence, couldn't be simpler and a three-word call on the emergency radio net – Golf Four Delta, for instance – will pin-point an incident within metres.

I gaze out at the faces in the room. For them, this must be pretty basic stuff – common sense applied to the terrifying intangibles of the unforeseen – but to a newcomer like myself it's deeply reassuring. Minutes earlier, I've shared a coffee with Ian Sheeley, the ATC boss at Brize Norton and this year's Flying Display Manager. He's here as an observer and just at the moment he's more interested in the ever-changing mosaic that used to be his flying programme, but even so he admits that today's little exercise has its uses. He's never yet completed a tour on an RAF station where aircraft, and sometimes aircrew, weren't lost.

Lost? I'm listening to Peter describing the basic emergency structures. How Supt Adrian Grimmitt, this year's Gloucestershire police Silver Commander, will be directing civil and police operations from the Emergency Control Centre in Building 1223. How the Silver Co-ordinating Group will – in the event of an incident – convene in

Building 1224 nearby. How Show Operations Control, or SOC, will be co-ordinating second-line support. How the three Crash Combines – Alpha, Bravo and Charlie – will spearhead the rescue and firefighting efforts. And how the three Mobile Response Columns, or MRCs – Red, Green, and Blue – will follow in their wake.

Peter moves smoothly on to the management of casualties. These are Brian Robertson's responsibility. I can see the Aldershot GP over on syndicate two. He nods as Peter talks of triage, reception and documentation and I wonder to myself whether he shares my fascination at Peter's choice of tense. The seriously injured *will* be stabilised. Next of kin *will* be comforted. This is the future definite. There are underlying assumptions beneath this seamless event-stream and one of them is the possibility – likelihood? – of something going wrong. What, when and how remains to be seen but you can't mix high-performance aircraft, ambitious airmanship, and the expectations of tens of thousands of people without the admission of an element of risk. The only real question to address is that of scale. How big is that risk? And what might be the consequences?

Before lunch, Peter proposes to offer a series of small-scale day-to-day incidents – nothing major, nothing unduly alarming – and it will be the job of the syndicates to come up with plans of action. After lunch, Peter will up the emergency stakes, outlining a series of events that will make front page headlines in papers all over the world. Limiting the fall-out from the catastrophe will be the job of the people in this room.

First, though, a little something to warm everyone up. A Ford Escort has come to rest at the mouth of Gate H. Slumped over the wheel is a man in his late sixties. His wife says he's been complaining of chest pains all morning. He's unconscious, she's very frightened, and the traffic is already backing up along the Kempsford road. What do you do?

The syndicates huddle together over their respective tables. They have just five minutes to sort this drama out. I join syndicate eight. It includes Jack Taylor, RIAT's Emergency Services Co-ordinator, and Tony Webb, Deputy Director for Public Affairs. Jack is brisk. He's been here before and in his opinion this isn't something that's going to unduly stretch the system. Call for an ambulance. Get the guy to the showground medical centre. Shift the car. Wave the traffic in. Next, please. Heads nod around the table. Then, thanks to Peter Atkinson, the plot thickens. The driver has in fact died. He's beyond help. So who certifies him dead?

'A doctor,' Jack growls. 'Who else?'

Fine, Peter agrees. But then there's the question of the police coroner's officer. This is a sudden death. Ought he to attend? And if he does, where's he coming from? One of the Gloucestershire police contingent suggests Cirencester. Cirencester is ten miles away. The roads are thick with show traffic. The wife's pretty distressed. Who looks after her? Who gets the coroner's officer through? And what happens to the body? The latter, clearly, ought to be ferried over to Brian Robertson's field hospital. Hangar 1205 has a temporary body store. But how does the body get there?

'Helicopter,' someone suggests.

Peter smiles. He's done his homework and he loves baiting the scenarios with these little cul-de-sacs. A helicopter despatched from the northside and returning with the dead body will cross the runway twice. That means two interruptions to the flying display. Anyone from Air Traffic got any views on that?

The arguments swirl on. Transfer him by road. Give the widow one of Heidi Standfast's information team. Tap Wally Armstrong up for ice to chill the body if it's a particularly hot day. Finally, all options exhausted, Peter brings debate to a halt. The driver is laid out in Building 1205. The coroner's officer is stuck in traffic the other side of the Crown at Crucis. The show goes on.

Two more minor incidents follow – a kidnapped child and a pedestrian bridge teetering on the edge of collapse – before we break for lunch. Back in Building 15, I run into Wally Armstrong. Yesterday, it seems, was a nightmare and today is even worse. The big southside diner and the catering tent over here on the northside, are both erected but try as he might he can't find any chefs. There are none available from the normal service sources and the rumoured recession has yet to creep as far as Gloucestershire. The market rate for a pretty indifferent agency chef is – Wally says – extortionate.

'But you haven't got a choice,' I point out. 'You'll just have to grit your teeth and pay it.'

'At £30 an hour?' he explodes. 'You've got to be joking.'

In the dining room, there's a queue for the roast pork and apple sauce. I'm due to have lunch with Tony Webb to sort out various problems with the Jumbotron screens. Paul has somehow found the money for two and that seems to have doubled his expectations about what we can provide. This, of course, is no surprise but when Paul himself appears he has yet more news. 'I've got you a ride in a Herc. It's on for Thursday, over at Lyneham.' He offers me a smile I don't quite trust. 'It'll be with the Tac Demo crew. You'll love it.'

I join Tony Webb shortly afterwards. Tony flew C-130s for seventeen years, earning himself an AFC in the process – and by the time we get to the gateau and cream I'm seriously alarmed. The Tac Demo is abbrieve-speak for eleven minutes of sensational flying. The guys take off in a very big hurry, throw the Herc all over the sky, land, go backwards, drop a Land Rover on the tarmac, take off again, pretend to be under fire, and then perform something called the Khe San approach. I press Tony for more clues to the latter but he's too busy laughing.

'Can you make notes and throw up at the same time?' he asks me. 'If not, it might be worth practising.'

Back at the Table Top, the afternoon's major incident is well under way. It's 12.30 on the Saturday of the show weekend. Ninety thousand spectators are waiting for the arrival of a trio of Harriers from 3 Squadron. As they run in towards the threshold, they collide with a flock of Canada geese. The Harriers are in 'V' formation. The pilot of the starboard aircraft loses control when his canopy shatters. He veers to the left and collides with the port aircraft, which banks at once to the north-east. The pilot of the starboard aircraft, meanwhile, manages to lower his undercarriage and land but loses control again, snakes off the runway and ploughs through the corporate enclosure and a section of the crowd before the aircraft breaks up in a car park, and catches fire. What happens next?

Already, the radio microphone is passing from table to table. There's a plea from the casualty bureau to be allowed to field the hundreds of incoming calls. Gordon Harris, from SOC, assures Peter that an ongoing cascade of information will flood every branch of the RIAT volunteer network. Brian Robertson confirms that his field hospital will have been brought up to full readiness and that the decontamination unit will have been activated to cover access at the front door.

Decontamination unit? Ian Sheeley puts me right. The Harrier, he explains, is made of composite materials, some of them toxic. Anyone exposed at the scene of the crash must therefore be hosed down.

Peter, meanwhile, is keen to push the story on. There are heavy casualties in the car park area. Some of them are clearly dead. Others are hideously burned. How do the responding resources co-ordinate with each other? His question hangs in the air while a young doctor calls for the microphone. He's not at all persuaded by this scenario. The Harrier has cut a swathe through the corporate enclosure and adjoining crowd areas. That, surely, is where the bulk of the casualties will be? There are murmurs of agreement.

Peter re-draws the area to be cordoned off by the incoming Mobile Response Column, then turns back to the syndicates. Seventy-three people have been confirmed dead. There are 361 seriously injured, including 27 major burns cases. Thanks to the presence of TV cameras at the show, the director is transmitting live to a global audience. How do you manage this breaking wave of media attention? What's the message you want the world to receive?

As I know only too well from my own career in television, this is far from fanciful and today's exercise now stretches to a mock press conference, to be conducted by Hugo Brooke, whose Chippenham company offers courses in media training. Tony Webb, the voice of RIAT, and Supt John Horam from Gloucestershire police, troop into an adjoining room to be quizzed on camera. I join them. For minutes on end, they agonise over a press statement. Hugo hovers over them. Keep to the facts. Stick to plain language. Don't be tempted to speculate about the cause. It's all good advice and as the camera rolls Tony Webb, grim-faced, addresses the world before Hugo weighs in

'You can't put it there.' Paul Bowen explains a parking problem to Lt Col Menskykov, pilot of the TU-22M *Backfire.*

Graham Hurley

Graham Hurley

In the absence of a towbar 50 ATC cadets, all RIAT volunteers, reposition 95 tons of Ukranian nuclear bomber.

Bad news for an ATC cadet during Tim Cairn's Emergency Services exercise ...

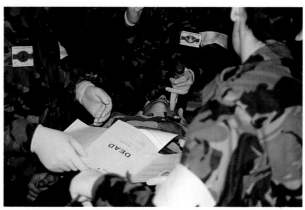

Graham Hurley

... and bad news from RAF Strike Command means a rapid rethink for David Roome's RAF 80th Anniversary Pageant.

The meetings go on and on and on, and on.

Graham Hurley

Graham Hurley

Graham Hurley

ABOVE & LEFT Friday 24th July. The Static Line on Apron Orange is nearly complete.

Peter March

Down and out. The starboard undercarriage of a German
Navy Tornado punches through the tarmac on Apron Blue.

Graham Hurley

Before the aircraft can be lifted,
a fuel bowser crew must pump out
Avtur from the starboard drop tank.

While crews work to recover the
Tornado, invited guests enjoy the British
Aerospace Gala Dinner in Hangar 1200.

Catherine Moubray

Air Chief Marshal Sir Richard Johns, Chief of Air Staff, delivers the keynote speech:

'Fly hard, fly well, fly safe.'

Catherine Moubray

The Hungarian MiG-29 climbs away on full re-heat during Saturday's air display.

Peter March

Peter March

Captain Gyula Vari, pilot of the MiG-29, and winner of the Friends of RIAT *As The Crow Flies* Trophy.

Behind the screens, Tony Howard sends live TV pictures ...

... to the Raytheon Jumbotron beside the Patrons Pavilion.

Graham Hurley

Graham Hurley

Graham Hurley

Who said aviation was glamorous?

A corporate hospitality suite awaits its lunchtime guests.

Catherine Moubray

Peter March

The SAAB SA-39 Gripen makes a slow pass ...

... in front of post-lunch VIPs.

Catherine Moubray

Peter March

The Spirit of Transport Past.

A DC-4 overflies waiting DC-3s during David Roome's celebration
of the 50th anniversary of the Berlin Airlift.

Peter March

The Spirit of Transport Present.

Lt Col Vaneev has been dissuaded from looping his An-72 *Coaler*.
Even so he later won the Lockheed Martin Cannestra Trophy for this display.

Peter March

ABOVE & BELOW A rueful David Roome watches the
final formation flypast in what remains of his
RAF 80th Anniversary Pageant.

Graham Hurley

Mating at 400 knots.
The French Mirage F-1 pair won
the Sir Douglas Bader Trophy
for this display.

Sqn Ldr Geoff Clark introduces
HRH The Duke of Edinburgh to the
controls of the C-17A Globemaster III.

A Rockwell B-1B bares all for the crowd.

Peter March

RIAT staffers de-brief aircrew at Sunday night's Hangar Party.

Catherine Moubray

Peter March

Having survived Sunday night's de-brief
a Tornado crew head for home.

The Ukranians try to do the same but have to return
to their parking slot. Why? No transponder.

Graham Hurley

We counted it all in.
Finance co-ordinator, Sue Vizor tallies the weekend's takings.

Graham Hurley

Graham Hurley

I counted them all out.
Sean Maffett checks Monday's Departures Board.

Catherine Moubray

Pilot Officer Chris Fopp congratulates Kevin Leeson (left) on winning the *Spirit of the Tattoo* Award at the Survivors Dinner.

All smiles now.

The perfect host. Capt Dan Jagt USAF's RIAT Project Officer addresses the Survivors Dinner while Paul Bowen looks on.

Catherine Moubray

with supplementary questions. Tony answers some of these, John Horam tidies up the rest. The policeman is visibly unhappy with his performance and insists on having a second go. This isn't altogether authentic – would he get the chance in real life? – but Hugo indulges him. Minutes later, we're back with the syndicates, watching the taped performance.

Tony Webb has finished his press statement. Now comes the first of Hugo's questions.

'Do you have enough medical facilities?' he asks.

Tony nods.

'Yes,' he says.

It's the perfect answer, unfudged, ungarnished, utterly factual, and it brings the house down. A little later, the Table Top finally over, I run into Heidi Standfast. Thanks to good company on her table, she's rather enjoyed herself.

'The guys were sound,' she says. 'In fact it was really funny.'

Funny? Seventy-three dead? Hundreds dying? Heidi nods. 'They asked us what outside agencies we'd call in.'

'And?'

'We insisted on the RSPB.'

A couple of days later, I take the train to London for the hosting brief at the RAF Club. With less than three weeks to go to the show, this is the moment when Amanda Butcher and Kevin Leeson have to expose the fine print of their VIP plans to the select band of Vice-Presidents, Vice-Patrons, and co-opted hosts, who will be the welcoming face of RIAT.

Kevin's presentation will be ad-libbed to forty-eight Powerpoint screens covering every nook and cranny of his protocol programme and I get the chance to update myself before the formal brief begins.

The RIAT year is a marathon for dozens of individuals but this is probably the week that finds Kevin closest to breaking point as the race for the tape begins. Since way before Christmas, he's been drawing up the broad outlines of his VIP programme, agreeing guest lists, extending invitations; and for the last couple of months, with guests confirmed, he's written fifty-six individual programmes, each one timed to the minute. Now, these plans must be agreed by the participants, vetted by their outer offices, approved by the sponsors and presented to Sir Roger Palin for comment. At any stage, in Kevin's phrase, the plot can be changed, and all too often it is. A mini-tweak here, a mega-tweak there, each adjustment triggering revisions that can all too easily roll through the entire programme.

It sounds to me like a nightmare – RIAT's SOP – and Kevin's blood pressure can't have been helped by the weeks he spent working out of Amanda's bookcase, the one corner left in the ever-more-cramped confines of Building 16. Does he, hand on heart, ever lose his temper?

He shakes his head. A snatched week clubbing in Ibiza has given him a wonderful tan and, for a man who also runs the whole of RAF Strike Command's Tornado engineering support, he seems remarkably composed.

'I got a little grumbly yesterday but it wasn't anything dramatic. This week is the worst – you're right – but as soon as we get over that bow wave of paper, the going gets a lot easier.'

RIAT is obsessed by paperwork but even by their standards Kevin's meticulously produced briefings are impressive. He's circulated something called the 'master phasing chart' for royal and VVIP guests, a detailed flow analysis in no less than seven colours. This little masterpiece is useful, as well as exceptionally pretty. At a glance, you can tell exactly where the Duke of Edinburgh or Prince Feisal of Jordan will be on the Sunday at any given moment. At 11.17, for instance, the Duke will be cruising slowly past a row of DC-3s, part of David Roome's Berlin pageant, while Prince Feisal will be chatting to recce experts on one of the SkyWatch displays. Each of these VVIP programmes is bolted together on the same template, a bit like trains running along the same track, each royal or VVIP separated by a carefully-measured time buffer.

I study Kevin's phasing chart a little harder. Without the clock, where would he be?

'Good question. Show-wise, we do everything in slots. Five minutes transit, fifteen minutes for the principal to do something, five minutes for the next transit, and so on.'

This sounds more than a little dull. I'm still trying to find a more tactful way of putting it when Kevin spares me the trouble.

'It's the only way to do it,' he insists. 'We build in a twenty-five-minute slip between each programme so basically we just time-shift down the day. That way, everyone knows exactly what's expected. It's good for the principals, good for the police protection boys, and of course the sponsors love it.'

This is an angle that has so far escaped me but the more I think about it the more central to the whole operation it becomes. Year on year, Paul and Tim are putting more and more resources into the corporate programme. Big companies bring RIAT all kinds of benefits – from direct sponsorship to enhanced profile – and a visit and a handshake from the Duke of Edinburgh means a great deal, especially it seems, for visiting Americans. That, surely, does absolutely no harm to the sponsorship prospects for next year. So should we start viewing the Duke of Edinburgh, and other members of the Royal Household, as super-volunteers, fund-raising for the cause?

Kevin gathers up his phasing charts. The hosting brief is only minutes away.

'My dear,' he murmurs silkily, 'perish the thought.'

Twenty-four hours later, a brief conversation with David Roome. He's been kind enough to check bits of this book for accuracy and he's phoned to let me know that the suggested revisions are in the post. He sounds uncharacteristically weary. I ask him why.

'You didn't know about the BBMF?'

The BBMF is shorthand for the Battle of Britain Memorial Flight – several Spitfires, two Hurricanes, a Lancaster and a DC-3. The aircraft are maintained and flown by the RAF for display purposes and figure importantly in both of David's tribute pageants.

'So what's happened?'

'They won't play ball.'

'Why not?'

'No idea.'

I'm staring at Ian Sheeley's latest running order for the flying programme. I've heard rumours from Sean Maffett that the BBMF are unhappy with Fairford but I didn't realise the situation was this serious. Not only are they refusing to depart from their usual display routines but it now appears that they have another engagement on the Sunday afternoon, over at RAF Wyton, near Cambridge. To meet Wyton's deadline, they must be away from Fairford by 15.30.

'But the RAF Eightieth doesn't even start until half past three.'

'Exactly.'

'So what will you do?'

'God knows.'

For the first time ever, David sounds just a touch rattled. Without the BBMF, he says, his RAF Eightieth pageant will be pure Emmenthal.

'How come?'

'Holes,' he says tersely. 'Bloody everywhere.'

RAF Lyneham is home for the RAF's fleet of fifty-five C-130 Hercules transports, an aircraft fondly known as 'Fat Albert'. The base sprawls to the west of Lyneham itself, a once-pretty Wiltshire village now encrusted with video shops, off-licences, and fast-food outlets. My joining instructions tell me to report to the main gate at 15.30. The Tac Demo Herc is to be airborne at 17.55. A couple of hours should give me ample time to meet the crew.

The Hercules operates with a crew of four on the flight deck. An aircraftman from 57(R) Squadron takes me across the base to the complex of offices and briefing rooms which serve as squadron headquarters. The captain on this year's Tac Demo crew is Flight Lieutenant Dom Stamp, a tall, friendly figure in an olive-green flying suit and a rather stylish pair of glasses. So far he's done nine years on the Hercules. If this sounds like a prison sentence, it plainly isn't.

'It's a lovely aircraft,' he says. 'It's sturdy. It's strong. It's got a good roll rate. And it does exactly what I tell it.'

The Hercules has been around for a while now, and when I enquire exactly how long, Dom grins.

'Longer than me,' he says.

'You're serious?'

'Yeah. The plane we're using today is older than I am. Coffee?'

I do the sums while Dom wrestles with the machine. He looks about thirty. According to Tony Webb, we're in for some exciting flying. The word he kept using was 'radical'. Just what have I let myself in for?

I'm still wondering about a final call to the wife when Dom returns with the coffees. He's got a couple of videos he'd like me to see. This way please.

I sit in the darkened briefing room while he sorts out the player. The first sequence shows white lights swimming in an ocean of green. The lights come and go. After a while, it occurs to me that we're sitting in a cockpit. I can just make out the latticework of the windshield and the onrushing blur that is the world outside.

'We call this NVG flying.' Dom's nursing his coffee. 'NVG stands for night vision goggles. If we have to, we can fly down to two millilux.'

'What's that?'

'It's a measure of ambient light. To the naked eye, two millilux would be pitch black.'

'And the goggles?'

'They magnify starlight to get that picture up there.'

I'm still staring at the screen. More white lights, dancing around ahead. I point them out. Dom nods. 'That's the Herc ahead of us.'

'*Ahead* of you? In total darkness?'

'Sure. He's using NVGs too.'

'What kind of height?'

'Two hundred and fifty feet.'

I close my eyes. I should definitely make the call. These guys are crazy. Two hundred and fifty feet? In formation? In total darkness? I make a mental note to upgrade Tony Webb. He's probably done this, too. Definitely a hero.

An hour or so later, we take a mini-bus out to the ramp. 57(R) Squadron is Lyneham's Operational Conversion Unit (OCU), introducing novice pilots to the mysteries of the Hercules, and the Tac Demo crew are all employed full-time as instructors. The co-pilot, Pete Astle, is himself an instructing captain but on the Tac Demo crew he flies in the right-hand seat. As the line of waiting Hercules on the parking ramp swings into view, I ask him how long he's been at it.

'Flying the Herc?'

'Yes.'

'Sixteen years, give or take.'

I nod, comforted. It's their lives, as well as mine.

We debus by the aircraft and I clamber up to the flight deck. It's infinitely bigger than I'd expected, with seats for the four-man crew (pilot, co-pilot, engineer, navigator), a tiny galley, and even a bunk tucked up against the rear bulkhead. There's a padded bench for visiting guests beneath the bunk and I make myself at home while Dom attends briefly to some paperwork. With the sun streaming in through the multi-panelled windscreen, I might be sitting in a slightly battered Victorian conservatory.

Dom pockets his biro and gives me the safety brief. There's a hole in the roof to crawl through if we come to grief but my best bet is to follow Bernie, the navigator. He has legendary escape skills and a finely developed instinct for staying in one piece. Dom gestures around the flight deck, indicating which bits I can hang on to if I fancy a wander round once we're airborne. The latter hasn't so far occurred to me – I can't rid myself of Tony Webb's wilder phrases – but I've brought a camera along and when I ask whether it's OK to use it Dom sees no problem.

'If you're using flash, just give me a shout before you press the button. Otherwise I might think something's blown up.'

Blown up? Already we're clattering down the ladder for a tour of the hold. The ramp at the back is open and the crew securing the lone Land Rover cast long shadows on the metal floor. Off-loading the Rover will provide one of the highlights of the display. After a tactical landing, the ramp will open and the Rover will roar off in a cloud of orange smoke. Dom gets Ian, the Loadmaster, to explain the fine points of this manoeuvre but I'm more interested in the tactical landing. Tony Webb has talked of maximum braking effort and throwing the props into reverse pitch and, as far as I can gather, this appears to be several millimetres short of a controlled crash.

We return to the flight deck. A NATO-issue sickbag has appeared on top of the notebook I'd left on the bench. Dom brews a pot of tea and invites me to sit in the left-hand seat while he explains how everything works. After the fifteenth dial, I've lost the plot but it doesn't really matter. I'm perched at the controls of a Hercules. The chatter of a returning helicopter comes through the open window, the engine throttles fall nicely to my right hand, and with no effort at all I've become the star of my own little fantasy. Is it too late to become a Hercules pilot? I don't think so.

Take-off has been briefed for 17.55. RAF Lyneham is hosting an exercise at the moment and there's a brief window between inbounds and outbounds for Dom to rehearse his Tac Demo routine. He and Pete Astle ease themselves into their harnesses and Doug – the engineer – straps himself into the central seat behind the control console. Bernie – the navigator – has plugged in my headset and I listen to the clipped chatter as Dom and Pete go through their pre-flight checks.

'Flap selector?'

'Aligned with flaps.'

'Clear No. 3 engine.'

'No. 3 cleared.'

'Turning 3.'

There's a whine from the inner starboard engine as the first of the four turbo-props spools up. The cockpit window is still open and I can smell the unburnt Avtur as the aircraft comes to life. With all four engines turning, the flight deck begins to rock slightly, and over Ian's shoulder the control panel has become a blur of gloved hands.

'Hydraulic contents?'

'Checked.'

'Door warning lights?'

'Out.'

'Taxi clearance.'

Pete contacts the tower for permission to leave the ramp. In Dom's ten o'clock I can see two more Lynx helicopters settling briefly on the tarmac. Last month's B-52 briefing at Fairford smacked of the real thing but this is in a different league entirely. Tony Webb's wind-ups are history. We're going flying.

Dom's right hand nudges the throttles forward and the Herc begins to bump slowly across the ramp.

'Ground idle?'

'Normal set.'

'Trim tabs?'

'Set for take off.'

'Auto-pilot?'

'Off.'

We turn on to the threshold of runway 25. It's still windy and the runway is briefly mottled with the shadows of racing cloud. The essence of today's rehearsal is timing – Dom's flying must squeeze the Tac Demo into the corset of Ian Sheeley's display programme – but the clock won't start ticking until we thunder in for our first run and break.

'Seats and harnesses?'

'Secure.'

'Take-off information?'

'VR 106. V2 119. Flap retraction 400 ft on the QFE.'

'Take-off clearance?'

'Obtained.'

Dom pushes all four of the throttles forward. We start to roll. Thirty seconds later, Pete calls 'VR' and we're lifting off. The climb-out lasts all of twenty seconds, then Dom hauls the big old transport into a steep climbing turn. By this point, I'm clamped to a solid bit of the galley, gazing out of the flight-deck window. Pretty bits of Wiltshire are hanging on the end of the starboard wing. Tony Webb was right after all. Making notes at 2G isn't as easy as you might think.

The plot calls for us to hold over Wootton Bassett while we await the OK to start the display. At 2,000 feet, Dom winds Fat Albert into a tight pattern of turns while Pete and Bernie peer out of the starboard window, waiting for another Herc to start his take-off run. At last he begins to roll. Our call sign is Ascot 683.

'Tower, Ascot 683. Permission to run in.'

The turn tightens even more and then the airfield swims into view. Dom lowers the nose and I ready my Canon Sureshot as the threshold fattens ahead of us. At 100 feet, Dom levels out and we roar down the centreline at 240 knots. A couple of shots capture the blue of grey over Ian's shoulder and I lower the camera in time to catch Bernie's eye. His right hand is making a vertical movement. He's suggesting I hang on to something solid again. I reach for the edge of the galley and brace myself for another of Dom's climbing turns. This time, the side of my face wants to part company with my skull but I tell myself I'm getting off lightly. At least we're not at 250 feet. And at least it isn't dark.

A tight right-hand circuit brings us back to the airfield. I'm far too busy trying to write everything down to worry about the tactical landing. Dom slams the Herc down and we shudder to a halt. As soon as Bernie calls green-on, I'm cleared to clamber down to the hold for another photie. By the time I get there, the Land Rover is bumping down the ramp in a fog of orange smoke. I take two shots in rapid succession and turn for the ladder to the flight deck. The ramp is already closing, and I can tell from the rumbling beneath us that we've started the take-off run. Back upstairs, the landscape's going the wrong way. Why on earth are we trundling backwards?

I try to frame a sensible question but it's too late. The aircraft comes to a halt, the engines howl, and then we're off again. I'm looking at Bernie. He's done this before. He's got my welfare at heart. What next?

We climb out to 500 feet and turn hard to starboard. Then I hear another rumbling behind us as Ian opens the rear door again. Pete, meanwhile, is peering out of the window, constantly updating Dom's mental picture of the airfield.

'Datum's in your three o'clock ... AOB's good ... datum's in your two o'clock ... in your one o'clock ...' Datum is the pilot's point of focus, in this case the control tower. AOB means angle of bank. Pete stops chewing gum for a moment, then wrinkles his nose. 'That smoke smells disgusting.'

He's right. As Dom dips the aircraft's nose for a low-speed flypast and climb-out, showing off the plane's innards to the imaginary crowd below, the remains of Ian's orange smoke is drifting across the flight deck. Ian's arm is reaching forward to brace himself, nicely framing the two pilots beyond. I steady myself for another shot, raising the camera. Shadows across Dom's flying suit. Bits of blue sky through the windshield. Lovely. It's at this point that I feel the lightest of taps on my elbow. Bernie again.

Pre-flight, Dom had given me a five-page briefing pack on the Tac Demo, including a helpful set of ribbon diagrams explaining exactly what happens when. I've left the ribbon diagrams on the bench beside my lap belt, and eight minutes into the flight I've completely lost track of where we are. Bernie's holding his right hand at an alarming angle. Could this be the 405-degree accelerating turn, followed by the sixty-degree AOB wingover? It could.

I reach for my precious bit of galley. The world outside has ceased to mean anything at all. Trees below us are growing sideways. A small red bus is driving straight up the windshield. I try and fight the G force but give up. When it stops, it stops. I think about risking another shot, scribbling another note, anything to take my mind off what might happen next. Thirty years is a long time to be an aeroplane. What happens if the wings fall off? Abruptly, Fat Albert emerges from the wingover. Ahead, the view is full of airfield. We roar down the runway at 100 feet again and then Dom pulls back on the column and I can suddenly see nothing but sky. Moments later, the starboard wing is near-vertical and Pete's voice is back in my headphones. 'Good turn . . . keep it coming round . . . good turn . . . good turn . . . datum's in your two o'clock . . . one o'clock . . . twelve o'clock . . . runway's on the nose . . .'

We're up at 1,000 feet. The aircraft is perceptibly slowing. I'm up with the plot at last, bracing myself for Dom's *pièce de resistance*. The Tac Demo ends with a manoeuvre dubbed the Khe San approach. The USAF developed it in Vietnam. It's supposed to shield incoming aircraft from small arms fire and in essence it means descending from altitude *within* the airfield perimeter. In plain English, that means a dive from a thousand feet, followed by a savage pull-out at the bottom. Dom is still throttling back. The aircraft appears to have stopped in mid-air. Below us, way off to the left, I can see our beloved camper van. Dear God . . .

Abruptly, Dom drops the nose. For a long moment I have no weight at all, which is a very strange feeling indeed, and I raise the camera for one final shot as the runway comes up to meet us. If the film survives the crash it will, of course, be the clinching evidence. Never mess with gravity. Never mistake wings and four turbo-props for salvation.

I take my shot. Beyond Dom and Pete, the runway has suddenly flattened. The aircraft lurches slightly as the wheels meet the tarmac, then I feel the comforting rumble as the brakes begin to bite. Seconds later, the landscape is nearly stationary. Dom's left hand reaches for the little nosewheel by his knee. Fat Albert turns for the traditional Tac Demo sign-off. It's Dom's voice in my head-set. 'Going for the bow. Ready, ready, now.'

Dom hits the brakes. The nose dips. We're back in one piece.

An hour later, I'm recovering in a pub down the road. After the second pint, I phone Tony Webb. He recognises my voice at once. 'How was it?'

'Fine,' I tell him. 'Piece of cake.'

I'm staying the night with Paul Bowen. Paul returns late after a board meeting in London and slumps down at the kitchen table, drink in hand. In nine months' planning for the coming spectacular, I don't think I've ever seen him so weary, so physically drained. Board meetings can be difficult. He's been battling for a new building to house Enterprises and constant tussles at board level have taken their toll. Only now, faced with eviction from Buildings 15 and 16 on health and safety grounds, does there appear to be some prospect of a permanent home. On top of this, of course, comes the looming prospect of the show itself. Endless meetings to chair. Endless decisions to make. Endless speeches to write. Endless holes to fill.

The mention of holes reminds me about yesterday's conversation with David Roome. I'm naturally keen to establish exactly what lies behind the squabble with the BBMF but one look at Paul tells me that this is neither the time nor the place. For weeks, people have been warning me about the run-in to the show – how gruelling it can be – and here in front of me is the physical evidence. The guy's exhausted.

After dinner, he begins to perk up. Tomorrow, he's to chair the day-long meeting that will troubleshoot the parking plan for more than 400 visiting aircraft. Putting all this sexy hardware in RIAT's shop window appeals to the showman in him, and to the weekend hobbyist who created the exquisite little model train lay-out upstairs. As the show approaches and the pace quickens, I've been thinking more and more about that roomful of carefully laid track and beautifully detailed rolling stock. It's the crudest of metaphors for something as complex and potentially overwhelming as the show but I fancy that the Paul Bowen who put together the train set is the same Paul Bowen who, tomorrow, will decide exactly what to do with several billion pounds' worth of aeroplanes. What it boils down to is control. To play God in your own backyard is immensely appealing. And it's simply a measure of Paul's boundless ambition that his backyard happens to be the biggest military airshow in the world.

True? Paul gives the notion some thought. Neither he nor Tim can resist making the show ever bigger, ever more ambitious, but the talk of playing God bothers him. Is he that autocratic? Doesn't RIAT belong to the volunteers?

'Of course it does. Without them, it wouldn't happen. But you two drive it. Without you two, it wouldn't even exist.'

He nods. This is beyond dispute. But what am I really trying to say?

It's my turn to think hard. A rekindled friendship after thirty years has given me a tremendous admiration for what Paul and Tim have achieved. But the price of that success is equally hard to ignore.

'You're knackered,' I point out. 'And you're knackered because the monster's out of control.'

'Rubbish. You really think that?'

'I do. I've seen the evidence. Here, tonight.'

'You're saying we can't hack it?'

'I'm saying you might go pop.'

His eyes return to his glass. He broods for a while.

'About tomorrow,' he says at last. 'That meeting about the parking plan.'

'What about it?'

'Some people think we've got too many aircraft. Not enough space.'

'And?'

He looks at me a moment, then raises his glass.

'They're wrong,' he says gleefully. 'You just watch.'

*

The meeting to get to grips with the parking plan begins next morning at 10.30, an hour late. The crisis over the BBMF has worsened overnight. There's no sign of any concessions on the part of Squadron Leader Paul Day, the BBMF's officer commanding, and Tim Prince has been doing the sums, should RIAT be driven to buying in replacement Spitfires and a Hurricane for David Roome's Berlin and RAF Eightieth tributes.

For the BBMF's Lancaster, the only specimen still flying in the UK, there can be no replacement but the money involved in plugging the other gaps will make a very large dent in RIAT's obsessively-guarded bottom line. The issue of whether or not the BBMF will adapt themselves to the demands of the Fairford weekend has now gone to Air Chief Marshal Sir John Allison, Air Officer Commanding-in-Chief of RAF Strike Command, and Tim is awaiting the call that might ease the log jam.

The parking meet takes place in Paul's office. Mel James has brought along Paul Emery, a key member of his Eng Ops team. John Thorpe, RIAT's Deputy Director, Air Operations, has driven over from his office at Boscombe Down, and Sue Allen is wedged in against Paul. Beside me at the table, looking after the big, wall-mounted airfield map, is Simon Boyle, a young RAF holding officer. It will be Simon's job to check Paul's wilder visions against the very real constraints of geography. We're trying to find homes for a medium-sized air force. Will there be enough room?

Paul, miraculously fresh after a good night's sleep, grips the meeting from the start. This year, he admits at once, there are not only more aircraft than usual, but a lot of those extras are on the large side. This in itself is an obvious problem ('challenge' is the word he prefers), but the difficulties with the jigsaw are compounded by the demands of David Roome's special pageants.

'There's going to be lots of movement around the airfield,' Paul warns, 'so that's something else we should be factoring in.'

Briefly, he outlines the broad principles behind his thinking. The acres of off-runway hardstanding are colour-coded for planning and organisational purposes, and to each Paul has already assigned specific categories of aircraft. The SkyWatch contingent will be on Apron Blue, to the east and south of the runway. The RAF line-up, part of the Eightieth birthday tributes will occupy Apron Orange. Apron Brown, along to the west, will be home to a line of USAF KC-135 tankers, plus a half-star of two B-1 swing-wing bombers flanking one of the venerable eight-engined B-52s. For smaller aircraft, Paul has found a berth on Apron Purple.

Returning to SkyWatch, Paul does a rapid calculation, dividing the total length of Apron Blue by the totalled-up wingspan of the aircraft he's designated to fill it. After leaving a bare ten feet between wingtips, he finds that he has roughly twice as many feet of aircraft as of concrete. This discovery appears to take him by surprise. He shows the figures to Mel James who does the sums again and comes up with exactly the same result. Whichever way you play it, the aircraft won't fit.

By now, Paul is looking for a scapegoat.

'It's an old map,' he announces. 'We need a new one.'

While Sue disappears to find an updated version of the airfield map, Paul broods about various overspill options and it's at this point that I begin to lose the plot, not because I'm not listening but because I suspect that the plot doesn't (yet) exist. This year, Paul and Tim are working the show – and the airfield – harder than ever. More planes for the static line. Pleasure flights in the DC-4. Press junkets on Lockheed's new C-130J. Major taxiing demands from David Roome's special displays. The list is endless, and as Sue returns with Catherine Iddon's updated site plan, it becomes obvious that something has to give.

It falls to John Thorpe, nerveless after umpteen airshows, to volunteer the answer.

'We've got to get rid of some of these bloody aircraft,' he says. 'I'll make a couple of calls.'

Paul vetoes the suggestion at once.

'No, you won't,' he says.

The new map is taped over the old one. With Apron Blue still resisting occupation by an armada of SkyWatch aircraft, Paul decides to transfer our attentions to Apron Orange. This will be home for the RAF's Eightieth anniversary tribute, and on one particular pan it's Mel's job to find spaces for two Hercules, a Puma helicopter, a Chinook and a Canberra, plus bucketfuls of Jaguars and Hawks, a Jetstream, a Dominie, and BAe's replica Eurofighter, manufactured largely in plastic.

'Just dot them in,' Paul tells him.

Mel mutters something I don't quite catch and his copy of the Apron Orange pan is black with little aircraft symbols before he spots a nasty glitch.

'Hang on,' he says. 'The Eurofighter's got to be northside on Friday night for the Gala dinner.'

Paul nods. Mel's right. BA are paying for the dinner and three of the featured aircraft on display inside Hangar 1200 will be theirs, including the showpiece Eurofighter 2000.

Mel tackles Paul head-on. 'So you're saying we break the line to tow it over?'

'That's right.'

'And midnight Friday, after the dinner, you want us to tow it back again?'

'Exactly,' Paul nods. 'It's BAe's dinner. It's their aircraft. They want it. They'll have it.'

Mel is still spelling out the challenge of returning the Eurofighter to its allotted space on Apron Orange. It's pitch dark and there are several hundred aircraft in the way.

'It's worse than tight,' he says. 'And anyway, the 2000 hates being towed too much. The thing's plastic. It's got no strength.'

'Too bad.'

'You're serious?'

'Always.'

Mention of the Gala dinner prompts Sue Allen to raise another problem. 'Amanda wants a Tornado for the hangar as well. Where's that coming from?'

Paul has found himself looking at an empty packet of cigarettes. He calls for his new PA, Jo, and asks her for reinforcements. Then he turns back to Sue.

'Get one out of the line,' he says. 'We've got hundreds on Orange.'

'But Amanda thinks they'll all be too dirty.'

'She does?'

Jo's back with a pack of 200 Superkings. Sue watches Paul strip off the cellophane, waiting in vain for an answer. Paul is more interested in Apron Black, a complex of parking ramps stretching south from the control tower. Here, he thinks, is a chance to do something really special.

He glances across at Mel. 'How long is a *Backfire*?'

Mel blinks.

'Quite long,' he says.

The *Backfire* is a supersonic swing-wing Russian bomber, a guaranteed crowd-pleaser. Paul is looking down at Sue's master plan. To the *Backfire*, he adds a U-2, an EA-6 Prowler, a Nimrod, and a couple of Boeing E-3 AWACs aircraft. He wants them nose-to-tail and he wants an estimate on the length of concrete they'll occupy. Mel busies himself with his *Observer's Book of Aircraft*. His fingers dance on the calculator beside his pad.

'Seven hundred and ninety feet,' he announces at last. 'With decent nose-to-tail separation.'

Paul is looking up at Simon, keeper of the plastic ruler. 'And how much have we got?'

Simon measures Apron Black from one end to the other. 'Eight hundred and thirty feet.'

'There!' Paul beams round. 'We step the aircraft up, height-wise. Put the U-2 at the front, then the *Backfire* behind it. It'll look sensational.' He pauses, struck by another thought. 'Does the U-2 want a citadel?' he asks Sue.

'No.' Sue shakes her head. A citadel is a double barrier around the aircraft with guards in between. The U-2, a high-altitude surveillance aircraft dating back to the Sixties, is evidently no longer shy of the world's attention.

Paul is still looking at Sue.

'Now, then,' he says cheerfully. 'Fighters.'

Sue reads out a list of fighters, all part of the SkyWatch display. In all, they number thirteen.

Mel's still gazing at Paul. 'So where do all these go?'

'Along the edge of Black, wheels on the concrete, tails overhanging the grass, noses pointing at the centreline display.'

'They can't.' Mel shakes his head. 'No way.'

'Why not?'

'The camber falls off badly there, and the surface is crumbling.'

He asks to see Sue's list again. The fighters include three recce F-4 Phantoms. These are big, heavy aircraft. The surface along the edge of Black simply won't take the weight.

'Plus there's a fuel problem,' Mel adds. 'Gas drips out of the aircraft after shutdown. It'll rot the concrete even more.'

At this point, Kevin Leeson appears at the open door. Some of the parking decisions may affect his protocol programme and he's keen to check on the kinds of aircraft his VVIPs can expect to see but Paul beats him to the draw. 'Two seats on the Gulfstream out of Northolt on Sunday morning?'

Kevin shakes his head. 'Full.'

'Really?'

The inflection Paul places on the word gives it the force of an order. Fred Crawley, the Board's Deputy Chairman, has two important guests he'd rather like to fly into the show on Kevin's VIP Gulfstream V, and what Fred requests he usually gets.

Kevin steps into the office a moment, gazing down at the paperwork spilling across the table: computer print-outs, airfield maps, scribbled calculations, umpteen crossings-out, in short ... the wreckage of this morning's attempt to turn mathematics on its head. Somehow, some way, berths must be found for all the attending aircraft. To me, the outsider, this is RIAT at its finest, a triumph of greed over geography, but not for a moment does Paul ever think of scaling his ambitions down. Size matters. He loves the sheer *numbers* of aircraft. If anything, he'd probably like more. The problems they bring with them – parking, specialist fuels, non-standard towbars – are simply more grist for the RIAT mill. This is what his team of managers are *for*. This is what the volunteers thrive on. Tease them with the impossible, and the best of them simply go away and deliver. That's why it's always worked. And this year will be no different.

Kevin departs to reconfigure his Sunday inbound. Paul, reaching for the map again, has had another thought about Orange.

'That Catalina . . .' he muses. 'How about we put it upstream of the fighter line?'

A Catalina is a 1940s amphibian, equally at home on water or concrete. More importantly, it isn't due to land until late Friday.

Mel James is sitting beside me. The implications of Paul's latest little wheeze are all too obvious. 'You want me to move the entire fighter line? For a *Catalina?*'

'Yep.' Paul grins at him. 'That's exactly what I want.'

Mel looks at him long enough to know that he's beyond help. Then he shakes his head.

'God's teeth!' he mutters. 'It's going to be a long night.'

Over lunch, I catch up with Tim Prince. The BBMF situation, he admits, is a definite worry and prospects for the show's climax haven't been helped by a conversation with the Red Arrows. Asked to fly a fin-flash in red, white and blue, they've refused point blank to depart from their standard display. They're also having grave reservations with the RAF tribute display's final manoeuvre, a breathtaking Vixen Break, with the BA development Eurofighter in the middle of the formation going vertical. If Fairford are serious about the Reds flying with Eurofighter, there might be a possibility of doing something a good deal more modest but there's no way they'll adapt their usual routines to accommodate Tim and Paul's splashy final bow.

Sue Allen has recently told me about a request from the Arrows for 200 complimentary tickets. At the market rate, that's nearly £5,000 worth of freebies. Aren't £5,000 favours like these supposed to work both ways?

Tim studies me for a long moment. Twenty-seven Air Tattoos have taught him the value of diplomacy.

'The Reds,' he says carefully, 'know they're the best in the world.'

After lunch, Mel James leads a recce to some of the parking ramps we've spent the morning trying to fill. Away from the office, out in the wind and the sunshine, the problems seem suddenly manageable.

We pause on the north side, at the mouth of Apron Green. Here, Mel was thinking of tucking away Lockheed's precious C-130J but a good look at the state of the tarmac persuades him that seven DC-3s might make better sense. In places the surface is roughened and pot-holed with use.

'Very Berlin,' he nods in approval. 'Suit the Daks nicely.'

We drive on. Across the runway, in front of the control tower, a row of hospitality chalets is going up. With the wail of rock music from the contractor's radios, and the flap-flap of unsecured canvas, comes the smell of rain in the wind. Gales are forecast for the weekend and many of the conversations in Buildings 15 and 16 are haunted by unvoiced worries about when this busy sequence of Atlantic lows will come to an end.

In front of the control tower, a scaffold is already in place for Sean Maffett's commentary booth and I'm still wondering whether he, too, has a wet-weather script when I rejoin Mel, John Thorpe and Paul Emery. They're walking the centreline, measuring the realities of Apron Black against Paul Bowen's plans for the U-2 and the *Backfire* and the rest of his precious SkyWatch tableau. Off to the right, I can see a huge loop of hardstanding, ideal for at least a dozen aircraft. Why didn't this figure in the morning's discussions?

Mel is busy pacing out the plan shape of a Nimrod. He looks up a moment, following my pointing finger.

'Paul wants it for VIP parking,' he says with an air of resignation. 'Interesting choice of priorities, don't you think?'

Returning to the north side of the airfield, we join a tiny group deep in conversation on the grass adjoining the northern taxiway. On Monday, there is to be a press conference for the local media. There'll be TV crews, and reporters, and stills photographers, and Patti Heady plans to entertain them with a band, and a small display of vintage aircraft, including a rare World War One biplane, a Curtiss Jenny. The Jenny will be coming from nearby Rendcomb, where it forms part of Vic Norman's impressive collection of classic aircraft.

We join the group beside the taxiway. Pilot Tim Senior has driven over from Rendcomb to recce the state of the outfield. The ground at

Fairford is honeycombed with rabbit warrens. There are holes everywhere and the Americans who run the base are seriously worried about this valuable biplane coming to grief. They've been talking to lawyers in Washington for most of the week and a detailed six-page insurance form, indemnifying the USAF against any claims, has gone to Vic Norman. Vic's hatred of paperwork is well known and the insurance situation has now reached stalemate. Along with comedian Tom O'Connor, the Curtiss Jenny will form the centrepiece of Monday's press conference. What happens if the bunnies write it off?

Mel puts the question to Tim Senior. Tim has just walked the ground and sees no problem. There's a narrow strip down the middle which is, he thinks, pretty safe. At this stage we're joined by Lt Col Frank Robinson, the USAF Base Commander. He, too, needs reassurance. He points off to the left, towards a highish mast about half a mile away.

'What about that fella?' he asks Tim. 'Isn't that a hazard if you're putting down here?'

Tim doesn't think so.

'We use a curved approach,' he explains. 'You can't see a thing dead ahead with these tail-draggers.'

The Colonel peers at him.

'Hey, fella,' he says, 'you ain't doing very much for my confidence here.'

Tim laughs.

'We land at thirty knots,' he says, 'so what's the problem?'

We return to the cars and it's at this point that I tumble yet another of RIAT's little secrets. While it's true that Paul delights in seeding each day with impossible demands, it's equally true that individuals like Mel James and John Thorpe get a real kick out of meeting them. Their appetite isn't simply for aircraft – the biggest, the noisiest, the fastest, the rarest – but for problems. They love meeting the impossible head-on. They love RIAT's refusal to use the word 'no'. They believe – absolutely – that any problem can be solved with a bit of initiative and a lot of nerve.

In the car again, heading back to Building 15, the pair of them –

with Paul Emery – are discussing RIAT's plans for '99. There's a full solar eclipse due in August and it can only be viewed from parts of the extreme south-west. Paul Bowen and Tim Prince are already talking to RAF St Mawgan, in Cornwall, about helping expand their Air Day and this involvement has now extended to a celebration of the solar eclipse. Paul has visions of a huge, open-air concert, something he likens to a middle-class Glastonbury. The only problem is the dates. Ideally, the air display and the solar eclipse would take place on the same day. Sadly, thanks to operational demands at St Mawgan, they can't.

We're driving in from the airfield. It falls to Paul Emery to voice the RIAT answer.

'Easy,' he says. 'We move the eclipse.'

The weekend comes and goes. A spectacular gale very nearly flattens the ever-lengthening line of hospitality chalets. Monday brings broken skies and dramatic sunshine. The Curtiss Jenny lands without disturbing a single bunny and Tom O'Connor amuses the local media. There's a good turn-out from the regional TV stations and I'm doing an interview with HTV about this book when I notice the distant 'V' of the Red Arrows, rehearsing over nearby Brize Norton.

Minutes later, amidst rumours that the Reds may make a surprise appearance for the benefit of the cameras, Tim Prince suddenly appears. He and Paul go into a huddle. It looks serious, and it is. Paul beckons me over.

'One of the Reds has gone in at Brize,' he mutters. 'Don't tell a soul.'

Lips sealed, I rejoin the journos for lunch. Tom O'Connor does twenty minutes of brilliant impromptu stand-up. Around 2.30, another summons arrives, this time from Paul's office. Tim's there and he's smiling. A bird strike downed Red Six, the synchro leader, Dave Stobie, moments after take-off. With no time to get the gear down, he pancaked the Hawk but walked away intact. Better still, Strike Command have just been on. The BBMF, after all, will be taking their place in Dave Roome's displays. No early departure on Sunday afternoon. No awkwardness over flying in non-standard vertical stacks.

I'm trying to define exactly how serious this little crisis has been. Tim looks at Paul. Paul grins.

'Pretty routine, actually,' he says. 'I always knew we'd resolve it.'

Tim glances back in my direction.

'That's code for serious,' he says. 'They had us bloody worried.'

Before leaving Fairford, I touch base with Tony Webb. Over the last couple of weeks, he and I have been involved in a minor stand-off with Paul over the Jumboscreens. Live pictures for these monsters are normally fed through cables from our outside broadcast control room but Paul is adamant that taxiways must be free from cables. The only other option is to use a couple of microwave links, but the quoted price of £7,000 is way beyond our budget. On a couple of occasions I've tried to change Paul's mind on the issue – arguing for the use of tiny half-inch ramps to protect the cables – but Paul isn't in the mind-changing business.

'Find another way,' he grunted. 'Run them underground.'

At this point, I'd bailed out of the argument, leaving time and deadlines to concentrate Paul's mind but Tony – spurred by Paul's challenge – had invested the best part of three days in finding a solution to the problem. From remote corners of the airbase came old maps, and digging expertise, and rumours of subterranean cable ducts. JCBs were borrowed, holes were excavated. Tony himself even qualified for a digging licence, *de rigueur* under USAF base rules. The trickiest problem was threading our cable under the southern taxiway, linking the control room to the big screen beside the concert venue, but finally Tony and his stalwarts located a BT duct, dug for victory, and pushed the cable through.

This story, of course, has a moral. It relates to Paul and his refusal to take no for an answer, and it's Tony who makes sure I don't miss it. As a newly qualified digger and ductman, he's quietly pleased with himself. 'We all said our leader was barking, didn't we? We all said it couldn't be done.'

'And?'

'He was right all along.'

*

That evening, Lin and I drive down to Bristol to meet Peter March. Peter was a teacher and schools inspector who abandoned the classroom for aviation journalism and he's been with Paul and Tim since the early Seventies. His knowledge of RIAT is unsurpassed, yet this intimacy is balanced by a remarkable ability to keep the beast at arm's length. His admiration for what Paul and Tim have achieved is immense but he knows, as well, the perils of getting too close to this monster they've created. RIAT, all too often, can eat you alive. From the earliest days at North Weald, Peter March is the only survivor.

Amongst his many responsibilities is the official show programme. Discussions about its style and contents have been going on since Christmas and the cover – in the hands of designer Graham Finch – was agreed two months ago. Yet only yesterday, fuelled by adrenalin and an irresistible urge to meddle, Paul has demanded changes. In the place of a nicely graduated blue/grey tint, he now wants a plain white background; in place of a classically good-looking typeface with drop shadow, he's asking for a much plainer font.

I'm looking at both versions. I can't begin to understand why Paul has countermanded his original decision. 'Don't you have any latitude?' I ask. 'Can't you just stick to Plan A?'

'No.'

'Why not?'

'Because he's the client. And because there are so many fingers in the pie now.'

By fingers, Peter means sponsors. Gulfstream's name appears on the programme's front cover, as it should, because they're paying for the production costs. Their view therefore forms an important part of the final consensus, and the longer Peter talks, the more obvious this latest change of plan becomes. Paul's playing safe. He's settling for something he knows won't rock the corporate boat.

This thought triggers memories from Peter. Back in the early Greenham Common days, he was programme editor, press officer, PR chief, and commander of the fly-posting squads. Everyone pitched in and the total budget for the show was less than £10,000. Now, a small army of deputy directors, co-ordinators, managers, and volunteers carefully attend to their individual responsibilities, and the projected budget for the '98 show is £2,860,496.

There is, of course, a compensatory windfall for the Benevolent Fund as the show gets more and more ambitious. Last year's cheque for £424,000 was the biggest ever, and paring down costs to the bare minimum is a way of life at Fairford. But hand in hand with expansion goes the relentless courtship of the major players in the aerospace industry, and this undoubtedly leaves its mark on Peter's programme.

'The space for editorial shrinks and shrinks,' he says ruefully. 'This year British Aerospace want two pages. Lockheed Martin want two pages. Even Meeks, the plant hire people, have a page of their own.'

'Don't you fight your corner?'

'Of course I do, and Paul and I have a space agreement, sixty–forty in our favour.'

This sounds reasonable. Squeezed by the sponsors, Peter is still hanging on to sixty per cent of the text. This gives him room for special sections on display items like David Roome's stacked displays for the RAF's eightieth birthday. So what's the problem?

Peter pulls a face.

'The agreement never survives,' he says. 'The show gets closer, other sponsors come on board, and guess who suffers?'

This, like the VIP car parks and a thousand other examples, is yet another straw in the wind of change that is sweeping over British air displays. To do anything on the scale of RIAT demands substantial sponsorship, and more and more of Paul's and Tim's time is devoted to securing industry support. For the way they've handled this development, Peter March has nothing but praise. 'No one else in the airshow world could have done what they've done. In fact no one's come anywhere close.'

Already, there are rumours of a huge sponsorship deal for the year 2000. Whether or not Paul and Tim will pull it off remains to be seen but Peter March has been more than impressed by the way they've mastered one of the steeper learning curves.

'They've been exceptionally clever. It's not just a question of courtship, it's a question of gently playing the major companies off against each other. Make a success of it for Lockheed Martin, and

British Aerospace will come on board. If they like what they see, it'll be Boeing next. And then Airbus, and GEC, and all the other major players. You reach a kind of critical mass; then everyone's scrambling for a piece of the action.' He shakes his head, looking at the wreckage of his precious front cover. 'Amazing, really.'

Back home for a breather before the final act of this extraordinary drama, I take delivery of an envelope from Fairford. Inside there's a sheaf of notes from Paul, an apron-by-apron analysis detailing the final outcome of Friday's parking meet. These are the fruits of Paul's weekend, bent over his desk, drawing in each of the hundreds of aircraft due to display at RIAT 98. Attached is a note in his neat, ultra-legible hand. *For your scrapbook*, it reads, *I know an anorak when I see one.*

I turn to Apron Black. Instead of the C-5B Galaxy, concert-goers will find themselves looking at a line of big AWACs aircraft. Of Paul's cherished line of fighters, overhanging the edge of the concrete, there's absolutely no sign. Looking down at the carefully-drawn arrows, each carefully tagged with the name and code number of a particular aircraft, I remember a comment of Mel James, out on the airfield, after the parking meet.

'Wait until the planes arrive,' he'd muttered. 'That's the time for the reality check.'

By the weekend, the show is almost upon us. I've enlisted my eighteen-year-old son, Jack, as a volunteer on Catherine Iddon's site team and we report at Gate F as instructed. For the next eight days we won't be setting foot outside the airbase.

The staff reception complex at Gate F, now fully functioning, is less the Taj Mahal, more a lookalike for the executive section of a large provincial airport. Deep blue carpet laps around the row of check-in desks. Flowers spill out of deep plastic tubs. There's even a chandelier hanging from the ceiling of the cavernous reception tent. This, as manager Gill Sharpe is the first to point out, is a world away from the cramped, threadbare chaos of even last year's show.

Queues of incoming volunteers have already formed at the desks, and after Jack and I have collected our passes, meal vouchers and RIAT baseball caps, I bump into Peter March. Since our get-together in Bristol a couple of days ago he's decided to make a fight of it over the programme cover, and to his amazement Paul has conceded the case for a classy grey/blue background tint. In one sense it's the smallest of victories but Peter's eyes are shining when he recounts the series of phone calls. There is, after all, room for negotiation. And 43,000 programmes – at £6 apiece – will look all the better for it.

At five o'clock, the base cinema fills with row after row of RIAT managers. Most of them, like me, are now hunkered down for the coming campaign. Trenches have been dug, supplies laid in, and when Paul and Tim mount the stage for the evening brief there's an unmistakable feeling of optimism in the air. This year's battle plan will succeed, whatever the old enemies – time and circumstance – have in store.

Paul is as brisk and punchy as ever. Sponsorship is breaking all records, Tom Watts is still selling exhibition space, the static display line will be longer than ever, and ticket sales are climbing strongly after the World Cup dip. This is truly excellent news but over the next two-and-a-half hours Paul and Tim sound a number of cautionary notes. There are warnings about not latching on to Follow Me vehicles in a bid to short-cut across the runway (one Volvo last year picked up a convoy of fourteen tailing cars). There are reminders about the need for strict discipline on the show's twenty-five radio nets (many spectators come armed with sophisticated radio scanners and might not appreciate the RIAT sense of humour). And finally, there's even an admission from Paul that this year's parking plan is, in his phrase, 'intimate'.

'It *is* very crowded,' he concedes. 'And it will look very good but I'm afraid it isn't vehicle friendly. So remember – cars and aircraft never mix.'

This reminder, while timely enough, is probably unnecessary. Most of the people here are veterans from previous shows. They know that Paul and Tim have the coming weekend firmly gripped. They understand the need for ground rules and they've experienced the chaos that can ripple from the smallest mistake. And when Sir Roger gets to his feet for the closing exhortation – *Attention to detail! Teamwork!*

The bottom line! – they're already anticipating their first pint of the evening. The show is in good hands. It's going to be a cracker.

Outside, in the mill of departing managers, I run into Sean Maffett. He seizes me by the elbow and steers me towards a quiet corner.

'Have you heard the latest?' he whispers. 'The RAF are refusing to fly Dave Roome's stacks.'

Over the next twenty-four hours, this alarming development unfolds. After modifications and approval by Geoff Brindle's Flying Control Committee, back last month, a formal letter setting out David Roome's plans for the Berlin and RAF Eightieth pageants had gone to Air Commodore Operations at the headquarters of RAF Strike Command, the officer responsible for display participation. Last Friday, David Roome and Les Garside-Beattie had driven up to Strike Command headquarters at High Wycombe to iron out any problems. Facing two Air Commodores, they realised at once that all was not well. The RAF were deeply unhappy about David's proposals. In their view, the plans for briefly coalescing stacks were inherently unsafe and they were not disposed to authorise the participation of RAF aircraft and crew. In other words, with just a week to go to the show itself, David's careful plans for the climax lie in ruins.

Monday dawns, windy and overcast. Over the weekend Paul and Tim have been working the telephones, lobbying figures in the upper reaches of the Ministry of Defence, trying to apply pressure to reverse Strike Command's decision, and this morning sees a three-handed RIAT delegation – Geoff Brindle, Les Garside-Beattie, and David himself – returning to High Wycombe to argue David Roome's case. With time so tight, it seems inconceivable that the RAF can simply cancel two-and-a-half hours of flying and over lunch, back at Fairford, Paul, Sean Maffett and I try to anticipate the outcome of today's confrontation.

In Paul's view, RIAT occupies the moral high ground. The formal proposal for David's birthday tribute has been lying on Strike Command desks for nearly a month. David Roome's pedigree in the arcane world of aerial choreography is beyond question. And, most telling of all, his meticulously developed masterplan has won the unanimous approval of RIAT's own Flying Control Committee – appointed by the Assistant Chief of the Air Staff under the direction of the Secretary of State for Defence. In their view, David's tribute pageant is both flyable and perfectly safe. If the likes of Brian Trubshaw, Chris Yeo, Rick Peacock-Edwards and Geoff Brindle are to be ignored like this, why bother with a Flying Control Committee at all?

The situation, in Sean's view, is unprecedented. Paul and Tim have never been shy of deadlines but with less than a week to go they now face the prospect of completely re-designing the last two-and-a-half hours of the show. Promises about vertical stacks and breathtaking airmanship are already in print. Last week's press conference has produced a wealth of anticipatory coverage and Heidi Standfast has also persuaded a number of regional newspapers to publish special Air Tattoo supplements. Most embarrassing of all, Peter March is even now standing over a Cornish printing press, monitoring the production of 43,000 souvenir programmes, each one detailing exactly what David Roome has in store for the flying programme.

I'm looking at the remains of my cheese salad, wondering how David Roome must be feeling. Here is the man who – at the RAF's own bidding – sent rivers of aircraft over Central London for the Battle of Britain's fiftieth anniversary. Here is the man who first turned Paul's proposals down and then went away and translated them into flyable lines in the sky. After five months of planning – all those grids, all those headings, all that split-second timing – has the show's spectacular climax really crashed and burned?

Paul picks at his pasty and chips. There's still no word about the outcome of today's meeting but the portents don't look good.

'On Friday they ordered Dave to go away and produce a Plan B,' he broods. 'At this stage in the game, that's bloody foolish.'

Sean nods, sympathetic. He's had his finger on the RAF's pulse for a long time now and he feels the heartbeat getting more and more irregular. In his view, they've become hidebound and inflexible. They have absolutely no time for concepts like the Theatre of the Air and this year their attitude to RIAT has occasionally verged on outright hostility. Already, this month, there have been the difficulties over the Battle of Britain Memorial Flight, and the Red Arrows. Now this bombshell. The original notion for an Eightieth anniversary tribute came from the RAF itself. How come, at this late hour, they've chosen to wreck it?

I'm still looking at Paul. Without clearance from the RAF, this part of the show won't happen. Given a firm thumbs-down, what does he do next?

A deep weariness briefly shadows his face. Then he shakes his head. 'We'll win,' he says tersely. 'We have to.'

The afternoon comes and goes. In the real world of the airshow, out of range of Strike Command's big guns, tents are still going up, mobiles are ringing and, in her office behind the Patrons' Pavilion, Caroline Rogers is weathering a tiny crisis over flowers. Caroline is Deputy Director for Business Development and to her falls the responsibility for keeping RIAT's corporate sponsors happy. It's a huge job and it gets bigger every year but as more and more aerospace money drops into the Benevolent Fund pot, the need to take care of the smallest details remains as important as ever.

Caroline Rogers cut her teeth in the frenzied world of catering. She has an honours degree in tact and the lowest blood pressure of anyone I've yet met. This afternoon's little drama features Michelle, the British Aerospace executive who had some trouble finding William's Kitchen at Nailsworth for the Gala Dinner tasting back in April.

For the show itself, Michelle is supervising BAe's impressive hospitality chalet. Already, she's found herself hopelessly overbooked – 260 acceptances for 100 table places – but Caroline has managed to solve this with the addition of an extra chalet. Now the time has arrived to give the interior decor some finishing touches.

This year's theme colour is red. A week ago, flower-wise, Michelle asked for birds of paradise 'or something orangey'. Caroline passed the request on to Tony Morris, the Cheltenham florist who supplies all RIAT's shrubs and flowers. Now, with three days left before the first corporate guests arrive, Michelle's having second thoughts. She's been to Tesco's. She's seen some nice little flowers. They're blue. They look a bit like violets. Might Caroline oblige?

Caroline is in the obliging business but time isn't on Michelle's side and Caroline needs to be clear about exactly what she's after. Michelle has the name of the little violet numbers. They're called *brodia*. Tony Morris is with us. He's driven over from Cheltenham to sort out the last of the shrubs. Like Caroline, he's used to the madness of RIAT but conversations like these are designed to test him.

The next ten minutes, for me at least, is the purest confusion. Is it to be eight vases or six? Does Michelle want twenty table posies or fourteen? Are they to be in red or orange or blue? Caroline has a master list and as the conversation develops, the neat lines of type disappear under a duvet of scribbled amendments.

Tony, meanwhile, is addressing himself to the practicalities. He has a wonderful Gloucestershire accent, bemusement hidden beneath the softest country burr.

'These violet things,' he says. 'They come from down Italy somewhere and they only deliver Wednesdays.'

Michelle looks puzzled. 'So?'

'It's Monday already.'

'But that gives you two days.'

'No, but the man down there, he leaves tomorrow morning in the truck. So if you go for the violets, I've got to phone the order through. You follow me?'

Michelle plainly doesn't. As the client, she wants the right to change her mind yet again. Caroline, very gently, suggests it's time to make a decision. Tony's right. If he leaves the order too late, the truck might be rumbling north without the violets. And what would Michelle do then?

Michelle is unpacking one of her bubble-wrapped vases.

'Easy,' she grins. 'I'd just go back to Tesco's. They're £3.99 a go, all done up in cellophane. You just snip and dunk.'

Caroline and Tony retreat from this exchange and hurry up the line of chalets to the big Patrons' Pavilion at the end. Lockheed Martin are sponsoring Patrons' this year and they've built a small concrete plinth outside the canopied entrance. This will shortly support steel models of best-selling Lockheed products – the F-117 Nighthawk stealth fighter, the C-130J variant – and Caroline wants to soften the concrete edges with a nice hedge. Lockheed executives think that's a good idea but want the hedge additionally to fend off trophy hunters. Tony must therefore come up with nature's answer to barbed wire.

'We could go for *berberis*,' he says at length. 'That's a kind of coppery, prickly hedge.'

'How prickly?'

'Very.'

Later in the afternoon, still awaiting word from High Wycombe, I join Paul and his young RAF holding officer, Tonia Glover, on a tour of the airfield. We end at the Flight Centre. Inside, the huge hangar is hung with signs for the benefit of incoming aircrew. HM Customs. HM Immigration. Passes and Permits. Accommodation. Flying Operations. Car Rentals. Snack Bar. It looks like a Lego airport, a tiny miracle of organisation, and behind a desk in the corner I find the resident weather man, Ian Matthews, seconded from RAF Benson, near Oxford. Over the past few months I've become just a little obsessed with weather charts. I can tell a cold front from a warm front, and nine times out of ten I can translate all those isobars into cloud patterns and the wet breath of a westerly wind. With the help of a world-wide data feed, Ian has drawn up forecast maps for the next five days. On Wednesday and Thursday a deep trough is due to sweep in from the Atlantic. This will bring a lowish cloud base with brisk south-westerly winds, gusting force six. This is far from ideal for the first wave of aircraft in Sue Allen's arrival plot but Friday brings a dramatic improvement. By then, the wind will have backed to the north-west, chasing the depression into the North Sea. Behind it, building nicely on Ian's charts, comes a big fat tongue of high pressure licking up towards the south of England. High pressure means sunshine, warmth, cloudless skies, a perfect day.

Leaving the Flight Centre with Paul, I shake my head in disbelief. He and Tim must be jointly sponsored by Hartley's. Jammy isn't the word. Paul pauses by his courtesy Daimler. He's been checking with Ian Matthews for the last three days.

'What did I tell you?' he says, beaming. 'Fortune favours the bold.'

Alas, not always. In the early evening, at last, comes news from High

Wycombe. Strike Command are still adamantly opposed to the vertical stacks and no amount of detailed briefing from David Roome, Les Garside-Beattie, and Geoff Brindle can alter their refusal to commit RAF aircraft and crew. Paul confers on the phone with Sir Roger Palin. As a retired Air Chief Marshal and Controller of the Benevolent Fund, Sir Roger wields considerable clout. Assured by the audit trail of paperwork stretching back to January, and angered by the RAF's refusal to participate in its own birthday celebrations, he is quite prepared to take the issue to the highest level, but after a long discussion, he and Paul agree that no time remains for an appeal. Arguing the case in front of the Chief of the Air Staff would, in all probability, swallow another two days. Asking David Roome to design and brief an alternative display in twenty-four hours would be both unreasonable and dangerous.

By the time I catch up with Ian Sheeley on Tuesday morning, David Roome's carefully nurtured Eightieth tribute has been officially binned. In its place, lying on Ian's desk in the Flight Centre, is a smudged, two-page fax, the fruit of David's labours overnight. The two-lap stacks of aircraft, grouped by type, have gone. Any attempt to explore new corners of the air display envelope has been abandoned. In its place, interwoven with solo displays and Missing Men formations, are five fly-bys, each composed of same-age aircraft. The first features an SE-5, a Curtiss Jenny, a Sopwith Camel, a Tutor, and a Magister. The last offers the crowd a Canberra, a Hawk, a Harrier, a Jaguar, and a Tornado. Each of these formations will fly the length of the crowd in line abreast. On paper it looks pretty ordinary and Ian agrees that on the day there's every chance that it will look no different to the kind of standard flypast dished up by every UK airshow. For this year, with the exception of the surviving Berlin Airlift, the Theatre of the Air is history.

Sean Maffett can scarcely believe it. He has his own copy of David Roome's fax and his disillusion with the service he knew and loved is near total. In the heat of this particular moment he suggests – only partly in jest – that next year RIAT should completely sever its links with the RAF and put together a show on the basis of a wealth of foreign and civilian contacts. Whether an Air Tattoo organised by the

RAF's own Benevolent Fund could ever do anything so radical is a moot point but, faced with explaining this sudden change of finale to a crowd of 100,000, Sean is sorely tempted to level the score.

At the end of the two-and-a-half hour tribute, Paul wants the RAF College Band to play live as twenty-one Tucanos soar overhead in their specially-rehearsed 'Eighty' formation. A medley of three numbers is to start with 'Happy Birthday' and Paul is bidding for an entry in the *Guinness Book of Records* for mass community singing as the crowd join in. Sean, who has just persuaded the band to mime to a pre-recorded CD in the interest of split-second control, is no longer convinced about the choice of music.

'Happy birthday?' he queries. 'Who cares?'

The morning slips by. Twenty-four hours from the arrival of the first aircraft, Wally Armstrong yo-yos between the north and south sides of the airfield, a radio in each hand. Thirty thousand pounds' worth of champagne for the corporate hospitality chalets has just arrived and a communications foul-up means there's nowhere to put the stuff. Where's the secure storage? Why hasn't it turned up on time? He shakes his head, lifting a radio as yet another voice repeats his call sign.

'The loos at Patrons' aren't working,' he announces. 'Any ideas?'

Over in her complex at Gate F, meanwhile, site manager Catherine Iddon is trying to cope with sudden demands for more portable crowd barriers. At a cost of £13,000, she's already hired nearly 2,500 of the things. Her budget is tight and at the height of the season for big public events there's absolutely no possibility of laying hands on any more. The UK has run out of crowd barriers. End of story.

'You'll just have to cope with what we've got,' she confides to the radio. 'And I'm sure you will.'

Coping is the day's big theme. At 3 p.m., a small meeting convenes in the office that Paul and Tim share in the shadow of the control tower. This building is officially designated 1108 and down the corridor, separate hives of activity, are Show Operations Control (SOC), the

Message Centre, the Comms HQ, and the big locked office where accountant Sue Vizor and her team will be counting all the incoming cash. The public days of the show are still seventy-two hours away but already the pace is frantic. Pausing for breath beside Paul's door, I catch Hugh Lohan's eye. This year, Hugh is working in SOC. Last year, he edited the daily newsletter. His knowledge of RIAT is broad, as well as deep.

'Remember,' he says, 'no plan survives contact with the enemy.'

Present for the meeting in Paul and Tim's office are Geoff Brindle, Ian Sheeley, Sean Maffett, Tony Webb, and Simon Boyle, the young RAF holding officer. Paul and Tim have an hour to dismember David Roome's heavily bandaged Eightieth tribute, and test it against the clock, ATC constraints, and the expectations of the crowd. David has spent all night re-configuring his masterplan. It would be entirely forgivable if one or two bits didn't entirely hang together.

The troubleshooting starts at once. The first formation will be led by a civilian pilot called Des Biggs. Does he have the requisite CAA display authorisation? If he doesn't, who else does? According to Ian Sheeley, David's revised plan calls for the formation to fly in stepped-up increments of ten feet. Is that too tight a gap? Will it display the aircraft to best effect? Shouldn't the Flying Control Committee – Geoff Brindle – be thinking in terms of fifty feet? These are questions that should have been answered months ago but Strike Command's sudden bombshell has moved events into a strange nether world. Are we really trying to bolt together this limp excuse for a birthday tribute at just three days' notice? Are the guys up at Strike *that* determined to wreck the party?

At this point, rain begins to lash the airfield and as the debate hurries on to the third of the formations – the Hurricane, Spitfires and Lancaster of the BBMF – I sense that we've hit rock bottom. All that planning. All that publicity. All those expectations. All that excitement. Gone.

This, though, is no time for recrimination. The last forty-eight hours have filleted David's pageant and the job for these men is to make the best of what's left. We're looking at serial 10. Before the BBMF run in for their flypast, two civilian Spitfires – flown by Andy Sephton and

Air Marshal Cliff Spink – have just taken off. The pace of David's Plan B is faltering. There's too much time between events. Too little is going on. It's Paul who voices the obvious solution.

'Let's have one of the civvie Spits display solo,' he says.

Geoff Brindle agrees.

'Never fails,' he says. 'Great idea.'

'Which one, then?'

'Andy Sephton. He does a great display.'

'How long?'

'Six minutes to land?'

Ian Sheeley has his finger in David Roome's fax.

'He doesn't land,' he points out. 'He flies back to the hold.'

'OK,' Paul nods. 'Five minutes, then. Let's make that Serial 10a for the time being. 15.57 to 16.02.'

'Remember the Blenheim breaking to land before him.'

'OK,' Paul frowns. '15.58 to 16.03. Agreed?'

Heads nod around the room. The first half hour of the tribute has been tightened by five minutes, and Paul's amendment now puts David's display exactly back on schedule.

'BBMF next?' Paul grunts. 'Straight fly past again?'

Sean Maffett nods.

'Yep,' he says. 'Even the air force can manage that.'

Towards the end of the programme, a line of modern jets fly in to complete the five formations. Mention of the Hawk triggers a comment from Ian Sheeley. He's heard on the Service grapevine that the RAF are staging a quiet practice at RAF Marham, up in Norfolk. Any debate about the order of these five aircraft – where they'll be placed in the line – is therefore academic. This decision, like so many others, has suddenly been pre-empted by the remorseless pressure of events.

After the fifth formation come the twenty-one Tucanos, flying the birthday figure. David's original script called for the black trainers to burst through an RAF fin-flash – red, white and blue painted in smoke – but the Red Arrows, too, have refused to join either the spirit or the letter of the Fairford birthday party and so the Tucanos will simply fly in from the north, denied the drama of their original entrance. There's still concern, though, that the Tucanos shall be given a firm commit time. Building the '80' formation is a tricky feat of airmanship and a succession of delays is the last thing they'll need.

Tim Prince is peering at David's timings.

'OK,' he says, 'let's give them a firm go-time. If we're running late on the day we'll just bin whatever gets in the way.'

We all return to David's script. What comes before the Tucanos?

'It's formation five,' Ian Sheeley announces. 'The Marham lot.'

There's a pause, then a collective chuckle. Formation five, the modern jets, will be the RAF's own contribution to the birthday finale. What sweeter revenge than to return the compliment and send them packing. It's unlikely to happen, of course, but just the thought of getting even puts a smile back on the faces around this room.

'I knew it,' Sean Maffett mutters. 'There *is* a God.'

That evening, at the regular progress meeting in the base cinema, Paul calls on Ian Sheeley to update the other managers on the latest revisions to David Roome's finale. Already, an alibi has been agreed in the form of an official RIAT explanation for this sudden departure from the heavily publicised programme. With the sweetest of ironies, the weather has suddenly become our friend.

Back in the meeting in Paul and Tim's office, Geoff Brindle had carefully plotted out the line.

'All this wind and rain has given us a headache,' he'd suggested. 'It's been very gusty, as you know, and the vintage aircraft are more than a bit vulnerable. They're non-radio. They're operating from Rendcomb. And putting them in with modern jets is pushing it just a wee bit too far. Thus the adjustments.'

This, of course, exactly echoes part of Strike Command's case but two hours later, in the base cinema, Ian Sheeley puts it a little more bluntly. He announces that the original birthday tribute has changed. The vertical stacks have gone. In their place, punters should expect something rather different. The phrase he uses is 'formation passes'. For David Roome, and five months of detailed planning, it's the saddest, bluntest epitaph.

That night, in the vague hope of tracking down my son, I go to a party at the far end of the airfield. Catherine Iddon's site team are having a premature celebration, twenty hours ahead of the showground's completion. Standing over the hissing barbecue, poking at the fat curls of sausage, is Support Services co-ordinator, Mel Kidd. He, too, is in the crisis-management business.

Mid-morning, word came from the complex of offices in Building 1108 – next to the control tower – that the loos were overflowing. Something clearly had to be done. But Mel smelled a rat. He'd been driving along the southern perimeter road only yesterday, with the car window open, and he had first-hand evidence that the system had only just been emptied. So how come the occupants of 1108 had refilled a 6,000 litre collection tank in just twenty-four hours? Had they taken the emergency evacuation plan just a little too seriously?

Mel somehow doubted it. Despatching a water ranger to investigate, he awaited developments. Within the hour, the ranger reported back. One of the contractors had parked a sentry box loo – one of the sort you put on building sites – beside 1108. He'd neglected to lock it, and pretty soon the loo was in constant use. Half a day later, it overflowed – with dramatic consequences. The walls between RIAT's many fiefdoms are paper thin. Word spread that the underground collection tank, rather than the portaloo, was full.

Mel gives his sausage a final turn. Moral of this little story? Always lock your thunderbox...

No plan survives contact with the enemy. Wednesday morning's first phone call brings news from Lin, my wife, that my mother has broken her thigh. At eighty-two, already in a state of some confusion, she's been rushed to hospital. For the time being, her leg is in traction. Later today, she'll undergo a two-hour operation to pin both ends of the broken femur. Lin will phone again once my mother has recovered from the anaesthetic. Everything is under control. I'm not to worry. This news gives the day a strange cast. There may, after all, be a world outside Fairford.

I'm not sure that David Roome agrees. I find him in the Flight Centre, manning the desk marked 'Flying Display'. He's looking slightly battered – resigned would be a better word – and, when I offer my sympathies for all that wasted effort, he just shrugs. Privately, he'd always regarded Geoff Brindle's Flying Control Committee as the real test of his Berlin and RAF Eightieth plans. If he was to encounter turbulence, it would be from the likes of Les Garside-Beattie and Chris Yeo, the men charged with giving the air display a clean bill of health. The possibility that his masters at Strike Command might be difficult was pretty remote. The thought that they might reject his plan entirely was inconceivable.

So what went wrong?

David has plainly been thinking of little else since his first meeting with the Air Commodores on Friday. In his view, they simply hadn't understood the letter sent to them in June, which summarised the events and was designed as an introduction to a detailed verbal brief he was expecting to deliver personally. Instead of calling for the full brief, they had chosen to work from the summary, and from there it was only a small step to talk of confliction where there wasn't any. They were making decisions on the basis of carelessly-drawn tracks that appeared to converge as the planes rolled out for the run past the saluting veterans. They were making no allowances whatsoever for the separations – both lateral and vertical – that David had been at such pains to maintain between aircraft.

As fast-jet pilots, both David Roome and Geoff Brindle have spent their service careers mastering the black arts of air defence. They know about confliction, about intercepts, about lots of aircraft weaving intricate patterns in the sky, but none of their collective experience, nearly 12,000 hours, seemed – at Strike Command – to count.

'It's the not-invented-here syndrome,' David says bluntly. 'We were trying to do something different – safely – and I'm not sure they really understood that.'

David looks glum for a moment. Already, yesterday's amended display brief is on its way by fax and E-mail to participating squadrons. It may raise the heartbeat in a number of watching veterans but it certainly won't fulfil the extravagant promises in the press and the souvenir programme. Was all that work really for nothing?

'Not entirely. We'll salvage something. We've still got ninety-seven aircraft and there'll be some nice moments but the sad thing is we're back to where we started. Aircraft will transit right to left. It'll be no different to any other puddle-jumping little show.' He gives me a rueful grin and then nods at my notepad. 'Good luck with the book,' he says. 'Shame about the display.'

Outside the hangar, in the last of the morning sunshine, I can hear the far-away whine of throttled-back turbo-props. There's an aircraft away to the east, easing down the glidepath. Moments later, I make out the distinctive nose-down shape of an incoming P-3 Orion. It's 09.23, the very first arrival. RIAT 98 is under way.

From Eng Ops, in Building 29, I hitch a ride with Mel James' wife, Denise. She's charged with the welfare of the refuelling, ground support and parking teams and her Land Rover is full of cold drinks, sandwiches, and sundry other nibbles. Across the top of the windscreen, in day-glo orange, a sticker reads FAIRY GODMOTHER.

We drive to the southside around the perimeter track. Everywhere I look, the airfield is coming alive. Shuttle buses, full of volunteers shipping out to their battle stations. Follow-Me jeeps and Volvos, ready to shepherd arriving aircraft to their parking slots. The Park and View enclosure beside the runway threshold, already packed with men in bulky anoraks, perched on collapsible ladders. A sight of these die-hard enthusiasts will, I know, bring a smile to Paul Bowen's face. At £9 each, the money is beginning to roll in.

We pause beside the enclosure to watch a little Swiss Air Force Learjet dancing in to land. The runway lights – red, green, yellow – stretch away towards infinity. As the Learjet touches down and the pilot throttles back, I hear the chatter of a thousand cameras. The spotters again, banging off that extra shot.

At the fuel farm, beside Gate A, I join Andy Chapman and Dave Jeffreys on one of the eight RAF fuel bowsers tasked to slake the thirsts of incoming aircraft. For Dave, an ops duty officer with Britannia Airlines at Luton, RIAT has become a regular highlight of his year. He rides shotgun on the bowser, handling all the paperwork and keeping track of the fuel bills. Andy, on the other hand, has never been to Fairford before. A service driver from RAF Marham, he was volunteered for the Air Tattoo and has still to grasp the sheer scale of the event. So far, mid-morning, only a handful of aircraft have arrived but he's seen the daily arrivals schedule and he knows that by Friday night these yawning spaces will be black with aeroplanes.

'Everyone comes here for the same reason,' he says. 'To be part of The Biggie. Whenever you mentioned Fairford back at Marham, everyone goes *Wow*.'

We head for Apron Green on the north side of the airfield, waiting for trade. As we round the runway threshold, I resist the temptation to duck as a big USAF C-141 Starlifter flares out at the end of the long descent. Dave, it turns out, has the two key qualifications for serious aircraft-watching: the memory of an elephant and the eyes of a hawk. The C-141 is halfway down the runway, shuddering under reverse thrust.

'She's in from Memphis,' he tells me. 'That's an eight-hour transit.'

We rumble on, Andy nursing the big Scammel. Eighteen thousand two hundred and fifty litres of highly volatile Avtur is all the incentive you'd ever need to avoid oncoming traffic, but Dave and I only have eyes for the sky to the east. A roar of jet engines on full throttle announces the arrival of a trio of RAF Jaguar GR1s from 41(F) Squadron. They roar down the runway at 100 feet before breaking to the south for the long turn towards the downwind leg. As they bank against the tumble of clouds to the west, Dave's radio comes to life. Our call sign is Jaffa. Boss Hogs hands out the refuelling assignments.

'Boss Hogs, Jaffa. Over.'

'Jaffa, Boss Hogs. Go ahead.'

'Yours is the Swiss Learjet. Apron Green.'

Dave has already found the little executive jet, rolling back towards us on the northern taxiway. He glances at Andy. 'Ever done a Learjet before?'

'Never.'

'It's open line. Half in one wing, half in the other. It leans right over when you're pumping.'

I'm back in the mysterious world of other people's expertise. 'Open line' evidently means you refuel the aircraft like a car. I'm wondering whether we might qualify for Bonus Points at the end of all this when the radio comes alive again. The Learjet has what Boss Hogs terms a 'negative requirement'. We're heading, instead, for a little twin-engined Islander, newly arrived from RAF Aldergrove, outside Belfast.

This, too, is parked on Apron Green. Andy hauls out the long refuelling hose and hands the refuelling nozzle to the aircraft's co-pilot, already standing on the wing. The Islander belongs to the Army Air Corps, and the fuselage behind the cockpit is packed with camera equipment.

The pilot, SSgt Mark Kingston, gives me the brief on the plane's capability. He's here to join the SkyWatch line-up, and he explains how the cameras in the back are equipped with prisms to supply panoramic shots as he sweeps back and forth over sites suspected of harbouring explosive devices. Only after his photographs have been analysed for trip wires and other booby traps, will the bomb disposal boys be released to work on the device itself. It's at this point that the SkyWatch theme begins to make hard operational sense, and I'm wondering about the wisdom of overflying unexploded bombs at 200 feet when I hear a yell from the co-pilot, up on the wing. Mark has been too busy talking to me to keep an eye on the fuel gauge. His mate with the nozzle is covered in Avtur.

Andy shuts off the fuel. The co-pilot jumps down from the wing. He's less than amused at becoming a walking fire risk but he's brought two spare flying suits and is already peeling off the one he's wearing.

'I'll dump it in the bath overnight,' he grunts. 'That should sort it.'

From the Islander, we return to the southside, prowling up and down, looking – unsuccessfully – for customers. Dave is complaining to Boss Hogs that this is lousy publicity for the book, a clever ploy to give us first refusal on the Ukrainian Tu-22M *Backfire* bomber, star of the static show and due in from Kiev any time now. It's Dave who spots it first. Those eyes again.

'There,' he says, pointing away to the east.

Thirty seconds tick by. Even with binoculars, I can see nothing but clouds. Finally, exactly where Dave had indicated, the distinctive nose-on shape of the sleek, swing-wing bomber swims into view. I track it down the glide path. Dave is beside himself with excitement. As it roars past, braking under reverse thrust, he's taking his tenth photo.

'I wonder where he's parking up?' he muses, back in the cab.

I think back to the parking meet, and Paul's subsequent re-write over the weekend.

'Black,' I say smugly. 'Over there.'

We wait in vain for the *Backfire*. Finally, nearly an hour later, it taxies towards us. We can see the aircrew up in the tiny tandem cockpits. The pilot eases the big jet on to the apron alongside Black, noses towards the edge of the concrete, and then shuts down. Minutes later, word comes from Paul Lindsay, Mel James' number two in Eng Ops, that the Ukrainians must be hard up for laughs. Parked so close to the grass, there's absolutely no chance of getting the *Backfire* out again. The customised towbar is stored in the belly of the escorting Il-76, a giant, four-engined, heavy-lift transport, but even with the towbar there's no room on the concrete for the tug. RIAT has just acquired its first-ever *Backfire*. On permanent loan.

Waved away from the *Backfire*, we motor slowly up to Apron Pink to refuel the Il–76. The engineer aboard is asking for 45,000 litres. We have 15,740 left. An accompanying bowser has a full load. But even between us, we don't have enough to satisfy this thirsty giant.

By the time we arrive, a large group of Ukrainians are supervising the off-load. They've heard about their *Backfire*'s parking plight and think the towbar might help. The towbar, naturally, is stowed at the wrong end of the enormous hold. The row of big steel containers, off-loaded from the Ilyushin, lengthens on the tarmac. By mid-afternoon, I'm riding on the back of a tug as we return to the *Backfire* with the towbar. The towbar alone is three times the length of a family car. For Paul Lindsay and his team, it doesn't look too promising.

Rounding the curve of Apron Black, the *Backfire* comes into view. Straining on each of the three wheels are twenty-plus air cadets. Paul Emery, another member of the Eng Ops team, has taken the situation by the scruff of the neck and given it a bit of a shake. When he suggested brute force, everyone said that muscle power alone couldn't shift a *Backfire* bomber. Yet here it is, moving.

I slither off the tug the moment it comes to a halt, and take a series of photos. This, I've already decided, is RIAT at its finest. Ninety-five tons of Russian bomber stuck fast on the tarmac? No problem.

*

At this point, I bid farewell to Andy and Dave and hitch a lift with John Thorpe. As Airfield Manager, John has a roving troubleshooter brief which he clearly relishes. Having spent the best part of a week preparing for the arrival of hundreds of aircraft, he's been tied up for most of the day trying to corral a surprise intruder.

Reports of a deer loose on the airfield came to him at 08.34. Broadcasting a general alert in case the animal strayed into the path of a landing jet, he led a convoy of four Follow-Me Volvos and Chrysler Cherokees to track the beast down. At the western end of the airfield, he finally spotted it. After a series of high speed manoeuvres, the deer was effectively trapped. The police, alerted by radio, opened a nearby gate. The Volvos closed on the deer, shepherding it towards the open gate. Two metres from the gate, a passing lorry on the road outside startled the deer. It bolted through the tiny gap between the cars and headed, once again, for the runway.

More high speed chases. More handbrake turns. Trapped once again, the animal was on the point of submission when a deer warden from the Cirencester animal rescue service turned up. He had the kit and the experience to deal with the problem. While he was preparing a dart to anaesthetise the beast, the deer did a runner for the second time.

We're sitting in John's Cherokee, listening to the chatter of radio traffic. Already, he's become Deer Hunter One. Lockheed's new C-130 J howls past. What next for the deer?

John gives me a withering look.

'We had the bugger well under control,' he says, 'until the expert turned up.'

By the time the airfield closes at six o'clock on Wednesday evening, seventy-four aircraft have been tucked away in their designated slots. In the vastness of the airfield they look almost insignificant, a calling card for the armada due to fly in tomorrow and Friday. Back in my room at the Visiting Officers' Quarters (or VOQs), I scribble notes to myself. Lin has phoned with the news that my mother is out of surgery, and thanks to Paul Bowen I'm able to dash back for a brief bedside visit. He has sole access to a Daimler and a driver – Sue Stafford –

for the duration of show week and he's put Sue and the car at my disposal for the ninety-mile trip back to Portsmouth.

It's a generous, touching gesture, entirely typical of this extraordinary organisation, and I'm walking back to the base cinema to rendezvous with Sue when one of the mini-buses stops to offer me a lift. Seconds later, outside the American BX store, the driver stops again. A dozen Jordanians, pilots and ground crew from the Royal Falcons display team have finished their duty-free shopping and they, too, would appreciate a lift.

They pile in, laden down with goodies. One of them in the seat behind me offers the driver a cold can of Pepsi. The driver thanks him and takes it. There's one for me, too, but I decline, explaining that even the sight of the stuff turns me over. We pull away from the kerb. Behind me I can hear the buzz of conversation, then laughter. I feel a tap on my shoulder. I turn round. A dozen hands are stretched towards me, each holding a can of ice cold Pepsi.

That night, Sue drives me through torrential rain to Portsmouth. My mother, recovering from surgery, gazes up at me from the hospital bed. I've been keeping her abreast of my Fairford adventures since October but her memory has been failing for years and a hefty shot of post-operative morphine doesn't help.

'Airshow?' she queries. 'What airshow?'

I'm back in my room at the VOQ by midnight. By dawn the rain has gone and by the time I make it into the Flight Centre the first wave of the day's arrivals are whining past on the northern taxiway. Inside the big hangar, I find Geoff Brindle manning the FCC's desk. As Chairman of the Flying Control Committee he's charged with meeting incoming show pilots, testing their display routines and ribbon diagrams against the FCC's own regulations. Yesterday, it seems, was especially interesting, not least because one of the Ukrainian pilots had some ambitious plans for his big An-72 transport, NATO codenamed *Coaler*.

'He wanted to loop it,' Geoff says wonderingly.

'Is that possible?'

'It may well be.'

'So what did you say?'

'Not on my airfield you won't.'

Geoff reaches for a pen. On the back of yesterday's arrival plan, he sketches the Ukrainian's show routine. The top of a loop will find the aircraft upside down. When Geoff vetoed this manoeuvre on safety grounds, the two men found themselves in what Geoff terms 'an AOB auction'. AOB is pilot-speak for angle-of-bank. An AOB of ninety degrees would stand the An-72 vertically on one wing. Beyond that, in aerobatic terms, it becomes a wingover.

The Ukrainian, Lt Col Alexiy Veneev, opened the bidding at 150 degrees. When Geoff finally settled at 110 degrees, he sensed his new pilot friend was genuinely offended.

'I'm not questioning his competence,' Geoff insists. 'Far from it. I'm simply here to give him as much latitude as the rules afford. An AOB of 110 degrees means he'll have to go away and re-configure. He's not happy but it'll be an interesting test.'

From the Flight Centre, I nip up to the USAF's Community Activity Center (CAC), where Tim Cairns – the RIAT manager co-ordinating the show's event services – is about to brief a couple of hundred ATC cadets. This afternoon Tim will be staging a major exercise designed to test the system to its limits, and the cadets have been cast as casualties. All week, Col Brian Robertson's 306 Field Hospital RAMC (V) has been taking shape in Hangar 1205, and a handful of his staff have now pitched camp on the patio outside the CAC. Their role is to make the casualties look as realistic as possible and their repertoire of critical injuries includes a big bowl of pretend blood for major flesh wounds, and *crêpe*-like discs of scorched cotton to mimic third-degree burns.

TA Sgt Loader is stirring the blood. Ingredients include water, food colouring, and generous squeezes of glycerine to make it thicker. The comic potential of this little scene is rich with possibilities, but Sgt Loader is keen to point out the darker side.

'You've got to know what a real wound looks like,' he says grimly. 'You've got to understand how wounds bleed.'

Inside the club, the big briefing room is packed with kids. For them,

287

this is obviously the perfect day out: a yummy packed lunch, big dollops of stage blood, and the chance to act their hearts out. The latter, for Tim Cairns, is especially important. They'll shortly become the victims of a major disaster. Some of them will die. Others will be unconscious. But the majority will still be on their feet, lightly wounded, traumatised, unable to comprehend the piles of burning wreckage and charred flesh.

'We want to make this as realistic as possible,' he tells them. 'And we're relying on you to give our blokes a hard time. The dead and badly injured can be pretty straightforward. It's the survivors who often make things tough for us.'

Around the room, I can sense a gleeful anticipatory stirring. His briefing over, Tim catches my eye.

'I've arranged for you to ride with the Red Column,' he says. 'They'll be attending the off-base incident.'

The emergency exercise is to start at 2.00. Before lunch, I'm due to attend Patti Heady's major press conference, over on the southside, and I hitch a lift around the perimeter track as a beautifully restored Constellation floats in to a perfect landing. Paul Bowen has been looking forward to this moment for months, and as little puffs of smoke blossom from the tyres I marvel at the world that he and Tim have created for themselves. Virtually any aircraft. From virtually anywhere in the world. Theirs. For the whole weekend.

By the time I make it to the Patrons' Pavilion, the press conference is over. A display for this book occupies a tiny corner of the big tented enclosure and it's very odd to see one of David Higham's team taking advance orders for something that has yet to be finished. What if one of Tim Cairns' scenarios comes horribly true? What if another night of RIAT hospitality sees off my last remaining brain cell?

Outside, in the fenced-off viewing area in front of Patrons', print journalists and television crews are watching one of the display rehearsals. Tony Webb's media team includes Harry Burgoyne, a C-130 Hercules pilot from nearby Lyneham. Harry and I have already shared a couple of nights in the bar, bonding over pints of Arkell's best, and now I join him as he peers upwards. 'What's that, then?'

Harry follows my pointing finger.

'The *Coaler*,' he says. 'The Ukrainian cargo job.'

I look up with renewed interest. The *Coaler* was the subject of Geoff Brindle's AOB auction. Lt Col Vaneev is the pilot who spent most of last night taming his wilder stunts for the benefit of the FCC. Now, climbing into a steep wingover, he appears to be stretching Geoff's indulgence to the limits. On the ground, the An-72 is a very odd-looking plane indeed – a short, fat fuselage with two jet engines on top of the main wing – but up in the air Lt Col Vaneev flies it with astonishing grace. At the top of the wingover, the plane appears – for a moment – to hang in the air; then it plunges into a near vertical dive, only to pull up into another soaring climb.

Harry is following the *Coaler* with some interest. Many thousands of hours at the controls of a Hercules have given him a healthy respect for gravity. When I ask him for marks out of ten, he offers a wry smile.

'There's always one display that worries me,' he murmurs. 'And right now I'm watching it.'

My third lift of the day – back to the northside to join Tim Cairns' bloodfest – puts me into the company of a USAF KC-135 crew, newly arrived from Kansas. The KC-135 is a big four-engined tanker, built around the Boeing 707 airframe, and for at least one of the crew – Master Sgt Earl Flower – Fairford is already an eye-opener. With the parking ramps beginning to fill, he stares out of the mini-bus window at the lines of Tornado fighter-bombers, neatly angled at forty degrees.

'It's big,' he mutters. 'So big.'

The driver glances up at him in the rear-view mirror.

'This is nothing,' she says. 'Tomorrow it gets really busy.'

'You kidding? There are *more* aircraft?'

I'm staring out of the window, too. The Constellation has found a spot for itself over on Apron Green. The Slovak display team, the White Albatroses, are readying their L39s for take off. While a Swedish Gripen, one of the new generation of composite fly-by-wire fighters, is taxiing back after an ear-shattering rehearsal.

Riding with these guys, I'm seeing the show through American eyes and for the first time I realise that Fairford has truly become a meeting point between East and West, between the two old rival Cold War blocs. From the States, B-1B bombers, and big old Buffs, and the giant bulk of the Galaxy heavy-lift transport. From the Ukrainians and the Poles and the Czechs and the Hungarians, MiG-29s, and Il-76s, and even the veteran MiG-21. All courtesy of RIAT and a year of incredibly hard work.

Earl Flowers' cigar is still unlit.

'Jeez,' he says. 'Just look at that ship, will ya? A *Backfire.*'

Snatching a plate of chips before joining Red Column, I bump into Sean Maffett. He's been pondering the commentary demands of David Roome's revised RAF birthday tribute and he's far from happy. Might I have time for the briefest chat?

We find a quiet corner in the Flight Centre and confer over coffee. Sean hasn't been sleeping too well. As the public voice of RIAT over the show weekend, he has to come up with some kind of explanation for the sudden absence of David Roome's finale stacks and he's not at all sure which line to take. Should he lie, and blame it on the weather, or on operational complications? Or should he tell the truth, and confess that the RAF have withheld their pilots and their aircraft on the grounds that they believe David Roome's original pageant to be inherently unsafe? The latter option is deeply attractive but would open far too many cans of worms. This, after all, is an airshow. Not a court of inquiry.

In the end, around dawn, Sean has settled for the barest of explanations. He hands me a sheet of paper. It reads: *You will have seen the descriptions in the programme about the stacks. For reasons entirely beyond the control of the Royal International Air Tattoo, these will not be appearing.*

Sean looks at me for a moment, his eyes deep-set with exhaustion. What do I think? Is it too blunt? Or will people glimpse the truth behind the curt, clipped phrases? I do my best to answer his questions. Frankly, as a spectator, I wouldn't care a stuff about the politics of aircraft acquisition, and the tricky interface between RIAT and Strike Command, but I've paid £24 for my ticket and another £6 for my souvenir programme, and I'm very much looking forward to the exciting piece of aerial theatre that closes the show. The curtain is supposed to rise at 15.34. Aircraft will twirl and pirouette. Display pilots will perform manoeuvres never before attempted. That, at least, is the hype. Now, of course, the stacks have gone, and in their place a series of aircraft will tramp steadily past, stage right to stage left. Do I care? Am I angry? Disappointed? Or what?

It's at this stage, oddly, that we both come up with the same thought. David Roome's ground-breaking pageant was – in essence – to be unrehearsed. What if it didn't work? And what, more importantly, if his revised display looks infinitely better than any of us currently expect?

We go back to Sean's draft explanation. He plans to expand it a little but the way he's phrased it – exact, toneless, factual – sounds just about perfect.

By now, it's close to 2.00 and Tim Cairns' emergency exercise is about to kick off. Bob Lamburne is the commander of Mobile Response Column Red, one of the three MRCs to test themselves against this afternoon's front-line rehearsal, and right now he's positioning his vehicles on the airside of Hangar 1205, Brian Robertson's field hospital.

For reasons that escape me, Tim Cairns has dubbed the exercise *Winged Warrior* and his scenario calls for a Harrier GR7 to plunge on to Apron Gold after what Tim calls 'a serious control malfunction'. A coachload of passengers about to embark on Concorde see the Harrier coming but are unable to do much about it. The aircraft and the coach burst into flames. Cue exercise.

I'm sitting in a red Land Rover with firemaster Robin Jackson when news of the incident comes through on the emergency net. The Green MRC is tasked to attend the conflagration on Apron Gold and through binoculars I track the twelve-vehicle convoy as it moves south across the runway against the pall of drifting smoke. Twenty minutes later, in Tim's grim fiction, a Latvian pilot – distracted by that same smoke – spins into a field one mile north-west of the airfield. This time, ground-zero is a camp site full of teenage kids. With Green Column fully engaged, the call comes for Red.

The camp site lies beside a narrow country lane. Red also boasts twelve vehicles – a mix of fire engines, ambulances, police vans, and four-ton trucks – and a lone cyclist pedalling towards us gets a nasty shock as we appear in full cry. The field with the tents is to our left. Drifting smoke obscures the remains of the camp site. The situation looks ugly.

Robin hauls the Land Rover into the field and we bump down towards the smoke. Behind us comes the first of the crash tenders. Robin kills the engine and we both get out. I'm still readying my camera when two youths emerge from the smoke and stagger towards us. One is called Kevin. Traumatised by the accident, he's hysterical about his pet dog. The dog's name was Morris. He was a collie. And, like twenty-six of Kevin's mates, he's just been incinerated.

I'm taking photos of this remarkable scene when a tall, bulky figure edges into my viewfinder. On the back of his fluorescent yellow jerkin it says PADRE. There are half a dozen padres amongst Tim's emergency teams – one indication of the darker consequences of watching high-performance jets – and this one is playing a blinder. He approaches young Kevin and does his best to comfort him. Morris is in safe hands. He's gone to the big kennel in the sky. All will be well.

Kevin is unconvinced.

'He's dead!' he howls. 'Mo's gone!'

As Robin's firemen plunge into the smoke, trailing hoses, the padre goes through it all again. How God cares for every living creature. How time will heal the deepest wounds. Kevin goes quiet for a moment, then he turns on the padre. He's had enough of all this consolation, all this talk of resurrection and deliverance.

'If there's really a God,' he sobs, 'how come we lost to Argentina?'

I'm still laughing when I'm arrested by a large man in camouflage fatigues. Exercises like these explore that strange no-man's-land between fantasy and real life, and it takes me a moment or two to realise that my captor means it. I'm press. I'm scum. I belong behind the cordon of plastic cones that already curtains the dead and dying from the world outside. With some difficulty, I persuade him that I'm with Robin Jackson, and that my presence is fully authorised. Reluctantly, he lets me go.

By now, the off-base incident is in full swing, and I wander round capturing image after image. Para-medics setting up drips. Kids huddled together in tearful groups. A green-clad doctor, hurrying from casualty to casualty, deciding which of the stricken to evacuate first. This process is called triage. It acts as a filter, making the very best use of resources, and I join one young victim in the back of a Land Rover ambulance for the ten-minute return journey to Brian Robertson's field hospital.

The casualty is a pretty student called Liz. She has a colourful head wound and Mike, the young male nurse riding beside her, suspects internal injuries. We bump out of the field and turn into the lane while Mike tries to administer comfort.

Liz peers up at him. She's been assigned a role before the incident began.

'Actually,' she confessed, 'I'm dead.'

We express our sympathies. Pretty soon, Mike is apologising for the state of the ambulance. It is, he says, 'a real snotter'. This makes Liz laugh. Encouraged, Mike starts quizzing her about college life. What's she studying? What does she want to do afterwards? As we turn in through Gate Q, back on to the airfield, the conversation is edging towards Liz's social life. Does she have any plans for this evening? Might she be going to the barbecue?

Liz braces herself as we roar down the northern taxiway.

'Depends,' she says sweetly, 'how long I'm dead.'

At the field hospital, laden ambulances are queuing at the big double doors. Inside, resus teams are working on the casualties from the earlier incident on Apron Gold. Half-close your eyes, and all of this could very easily be for real.

I find Brian Robertson standing alone in the shadows, monitoring the performance of his 220-strong team. He's been eager to fine-tune this machine of his since the day he arrived, and so far he's pleased with what he's seen. His prime responsibility is to save lives and stabilise the critically injured but there's another dimension to these macabre *tableaux*, and it's an observer from RAF Waddington who voices it.

'Its all about legal liability now,' he says. 'So you have to plan for the worst. Second at the scene of any incident, after the firemen, are the lawyers.'

This may well explain why Paul and Tim are taking such an intense interest in the success of *Winged Warrior*. Recent changes in the law might make them personally liable in the event of a major disaster, a possibility neither of them can afford to ignore. Mulling this over, I bump into Supt John Horam. He was the police spokesman who shared the mock press conference at the recent Table Top exercise, and he heads the operations team that Gloucestershire Police have put together for this year's airshow. This is the first time he's seen the field hospital in action and he finds it deeply worrying. Not because it's not superbly organised but because the images it offers compel a degree of introspection.

'This thing is worrying me to death,' he confesses. 'Thank God it's only a rehearsal.'

Back in the Gulfstream Flight Centre, I end the afternoon with Geoff Brindle and Les Garside-Beattie. They've spent the bulk of their day watching display rehearsals, and matching their own professional assessments against my own lay impressions is fascinating.

I was especially impressed by the Hungarian MiG-29 pilot, a Capt Gyula Vari. The MiG-29 is a big, heavy, immensely powerful Russian-built interceptor and in Capt Vari's hands it parcelled bits of sky with tightly drawn ribbons of curling brown smoke. His trademark tailslide – a vertical climb that slows and slows until the aircraft stops in mid-air and begins to sink backwards – it is breathtaking, but there were other bits of Capt Vari's repertoire that were equally heart-stopping.

Fair?

Geoff Brindle is looking amused. As an ex-Lightning pilot he has all the time in the world for fast jets, and none at all for fancy phrases. In his view, a pilot is either competent or off-the-plot. Competence of the standard he admires is much rarer than you might think, and – yes – Capt Vari was very definitely competent.

This seems to me to be pretty grudging praise but the longer Geoff and Les analyse Capt Vari's rehearsal, the more I glimpse the subtleties of the display pilot's trade. His first pass towards the crowd ended in a full afterburner climb. This evidently took him closer to the crowd line than the FCC allows and, when I look confused, it's Les who reaches for pencil and paper.

'It's all about vectors and energy,' he says, doodling a MiG on the back of an envelope. 'The guy pulls into a climb but some of that forward energy is still carrying him towards the crowd. He knew he'd done it. He didn't need us to tell him.'

I nod, still thinking of poor Capt Vari. Was there *anything* he'd done right? Wasn't his Cobra just sensational?

Les nods. His Cobra was fine but what really impressed him was the guile with which the Hungarian had used the clouds.

'Clouds?' I'm lost.

'Yeah. The guy has a display routine. He's topping at − say − 2,000ft. There's some fluffy Cu around and lots of bits of blue sky. Now the mark of a good pilot is the ease with which he can use all that, just make tiny adjustments so he's making best use of the scenery.'

I nod, trying to replay Capt Vari's display in my mind. Les is absolutely right. Wherever there were holes in the clouds, he was up there amongst them showcasing the MiG's fabulous body against the fluffy white clouds. At the time it had never occurred to me that this was anything but accidental. Now, thanks to these experts, I know different.

Geoff Brindle directs my attention to a couple of aircrew occupying a sofa across the hangar. They're both bending forward, locked in conversation.

'They're Swedish,' Geoff confides. 'The guy on the right is the Gripen pilot. The other one's his boss.'

The Gripen rehearsal had followed the MiG's display. To little me, amongst the watching pressmen below, it had been another sensational routine, thunderous horsepower garnished with exquisite airmanship. Am I wrong?

Geoff smiles. The senior of the two Swedes has a hand extended. It climbs and twists at the same time. The other Swede, the display pilot, nods. These hand movements are a kind of pilots' Esperanto, but so far I've yet to complete the course.

I turn to Geoff. 'What's he saying?'

'He's saying he cocked it up.'

'Cocked what up?'

'The upward roll. You probably remember. He completed it in cloud and came out in completely the wrong position. He knew he'd done it, just like the Hungarian guy. In fact he's already applied for a second rehearsal.'

Mention of a second rehearsal prompts me to mention the *Coaler* pilot, Lt Col Vaneev. Harry Burgoyne, who should know a thing or two about heavy transports, had his doubts about the Ukrainian rehearsal. Did the good Colonel stick to the agreed 110 degree angle of bank?

Geoff gives me an emphatic nod.

'He did,' he says, 'and we thought he performed beautifully. He flew it like a glider. It had everything. It was nicely centred. He captured the display line. He did exactly as we'd asked.'

I blink, still watching the conversation on the sofa. At the end of Sunday's show, Geoff Brindle and the rest of the Flying Control Committee must decide the winners in a series of competitions. I'm not sure of the odds on Col Vaneev but I sense he might be worth a quid or two.

The conversation on the sofa at last comes to an end. The Gripen pilot, chastened, heads for the coffee machine. Geoff and his committee operate a yellow card/red card penalty scheme for air display transgressions. Has anyone been warned yet? Has anyone been sent off?

Geoff swaps glances with Les. Sometimes these guys can be positively masonic.

'It's early days,' he says mischievously. 'Stay tuned.'

Friday is just twenty-four hours away from the show. For little me, the weekend will be the big test for the Jumbotron screens, and with the sky black with arriving aircraft it's time to do some serious tape-editing, preparing archival packages to drop into various elements in the eight-hour display programme. This kind of work can be time-consuming and I've promised Tony Webb at least half a day away from the orgy of note-scribbling that will one day become this book. First, though, I meet Alan Foulis.

He's driving one of the white mini-buses that cart the aircrews around and he stops to give me a lift. We're talking within seconds. Have I heard about his little adventure on Wednesday? I haven't.

As we potter around the perimeter track, pulling over for taxiing Tornados, he tells me what happened. The task was simple. He was to drive over to RAF Brize Norton, pick up the Ukrainian crew of a civilian Il-76 from their overnight accommodation, drive up to RAF Lyneham and reunite them with their aircraft. The big cargo plane was to form part of the RIAT static line, and it was their job to fly it the fourteen miles back to Fairford.

Alan got on with the job. The Ukrainians were waiting for him at Brize. An hour or so later, he was driving in through the gates at Lyneham. Pulling up beside the towering Il-76, he prepared to wave them farewell. They wouldn't hear of it.

'What do you mean?'

'The cargo ramp was down at the back. They just waved me on.'

A sleek Mirage 2000 is on short finals ahead of us. It takes me a couple of seconds to realise what Alan is saying. I turn to stare at him.

'They gave you a lift back? You and the van? In the Il-76?'

He nods, grinning.

'Seven minutes door to door,' he confirms. 'I counted every second.'

For the next three hours, locked in a portacabin with editor Alastair Chapman, we prepare a dozen or so archival sequences, cutting black and white pictures to play into the live coverage we'll be offering of the show itself. Images of SE-5s and Sopwith Camels and Hurricanes and Blenheims flicker on the screen before us as B-1B bombers and F-16s thunder overhead. It's the oddest feeling, butting one era against another, but Alastair does a fine job and we're through by lunchtime.

Returning to the sunshine and the mayhem outside, I run into my wife, Lin, and Tony Howard who will be handling the bulk of the live direction. Tony taught me everything I know about television and he's also one of my oldest friends. I'm only too aware of how under-briefed he's been about the coming weekend but the two-hundred-metre walk from the VIP car park to what Tony Webb has christened 'the media village' seems to have given him a clue or two.

He's watching a pair of French Mirage F-1s trying to mate overhead at 400 knots. The noise is unbelievable.

'Christ,' he says at last. 'What have you let me in for?'

Over snatched lunch in the mobile control room (or 'scanner') we discuss our war plan. The screens are to be operational from 07.30 to 20.30.

'That's Zulu,' I add, showing off.

'Zulu?'

'One hour behind local. GMT basically.'

He resists asking about GMT. Far more to the point is the prospect of this huge wodge of live direction. Tony is never less than a rock in these situations but after thirteen hours he wouldn't have a brain left. Not that he'd ever admit it.

'The first couple of hours we'll be playing out videos of old airshows. Live starts at quarter to ten. There are two archival packages, one for Berlin, one for the RAF Eightieth at the end. After the show ends we do a live concert. I'll be there for whenever you want me.'

Something even noisier than the Mirages is trying to fly into the scanner. I'm not very good at lip-reading but I more or less get the gist.

'No problem,' I think he says.

By now, the static display line is filling up fast. Aircraft are landing at two-minute intervals from the east and the enclosures in front of the hospitality chalets are a swirl of corporate guests. Lunched and happy, they're emerging to watch the first of the afternoon's rehearsals. The wiser individuals wear ear plugs. The rest are probably oblivious.

Lin and I have an invitation to the Raytheon Aircrew Enclosure. Manager Liz Haarlar has promised a big gathering of pilots and that's exactly what we find. Striking up conversation with total strangers isn't easy, and fast jet pilots can be formidably remote, but Lin and I strike lucky first time, settling down with a couple of Luftwaffe Tornado jockeys.

Capt Michael Sauer flies out of Norvenich, near Cologne, piloting the Air Defence version of the Tornado. Paul Neumann, on the other hand, flies an ECR Tornado, specialising in recce and surveillance missions. For a while they talk easily about the show, how impressive it is, how pleased they are to be here. Colleagues in the German navy have warned them that Fairford has got too big, and too impersonal, but so far they've had a great time. Nothing of an equivalent scale appears to exist in Germany – or anywhere else in Europe – and they're more than happy to spread the word.

At this point, a group of Ukrainians settle at a neighbouring table and their appearance prompts Michael to ponder the new shape of European military aviation. Squadron exchanges with the old eastern bloc countries are now common but it's sad to see a once proud empire reduced to such straitened circumstances. Large consignments of out-of-date drugs are regularly sent to Kiev, and departing Ukrainian transport aircraft often fly out with huge cargos of technically illegal tyres. German regulations stipulate a certain minimum of tread, enough rubber to keep Ukrainian cars on the road for years.

Away to the right, a blast of afterburner announces the appearance of Capt Gyula Vari, the Hungarian MiG-29 pilot. Conversation for the next eight minutes is quite impossible, but I watch the faces of the German pilots as the MiG powers through Capt Vari's display routine. Reunification presented the Luftwaffe with a squadron of MiG-29s from the old East German air force, and they still fly from their base up in Laage, providing a taste of close-quarters combat for a succession of eager NATO and USAF fighter jocks.

With Capt Vari back on the ground, I'm curious about the strengths and weaknesses of the now-legendary Soviet fighter. How does the MiG-29 perform against, for instance, the Tornado?

Michael and Paul exchange glances. The Tornado, they say at once, makes an ideal low-level bomber. Down at 200 feet, even in bad weather, it flies like a Mercedes. The MiG, on the other hand, has big problems in the low-level role. Over 420 knots, unless you keep the stick forward, it tends to fly up. This, of course, is fudging the issue. I'm thinking *Top Gun*. Head to head, who blinks first?

Another pause in the conversation, slightly warier than the first, then the frank admission that, yes, the Tornado is underpowered. Ask any fighter pilot for an ideal mount and he'd very probably elect for an F-16. The conversation comes to a halt again while a B-52 takes off. Michael is watching the Hungarian MiG taxiing back to Apron Green on the far side of the airfield. He's looking extremely thoughtful and when the B-52 has climbed out to the west, he talks softly about the recce missions he's been flying over Bosnia. How mid-air refuelling keeps himself and his navigator in the air for hours on end. How Serbian radar units often lock on to them. How the Luftwaffe pilots wear American flying suits, and carry neither rings nor wallets nor patches. How the bulky escape kit includes a P8 pistol, a GPS, an edible map, a printed ransom offer, and $2,000. This is military flying for real, and only three weeks ago Paul and his fellow pilots in the recce squadron were discreetly warned about the possibility of a live war in Kosovo.

Paul is looking hard at what remains of his Diet Coke.

'The Serbs fly the MiG-29,' he says, quietly.

We emerge from the Aircrew Enclosure to find the Catalina flying boat inching into its static slot on Apron Orange. Back at the parking meet, it was Paul Bowen's idea to showcase this glorious old amphibian in the very middle of the Apron Orange static line, but settling at a shallow angle to its neighbours it looks slightly odd amongst the purposeful shapes of the A-10 Warthog, and the F-15 Eagle. John Thorpe, supervising the final adjustments to the Catalina's weekend pose, is worried that the long spread of the high wing may be intruding too far into the taxiway, but the pilot – John Alsford – has met Sue Allen's plea for an earlier arrival slot, and is determined to display his pride and joy to the best possible effect. His plans for this afternoon, now abandoned, revolved around preparations for Seawing 2000, a millennium seaplane meet. Promotional excursions on the south coast, including touchdowns on Southampton Water, have now been postponed until Monday.

Mid-afternoon on Friday also sees Tom Watts, RIAT's doughty Exhibition Manager, opening the airfield to the long convoy of traders who will be filling the 400 sites Tom has so far sold. Many of these nut-brown men and women spend the summer moving from event to event, and the cannier ones – dealing strictly in cash – have held off until the last possible moment before parting with their bulging rolls of £20 notes. A modest pitch (or 'stance') will cost them £350 for the weekend, and it's the weather that makes the difference between a fat profit and a despairing loss.

Down at Gate J, with Tom Watts, I watch the procession of vans and trailers bumping up towards Apron Violet. The Hog Roast. The Fish and Chip Bar. The Hat Shop. The Fresh Bread Feast. The DoNut Surprise. Aviation Artifacts. Candy Floss Heaven. Over in the Flight Centre, forecaster Ian Matthews has confirmed the arrival of a high pressure system and the smiles on the faces of these traders is all the evidence I'd ever need that tomorrow – after weeks of atrocious weather – is set fair.

After the fifth burger bar rumbles past, Tom admits that he'd like to drag this important corner of the Air Tattoo a little more upmarket but Paul's and Tim's city has been taking shape all morning and it's begun to occur to me that the mix of hunky high-tech aircraft, thunderous display flying, and cheerful funfair ambience is – for the general public – just about right. The cool, carpeted spaces of Caroline Rogers' VIP chalets are a world away from the noise and bustle of the static line, but for a native of Clacton-on-Sea like me there are bits of Fairford that are very familiar indeed.

Tom bends to the window of an incoming van to answer a query about changing pitches. His thirty-strong volunteer force are briefed to keep an eye on traders who swap one allotted position for something more tempting but in this case there appears to be room for manoeuvre. The problem solved, Tom waves the van on.

I still can't believe the weather. After weeks of wind and rain, how can it suddenly come good like this?

Tom runs a hand over his face. Like more or less everyone else I've met, he hasn't slept for days. 'It's luck. You either have it or you don't.'

'And Paul and Tim?'

'Have it,' he nods. 'In spades.'

Really? Returning to the media village to touch base with Tony Howard in the OB scanner, I spot a line of cones further up the big east/west taxiway on which the static line is nearly complete. The cones have been deployed by an Incident Team, and beyond them I can see the dark grey bulk of a German navy Tornado. One wing has dropped. There are firemen running out hoses, Land Rovers with flashing headlights, guys from Eng Ops talking urgently on two-way radios. Is this another of Tim Cairns' scenarios? I rather doubt it.

Attempts to breach the security cordon in front of the cones come to nothing. Then, a stroke of luck. In attendance is Robin Jackson, firemaster on the Red Mobile Response Column. We're old campaigners now, veterans of Thursday's off-base incident, and he takes me through to the gaggle of engineers crouched beneath the Tornado's starboard wing.

Being towed to its parking slot on Apron Blue, the tug and the Tornado had made a detour to avoid a vehicle blocking the taxiway. The asphalt on the edges of the taxiway is laid to a lesser load-bearing specification than the broad strip that runs down the middle. A fully laden Tornado can weigh twenty-eight tons. At first, the detour had been troublefree. Then, abruptly, the aircraft's starboard wheel had disappeared through the blacktop, bringing the heavy jet to an abrupt halt.

I'm looking at the damage. The hole punched in the tarmac is substantial. The upper surface of the tyre is just visible but the Tornado is very definitely down on one knee, the big air-to-ground missile hung from the aircraft's belly now inches from the asphalt.

I raise my camera for a shot but a fireman warns me not to. A bowser crew are pumping out the Tornado's tanks, offloading six tons of Avtur as a prelude to whatever happens next. You can smell the fuel vapour in the air and only when I guarantee not to use the flash am I finally allowed to take photographs. Converting an accident into a fireball is the last thing these guys need.

The crippled Tornado, with its ever-widening circle of cones and emergency vehicles, has brought all movement along Apron Blue to a halt. Mid-afternoon, there are still eighty aircraft to park. How long before the Tornado is back on its feet again?

Robin, like everyone else, isn't at all sure. There are hardened points on the airframe to permit jacking but the big hydraulic jacks, like the undercarriage, could easily punch through the thin crust of asphalt. Airbags are another solution, but there are none available on base. Rumours that Gloucester Fire Headquarters might be able to come up with something may – or may not – be true. The only other alternative is to seek help from the RAF's Aircraft Recovery and Transportation Flight at RAF St Athan, in South Wales. This specialist unit, dubbed 'the crash and smash team', has the kit and the expertise to extricate the Tornado, and a stand-by call has already gone through, but St Athan's is a couple of hours away by road and the deadlines are getting tighter by the minute. Fairford's gates will be opening to the public at half past six tomorrow morning. By then, the static line must be complete.

Back in our room at the VOQ I make call after call, trying to keep abreast of the situation. Paul is insisting that I attend tonight's Gala dinner – Amanda Butcher's extravaganza in Hangar 1200 – but just now the thrombosis on Apron Blue seems a great deal more important. What if the blockage proves immovable? What if Mel James' precious static line includes a one-legged German fighter, and a queue of waiting aircraft behind it? I finally get through to John Thorpe, who has no doubts that the next few hours will provide some kind of solution. With the fuel off-loaded, he and Paul Lindsay have already carved a path for taxiing aircraft around the crippled jet. The guys from St Athan are loading their big transporter and should be leaving within the hour.

Sensing, quite wrongly, my disappointment, he chuckles.

'Got a title for the book yet?' he says. 'How about *Tornado Down?*'

At half past seven, I join the throng of dinner jackets on the apron in front of Hangar 1200. Amanda has been planning this event since well before Christmas, and with six-figure sponsorship from British Aerospace she's determined to match the glowing reviews she won for last year's USAF birthday celebration.

There are rumours that the interior of 1200 looks sensational but for the time being we move from group to group, sipping champagne, nibbling William Beeston's delicious canapés, and marvelling at Amanda's luck with the weather. The wind has dropped almost completely, leaving a warm, still evening. Swifts twist and loop above our heads and over to the west, gauzy curtains of cloud are gilding nicely. Might the BA budget stretch to the perfect sunset?

A fellow guest at tonight's dinner is Orion's editorial director, Simon Spanton. Simon has been editing my novels for years now, and we're close friends. This book is partly his idea and he's as passionate about aircraft as I am. An afternoon in front of the Orion Media Centre tent hasn't done much for his eardrums but we're still discussing the finer points of Capt Vari's MiG-29 display when the bandmaster brings Beating the Retreat to a halt, and raises his baton.

Conversation is suddenly stilled. On the other side of the Apron I can see Sir Adrian Swire, chairman of the RAF Benevolent Fund, cocking an ear. The band tiptoe into the plaintive opening bars of 'The Evening Hymn'. For a second or two, the music engulfs us. Then, magically, I hear the far-away growl of Merlin engines. Simon and I exchange glances. Heads are looking skywards. Then, low over the hangar, swoop a pair of Spitfires. As the music swells they soar away to the west, banking left and right, those unforgettable wings silhouetted against the evening sun. The sound of the Merlins slowly fades. The RAF ensign lowers. The music comes to an end. From a week bursting with unforgettable images, this is the one moment I'll treasure for ever.

The Gala Dinner occupies the rest of the evening. Amanda has transformed the bare, bleak spaces of Hangar 1200 into an enormous cave. The walls are hung with black cloth, liberally spangled with thousands of tiny bulbs. Softly lit aircraft provide a backdrop to dozens of beautifully dressed tables and a complete line of RAF squadron standards have been carefully positioned behind the top table. Like so many corners of the Tattoo, this setting has an almost magical quality, an artful mix of theatricality and nostalgia, garnished with fine wines, exquisite food and good conversation. Five hundred and eighty guests tuck into William Beeston's sole pana with lemon gréss and ginger followed by roast fillet of beef. A small musical ensemble play throughout the meal, and with the port come the speeches.

Sir Roger Palin takes the microphone on behalf of the Benevolent Fund. He thanks the sponsors for their support, shares his vision for the coming years, and provokes a huge round of applause when he thanks Paul and Tim and RIAT's volunteer army for all their hard work. John Weston, chief executive of British Aerospace, takes up the running and offers a witty reply. But it falls to Air Chief Marshal Sir Richard Johns, Chief of the Air Staff, to somehow compress the essence of this extraordinary event into a single phrase. He's talking about the coming weekend and from the top table he's looking out over the heads of hundreds of invited aircrew.

'Fly hard,' he tells them. 'Fly well. Fly safe.'

By the time I get up next morning, the public gates have been open for an hour. I walk the mile from the VOQ to the Gulfstream Flight Centre, battling the aftermath of the Chateau Cantermerle. It's a perfect day, a blue, blue sky broken only by a single contrail pluming behind a high-flying eastbound airliner. Across the airfield, beyond the runway, I can see a multi-coloured nest of tethered hot-air balloons, rising slowly in the still air. The morning arrivals – mainly charter aircraft full of visiting VIPs – have yet to touch down and the near-silence after all those hectic days of preparation is slightly unnerving. Even the agents of darkness appear to be on our side. At the main gate, the security placard announces THREATCON: NORMAL.

In the managers' tented mess, alongside Building 15, I have breakfast with Paul Lindsay. As Mel James' number two in Eng Ops, he's been up most of the night sorting out the German navy Tornado, and he's only too happy to tell me what happened. The crash and smash boys from RAF St Athan finally arrived around 20.00. They brought with them a custom-made Tornado sling on the big Queen Mary transporter and they used air bags to support the aircraft's wings while a heavy lift crane hired from nearby Swindon eased the Tornado upwards. Checks on the affected undercarriage oleo revealed a hydraulic leak and minor damage around the brake unit but, much to the relief of the German navy aircrew, their precious Tornado was finally put to bed in its allotted parking slot at ten minutes past midnight. All that remained at the site of the incident was a gaping hole in the asphalt and a working party from the Site Team had the ramp operational again by dawn.

Tim Prince had stayed with the incident throughout the night, winning a nod of respect from Paul Lindsay.

'That's leadership by example,' he grunts, buttering his third slice of toast.

The morning's display brief for participating aircrew takes place in the base cinema at 8.15. More than a hundred pilots nurse coffee and danish while Geoff Brindle opens the proceedings. He's wearing his number one uniform with the top button undone in archetypal fighter pilot style. Behind him, up on the stage, stand Ian Sheeley and Tim Prince. Tim, to my surprise, has had time to slip into a suit and looks remarkably fresh.

Every pilot's day begins with the Met brief and it's Ian Matthews who passes on the good news about the area of high pressure that has magically inserted itself between a seemingly endless series of Atlantic depressions. By tomorrow afternoon, he warns, the anti-cyclone will have been chased east by yet another incoming front but for today we can expect broken cloud to 5,000 ft, freezing level at 7,000 ft, light westerly winds in the range five–eight knots, and a maximum ground temperature of twenty-one degrees C.

After Ian Matthews comes Ian Revell with the air traffic overview and a word or two about emergency procedures. A Priority Two incident, he says, will be fitted in around the display, while a Priority One will stop the flying programme entirely. I glance round at the watching aircrew. Most seem more interested in their danish than the small print of Tim Cairns' emergency arrangements, and when I turn back to the stage it's Ian Sheeley who's entering a plea for pilots to keep to the planned schedule. The flying programme is over eight hours long. Parts of it are extremely complex. Any slippage will give Ian and his team problems they can do without.

Geoff Brindle stands up again, reminding display pilots about FCC rules. No flying below 100 ft straight and level. No flying beneath 300 ft in the turn. And a minimum of 500 ft when pulling out of any vertical manoeuvre. Geoff is warming up now. Twenty years ago, his would have been one of the faces behind me in the stalls and he understands the temptations of display flying only too well.

'You're only cleared to fly low-level over the airfield,' he warns sternly. 'So don't hide behind the trees, because it upsets the locals quite a lot.'

He lets the ripple of laughter subside; then adds a postscript. The validations over the last couple of days, he says, have gone well. He and his FCC colleagues have watched some really good, really crisp displays.

He pauses, eyeing the assembled aircrew. Then he smiles. 'Gentlemen, the field is yours. The air is yours. Go to it. And good luck.'

At Building 29, Eng Ops, I hunt for Mel James. I've booked myself an interview with the Hungarian MiG-29 pilot, Capt Gyula Vari, and the last thing I need is to get arrested en route. Security in the active parts of the airfield is extremely tight and it's only top RIAT brass like Mel who can unlock this ring of steel.

Mel drives me down to Apron Green. Beside the MiG, we get out of his Cherokee Jeep. Back in November, Mel had gone into considerable detail about the foibles of Soviet aeronautical engineering. At the time the lecture hadn't meant very much but now he squats beneath the MiG's wing, pointing at a feature above the undercarriage housing that looks suspiciously like impact damage. The line of rivets stitching the metal seems intact but the fuselage bulges in all the wrong places.

'Traffic accident?' I enquire.

Mel gives me a brisk shake of the head.

'That's a double curvature structure,' he says. 'Perfect example.' His finger lowers towards the undercarriage. 'Tell you something else, too. Every time these guys come back from a display, they ask for technical water. At first I hadn't a clue what they meant but they just want the stuff out of the tap with not too much crap in it.'

'Why?'

'To cool the brakes, of course. They just chuck bucketfuls all over the wheels.'

With Mel returning to Eng Ops, I look for Capt Vari. The MiG's ground support crew are sucking on cans of Tango at the edge of the ramp. Behind them, on the grass, is a litter of drop tanks, oil cans, and assorted spare wheels. When I ask for Capt Vari, the crew chief indicates a crop-haired individual in a flying suit, deep in conversation with another pilot, some thirty metres away. I know he's seen me, and as the airfield begins to come alive I'm only too happy to wait my turn.

Half an hour or so later, he strolls across. He's my height, about 5' 11". He has a firm handshake and a ready smile. When I ask him to go through his show display with me, he obliges at once. His English, unlike his flying, is less than perfect but when we get to manoeuvres he can't put into words, his hands come to the rescue. That language, again. Pilots' Esperanto.

'I take off on twenty-seven,' he says, nodding across the airfield towards the main east/west runway, 'and there I use full afterburner. I go into a hard pull-up. Nine G.'

Still mesmerised by the memory of the MiG's afterburner – two hot circles of fire with a plane attached – I don't immediately grasp the significance of what he's just said. Nine G is anatomically impossible. Nine G is when your body weighs not ten stone, but ninety. Nine G is the darkness at the very edge of the human envelope.

I offer him a forgiving smile. Language is tricky stuff. Mistakes happen all the time. '*How* many G?'

'Nine.'

'*Nine?*'

Over Capt Vari's left shoulder, the wing of a B-1B bomber gleams in the sunshine. I stare at it for a moment, letting the figure settle in my memory. It's not simply the fact that this man pulls more G than the average astronaut. It's the fact that it doesn't even raise a shrug. Nine G, for Capt Vari, is pure routine. You and I take the bus to work. MiG pilots pull nine G.

Unaware of the turmoil in what's left of my brain, Capt Vari has now reached the top of his afterburner climb and is descending through a couple of ninety-degree turns into a specially modified Cobra, a snake-like dance in front of the crowd that appears to defy all the rules of aerodynamics. Emerging from the Cobra, he punches in the afterburner again, turns upside-down for a while, then lowers the undercarriage for a high alpha pass. High alpha is the cue for his right hand to come towards me, sharply angled upwards. In the *SAS Survival Handbook* this is the recommended way of snapping an opponent's head off, and I'm musing on just what an appropriate metaphor this is when Capt Vari hits the afterburner for the third time and powers upwards in an eighty-degree climb. The climb slows and slows until the MiG is hanging in mid-air. By now, I'm back in the plot.

'Tail slide,' I suggest.

Capt Vari nods. I suspect he's beginning to enjoy this little per-formance – impressing the hell out of a stranger without the nuisance of nine G – but I've no time to check because already the big hands are rolling right and left before hauling the big fighter into a hard afterburner turn. After this comes a pull up and a sharp turn to the left – a mere seven G – before he balances the MiG vertically on one wing and flies a knife-edge the length of display line. After that comes a climb, two climbing rolls, another hard turn, plus three more rolls before he points the nose to the sky and whacks in the afterburner. Thundering upwards, he lets the speed decay into another tailslide before turning the MiG upside down for one final inverted pass and a departing wing waggle to say goodbye.

He pauses apologetically, as if I might be bored.

'Then I bring in flap and undercarriage,' he says sweetly. 'For the landing.'

I nod. Even my pen won't perform properly. *Nine G?* I give it a shake, wondering what kind of supplementary question can possibly do justice to this super-hero.

'You *enjoy* all this?' I suggest hesitantly.

He smiles again, the eyes invisible behind the aviator shades.

'Sure,' he says. 'Why not?'

For the next couple of minutes I trawl backwards and forwards over his flying career. How he trained on L29s and L39s. How he graduated to the MiG-21. And how, in 1995, he was finally chosen as one of the Hungarian Airforce's two official display pilots. As he talks me through the finer details my eyes keep straying to the MiG, parked beside us. This, remember, is the interceptor favoured by the Serbians, the all-too-fleeting silhouette that Luftwaffe pilots are beginning to take very seriously indeed. Is it really as formidable as it seems? Might all those amazing display routines translate into rows of tiny Tornados beneath the cockpit canopy?

Ever tactful, Capt Vari shrugs the question aside. Just now, the Hungarian Airforce are contemplating the difficult transition from Warsaw Pact to NATO. By 1999 they could be flying alongside their old enemies in the west. That will mean new tactics and new equipment for the likes of Capt Vari but when I press him on the likely outcome of a head-to-head with – say – an F-16, he at last takes the question seriously.

He gestures back at the MiG. The airframe, he says, is very strong and there's lots and lots of power, but the visibility from the cockpit is not so great.

He nods, wanting me to understand.

'For a fighter pilot,' he says, 'to see good matters a lot. If I can see my enemy, it's worth an extra engine.'

That, if I may say so, is extremely well put and I'm still writing it down when he starts to tell me about the workload. Compared to western fighters, the MiG is pretty crude. There's no terrain-following radar. No mega-fast master computer. Instead, the pilot does it all himself.

He gestures back towards the MiG.

'Work, work, work,' he says. 'All the time.'

I still haven't quite reached the bottom of the puzzle. Fly Capt Vari's MiG against an F-16, and who calls the shots?

As it happens, a couple of F-16s are parked across the ramp, both emblazoned with colourful Tiger paint schemes. Capt Vari eyes them for a moment, then smiles.

'I flew against F-16s last month,' he says softly. 'And it was real easy to catch them.'

By half past eleven, in time for David Roome's Berlin Airlift tribute, I'm back in the OB scanner with Tony Howard. One of the archive packages I cut yesterday morning is specially tailored for this display and for the next fifty-five minutes our cameras track a succession of piston-engined veterans as they drone around the circuit, sandwiching solo routines between stream take-offs and landings.

The sheer elegance of aircraft like the DC-3, DC-4, Lancaster and Lockheed Constellation makes for wonderful pictures. The standard of the camerawork is already very high – I've had the briefest look at one of the Jumbotron screens, and some of the shots have been breathtaking – but, given a chance to linger on these beautiful old machines, easing into pose after pose against a perfect sky, our cameramen excel themselves. The close-ups, in particular, defy description. In the air and on the ground they give us endless opportunities to mix away to the grainy black and white footage of their forebears at Gatow, Tegel and Tempelhof, and this blend of wonderful airmanship and rich nostalgia adds exactly the dimension I've been promising Paul and Tim.

Across the airfield, on the northern taxiway, the DC-3s roll to a halt beside a waiting convoy of veteran lorries. Even that tiny percentage of the crowd lucky enough to be at the very front of the enclosures can see little of the distant flurries of activity but one of our cameras is positioned beside the taxiway, sending pictures back by microlink, and anyone within range of one of our Jumbotrons has a perfect view.

The Berlin pageant over, I take time to stroll amongst the crowds on the static line. The airfield car parks are almost full now and there are rumours of a six-figure attendance. Quite what they'll make of David Roome's revised RAF birthday tribute is anyone's guess but for now I'm still marvelling at the way an empty airfield has so suddenly become a bustling city.

I, of all people, should have anticipated this dizzying transformation. For the best part of a year, I've been tracking the handful of men and women charged with building the airshow, yet 750 pages of notes, umpteen conversations, and a privileged seat in the dress circle have quite failed to prepare me for what I'm seeing.

A month ago, the veterans of Buildings 15 and 16 were warning me about something they called momentum. Once it starts, they said darkly, nothing can stop it. At the time, I made a note of the word, momentum, and thought little more about it. Then a week or so later, one or two of them began to talk in surfie language. The time for planning, and flow charts, and all the other grown-up stuff, was over. The biggest wave you've ever seen was shaping on the far horizon, and once it arrived you had no choice but to hang on like grim death and go with it. This, once again, I put down to exhibitionism or first-night nerves. But now, baptised by a little of the fire myself, I realise just how right they were.

It's a huge, huge event, meticulously organised, and quite suddenly it's upon you. A hundred thousand people. A final figure of 441 aircraft. Seven hundred and fifty thousand gallons of fuel. Accommodation for 1,750 aircrew. Buses and vans and hire cars to run them around. *Cordon bleu* cuisine for thousands of VIPs. Individual welcomes for dozens of foreign air chiefs. A special hallo for HRH the Duke of Edinburgh. A complete field hospital. Four thousand five hundred volunteers. Twenty thousand cars. And enough bars and burger stalls and hog roasts to feed – yes – a complete city.

My son, Jack, has transferred from the site team and joined us in the scanner. His knowledge of aircraft is encyclopaedic and his job over the weekend is to identify upcoming display items for Tony Howard. Just now, he's taking a breather with yours truly and half-way down the static line we find ourselves discussing this conjuring trick that has produced RIAT98.

It's already more than obvious that the last week has stretched Jack and his liver to the limit. He's been working fourteen hours a day, made friends he'll never lose, and swallowed countless pints of Arkell's; and, when I try and express something of my wonder at the magical appearance of this weekend city, he knows at once what I mean.

'It's not just the obvious things,' he says. 'It goes much deeper than that.'

The site team, notoriously, plug themselves into everyone else's business and in seven short days Jack has been mapping RIAT's underworld. He understands how to work the black market that apparently exists in the manager's blue meal tickets (I have two – why didn't he ask me?). He's an expert on blagging the special tools he might need for roping and staking, or the erection of signs. He knows how desperate the old eastern bloc aircrews are for hard currency (the *Backfire* pilot tried to sell him his leather belt for $5). And he cherishes, above all, the fierce tribal loyalty that bonds his own little group.

The site team, like umpteen other bits of the RIAT empire, have their own radio net. They chatter all day, hunting for gossip, passing on tips, skewering some hapless individual on the end of an elaborate wind-up. Jack's best mates are Nico, Zulu, Fawkes, Gucci, Simple and Windy. His own call sign is Gringo. Lost to reality, he now belongs to another world.

On the way back to the OB scanner, we pass the ill-fated German navy Tornado. Jack, as it happens, was one of the site Team tasked with clearing up after the crash-and-smash boys from St Athan had put the aircraft back on its feet. He was there to help fill in the hole in the tarmac and he had a perfect view of what lay at the bottom of it.

We're strolling back towards the media village. For the second time today, I haven't quite kept up.

'So what did you find?' I ask him.

Jack nods down Apron Blue. To the right of the taxiway lies the big Jumbotron screen beside the concert venue.

'Television cables,' he says, 'and they looked pretty new.'

It's at this point, while I'm still mulling over Tony Webb's role in downing the German Tornado, that something rather alarming happens. The French aerobatic team, the *Patrouille de France*, are nosing out of Apron Green, preparing for their twenty-five-minute display. Overhead, an Italian G-222 is putting the final touches to a wonderfully elegant solo performance. And then, quite suddenly, the entire air traffic control team appear on the balcony in front of the control tower and begin to dance.

Jack and I stare up at them in wonderment. Over the whine of the G-222 I can hear music. It sounds like the charleston. What on earth are they up to? Why aren't they crouched over their consoles, saving us all from immolation?

Through a pair of borrowed binoculars, I take a closer look. The ATC team are led by Julie Morrissey, a high-flying air traffic controller from the CAA Safety Regulation Group at Manchester's international airport. Last time I met her, I was struck by the steadiness of her gaze and by a certain professional briskness, but here she is – arms flailing, legs kicking – while the G-222 throttles back over the distant line of hangars and eases into a long right-hand turn before landing.

I glance at Jack. Even he doesn't know what's going on. Why compete with all these glorious aeroplanes when half the people in the crowd wouldn't know the charleston from an epileptic fit? I make a mental note to find out later and return to the cool sanity of the OB scanner. Tony Howard is gazing at a tight shot of eight beautifully framed French alphajets.

'So what happens next?' he enquires.

The long hot afternoon crawls past. My enquiries about the ATC team meet a wall of silence. Rumours filter through that David Higham's Sky High Village is breaking all trading records and a press release from Patti Heady arrives, detailing a mercy mission only four hours earlier by the crews of two of our resident helicopters.

A water skier had entangled himself in wire on one of the nearby lakes. Saved from drowning, he'd been treated on site by a medical team flown in by the big yellow Sea King, parked over on Apron Green. The police Osprey had also attended and the skier is now recovering at St Margaret's Hospital, Swindon. As an inspired piece of PR, this is ample evidence of the long reach of RIAT's emergency resources, and the press release as good as says so. In the words of Show Operations Contingency Planner, Peter Finch, 'As part of the community, this was a responsibility we were happy to undertake. During this incident, at no time was safety at the airshow endangered.'

At 15.34, David Roome's RAF Eightieth birthday tribute begins, as planned, with two helicopters running in from the north towards the crowd line. Trailing RAF ensigns, they split left and right and I watch the much-publicised Sea King on one of Tony Howard's TV monitors as the big, yellow helicopter chatters down the display line.

Camera four, meanwhile, has picked up the distant shapes of the Tiger Moths, closing the airfield from the east. They're holding a Diamond Nine formation and at the end of the telephoto lens they seem to be dancing in the heat. Minutes later, they make their stately way overhead – a lovely shot on camera five – leaving the runway clear for a Blenheim and a Harvard to take off.

From our perch in the OB scanner there are plenty of pictures – taxiing aircraft, disappearing Moths, and the hazy smudge of the next incoming formation preparing to run in. Watching one of the Jumbotrons, David's revised display might just raise the blood pressure amongst older members of the crowd, and Sean Maffett is certainly doing his best to decorate David's cake with a little icing of his own, including 'live' help from the head of the MoD's Air Historical Branch, Sebastian Cox. But as the pageant develops, the gaps between anything dramatic happening become more and more obvious.

One of the great merits of David Roome's original plan for stacks was its sheer novelty. This had never been tried before and everyone knew it. Now, though, the RAF has preferred to celebrate its own birthday with a series of simple fly-bys and less than half way through the pageant I'm beginning to wonder how many people have lost the thread.

From the OB scanner, we're pumping in yards and yards of archive film – Royal Flying Corps stringbags to underpin the first formation, Battle of Britain combat footage to spice the solo Spitfire display – but only a tiny percentage of the crowd will be anywhere near a Jumbotron screen, and as we get closer and closer to the show's finale I'm wondering what David Roome must be feeling. This isn't at all the extravaganza he'd planned. Puddle-jumping would be one of the kinder verdicts.

The archive inserts at an end, I leave the live coverage to Tony's inspired direction and return to the static line. The big southern taxiway is still black with people and for the first time it occurs to me that – for most visitors – the flying display is no more than an extra. These people come for a family day out. They come to ogle the parked aeroplanes, and buy T-shirts, and indulge their kids, and take the odd glance skywards when something especially noisy happens. Most of them don't seem to have much interest in following every wrinkle in the flying programme – which is probably just as well because at least two lines of burger bars, exhibition displays, and hospitality chalets fence them off from the airfield. There's provision, of course, for the hardened aircraft spotters – extra cash buys you a grandstand seat in the RIAT enclosure, or the FRIAT pen, or the Jubilee Gardens – but most folk seem content to simply bimble along, taking in the odd whiff of Avtur, their attention only occasionally drawn skywards.

There are very definitely exceptions to this rule and the RAF's own display team, the Red Arrows, is one of them. The Eightieth tribute ends with the Red's new display and at this point the flood of humanity along the static line comes to a halt. Fathers crouch beside sons, pointing upwards. Mothers shield their eyes against the sun. For twenty-five wonderful minutes, we all watch the longest firework in the world and at the end of it all there's a spontaneous round of applause. A hundred thousand people can't be wrong. The Reds really are the best in the world.

Minutes later, I run into David Roome at the foot of the tower. It seems unkind to ask how he's feeling but I do so anyway. He shrugs. The last two-and-a-half hours haven't been the jolliest moments of his life but his real regret is the loss of the vertical stacks. He's still convinced they would have worked. He knows they were flyable.

He looks me in the eye. 'I briefed the guys at one o'clock … and you know what they said?'

I shake my head. 'Tell me.'

David tilts his head skywards. Curls of red, white and blue smoke still hang in the air. The Red Arrows have left the crowd happy but much of the previous couple of hours has been all too forgettable.

'They couldn't believe this was all I wanted them to do.' David shrugs again. 'Pathetic, isn't it?'

After the flying display comes the evening concert. The German navy Tornado has mercifully spared our cable so we're still able to feed the big Jumbotron screen beside the stage with pictures. The Band of the RAF College at Cranwell, with the Steven Hill Singers, provide a two-and-a-half hour medley to ease the rush for the exit gates; and we exhaust every inch of available archive in the battle to provide something extra on top of the live pictures. In broad terms, it seems to work and there's a biggish crowd waving Union Jacks at the end.

By half past eight, Tony and I are exhausted. Tony, especially, has spent most of the day in the OB scanner and he must have broken the world record for live direction. We're both agreeing that a shower and a few beers would be nice, when Paul Bowen appears. The VIP barbecue out at Rendcomb is well under way. We're leaving at once.

This, for little me, is something of a test. So far, I've weathered the RIAT storm in pretty good shape. I've been writing notes, and making friends, and plotting the curve of this book non-stop for seven days. The most sleep I've managed in one night is three hours. But, just now, I'm knackered.

Paul gazes at me, amused. Then he tosses a bunch of car keys in my direction.

'Yours is the Range Rover,' he says. 'Follow me.'

Lin and I do his bidding. We don't talk much during the half-hour journey. By the time we arrive, it's nearly dark. Vic Norman's grass strip is black with fleets of executive limos. In the hangar, beyond a circle of tables, an RAF band is playing Glenn Miller classics. Out on the flight line, an immaculate Super Stearman TT-17 is taxiing in after the last of the VIP jollies. The air smells of Avgas and charring steak in roughly equal proportions. I begin to perk up. Paul's right. What's exhaustion compared to this?

We stay for a couple of hours. The conversation is warm, the food is exquisite and the VIPs are glowing as the band plays on. I eat my bodyweight in lamb chops, play footsie with my wife and after chocolate roulade and strawberries there's a twenty-minute firework display before the chauffeurs gather their charges and the impromptu car park begins to empty.

On the way back to our borrowed Range Rover, I encounter Amanda Butcher. First the Gala dinner. Now this.

'That was incredible,' I tell her. 'You should join the Magic Circle.'

Sunday morning dawns cool, with a high blanket of thin grey cloud. Ian Matthew's weather charts are promising a cold front by late afternoon, and there's definitely a change under way, but, for the time being, Paul and Tim's luck is holding. There's little immediate prospect of rain and the cloud base won't interfere with the flying.

Inside the Flight Centre, Ian Sheeley is preparing for morning prayers, the twenty-minute brief for all participating display pilots. The start of yesterday's flying programme suffered a direct hit when the White Albatroses display team got caught in a traffic accident and failed to make it in time to open the show. The team manager was mortified that his seven Aero L-39s were unable to launch but this morning he made sure they were up before dawn and, when Ian arrived at the Flight Centre at 7.00, he found them all waiting outside.

Yesterday's non-appearance of the team in the flying programme nearly had the makings of a diplomatic incident. The visiting chief of the Slovak Air Force, alerted to what had happened, was lobbying vigorously for the White Albatroses to replace the Red Arrows at the show's finale, and was puzzled at Tim Prince's refusal to do any such thing. This morning, though, the L-39s have been given a compensatory display slot, minutes ahead of the Berlin Airlift pageant.

Another casualty from yesterday's programme was the McDonnell Douglas EF-18 Hornet, from the Spanish Air Force base at Torrejon. Incoming VIP flights and a delayed arrival by Concorde forced Ian to cancel the Hornet's contribution to the SkyWatch segment of the morning's flying, and tempers only improved when he promised the Spanish a prime spot in today's display. National pride again. And an absolute determination to fly the pants off all the other *perros calientes* in the show.

With morning prayers now only minutes away, members of Geoff Brindle's Flying Control Committee pause by the coffee machine before strolling over to the base cinema. Post-match analysis of yesterday's show has already binned most of the RAF's revised Eightieth birthday tribute. It lacked punch. It lacked coherence. It looked, in a word, very, very ordinary. Roger Beazley, in particular, regrets that there's been such a major disconnect between the airshow and the powers-that-be. In combat terms, he says, David Roome's plans couldn't possibly survive such flak. His pageant has crashed and burned, a source of enormous regret.

There are plaudits, on the other hand, for some of the individual displays. In Geoff Brindle's opinion, Alan Wade's performance in the Little Slingsby Firefly was airmanship of a very high standard indeed;

and he liked, as well, the Tornado F3's routine from 25 Squadron at RAF Leeming. The Tornado is not a naturally agile aircraft and – in his view – Flt Lt Pete 'Willie' Hackett positioned the heavy jet very nicely. Before we leave the hangar, I ask him about the figure 80, flown across the crowd by the twenty-one Tucanos of No 1 Flying Training School at Linton-on-Ouse. This birthday tribute has provided moments of light relief in various planning meetings over the year but on the day Geoff was rather impressed with the result achieved by Squadron Leader Karim Sachedina.

'You could actually see the 80,' he says with a twinkle. 'Most of these stunts end up looking like a clatter of bits.'

Down beside the VIP reception centre, shortly afterwards, I find British Airways steward Antony Maslin fussing over an insect smudge on the windscreen of his courtesy V8 Daimler. As one of the volunteer chauffeurs on Kevin Leeson's protocol team, he's tasked to pick up royalty and VVIPs from a variety of incoming executive jets, and chauffeur them around the show. One of this morning's show guests will be HRH the Duke of Edinburgh, and Antony's preparations for the royal presence began with a determined attempt to give the car a good wash. Half an hour's hard labour with a bucket and a chamois left an immovable pattern of dust marks and only the intervention of the USAF fire chief saved the day.

'He used a hose on it, and I flew round behind him with a dry cloth,' he gasps. 'I couldn't bear to let Kevin down. I was absolutely dripping with sweat.'

From Building 29, on the northside, I motor slowly around the perimeter track. Each day's movement on the runway begins with a cavalcade of emergency vehicles. Lights flashing, sirens blaring, they drive from east to west, a convoy of fire tenders, ambulances and assorted trucks, designed to offer the most graphic reassurance to the tens of thousands of watching spectators who have already turned up. None of the crowd will have sat through the Table Top or memorised the racier bits of Tim Cairns' emergency operations order, but this carnival start to the day couldn't be sending a clearer message. We take safety very seriously indeed. Your lives are in our hands.

Behind the crowdline, and at various points around the airfield, little colonies of hot air balloons have reappeared, each of them shaped and branded. A Chubb fire extinguisher. The Britannia Building Society's piggy bank. A giant Bertie Bassett Liquorice Allsort, his big pink head gravely nodding in the light westerly breeze. The balloons have been up, like the Slovak aerobatic team, since dawn, marshalled and organised by the RIAT balloonmaster, Ian Cheese. They'll deflate in time for the two Sea King helicopters from RNAS Culdrose to open the display programme, but collectively they sound the opening note in this day-long symphony of flight.

I pause beside the Barbour balloon, tethered to a series of fire hydrants, and watch a line of Second World War trucks, jeeps and staff cars motoring slowly past en route to the northern taxiway. In a couple of hours' time, this little convoy will form part of the Berlin Airlift pageant, period-perfect close-ups for the feasting eyes of Tony Howard's camera five.

Behind the convoy come a couple of white mini-buses, both full of aircrew. Booted legs protrude through the open side door. Hands stifle yawns. The first bus carries a contingent from the 193rd Special Operations Wing of the US National Air Guard en route to their C-130 Hercules. The second is taking half a dozen Ukrainians to the distant bulk of their waiting An-72. Both buses grind to a halt to watch the eight Alphajets of the *Patrouille de France* easing gracefully on to the runway for their early departure back to Paris.

Wherever you look, there's fresh evidence of what Paul and Tim have managed, yet again, to confect for the public's consumption, and watching all the elements falling into place it's impossible not to reflect a little. They might have started their careers as traffic controllers with a hands-on gift for organisation but the twenty-seven intervening years have turned to them into something else. For nine months now, I've been searching for that single word that most perfectly describes what they've become and this morning, watching the public streaming into this weekend city of theirs, I suspect I've found it. The pair of them, in the long tradition that stretches back to the Hendon Air Pageants of the Thirties, are showmen.

*

I find Tim alone in his office in Building 1108. Like Paul, he revels in confronting the impossible and at the heart of this morning's crisis lies the elegant white shape of Concorde, parked up on Apron Gold. The supersonic airliner will be at the show all day, waiting to take 100 charter passengers back to Heathrow. This sub-sonic flight forms part of a special package, marketed – with Goodwood Travel – through RIAT. For £225 you get a ticket to the show, a souvenir programme, oodles to eat and drink, and the chance to boast afterwards that you've flown on Concorde. This isn't cheap but every one of the 100 tickets has gone.

Tim is staring at the phone. British Airways Operations have just confirmed they want their baby back. Overnight, two other Concordes have been taken out of service. Fare-paying passengers, expecting to fly supersonic, are waiting at Heathrow. The big white bird must be airborne from Fairford at 10.30. Sorry, folks, but business is business.

Tim, naturally, is less than thrilled by this bombshell. A bus to Swindon station and the 20.04 to Paddington doesn't have the same appeal as Concorde, and he shudders at the thought of 100 angry punters, thirsting for RIAT's blood.

I settle into the sofa beneath the window. BA are making noises about the small print in the charter contract. If it comes to a tussle, they can cite 'overriding operational difficulties'. What does Tim do now?

Tim isn't altogether sure but he's spent a great deal of time over the last two months fine-tuning every passing second of the air display programme and he – above all – knows that no slots exist for an unannounced Concorde departure. Taxiing will take five minutes. Engine run-up maybe ninety seconds. Take-off and climb-out, allowing for wake turbulence, another couple of minutes. That's eight minutes in all, or one complete display. The delays in yesterday's programme, due to extra VIP arrivals, rippled on through the entire display. The cancelled Spanish Hornet pilot, for one, was incandescent. Is all this to happen again?

'It's a safety issue, too,' he says. 'And there, I'm afraid, it's out of my hands.'

He's already talked to Geoff Brindle and he knows that the Flying

Control Committee won't budge. With a movements plot as complex as this one, an unscheduled Concorde departure is a risk too far. The big bird stays.

The phone rings. It's British Airways again. The issue has advanced through several layers of management. Holding Concorde hostage is totally unacceptable. They definitely want their aeroplane back.

Tim listens, unruffled. I can hear the big guns booming, from my seat across the room. Finally, he bends to the phone.

'I'm really, really, sorry,' he says regretfully. 'I've done my level best to change their minds but the truth is we can't rip-shit any more. The FCC are immovable on this one. They just won't mess with the flying display. Not in today's climate. I've tried my damnedest. You know I have. But there's just no way.'

The conversation goes on and on and I finally tip-toe out before the issue escalates any further. Concorde, I suspect, will be spending her day on Apron Gold, as scheduled. Admiration is too small a word . . .

The portacabin across from Show Operations Control houses the admissions team responsible for ticket sales at the show gates, and car parking thereafter. The team is headed by Peter Williams, a high-flying police superintendent from Dorset who looks – and occasionally acts – like Jack Nicholson. Peter, with his oppo, manager Mark Williams, has been up since dawn dealing with the flood of cars sluicing in through the network of narrow country lanes.

Peter's already estimating yesterday's crowd at a fraction under 100,000 but reports on local radio stations about traffic accidents and huge tailbacks have thinned this morning's attendance. I've bumped into Peter on a number of occasions throughout the year, and I've never been less than impressed at his accounts of the pressures the show itself exerts. This morning, tucked away in their little office, he and Mark are drinking coffee.

We talk about the crises that yesterday didn't produce. By 11.00, the on-airfield car parks – all seven of them – were virtually full. Drivers were good as gold. The police had the traffic moving nicely. A couple of suspect packages turned out to be abandoned rubbish.

Only at the end of the day was Peter really put to the test.

Under the new arrangements to speed the exit flows, Peter hands over to a brand-new team under ex-police superintendent, Roy Denning. As yesterday's flying programme came to an end, and the car parks began to empty, Peter and Mark drove over to Gate P. Curious to sample immediate reaction to the show, Peter made a point of saying an individual goodbye to each departing car. Around a thousand cars bumped past and Peter now reports that the huge majority had enjoyed themselves. This is good news, of course, but it's something else that strikes Mark.

He's half way through his second danish and he still can't get over it.

'Trying to find a thousand ways of saying goodbye.' He shakes his head. 'Why does he bother?'

Outside again, I bump into Amanda. She's just had a call from Rendcomb, Vic Norman's grass strip away to the north-west. Jonathan Smith, the manager charged with organising last night's VIP barbecue, had been clearing up at the airfield this morning when the eight French Alphajets of the *Patrouille de France* swept over the perimeter fence in perfect 'V' formation. They crossed the airfield at fifty feet, pulled into a loop, and then – a minute later – were gone. It was, he confessed breathlessly, the eeriest experience, and only when he made enquiries did he realise why the French had gone to the trouble of giving this impromptu salute. Vic had thrown a barbecue on Friday for all the attending aerobatic teams, and the French – *en route* home – had dropped in to say thank you.

With the flying programme back at Fairford about to start, I find Sean Maffett aloft in his commentary position on a scaffold in front of the control tower. He's unhappy about yesterday's Eightieth anniversary finale. On top of the RAF's failure to come up with the agreed goods, British Aerospace had been at pains on Friday to get Sean to downplay any excitement about Eurofighter's part in the climax to David Roome's revised pageant. They'd sent a fax asking him to 'condition the audience's expectations'. Eurofighter, they said, was not going to do any aerobatics – as it had done at Berlin and would do at Farnborough. Sean reluctantly agreed to this request, and yesterday he'd done his uncomfortable best to make sure the audience was duly conditioned.

So here we are on Sunday morning and the public relations executive from BAe chooses exactly the wrong moment to climb Sean's ladder for a chat. His name is Andy Cross and he wants to know how it's all been going.

'Deeply pathetic, since you ask.'

Andy blinks. Sean is wearing a badged flying suit and his trademark baseball hat and he wants to know why, when he'd fulfilled his side of the bargain, British Aerospace reneged on its Eurofighter promises. In earlier correspondence, they'd pledged themselves to three manoeuvres. Yesterday, at the climax of the eight-hour flying programme, they'd managed only one and a bit.

'And that was pathetic, too,' Sean points out. 'One loose circuit, a steepish climb, and off home. How I am supposed to explain that?'

Andy is looking a little hurt. All this isn't as simple as it might seem, as Sean knows. Full-blown displays are absurdly expensive. If Fairford gets one, then other airshows in other participating countries will want the same treatment. We're talking millions of pounds here. Money that doesn't exist within the development programme.

Sean is watching a French Etendard through a pair of battered binoculars. 'Your bloke was in the wrong position, too.' He adds, 'When he joined up with the Reds, he was supposed to be abeam the wingmen. That would put him in the middle of the back row of the formation. You know what actually happened?' He lowers the binoculars and glances at Andy. 'He was way behind.'

At this point, onlookers dissolve into slightly nervous laughter. Sean is famously committed to accuracy. Every time he commits himself on air, his reputation is at stake. On the basis of promises, he'd prepared the ground for Eurofighter. What the public actually saw was a limp excuse for an air display, much like the rest of the RAF Eightieth tribute.

'Pathetic,' he murmurs again, reaching for his microphone.

*

Sunday's flying programme gets under way. Down in Show Operations Control, co-ordinator Brian Hughes is cautiously assessing the weekend's success. Paul and Tim now devote a great deal of their time at the show to carrying the RIAT torch amongst the major VIPs, and Brian – in the view of one Tattoo veteran – is Paul's and Tim's representative on earth.

A retired Group Captain with thirty years' experience in the RAF police, Brian now acts as a security consultant for a major city bank. He's been with RIAT since the early Greenham Common days, and has become a by-word amongst the older volunteers for a very special brand of nervelessness. Saturday, he says, is always a rehearsal for Sunday. That, to me, suggests a degree of chaos on the show's first public day, but Brian dismisses the thought. This year's show has gone like clockwork. Lots of little incidents, but nothing on the scale of past upsets. This is hardly the stuff of major drama but nine months prowling around with my notebook and my pencil has taught me that the best stories are always in the minor key. Has *nothing* happened worth a mention?

Brian frowns, flicking back through the SOC log. Finally, he alights on something that might just take my fancy.

It's the old story about the punters who arrived in a friend's car, got separated early on and ended up clueless about where the car was parked. They hadn't taken the registration. They didn't know the make. They couldn't even remember the colour.

This seems wildly improbable. Wasn't there *anything* they'd seen to guide them back to their precious friends?

Brian at last smiles.

'A balloon,' he says. 'They parked near a big yellow hot-air balloon.'

'And?'

'The balloon had gone.'

Down the corridor from SOC lies the cash office. Both doors are locked but I've got to know the accountant, Sue Vizor, and she answers my plaintive knock. Inside, I find desks piled with pound notes, and scales weighed down with fat yellow bags of coins. Sue and her twelve-strong team have been here since dawn on Saturday, issuing floats to programme-sellers and the men and women from the local Lions Clubs who man the admission gates. Leather-clad bikers run the cash in and out of this busy little strong room, and since 10.00 on Saturday, when the serious money began to roll, the sums on Sue's calculator have been getting longer and longer.

Sue has just completed a print-out of yesterday's takings. The revenue is already sub-divided for analysis purposes and she shows me the figures. The sale of aircraft checklists – a spotters guide to aircraft in the static line, at £2.50 each – produced £11,704.09. Souvenir programmes, clad in Peter March's elegant blue-grey tint, yielded a heartening £99,980.21. And spectators parting with money on the gate – rather than buying tickets in advance – paid no less than £151,907.85. In all, yesterday's show raised a whacking £338,774.07. When it comes to money, I'm as naive as the next guy. Was it all cash? And did it all come through here?

Sue is an office clerk turned self-taught accountant. Like so many at RIAT she has won her spurs through merit and now keeps track of the millions of pounds that flow back and forth through Enterprises' books. Over the show weekend, she has a five-strong team from Lloyds to help her bank the ever-growing piles of currency that brighten the desks in this room, but the hands-on responsibility remains her's. With the show weekend over, Sue and her tiny full-time staff of three must field a tidal wave of invoices from suppliers and participants. It will be months before they can compute the final figure that will go on to the cheque Paul and Tim present to the Benevolent Fund.

I'm still wondering about the money. Already, more than a quarter of a million pounds has gone through this office. Today may produce a similar figure. Divide half a million quid into notes, and the piles would reach the ceiling.

Sue nods.

'And money's filthy,' she says. 'You try counting it all weekend.'

Outside again, the sun has appeared. The crowds along the static line are noticeably thinner than yesterday and I make my way down towards the Patrons' Pavilion, the grandest of the little encampment of hospitality chalets which occupy prime position along the very centre of the crowd line. Access to Patrons' is barred by a posse of RAF policemen who check passes and trade polite small-talk with a never-ending trickle of elegant women in amazing hats.

One of my five badges will doubtless get me into patrons' but the largest of our two Jumbotron screens is positioned alongside and I linger for a minute or two, watching the pictures. Tony Howard and his cameramen are pulling in some scorching shots and I gaze in awe as a Tornado GR1 thunders skywards in close-up against a blur of cloud. This morning we've introduced a system for posting lost kids on the screen – red lettering against the soaring Tornado – and I instinctively check the spelling as news arrives from Show Operations Control that Ben Gorrod (eleven) has gone missing. We've deliberately kept description to the bare minimum and the results can be comical. Ben has a blue/yellow top, and a blue bottom. Really?

Behind the line of tented chalets, a series of interlinked offices provides the nerve centre for Kevin Leeson's protocol operation. This morning, he's fielding not one but two Royals – HRH the Duke of Edinburgh, and HRH Prince Feisal of Jordan – but when I catch him eyeing a tray of canapés, he seems remarkably calm. The programme is running like clockwork, Antony's newly washed car looks immaculate and – at 11.09 – he's even got time for his 08.00 pee. Grabbing his service cap and two perfect roundels of smoked salmon, he dives for the exit.

In the room next door, Bob Arnott, Patrons' Pavilion co-ordinator, is contemplating last-minute adjustments to the lunchtime seating plan. Of the forty-four nine-place tables in the Patrons' Pavilion, four are of extra-special interest to Caroline Rogers' team and while the Tornado overhead pulls into another floor-wobbling full afterburner climb, I browse through the T-cards listing the guests. The tables have been tagged with gloriously martial codenames – Nighthawk, Raptor, Hercules, Fighting Falcon. I've no real feel for the weight of individual celebrity but a passing glance suggests that Nighthawk – with Sir Adrian Swire, Air Chief Marshal Sir Richard Johns, USAF General Jumper, and HRH the Duke of Edinburgh – might offer a glimpse or two into the upper reaches of the military establishment. Looking up again, I catch Caroline's eye.

'Would you like a nibble?' She nods at the tray of canapés. 'Only Kevin seems to be setting a trend.'

Back outside, fortified by the plumpest *langouste* I've ever seen, I can't resist a second peek at the Jumbotron screen. The Tornado has gone. In its place, against a big wide shot of the showground area, comes another message from Show Operations Control. This time I get no further than the first line. LOST ADULT, it says in heavy red letters. I look round in wonderment. Lost *adult?*

Beyond the Jumbotron lies David Higham's Sky High Village. Sue Vizor has already enthused about his sales performance yesterday, and now seems a good time to offer my congratulations. Our day out at the Birmingham Spring Fair seems a lifetime ago but the gambles he took with the merchandise on display there have obviously paid huge dividends.

The big tent is packed with shoppers but of David there's no sign. Volunteer manager, Charles O'Brien, does the honours with his radio. 'Sky Leader, Sky Leader, Village Idiot, over.'

I should be getting used to all this call-sign chic by now but curiously I'm not. The workings of the radio nets remain as big a mystery as David's feel for the shopping needs of the great British public.

Finally he turns up. He doesn't even have the grace to look knackered.

'Have you seen the figures?' he says at once. 'Nearly twenty per cent up on last year. Fantastic.'

He gestures round at the swirl of eager buyers. Each of these men and women, to David, represents a credit card, or a cheque book, or even hard cash. He's put temptation after temptation in their path and – to his enormous satisfaction – they're gorging themselves.

'We're smashed on T-shirts,' he says. 'Completely sold out. And look at this...'

He steers me towards a pile of boxed screensavers. They feature a clever aviation graphic, and at £14.95 each he's so far sold 102.

'Fifteen hundred quid,' Charles confirms.

The list goes on. Avia watches. RIAT calendars. Books. Videos. A honey trap of consumer goodies, each of them pushing the sales curve relentlessly upwards. David pauses for breath. I'm still thinking about the Avia watches.

'How much are they?' I enquire.

'£94.50 each.'

'And what's the profit margin?'

'Bloody healthy.' He grips me by the arm again. 'Don't print that.'

Dazed by David's euphoria, I emerge in time to watch a C-130 Hercules pulling off the runway into a steep climbing turn. There's something about the paint scheme that seems familiar and I'm tussling with a serious bout of *déjà vu* when the show commentary – Mike Whitehouse this time – gives me the only clue I need.

'Welcome to RAF Lyneham's Tac Demo flight,' he announces. 'Just sit back and enjoy the next eleven minutes.'

I need no further invitation. Up there are Dom Stamp and the boys, the magicians who threw me around the Lyneham sky, rearranging bits of the landscape until I'd completely lost track of whether we were airborne or back on the ground. For the promised eleven minutes, they swoop and turn and bank and climb, hauling the game old transport through the ribbon diagrams that even now grace my study walls. At the end of the display, as Dom closes the threshold at 1,000 feet, I'm practically counting the seconds until he pushes the nose down, plunging Fat Albert towards the runway. Moments later, there's a roar as Dom flattens the dive, greases the wheels on to the runway and then pulls the props into reverse. Beside me, a ten-year-old is staring up at his dad.

'That was well scary,' he says. 'I thought he was going to crash.'

For a moment, I'm tempted to agree.

'Me, too,' I'd like to say. 'Me, too.'

My last call of the day takes me over to the ritzy new premises at Gate F, where Gill Sharpe is handling arrangements for the evening's traditional hangar party. This will be RIAT's annual thank you to the volunteers and aircrew who have made the last two days possible. Admission is strictly by ticket and Gill has a problem.

'The hangar holds 2,000,' she says. 'I have 3,000 tickets. And 4,000 want to come.'

This, to me, sounds pretty conclusive. Mathematics is an exact science and Gill's problem is beyond solution. There is, of course, one obvious answer but, before I suggest it, I wonder aloud about the other bits of Gill's job. Over the past month or so, she's been finding beds for 4,000 volunteers. Billets vary from the Distinguished Visitor Suites in the Visiting Officer Quarters (DVSVOQ!!) – complete with kitchen, two bathrooms, and 10,000 TV channels – to a camp bed in gash accommodation with a shared portaloo and umpteen neighbours. This is just one symptom of the class structure that has begun to infect RIAT but Gill – an ex-army officer with a resilient sense of humour – doesn't think there are any huge gripes. The show has gone well, the new Gate F complex has worked like a dream, and the truth is that most volunteers will return for another dose of RIAT next year.

'I think it's the people,' she says. 'I don't think it's the planes at all.'

She's probably right. Getting the airshow on its feet is incredibly hard work but the after-hours social pace is unremitting. Which brings us nicely back to the hangar party: 4,000 into 3,000 doesn't go. Why not ask Paul to work another little miracle?

Gill smiles. That's exactly what she's done.

'And?'

'We're printing another thousand tickets.'

By 5.30, the flying programme is drawing to a close. A ledge of cloud is creeping in from the west but enough altitude remains for the Red Arrows to produce another awesome display. Up on the control tower balcony, Geoff Brindle's Flying Control Committee have compared notes to decide on the winners of various aerobatic trophies. Capt Gyula Vari, the Hungarian MiG-29 pilot, is pipped for the Superkings Solo Jet Aerobatic Trophy but wins the *As The Crows Flies* Trophy, awarded by the Friends of RIAT. Lt Col Alexiy Vaneev, meanwhile, wins the coveted Lockheed Martin Cannestra Trophy for his glider-like performance in the AN-72 *Coaler*. The trophies, I'm told, will be awarded at the hangar party before events get out of hand.

*

This sounds immensely promising but Lin and I arrive late at Hangar Zoo, after coaxing another two-and-a-half hours of live big screen pictures from the evening concert. Exhausted again, we queue for the traditional omelettes. There's a choice of four fillings and the nice lady with the frying pan insists I have the lot.

An hour or so later, swollen with omelette, Lin and I join the many-headed monster on the dancefloor. Fighter pilots, transport crews, nurses from the field hospital, and volunteers from every corner of the RIAT empire jostle and sway to the hot rhythms of Fabba. At one point, there's a spectacular tussle over a stuffed pink pig. At another, a human pyramid climbs unsteadily towards the hangar roof. Most of us are drunk. Most of us are knackered. And most of us are very, very happy. The dancing lasts to way past midnight. At the door to the bar outside, with the music still pulsing from the band, I take one last glance back. On Friday night, this was the venue for the Gala Dinner. It seems like an age ago.

Monday is goodbye day. In the Gulfstream Flight Centre, aircrews jockey for departure slots, constrained by the iron corset of Sue Allen's masterplan. From 08.30, local time, 400-plus aircraft will be lifting off at two-minute intervals in a non-stop stream of outbound aircraft which will, for one brief day, make RAF Fairford one of the busiest airfields in Europe.

At the weather desk, Ian Matthews and his Met team are briefing individual pilots on what they might expect *en route* back to their home bases. Capt Thomi, leader of the *Patrouille Suisse*, is gazing at the map on the screen of Ian's mobile outstation. He and his six Northrop F-5E Tiger IIs have filed for the transit back to Switzerland. The flight will take them an hour and twenty minutes but right now he's more interested in the cluster of little green triangles guarding the alpine approaches to northern Italy. The green triangles signify thunder storms, unwelcome news for any pilot.

Ian briefs him on the small print. Local cloud base down to 500 ft. More cloud and westerly winds *en route*. Thunder cloud topping at 39,000 ft over the Alps. Thomi, emotionless, takes it all in. His six F-5Es, plus a spare, will depart in what he calls 'a snake' – a vic of three, another vic, and then a singleton. Weather permitting, they'll re-form *en route*, and then revert to the snake for the let-down into their home base at Payerne.

Ian shakes him by the hand.

'*Bon voyage*,' he says.

Other crews for the weather brief press forward. Lt Col Mykola Menskykov, the *Backfire* pilot, is returning to the Ukraine. There are thunderstorms over eastern Poland but the weather in Kiev is pretty nice. The crew of a USAF C-141, on the other hand, is westbound. Over the Atlantic, the jetstream is currently running east at 150 knots, so they'll route either north or south, avoiding the torrent of high-altitude wind that would stretch their journey time by hours. The faces at the counter change and change again. Dutch F-16 pilots. The Italian G-222 pilot. Two RAF Tornado jockeys. Beyond them, more aircrew crowd around the coffee machine, or lounge on the wicker framed sofas, comparing notes. It's been a great weekend. Time to haul ass.

Out on the airfield, John Thorpe is busy unpicking the tightly knitted lines of parked aircraft. Already, gaps are appearing as Tornados, Jaguars, and the Italian F-104 Starfighter whine slowly down the big taxiway that loops round towards the eastern end of the runway.

The USAF spy-in-the-sky U-2 wants to be airborne at 10.34. The aircraft has a wingspan of eighty-two feet, and John and I have to move the traffic cones before it can begin to taxi. As the sinister black shape glides past, the pilot lifts a hand in salute. He'll be crossing the Atlantic at 60,000 ft, way above the weather, and the special pressure suit he wears, complete with sealed, full-face helmet, imposes enormous physical restrictions. John watches him ease past the cones. A test pilot himself, he doesn't envy Maj Dominick M Eanniello his next seven hours.

'The junior spaceman kit was never for me,' he says. 'You can't even scratch your nose in that helmet.'

Away to the right, the *Backfire* has once again been repositioned. After the *débâcle* with the German navy Tornado, Eng Ops crews checked beneath other aircraft for signs of subsidence. When they got to the big Ukrainian bomber they discovered the tarmac beginning to fracture around the main undercarriage. Another couple of hours, and the plane – along with RIAT – would have been in serious trouble. Not even the team from St Athan can lift ninety-five tons of heavy bomber.

With aircraft now launching in a steady stream, we return to SOC where, at last, I have a chance of solving the riddle of Saturday's spontaneous entertainment. Just why were Julie Morrissey and her ATC team doing the charleston?

The plot behind this bizarre caper takes me a while to crack. In some quarters, the ATC team are thought to be a little outside the social loop. They tend to keep themselves to themselves. They need a bit of jollying. The answer? Kidnap their badger.

Many of the RIAT teams adopt mascots. The ATC lot, this year, arrived with a winsome toy badger. They propped it up in one of the control tower windows where it had a nice view of the aeroplanes, and they introduced it to Grommitt, another pet member of the ATC family. The badger, naturally, was extremely happy. Then, on the Tuesday evening before the show weekend, it mysteriously disappeared.

Early on Wednesday, the ATC team arrived at the tower to find a ransom note waiting for them. The note specified a series of demands. Attached, was a Polaroid of the badger, Zippy-tied to the bottom of a radiator. Within minutes, a second note from the raving insane animal takers (RIAT – geddit?) arrived by fax. The dial-back number had been electronically erased and the blunt message extended the ransom deadline by a couple of hours. If the demands weren't met in full, the badger was history.

Julie and her team played tough. More notes arrived. Then, increasingly worried about the badger's welfare, the ATC team agreed to meet the ransom demands at least in part. One can of Pepsi was therefore left at a particular location, while a cross specifying compliance appeared in the designated control tower window.

It wasn't enough. An audio tape arrived, containing an interview with the badger. A gravelly-voiced interrogator spelled out the consequences of messing with the kidnappers. The poor badger sounded terrified. Something had to be done.

The ransom demands escalated. With them came a second Polaroid. This time, the badger had been gaffer-taped to the nose wheel of a B-1B bomber. Unless Julie caved in, he'd be accompanying the USAF crew on their Friday rehearsal. In the nose wheel bay.

Julie, at first, refused to concede. On Friday, she sweated through the B-1B's rehearsal routine. Her binos misted. She developed a nervous shake. Finally, overcome with guilt, she signalled her acceptance of the latest set of demands. Yes, she'd dance the charleston in full view of Saturday's crowd. And yes, her entire team would be there with her.

The charleston over, the final note arrived. If Julie cared to look beneath the table she'd knelt on to tape the cross on the window, she'd see a radiator. Zippy-tied to the bottom of the radiator, she'd find her little fluffy friend. Julie followed the instructions. And there – a little upset and a lot thinner – was her precious badger. Throughout the kidnap crisis, he'd never left the tower.

By lunchtime on Monday, I've assembled the entire Badger File. The identity of the kidnappers? My lips are sealed.

By early afternoon, all over the airfield, the weekend city is vanishing in front of our eyes. Sean's scaffold tower has already gone. The first of the hospitality chalets is a neat pile of folded canvas. Cranes are lifting portaloos on to the backs of flatbed lorries. It will be September before everyone can clear a date in their diaries for a collective post-mortem on the success of the weekend but already individual teams are getting together, comparing notes.

The technical term for this exercise is 'hot wash-up', and as far as I can tell the feeling about the show is pretty positive. Last year's crowd, lured by the B-2 Stealth bomber, was truly exceptional but this year's attendance – on the basis of rough figures – already looks extremely good, and Paul Bowen anticipates a hefty surplus after the show has met all its costs.

'People in this business criticise us for the amount of money we spend on the show,' he admits, 'but that money is an investment. Put lots in, you get lots out.'

It's true. Last year's show cost £2.3 million. Six months later, a cheque for nearly half a million pounds went to the RAF Benevolent Fund. This year's budget is larger still and once again the Ben Fund can expect a big donation.

Successful then?

Paul nods. Now is not the time for faint hearts.

'Very,' he says, firmly.

At 15.05, the grassy knoll in front of the control tower begins to fill with RIAT staffers. The word has gone round. The *Backfire* is about to depart. We wait and wait. The sleek, grey bomber is holding just short of the threshold, the strobe light beneath the belly already winking. Nearly an hour ticks slowly by. Finally a pair of yellow steps appears, not a good sign, and minutes later word comes from the tower that the *Backfire* doesn't have a transponder.

The transponder enables radar controllers *en route* to track and identify the beast. The ATC centre at West Drayton are happy to let it through to the edge of UK airspace without a transponder but other European control centres are saying 'no'. No transponder, no transit. Finally, the crew climb down from their cockpits and file on to a bus. RIAT will work the system to find a way for the *Backfire* to fly home but, in the meantime, Lt Col Menskykov and his crew must steel themselves for another couple of nights of RIAT hospitality.

At 17.00 comes the last of the managers' meetings. Tim Prince rattles through a checklist of key reminders for the men and women charged with de-rigging the train set. By Friday next, the airfield must be handed back to the USAF. Not a scrap of litter. Not a shard of glass. Not a single shred of evidence that these bare, windswept spaces have played host to 180,000 people and 441 aircraft. Tim's list of planes lamed by the show now extends to six. Support crews will shortly be flying in with bandages and spares. The weekend, he concludes, has been a bloody marvellous effort. You're all knackered. You're all sick to death of aeroplanes. But spare a thought, please, for the crew of a westbound KC-135 that left this afternoon. They blew a tyre on take-off and elected to carry on. Crash crews await them at their home base in the States.

He pauses.

'Eight hours concentrates the mind wonderfully,' he says. 'Let's wish them a happy landing.'

In the event, the KC-135 makes it home without incident but late that same afternoon word comes that the Catalina amphibian, star of Apron Orange, has crashed in Southampton Water. Details are unconfirmed but at least two VIPs on board, including the Mayor of Southampton, have been killed.

Only later, from Emergency Services Co-ordinator Jack Taylor, do I learn more. His son, Alex, is a police sergeant based in Southampton. He, too, is a RIAT volunteer. Returning to work from the show, he'd barely had time to sit down at his desk before the phone rang with news of the disaster. With the bodies recovered, it was Alex's job to search the wreckage for evidence for the inquest. From the cockpit, he retrieved a pile of RIAT paperwork and a flight plan charting the pilot's route from Fairford to Southampton.

I'm writing as fast as I can. This year, once again, RIAT has mercifully been spared what people like Jack call 'an incident' but the tragedy at Southampton is evidence enough that even the prettiest aeroplanes can cheat gravity just once too often. Before Jack leaves for his own drive home, I need to know exactly what perch his son occupies in the RIAT family tree.

Jack looks at me for a moment.

'He's the leader of one of the Mobile Response Columns,' he says at last. 'Strange, isn't it?'

That evening, back in the Patrons' Pavilion, 250 of us attend the show's last function. Dubbed 'the survivors' dinner', it offers the chance to unwind and relax once the crowds, and the aeroplanes, have gone home. Good food, good wine and good company untangle the weekend's tougher knots and the mood is festive. If anything, it feels like an enormous family Christmas.

Courses come and go. Glasses are endlessly recharged. Then, with the disco readying on the dancefloor at the back, come the speeches. For Sir Roger Palin, this is his last show and his last survivors' dinner as Fund Controller and Chairman of Enterprises. In October, after five successful years he will be handing over to Air Chief Marshal Sir David Cousins.

Sir Roger, in my brief experience, addresses audiences like the fighter pilot he once was. He comes in fast and hard and favours a style of delivery he himself might describe as 'punchy'. Tonight, though, his manner is softer, and altogether more thoughtful. He reflects on five busy years at the helm of this extraordinary organisation and on membership of a team that he obviously cherishes. He offers a graceful tribute to Paul, and Tim, and to the thousands of others without whom the last two days would never have happened. Then, as his speech draws to an end, he confides that his days at Fairford are not, in fact, over.

'I'll be back,' he promises. 'As a volunteer.'

This gesture, and all his hard work, wins warm applause. Paul and Tim present him with a framed memento depicting five airshow posters signed by the RIAT management team. Afterwards there are more speeches, and the award of commemorative certificates for the longest-serving volunteers. There is, as well, the presentation of a little silver Lancaster in recognition of the one individual who, in Paul's and Tim's view, has done most to embody the Spirit of RIAT. This year, the award goes to Kevin Leeson for his success in smoothing the paths of umpteen VIPs.

By now, I've been around long enough to know that this award is more than justified – Kevin's truly played a blinder – but in some quarters the presentation is less than welcome. RIAT is getting bigger and bigger, as it must. Without commercial sponsorship, and all the VIP trimmings that come with it, that expansion simply wouldn't happen. It's inevitable, therefore, that this corner of the Fairford operation becomes increasingly vital.

But with all the plaudits from the likes of Lockheed Martin and British Aerospace, comes a grumble of concern from another quarter. Some of the volunteers are feeling left out, passed over, ignored. The old spirit, they say, is vanishing, swept away by RIAT's infatuation with big business. We, too, matter. Without us, they murmur, RIAT simply wouldn't exist.

This, of course, is equally true but tonight is not the time to debate the issue. People have been working non-stop for over a week. They're tired and perhaps a little over-emotional. Words exchanged in the heat of the moment will – tomorrow – be withdrawn.

Past midnight, buses run us back to our various billets. The following morning, it's time to say goodbye. The list of people who have become friends is endless. For most of them, this chilly, post-show Tuesday is the briefest pause in an increasingly hectic year.

Next week, Paul and Tim plan a flying visit to RAF St Mawgan to discuss arrangements for next year's solar eclipse extravaganza. David Higham, meanwhile, is plotting the launch of his Christmas catalogue. Heidi Standfast is thinking hard about the autumn concert tours. Clive Elliot is dreaming up new targets for his corporate hit list. While Gill Sharpe is getting ready to pen 4,000 individual thank-you letters, every one destined for a volunteer.

For each of these men and women, and for many more, it's absurdly difficult to find the words to say goodbye. How do you sum up ten unforgettable days? How can you do justice to such a huge adventure? In the end, of course, it's a mumble and a hug and a kiss, and a promise to stay in touch. We might have been through a war together. And that, in a way, is what we've done.

Back at the campsite, where our son Jack has been living for the last week and a half, we ready our old VW van for the journey back to Portsmouth. Out on the airfield, his mates on the site team are still hard at work and his own goodbye has an eloquence I can only envy.

He stands beside the van, a borrowed radio to his lips.

'Windy? Gringo here. Thanks for everything. Top stuff ... Zulu? ... Catch you sometime. Great party. Loved the kaks ... Nico? Good one, mate. Brilliant time. Take care ...' He signs off, lowering the radio. 'Wild.' He shakes his head. 'And completely mad.'

....

CHAPTER TWELVE

Friday, 7 August 1998

The following week, I return to Fairford. The publishing deadline to get this book ready for David Higham's Christmas catalogue is brutal even by RIAT standards and producing 40,000 words in five days has left its mark. Paul and Tim need to check various passages for accuracy and that means delivering the manuscript personally.

Paul is back in his office in Building 15. The trip to St Mawgan has been extremely productive, and he's now returned to tackle the aftermath of the show. Post-RIAT reviews in the aviation press have been merciless. Mark Ashley, in *Aircraft Illustrated*, described the Saturday flying display as 'noticeably disjointed, with long gaps between items which is most unlike previous Air Tattoos'; while Alan Warnes, in *Air Forces Monthly*, was even more damning. 'There I was,' he wrote, 'hoping to see a mass fly-past of all the different types operated by the RAF past and present, and what did I get? Dribs and drabs of aircraft flying through...'

Paul reads these comments aloud, then leans back in his chair, only too aware of the consequences of the RAF's last-minute decision not to fly David Roome's finale pageant. Sir Roger Palin has taken up the cudgels with RAF Strike Command and he's absolutely determined to protect RIAT from a repeat of this *débâcle*. But the evidence in cold print, and on the Internet, is there for all to see. For once, in the eyes of the aviation world, RIAT has taken a backward step.

Paul abandons the press cuttings and turns to a pile of photographs.

He flicks through them, sliding the odd gem across the desk. The Ukrainian *Backfire* pilot, newly arrived from Poltrava, beaming down from his cockpit at the circle of raised cameras. Two foreign air chiefs, locked in conversation at the SkyWatch Symposium at Church House, Westminster. A nameless fighter pilot, upside down at the hangar party. The magnificent reception at Apsley House, the table set for the Thursday VVIP dinner. These are images from corners of the Air Tattoo not reflected in the pages of the aviation press. They proclaim the success of twelve months of incredibly hard work and each of them triggers a fresh memory.

For a while, we swap stories from last weekend. Mine keep trailing off into silence. The last fortnight has left me more exhausted than I can describe. The manuscript lies on the floor beside me, wrapped in a plastic bag, and I'm quite keen to get home for a good night's sleep.

At length, Paul turns to next year. He's undeniably stung by the criticisms of last week's show and he's determined to make good the damage. He pulls a letter towards him. It carries confirmation of a huge sponsorship deal and there's a figure with lots of noughts in the second line.

'I've been thinking hard about '99,' he says. 'We need more big screens, lots more. And we need to think a lot harder about the concert, and the music, and the archive film. It was a bit of a scramble this year. Next year we'll start earlier, much earlier.' He looks up. 'Agreed?'

I'm gazing at him across the desk. For reasons I don't understand, he keeps slipping out of focus.

'We?' I query feebly.

He glances up at me a moment, then returns to the letter.

'Yes,' he smiles. 'We.'

Appendix I

Map

Appendix II

David Roome's notes for
80th Anniversary Pageant

The Royal International Air Tattoo 1998

RAF Fairford 22–27 July 1998
ISSUED FOR GUIDANCE ONLY
Valid only during RIAT **98**
Consult RIAT Air Operations Order for Full Briefing Details
Static aircraft park south of Runway 09/27
Spectator Enclosures south of Crowd Line
Flying display aircraft park north of Runway 09/27

Aircraft Parking Aprons

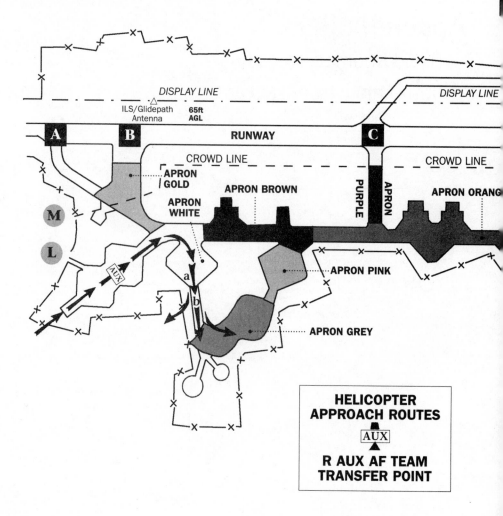

(original in colour)

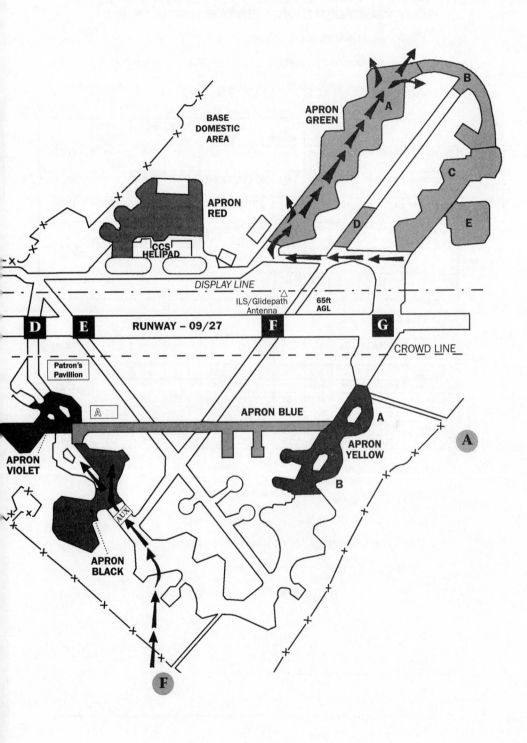

RIAT98 FINALE - THE 80TH ANNIVERSARY OF THE RAF

1   1534   Firefly (RAF20) take off to hold

2   1535   Sea King (RAF45) and Puma (RAF63) with RAF Ensign each +'80' (~~Becombes?~~)

3   1536   Tiger Moth Formation (CIV37) at Datum

4

Type	Lift off	G/S k	Ht ft	Up wind	Turn	Down wind	Turn	To Datum	Datum
Brisfit CIV20	1537 date.	45	200	1:00	:30 (15° AOB)	1:45	:30	:30	1541:15
Gladiator CIV21	1537:45	75	300	1:00	:25 (25° AOB)	1:25	:25	:30	1541:30
Spitfire CIV19	1538:30	120	400	0:45	:25 (35° AOB)	1:15	:25	:30	1541:50
Meteor CIV25	1539:15	150	500	:40	:30 (40° AOB)	:45	:30	:20	1542
Hunter CIV27	1539:30	210	600	:40	:35 (45° AOB)	:35	:35	:30	1542:25
F3 RAF?	1539:45	240	700	:30	:35 (50° AOB)	:40	:35	:30	1542:35

Into second circuit

Type	Datum	G/s k	Ht ft	Up wind	Turn	Down wind	Turn	To Datum	Datum	
Brisfit	1541:15	45	200	:45	:30 (15° AOB)	1:15	:30	:45	1545	✓
Gladiator	1541:30	75	300	:30	:25 (25° AOB)	1:25	:25	:45	1545	✓
Spitfire	1541:50	120	400	:40	:25 (35° AOB)	1:15	:25	:25	1545	✓
Meteor	1542	150	500	:25	:30 (40° AOB)	1:05	:30	:30	1545	✓
Hunter	1542:25	210	600	:25	:35 (45° AOB)	:35	:35	:25	1545	✓
F3	1542:35	240	700	:15	:35 (50° AOB)	:35	:35	:25	1545	✓

Brisfit return to Rendcomb.

Spitfire, Meteor, Hunter and F3 clear behind crowd to Hold.

5   1546   Gladiator land

6   1547-1554   Firefly (RAF20) aeros and land

7   1555-1557   Meteor, Hunter and F3 break to land

8   1558   3 x Spit (RAF2, RNLAF4, ?) take-off for Serial 11

1

17/06/98

9

Type	Lift off	G/S k	Ht ft	Up wind	Turn	Down wind	Turn	To Datum	Datum
Tutor CIV22	1559	60	200	1:10	:30 (20° AOB)	1:30	:30	:35	1603:15
Magister CIV23	1559:45	75	300	1:00	:25 (25° AOB)	1:25	:25	:30	1603:30
Harvard CIV35	1600:30	120	400	0:45	:25 (35° AOB)	1:15	:25	:30	1603:50
Vampire CIV26	1601:15	150	500	:40	:30 (40° AOB)	:45	:30	:20	1604
Gnat CIV28	1601:30	210	600	:40	:35 (45° AOB)	:35	:35	:30	1604:25
Hawk RAF22	1601:45	240	700	:30	:35 (50° AOB)	:40	:35	:30	1604:35

Into second circuit

Type	Datum	G/s k	Ht ft	Up wind	Turn	Down wind	Turn	To Datum	Datum
Tutor	1603:15	60	200	:40	:30 (20° AOB)	1:35	:30	:30	1607
Magister	1603:30	75	300	:50	:25 (25° AOB)	1:20	:25	:30	1607
Harvard	1603:50	120	400	:45	:25 (35° AOB)	1:10	:25	:25	1607
Vampire	1604	150	500	:25	:30 (40° AOB)	1:05	:30	:30	1607
Gnat	1604:25	210	600	:25	:35 (45° AOB)	:35	:35	:25	1607
Hawk	1604:35	240	700	:15	:35 (50° AOB)	:35	:35	:25	1607

Tutor and Magister return to Rendcomb.

Harvard, Vampire, Gnat and Hawk clear to eastern hold.

10   1608 - 1615   Tucano (RAF37) take-off, solo aeros and land.

11   1616   WWII Missing man (4 x Spit)

12   1617   Harvard break to land

13   1618   Squirrel land from BZN with RAFAT Manager

14   1618   Vampire, Hawk and Gnat all on break to land at 300k

15   1621   4 x Spit break to land

16   1624-1632   Solo Jaguar (RAF40) take-off, aeros and land

17   1633   Source Aviation 3 Vampires (CIV29) take off to hold

18

Type	Lift off	G/S k	Ht ft	Up wind	Turn	Down wind	Turn	To Datum	Datum
SE-5 CIV32	1634	45	200	1:00	:30 (15° AOB)	1:45	:30	:30	1638:15
Curtiss CIV36	1634:45	75	300	1:00	:25 (25° AOB)	1:25	:25	:30	1638:30
Hurricane RAF53	1635:30	120	400	0:45	:25 (35° AOB)	1:15	:25	:30	1638:50
Venom CIV30	1636:15	180	500	:40	:30 (45° AOB)	:45	:30	:20	1639
Harrier RAF?	1636:30	210	600	:40	:35 (45° AOB)	:35	:35	:30	1639:25
Jaguar RAF17	1636:45	240	700	:30	:35 (50° AOB)	:40	:35	:30	1639:35

Into second circuit

Type	Datum	G/s k	Ht ft	Up wind	Turn	Down wind	Turn	To Datum	Datum
SE-5	1638:15	45	200	:45	:30 (15° AOB)	1:15	:30	:45	1642
Curtiss	1638:30	75	300	:50	:25 (25° AOB)	1:20	:25	:30	1642
Hurricane	1638:50	120	400	:45	:25 (35° AOB)	1:10	:25	:25	1642
Venom	1639	180	500	:25	:30 (45° AOB)	1:05	:30	:30	1642
Harrier	1639:25	210	600	:25	:35 (45° AOB)	:35	:35	:25	1642
Jaguar	1639:35	240	700	:15	:35 (50° AOB)	:35	:35	:25	1642

SE-5 to Rendcomb (Sat) and Boscombe (Sun), Jenny to Rendcomb.

Hurricane, Jaguar, and Harrier clear to eastern hold.

Venom clear to join missing man at Serial 21

19   1643-1655   Harrier (RAF7) take-off, aeros and land

20   1656   Hurricane break to land

21   1657   Early jet Missing man (3 x Vampire 1 x Venom)

22   1658   Jaguar and Harrier break to land

23   1700   ~~GR1(Sat)/F3(Sun) take off to hold~~

24

Type	Lift off	G/S k	Ht ft	Up wind	Turn	Down wind	Turn	To Datum	Datum
Hind CIV24	1701	75	200	1:00	:25 (25° AOB)	1:25	:25	:30	1704:45
Blenheim CIV33	1701:20	90	300	:45	:30 (25° AOB)	1:20	:25	:30	1704:50
Lancaster RAF54	1701:55	120	400	0:45	:30 (30° AOB)	1:15	:25	:30	1705:20
Canberra RAF9	1702:45	180	500	:40	:30 (45° AOB)	:45	:30	:20	1705:30
GR1 RAF?	1703:05	240	600	:30	:35 (50° AOB)	:40	:35	:30	1706:05

Into second circuit

Type	Datum	G/s k	Ht ft	Up wind	Turn	Down wind	Turn	To Datum	Datum
Hind	1704:45	75	200	:45	:25 (25° AOB)	1:15	:25	:45	1708:30
Blenheim	1704:50	90	300	:50	:30 (25° AOB)	1:25	:25	:30	1708:30
Lancaster	1705:20	120	400	:40	:30 (30° AOB)	1:10	:25	:25	1708:30
Canberra	1705:30	180	500	:25	:30 (45° AOB)	1:05	:30	:30	1708:30
GR1	1706:05	240	600	:15	:35 (50° AOB)	:35	:35	:25	1708:30

Hind return to Rendcomb.

Blenheim, Lancaster, Canberra and GR1 clear to eastern hold.

25	1710	4 x F3 (Missing man formation) take-off to hold
26	1711-1719	Singleton GR1 (RAF18) aeros and clear to hold (Sat) [F3 (RAF51) on Sun]
27	1721	3 Vampire, 1 Venom break and land
28	1722	GR1(Sat)/F3(Sun) break to land
29	1724-1732	Taxi past: CAF CzAF FAF RNLAF RNZAF RNoAF PolishAF SlovakAF?
30	1733	Present day Missing Man (4 x GR1)
31	1734	Blenheim at 3nm finals to land, Lancaster at 4nm
32	1736-1738	Blenheim and Lancaster land
33	1739	Canberra on the break to land
34	1741	5 x Tornado (missing man formation + GR1(Ser24) break to land
35	1745	RAFAT 'Flash' through which Tucano '80' fly (Tucanos at 5nm)

4   17/06/98

36	1747	Tucano '80' (RAF38) at datum (north to south)
37	1750-1808	RAFAT (RAF1)
38	1800	EF2000 joins western hold
39	1810	RAFAT join with EF2000 (CIV5) at western hold) *Reds 'sugary shut gear'.* (Reds 1-7 in Big 7, with Synchro going direct to BZN))
40	1812	RAFAT 7 + EF2000 in line astern on Red 1, 2 orbits culminating in EF to vertical and RAFAT vixen break, then to BZN
41	1815	Close